TERRORISM, ECONOMIC DEVELOPMENT, AND POLITICAL OPENNESS

To what extent are terrorism and development related? What are the relative weights of the economic, political, and social aspects of development? What is the development effect of different responses to terrorism? This volume addresses these crucial questions, synthesizing what we do know about the development links with terrorism and pointing out what we do not know. Contributors to this volume examine the economic and fiscal costs of terrorism and the response to terrorism. They conclude that the economic costs of terrorism in rich countries are low relative to the economic costs of combating terrorism; both are likely high in poor countries. They also report evidence on how development affects terrorism. This work supports the hypothesis that political development – political openness and the quality of government – is inversely associated with the emergence of terrorist organizations. Though less clearly, it also supports the proposition that national economic development – mainly international openness – can moderate terrorism.

Philip Keefer is a Lead Research Economist in the Development Research Group of the World Bank. Since receiving his Ph.D. in economics from Washington University in St. Louis in 1991, he has worked continuously on the interaction of institutions, political economy, and economic development. The issues addressed in this work range from the effect of insecure property rights on economic growth to the effect of political credibility on the fiscal and monetary policy choices of governments. His work has appeared in numerous economics and political science journals, including the *Quarterly Journal of Economics*, the *Review of Economics and Statistics*, the *American Political Science Review*, and the *American Journal of Political Science*. Dr. Keefer has worked intensively in or on numerous countries, including Bangladesh, Brazil, the Dominican Republic, Ghana, Indonesia, Mexico, Nepal, Pakistan, Peru, and the Philippines.

Norman Loayza is a Lead Research Economist in the Development Research Group of the World Bank. He was born in Arequipa, Peru, and received a Ph.D. in economics from Harvard University in 1994. Since then, he has worked at the research group of the World Bank, with an interruption of two years (1999–2000) when he worked as senior economist at the Central Bank of Chile. Dr. Loayza has studied several areas related to economic and social development, including economic growth, social conflict, and crime and poverty alleviation. He has edited five books; is coeditor of the book series Central Banking, Analysis, and Economic Policy; and has published more than 30 articles in professional journals, such as the *Journal of Monetary Economics*, the *Review of Economics and Statistics*, the *Journal of International Economics*, *Economic Development and Cultural Change*, and the *Journal of Law and Economics*.

Terrorism, Economic Development, and Political Openness

Edited by

PHILIP KEEFER

The World Bank

NORMAN LOAYZA

The World Bank

CAMBRIDGE
UNIVERSITY PRESS

CAMBRIDGE UNIVERSITY PRESS
Cambridge, New York, Melbourne, Madrid, Cape Town, Singapore, São Paulo, Delhi

Cambridge University Press
32 Avenue of the Americas, New York, NY 10013-2473, USA

www.cambridge.org
Information on this title: www.cambridge.org/9780521887588

First published 2008

Printed in the United States of America

A catalog record for this publication is available from the British Library.

Library of Congress Cataloging in Publication Data
Keefer, Philip.
Terrorism, economic development, and political openness / Philip Keefer, Norman Loayza.
p.   cm.
Includes bibliographical references and index.
ISBN 978-0-521-88758-8 (hardback)
1. Terrorism.   2. Terrorism – Economic aspects.   3. Terrorism – Political aspects.
I. Loayza, Norman.   II. Title.
HV6431.K38   2008
363.325–dc22   2007029941

ISBN   978-0-521-88758-8 hardback

Contents

v

List of Tables

List of Figures

Contributors

Justin L. Adams is a director of economic studies at Forward Observer, a political economics consulting firm in Sacramento, California, whose previous research at RAND included defense economics and international economic development.

S. Brock Blomberg is a professor at Claremont McKenna College with appointments in the economics department and the politics, philosophy, and economics program. He has written extensively on the economics of terrorism in journals, books, and newspapers. He has held appointments on the president's Council of Economic Advisors, the Federal Reserve Bank of New York, the Federal Reserve Board of Governors, the International Monetary Fund, Harvard University, Wellesley College, and the University of Southern California.

James Dertouzos is a Senior Economist who has worked on a variety of policy issues at RAND since 1979, including public sector resource allocation, civil justice, and market regulation.

Arindam Dutta is a doctoral fellow at RAND and a consultant for the World Bank, focusing on the economics of international health, development in South Asia, and program evaluation.

Walter Enders, a Professor of Economics and Lee Bidgood Chair of Economics and Finance at the University of Albama, was selected as the 2004 recipient of the Blackmon-Moody Award, one of the highest honors bestowed on faculty at the university. In 2003, the National Academy of Sciences selected him as a corecipient of its Award for Behavioral Research Relevant to the Prevention of Nuclear War. Professor Enders and Professor Todd Sandler (see p. xvi) were chosen "for their joint work on transnational terrorism using game theory and time-series analysis to document the cyclic and shifting nature of terrorist attacks in response to defensive counteractions," according to the announcement by the NAS.

Susan S. Everingham is the Director of International Programs within RAND's National Security Research Division, whose earlier work focused on mathematical modeling of defense systems, cost-benefit analysis of drug and criminal justice policies, and military personnel management.

Gregory D. Hess, the Russell S. Bock Chair of Public Economics and Taxation, is currently the dean of faculty and vice president for academic affairs at Claremont McKenna College. He is a graduate of the University of California, Davis, and earned master's and doctorate degrees at The Johns Hopkins University. Before coming to CMC, he was the Danforth-Lewis Professor of Economics at Oberlin College and a lecturer at Cambridge University and Fellow of St. John's College. He has served as an economist at the Federal Reserve Board in Washington, DC, and has been a visiting scholar at the Bank of Japan, the International Monetary Fund, and the Federal Reserve Banks of Cleveland, Kansas City, and St. Louis. His teaching and research interests include macroeconomics, public finance, monetary policy, macroeconomics, and political economy.

Philip Keefer is a Lead Economist in the World Bank's Development Research Group. His work focuses on the effect of political and social institutions on development. Before joining the Bank in 1994, he was Associate Director of the IRIS Center at the University of Maryland. In 1989–1990, he worked with the Instituto Libertad y Democracia in Lima, Peru. He received his Ph.D. in economics from Washington University in St. Louis, in 1991.

Alan B. Krueger is the Bendheim Professor of Economics and Public Affairs at Princeton University. He is currently editor of the *Journal of Economic Perspectives*, the most widely read journal in the economics profession. A prolific author, he has published widely on the economics of education, income dispersion, technological change, labor demand, social insurance, health economics, and environmental economics. Named a Sloan Fellow in Economics in 1992 and a National Bureau of Economic Research Olin Fellow in 1989–1990, he was a Fellow of the Center for Advanced Study in the Behavioral Sciences in 1999–2000. After a brief stint as Chief Economist at the U.S. Department of Labor, he was elected a Fellow of the Econometric Society in 1996. The following year he received the Kershaw Prize, which is awarded to a scholar under the age of 40 who has made distinguished contributions to public policy analysis. He received a B.S. with honors from Cornell University and a Ph.D. in economics from Harvard University.

David D. Laitin is the Watkins Professor of Political Science at Stanford University. He received his B.A. from Swarthmore College and his Ph.D. from the University of California, Berkeley. He is a member of the American Academy of Arts and Sciences. He has conducted field research on issues of language, religion, and nationalism in Somalia, Yorubaland (Nigeria), Catalonia (Spain), and Estonia. His books include *Politics, Language and Thought: The Somali Experience* (1977); *Hegemony and Culture: Politics and Religious Change Among the Yoruba* (1986); *Somalia: Nation in Search of a State* (1987, with Said Samatar); *Language Repertoires and State Construction in Africa* (1992); and *Identity in Formation: The Russian-Speaking Populations in the Near Abroad* (1998). He has also conducted research on civil wars and international terrorism, most of it in collaboration with James Fearon ("Ethnicity, Insurgency and Civil War" in the *American Political Science Review* [2003]) but also with Eli Berman and Alan Krueger.

Eric V. Larson is a senior policy researcher whose past research has focused on national security and defense planning issues, including the war on terrorism.

Fernanda Llussá is an Assistant Professor of Economics and Business at the Universidade Nova de Lisboa, in Portugal. She completed her Ph.D. in economics at the University of California, Los Angeles in 2003. Her master's degree at Fundação Getúlio Vargas, in Brazil, resulted in the thesis "Credibility and Public Debt Management: A Case Study of Brazil," awarded a National Prize in Economics by Banco Nacional de Desenvolvimento Econômico e Social (BNDES) and later published as a book. Professor Llussá has conducted research at the Harvard Institute for International Development; on geography, institutions, and state growth in Brazil; and her current research interests, including the effect of aggregate shocks on institutions and economic growth, have resulted in several publications in refereed journals.

Norman Loayza is currently lead economist in the research department of the World Bank. He was born in Arequipa, Peru, and pursued high school and general university studies in Lima. He obtained a B.A. from Brigham Young University, specializing in economics and sociology, and continued his studies at Harvard University, where he received a Ph.D. in economics, in 1994. Since then, he has worked at the research group of the World Bank, with an interruption of two years (1999–2000) when he worked as senior economist at the Central Bank of Chile. Dr. Loayza has taught postgraduate courses and seminars at the University of the Pacific in Lima, the Catholic University of Chile, and the University of Sao Paulo.

Nicholas Sambanis is Associate Professor of Political Science at Yale University. He received his Ph.D. from Princeton University's Woodrow Wilson School of Public and International Affairs in June 1999. His publications have appeared in several journals, including the *American Political Science Review*, *World Politics*, the *Journal of Conflict Resolution*, *Perspectives on Politics*, and the *Journal of African Economies*. He is the coauthor of *Making War and Building Peace*, a book about United Nations peacebuilding published by Princeton University Press in 2006. He is coeditor of *Understanding Civil War: Evidence and Analysis*, two volumes of case studies on civil war, published by the World Bank in 2005, and is working on a book on the causes of self-determination movements and secessionist civil war. Professor Sambanis is researching questions on violent civil conflict; the interaction of economic development, political institutions, and civil war; and the uses of international organizations to prevent or resolve large-scale political violence.

Todd Sandler is the Robert R. and Katheryn A. Dockson Professor of International Relations and Economics at the University of Southern California and the Vibhooti Shukla Professor of Economics and Political Economy at the University of Texas at Dallas. Professor Sandler applies theoretical and empirical models of economics to the study of international political economy, defense, environmental issues, and public finance. He is particularly interested in the application of game theory (noncooperative and cooperative) and microeconomics to issues in international relations. His current work focuses on the formation of international environmental agreements and regimes. Another facet of his work analyzes alliances, intergovernmental agreements, and the design of supranational structures. He is also working on new papers on transnational terrorism, global public goods, and a new book, *The Political Economy of Terrorism*.

Jacob N. Shapiro is a graduate student in political science at Stanford University and CISAC predoctoral Fellow. His research focuses on the role of economic motivations in terrorist organizations and on the organizational challenges these groups face. As a Naval Reserve officer, he was assigned to the Office of Naval Intelligence and the Naval Warfare Development Command. Prior to attending Stanford, he served on active duty at Special Boat Team 20 and onboard the USS *Arthur W. Radford* (DD-968). He received his B.A. in political science from the University of Michigan.

José Tavares is an Assistant Professor of Economics at Universidade Nova de Lisboa and research affiliate at the Center for Economic Policy Research in London. He holds a Ph.D. in economics from Harvard University and has specialized in macroeconomics with a focus on the political economy of fiscal policy and economic growth. His research has been published in academic journals in Europe and the United States, including the *Journal of Monetary Economics*, the *Review of Economics and Statistics*, the *Journal of Public Economics*, and the *European Economic Review* and also appeared in edited volumes of Harvard University Press, MIT Press, and Cambridge University Press. He has undertaken research projects for the World Bank, the Asian Development Bank, the Harvard Institute for International Development, and the Banco de Portugal. His work has received comments in the general press in the United States (*New York Times*) and in Portugal.

Gregory F. Treverton is director of RAND's Center for Global Risk and Security. Earlier, he served as president and director of studies of the Pacific Council on International Policy, an initiative rooted in the American West to bring together leaders interested in international matters and their effects on domestic affairs. At RAND, he has directed the Intelligence Policy Center and the International Security and Defense Policy Center, and he serves on the faculty of the RAND Graduate School. Before joining RAND, Dr. Treverton served as vice chair of the National Intelligence Council, overseeing the writing of America's National Intelligence Estimates (NIEs). He has been Senior Fellow and Director of the Europe-America project and of the project on America's Task in a Changed World at the Council on Foreign Relations in New York.

Overview

Terrorism, Economic Development, and Political Openness

Philip Keefer and Norman Loayza

Terrorism is as old as war, but only with the attacks of September 2001 in New York and Washington, March 2004 in Madrid, and July 2005 in London did it become a central concern of governments in the rich countries of the West. This concern prompted policy makers to focus on the potential links to development of both terrorism and the response to terrorism, quickly revealing important lacunae in the literature. To what extent is terrorism related to development? If development is a determinant of terrorism, what are the relative weights of the economic, political, and social aspects of development? And what is the development effect of different responses to terrorism? This volume addresses these crucial questions, synthesizing what we know about the development links with terrorism – and pointing out what we do not.

Policy makers and scholars are concerned with development-terrorism links in both directions: the economic effect of terrorism, but also the development roots of terrorist activity. This volume bridges both, first with contributors who examine the economic and fiscal costs of terrorism and the response to terrorism, and second with others who assess how development affects terrorism, drawing on existing linkages and also reporting on new evidence. The first is a much-investigated issue. Nevertheless, as chapters by Enders and Sandler and Treverton et al. demonstrate, evidence is much more abundant about the costs of terrorism in developed countries than in poor countries. Enders and Sandler also find that the economic costs of terrorism appear to be low in rich countries and, in all likelihood, high in poor countries.

A contentious debate surrounds the second question. Does terrorism relate to development? If it does, is it the economic or another dimension of development that matters? On the one hand, the contributors to this volume present consistent empirical support for the hypothesis that political openness and the quality of government are inversely associated with the emergence of terrorist organizations. On the other hand, the research presented here points to continued dispute about the role of economic development. The question is difficult to answer, however, because factors identified as having a significant effect on terrorist activity – such as governance, political openness, and trade openness – also significantly affect incomes.

A key question that we do *not* take up in this volume is the development effect of the largely military and security-based response to terrorism. This is undoubtedly an important and difficult question, but little research on the development effect of either type of response has been carried out. The direct and short-run development costs of military intervention are likely to be large but are unknown with any precision; research into the much more contentious issue of the long-run effects of military intervention on the development of countries that are sources of terrorism is practically nonexistent. Many of the security-based responses to terrorism restrict the free movement of labor and goods from countries thought to harbor terrorists into North America and Europe and also stymie the flow of capital into and out of those countries. These measures certainly have a development effect; whether this effect is large in absolute terms, or relative to the net benefits to richer countries (recognizing that richer countries also incur an economic cost from such restrictions), is unclear.

The unprecedented terrorist attacks of 9/11, which froze financial markets and brought air transportation to a halt in the United States, are a focal point of some contributors: if the costs of terrorism were not dramatic in the case of 9/11, the economic costs of terrorism are unlikely to be the main threat confronting large, rich countries. Both Enders and Sandler and Treverton et al. examine this case. Enders and Sandler conclude that the economic consequences of the 9/11 attacks were large, but fleeting, leading to a small drop (in percentage terms) in national income ($90 billion over a period in which the U.S. economy generated $10 trillion worth of goods and services). Growth dropped briefly but quickly returned to its pre-attack path.[1]

Enders and Sandler note, though, that in areas that are still rich on a per capita basis but that have economies much smaller than that of the United States, the economic effects may be large, particularly when the terrorist

---

[1] It can be argued that the costs of 9/11 are low precisely because of the large security response by the U.S. and other nations' governments. However, even counting the costs of this security response, the economic consequences of 9/11 remain small in proportion to the size of the U.S. economy.

threat is endemic. They cite evidence from the Basque Country in Spain showing that chronic terrorism can drive income per capita 10 percent below where it would otherwise be, for at least as long as the terrorist threat persists. In addition, even within large rich countries, some industries, such as those connected with travel, suffer disproportionately (even these fully recovered in the United States, however).

Poor countries are also frequent targets of terrorist activity, but scant evidence exists about its economic effects. Enders and Sandler conclude that the available evidence indicates that the costs of terrorism are much greater in small, poor countries. Why the difference between large rich and small poor countries? The reasons are intuitive: large, diversified economies are better able to shift resources to less affected sectors. Moreover, rich countries tend to have well-functioning policy institutions that can respond to shocks adroitly and with ample information.

Treverton et al. focus more narrowly on the budget costs of the response to terrorism in the United States and Britain. Using a number of approaches, they estimate that the incremental increases in U.S. government expenditures that can be traced to 9/11 amount to \$19–\$26 billion per year, most of which has gone to domestic security, or \$69–\$96 billion if the military operations in Afghanistan and Iraq are included.[2] Of these expenditures, \$2–\$4 billion represent incremental annual spending on development assistance. Their evidence does not suggest that wealthy countries have increased assistance to offset the costs of terrorism for the poor countries victimized by terror.

From the discussions in Enders and Sandler and Treverton et al., as well as the review in Llussá and Tavares, we can draw conclusions about the nature of the economic threat to large, wealthy countries posed by terrorism and about the types of policies adopted, at least by the United States, in response to it. Most of the remaining contributors to this volume, by looking explicitly at the development roots of terrorism, offer analyses that help to frame the evolution of policy in the future. They examine the extent to which low incomes directly lead to terrorist activity. However, they also examine other factors, such as weak governance, political openness, and openness to the rest of the world; these other factors may affect both poverty and terrorism

---

[2] Their estimates of war costs are conservative, based only on cash outlays for the war. Bilmes and Stiglitz (2006) estimate that war costs to date would be approximately 50% higher if one takes into account the increment of total indirect defense spending that should be attributed to the wars, payments made to cover injured and disabled veterans, and the interest on government debt incurred to finance the war.

and, therefore, exercise both an indirect influence (through poverty) and a direct influence on terrorism.

As the thorough literature review in the chapter by Llussá and Tavares makes clear, comprehensive studies that address the long-run determinants of terrorism are scarce. Policy makers have nevertheless expressed support for three possibilities – poverty, weak governance, and lack of openness. In a 2005 speech, the Secretary of State for International Development of the UK, Hilary Benn, argued that "terrorism can plant its roots in poverty. Corruption, poor governance, economic mismanagement and a lack of representative politics all can play a part in alienating and radicalising poor people."[3] Andrew Tobias, Administrator of the United States Agency for International Development (USAID), echoed these ideas in April 2006, pointing out that "the locus of national security threats has shifted to the developing world, where poverty, oppression, injustice and state indifference are exploited by our enemies to provide haven for criminals and the planning of criminal acts."[4] The Danish Ministry of Foreign Affairs notes that the connection between good government, economic development, and terrorism has been assumed, not demonstrated, but accepts as an operating principle "the fundamental assumption that people will be less inclined to embrace extremist fundamentalism and terrorism when they live in an open, democratic society based on the rule of law, where they may exert an impact through free exchange of opinions and democratic participation, and where conflicts are resolved through negotiation."[5]

Cross-national evidence identifies a nuanced role for *economic* development in reducing terrorist activity. Chapters by Blomberg and Hess support policy maker conclusions that poverty drives terrorism, finding that higher incomes impede terrorist activity. Krueger and Laitin, on the other hand, find little economic foundation for terrorist origins. Why the different conclusions? Krueger and Laitin investigate the overall effects of income across all countries. In "From (No) Guns to Butter," Blomberg and Hess argue that the effects may differ between richer and poorer countries. Looking at these two groups of countries separately, they find that higher incomes significantly reduce the threat of terrorism in poorer countries, while the

---

[3] Hilary Benn, Secretary of State for International Development "Connecting People and Places," Development Studies Association, September 8, 2005. http://www.dfid.gov.uk/news/files/Speeches/dsa-connect-pandp.asp.

[4] Speech to InterAction April 10, 2006. http://www.usaid.gov/press/speeches/2006/sp060410.html.

[5] "Principles Governing Danish Development Assistance for the Fight against the New Terrorism." Ministry of Foreign Affairs of Denmark 4.

opposite holds in richer countries. Pooling all countries, the two effects would cancel out. The aggregate result may then mask the important role of economic development to offset terrorist threats to poorer countries. Because of methodological and data challenges, however, we must recognize that the issue is not yet resolved.

In contrast to the lack of conclusive evidence on whether the poverty of nations is a determinant of terrorism, the evidence is more uniform that individual poverty does *not* make people more likely to support or participate in terrorist activity. In a survey of 6,000 Muslims from 14 countries, the poorest respondents were the *least* sympathetic to terrorism (Fair and Haqqani 2006). Krueger and Laitin, Laitin and Shapiro, and Llussá and Tavares, in this volume, review evidence showing that individual terrorists are neither poor nor uneducated.

The second question of concern to this volume's contributors is whether weak governance and closed political systems foment terrorism. Results in Krueger and Laitin and Blomberg and Hess, though using substantially different approaches, coincide in finding that terrorism is more likely to originate in countries that exhibit closed political systems. Their findings lend strong support to policy maker assertions that good governance and political responsiveness to citizens are fundamental deterrents of terrorism.

Krueger and Laitin and Blomberg and Hess also agree that the economic characteristics of countries affect whether they will be the *target* of terrorist activity. This leads to a provocative dichotomy. The origins of terrorism seem to be in countries that suffer from political oppression; the targets are countries that enjoy economic success.

Economic openness is another factor that affects both economic development and, potentially, terrorism. In "The Lexus and the Olive Branch," Blomberg and Hess turn precisely to the question of terrorism and globalization. Using an innovative approach to explore this question directly, they examine every country-pair in the world (for which data are available). Not only is it the case that poor, nondemocracies are more likely to be the sources of terrorism in rich, democratic countries but also that more trade reduces terrorism between country pairs. Although these results are intuitive in view of recent terrorist attacks in rich countries, they emerge from estimates based on thousands of terrorist episodes recorded in the data.

Blomberg and Hess and Krueger and Laitin focus on cross-national terrorism, the greatest concern of developed countries. Not least because domestic terrorism can lay the groundwork for cross-national terrorism (the infrastructure of domestic terrorism can be used to project terror internationally), the sources of domestic terror are also important. In his chapter, Sambanis analyzes domestic terrorism and finds that many of the same causal factors as for transnational terrorism emerge. Globalization, for example, has a dampening effect not only on cross-national but also on domestic terrorism. Moreover, Sambanis identifies striking similarities between the causes of civil war and those of terrorism. The exception is precisely economic development: civil war is significantly more likely in poorer and less open countries, while (lack of) openness alone matters most for domestic terrorism.

The conclusion that terrorists are driven not by personal poverty, but by the political and economic climate of the countries from which they come raises new questions. Why should the social environment be more important than individual income? Why are terrorist organizations more common in countries with difficult political climates? In their chapter, Laitin and Shapiro provide reason to believe that the answer lies in the challenges of constructing a terrorist organization. Even though terrorism is not a purely ideological phenomenon, terrorist organizations depend on ideologically motivated, educated recruits. Unlike, for example, trench warfare, terrorism requires individual initiative and the exercise of judgment. Close monitoring by terrorist leaders of their "employees" is not possible. Ideological commitment helps solve part of this contracting problem. So also does an emphasis on recruiting well-educated individuals, who are most likely to come from more prosperous families.

Laitin and Shapiro emphasize that terrorism is not simply the direct outcome of irrational behavior. Terrorism is a complex strategy to achieve economic and political goals, having roots in distinct cultural and religious differences and using ideological commitment to sharpen its organization. Their conclusion is not surprising and could extend to the role of cultural and religious factors in social conflict throughout history. The One Hundred Years War is just one example of prolonged conflict in the West in which religious motivations were intertwined with other serious economic and political differences.

Their argument explains why terrorists themselves are rarely poor and why terrorist organizations are most likely to emerge in politically closed countries. On the one hand, terrorist organization is difficult and requires individuals with substantial human capital, which is more prevalent in families rich enough to educate their children well. On the other hand, to persuade such well-educated, relatively prosperous individuals to join a terrorist organization in democratic countries is difficult: the ideological payoffs are fewer and peaceful alternatives to terrorist methods are more abundant and effective. This also explains the paradox that individual poverty is less associated with terrorist activities than national poverty. National incomes and the political responsiveness of national governments are closely related: political environments that are repressive enough to facilitate terrorist recruitment are less likely to attract substantial investment and entrepreneurial activity.

The conclusions of contributors to this book demonstrate substantial overlaps with policy maker beliefs about the underlying sources of terrorism. Ideology is important, especially in facilitating terrorist organization; political openness and responsiveness to citizens matters, though perhaps mostly in their effects on ideological commitment; economic development plays a nuanced role, which policy makers have also noted – to the extent that low income per capita drives terrorism, it is likely because of underlying factors that affect both national income per capita and the emergence of terrorist organizations. Research does not identify easy policy alternatives but does underline the potential for development interventions as a way to counter terrorist threats.

Broadly speaking, policy makers have four options to draw upon in their response to terrorism: defensive (homeland security); broadly offensive (detecting and eliminating terrorist organizations even if this implies fighting an international war); narrowly tactical (focusing on the individuals and groups who are on the fence between becoming terrorists or not); and developmental (correcting the deep social and economic conditions that breed terrorists). These options are not necessarily mutually exclusive – the military defeat of governments in Germany and Japan in World War II preceded successful economic and institutional development efforts in those countries. However, military objectives usually do not include economic and political development, and development strategies usually have little effect on short-run terrorist threats.

The budget information from Treverton et al. indicates that security and military expenditures have consumed the lion's share of antiterrorism resources in the United States. Development expenditures unrelated to military training or to the military engagements in Iraq and Afghanistan increased, at most, by $4 billion annually in response to the 9/11 attacks, as little as 5 percent of the annual increased expenditures that they trace to the U.S. response to terrorism. However, development assistance, as outlined in USAID's antiterrorism program, does target the full range of development outcomes that research suggests support the emergence of terrorism, emphasizing elections, education, and economic assistance.[6] More generally,

---

[6] http://www.usaid.gov/policy/par05/USAID_PAR05_Highlights.pdf.

and independent of concerns about terrorism, bilateral and multilateral aid agencies are in the midst of a concerted effort to improve governance in poor countries.

The incremental spending on development assistance that can be directly linked to 9/11 is nevertheless small. It is, therefore, worth reflecting on whether the evidence about the links between terrorism and development might justify a greater focus of counterterrorism resources on development objectives, particularly on governance-related development interventions. Policy makers, while recognizing the importance of development in reducing the long-run threat of terrorism, might nevertheless focus on military and security responses to terrorism for two plausible reasons: the instruments of development agencies for improving governance and political accountability may not be sufficiently effective; and even if development instruments do effectively address the root causes of terrorism, they do so too slowly to mitigate clear and present dangers the growing terrorist threat poses.

Regarding the first point, there is no doubt that debates continue to rage about the efficacy of international assistance. These debates often turn precisely on the difficulties that donors have in persuading government elites to sacrifice their private rents to provide economic and political opportunities to citizens. However, in response to threats to their security, wealthy countries have made it abundantly clear that they are willing to exert pressure on governments that goes far beyond the typical financial conditionality that donors, particularly multinational donors, can apply. The contributions to this volume underline the priority that donors should give to accountability in their development programs in these circumstances.

Hesitation to fully incorporate development concerns into a counter-terrorism strategy may also be due to doubts about the efficacy of political development assistance in particular. Research has made substantial progress in identifying specific political features of countries that improve government accountability and performance. Ample evidence suggests, for example, that elections alone are entirely insufficient to ensure the good governance essential to prevent terrorism. If one compares poor countries that hold competitive elections with those that do not, for example, there is little difference in governance performance, as Table 0.1 indicates. Poor democracies and nondemocracies exhibit similar measures of corruption, of bureaucratic quality and the rule of law, and of broader measures of policy accountability, such as secondary school enrollment. Nevertheless, analyses have pointed with some precision to additional factors that are needed to ensure more effective citizen oversight of governments, including citizen information about political performance (see Keefer and Khemani 2005).

Table 0.1. *Elections and good government*

	Poor nondemocracies (#)	Poor democracies (#)	Rich democracies (#)
Corruption, 1997 (0–6, least corrupt = 6)	2.7 (25)	2.9 (34)	4.1 (49)
Bureaucratic quality, 2000 (0–6, 6 = highest quality)	2.3 (28)	2.4 (30)	4.6 (51)
Rule of law, 2000 (0–6, 6 = highest quality)	3.7 (28)	2.9 (30)	4.6 (51)
Gross secondary school enrollment, 1998 (% of school age children enrolled)	39.8 (34)	45.7 (25)	95.8 (48)

Note: Table reprinted from Keefer (forthcoming), Corruption, Bureaucratic Quality and Rule of Law from Political Risk Services, *International Country Risk Guide*. All other indicators from *World Development Indicators*, The World Bank.

The delays with which development efforts take hold are a more likely reason to focus budget allocations on security responses, if one believes that the threat of terrorism is large and imminent. Countries routinely confront a spectrum of security threats, ranging from armed conflict with other sovereign nations to crime. It is useful to compare the response to terrorism with country responses to threats at either end of this spectrum to better assess how development assistance might usefully fit into future counter-terrorism strategies.

As Enders and Sandler emphasize, a defining characteristic of terrorism is the intent of terrorists to create a perception of risk among the general population that is large relative to the size and capabilities of the terrorist group. To the extent that the menace of terrorism rises to the level of national security threats characterized by massed hostile armies and blocked sea lanes, no rational government would consider leavening its military response with development assistance; such assistance would await the resolution of the military conflict.

It is possible, for example, that countries might foment terrorism in lieu of conducting international warfare by traditional means, particularly if they are poor and their enemies are rich and have well-endowed conventional armies. To the extent that this is true, a military response to terrorism is a natural and potentially least-cost method of reducing terrorist activities. It seems difficult to characterize terrorism purely in this way, however, as a manifestation of government-government conflict. Even if in some cases transnational terrorism has been an instrument of governments, it is also evident that when supportive governments fall, terrorist organizations continue to operate, suggesting either that they are not particularly dependent on the support of governments or that the supply of those supportive governments is large.

Crime lies at the other end of the security spectrum from war. It imposes greater risks on citizens in developed countries than does terrorism, at least measured in number of lives lost. To take one example, in the United States, the Federal Bureau of Investigation reports approximately 16,000 murders per year over the past decade (16,528 in 2004). This is approximately six times the number of people who died on 9/11 and more than a thousand times greater than the number of Americans who died in terrorist incidents in a typical year prior to 2001.[7] Compared with the Enders and Sandler estimate of the economic costs of terrorism (that the *total* cost of the 9/11 attacks to the U.S. economy was $90 billion of lost output), Anderson (1999) estimated the cost of crime in the United States to be more than $1 trillion *annually*.

The response to crime also routinely includes a mix of policy options (military/police, defensive/security, developmental, tactical). With respect to the allocation of effort among different crime-fighting strategies in the United States, the latest figures on total criminal justice expenditures, from 2003 (covering city, state, and federal governments and including police, courts, and corrections) amounted to $185.5 billion, of which $83 billion went to police. It is difficult to quantify the costs of U.S. efforts to pursue a "developmental" strategy to reduce crime. However, economic assistance to the poor is roughly similar to the economic development strategies that donors have adopted to mitigate terrorist threats in poor countries. Such assistance includes public education, including special education programs; health care (through Medicaid); social interventions of various kinds; and direct transfers.

If one looks only at money transfers to the poor, excluding all other government programs, the proportion spent relative to criminal justice expenditures is far larger than the ratio of developmental assistance to homeland security and military operations in the U.S. government's counterterrorism strategy. The Department of Health and Human Services spent $48.7 billion in 2005 (the latest period available) on the Administration for Children and Families program.[8] The Social Security Administration spent $40.9 billion

---

[7] http://www.fbi.gov/ucr/cius_04/offenses_reported/violent_crime/murder.html.

[8] Department of Health and Human Services. *Budget in Brief.* 2007. http://www.hhs.gov/budget/07budget/2007BudgetInBrief.pdf.

on the Supplemental Security Income program in 2005.[9] The total outlays exceeded the total costs of policing in 2003 by more than $6 billion.[10] Compared with the war on crime, the war on terror devotes many fewer resources to development.

The interaction of immediate and fundamental responses to crime highlights the potential importance of both a security and a development response to terrorism. Evidence shows that income inequality is a major determinant of the incidence of violent crime but so also is the strength of the police, with opposite effects on crime, of course (see Fajnzylber, Lederman, and Loayza 2002). In the long run, the only way to ensure that crime is no longer a large social concern is by reducing the disparities in income and associated social ills. It can be argued that Scandinavian countries have achieved this. However, the policy response to high crime in the short run is best directed to deterring those people who are on the verge of committing a crime (the marginal actor). This is where strengthening the police and applying more severe penalties can be effective. They modify the incentives of the *marginal* actor, the people or groups considering whether or not to adopt (in the case of terrorism) the terrorist option to advance their objectives.

Of course, other approaches can affect the incentives of marginal actors by directly addressing the grievances of terrorists, which range from the religious or nationalistic to the purely economic (e.g., land redistribution). This volume has little to say about the nature of terrorist grievances and the desirability of addressing them directly. There is little dispute that they matter, however: intensely ideologically motivated terrorists operating in a reasonably sympathetic environment are willing to endure greater hardship and make demands that are more difficult for the targets of terrorism to meet.

Sambanis and Laitin and Shapiro, in this volume, argue that the structure and *modus operandi* of terrorist organizations vary considerably. They depend on the quality of government institutions, their degree of popular support, the sources and magnitude of funding they receive, and their

---

[9] http://www.ssa.gov/budget/2007bud.pdf. Social Security Administration: The Fiscal Year 2007 Budget, Press Release.

[10] These are underestimates, excluding other expenditures with a strong antipoverty component. For example, Medicaid in 2005 cost the federal government $181 billion, children's health care another $5 billion, and discretionary spending for children and families, including $7 billion for Head Start, amounted to another $13 billion. Department of Health and Human Services. Budget in Brief. 2007. http://www.hhs.gov/budget/07budget/2007BudgetInBrief.pdf. http://www.ssa.gov/budget/2007bud.pdf. Social Security Administration: The Fiscal Year 2007 Budget, Press Release.

degree of internal cohesion. This calls for more detailed data than simple event counts to understand the dynamics of terrorism. Most importantly, however, this observation underscores the need for a specifically designed tactical response to fight terrorist organizations. This tactical approach – focused on the incentives of the marginal actor and the structural weaknesses of the terrorist organization – is likely to be the most successful in the short run. In the long run, however, terrorist organizations would keep reappearing and in different shapes unless their fundamental causes are removed. This is where a development response becomes relevant.

At any rate, the object of the book is not to identify the ideal strategy to fight terrorism but to point out that economic and political development are key concerns. Policy makers around the world embrace this conclusion, though in the immediate aftermath of significant terrorist attacks, most policy change and fiscal effort have been dedicated to security and military responses to terrorism. If the analogy to crime is reasonable, however, it appears that the intense security and military focus of the response to terrorism could be leavened with greater incremental attention to the development agenda.[11] The contributions to this volume provide substantial support for an incremental shift toward greater development emphasis – improving governance, promoting international integration, and raising income opportunities – as counterterrorism policy evolves.

References

Anderson, David A. 1999. The aggregate burden of crime. *Journal of Law and Economics* 42(2): 611–42.

Benn, Hilary. 2005. Connecting people and places. Speech given at the Development Studies Association, September 8. Department for International Development, United Kingdom.

---

[11] This is especially so because it appears that much more is spent to prevent a death from terrorism than to prevent murder. Assuming that all expenditures on criminal justice in the United States were intended to prevent murder, expenditures to combat crime amount to approximately $11 million per victim. In response to the 2,500 deaths of September 11, U.S. antiterrorism expenditures (not including those that airlines and others were required by law to undertake) increased by $69–96 billion per year, including the cost of the military response. Assuming that terrorist attacks were expected to continue at this level from 2001 onward then the figures from Treverton et al. suggest that public policy valued the prevention of terrorist deaths at approximately $28 million per death. The expenditures per death would be much larger, by a multiple of hundreds, if the expected lives lost to terrorism from 2002 onwards were closer to the average over the years prior to 2001. The figure would be much lower than $28 million, though, if policy makers expected a substantial escalation in deaths from terrorism (e.g., from biological or nuclear threats).

Bilmes, Linda, and Joseph E. Stiglitz. 2006. The economic costs of the Iraq War: An appraisal three years after the beginning of the conflict. Paper presented at the meetings of the American Economic Association, January.

Fair, C. Christine, and Husain Haqqani. 2006. Think again: Islamist terrorism. *Foreign Policy* (January 30): http://www.foreignpolicy.com/story/cms.php?story_id=3359& page=1.

Fajnzylber, P., D. Lederman, and N. Loayza. 2002. What causes violent crime? *The European Economic Review* 46(7): 1323–57.

Keefer, Philip. Forthcoming. Beyond elections: Politics, development and the poor performance of poor democracies. In *The Oxford Encyclopedia of Comparative Politics*, ed. Carles Boix and Susan Stokes.

Keefer, Philip, and Stuti Khemani. 2005. Democracy, public expenditures, and the poor: Understanding political incentives for providing public services. *The World Bank Research Observer* 20:1 (Spring): 1–28.

Ministry of Foreign Affairs, Denmark. n.d. Principles governing Danish development assistance for the fight against the new terrorism. http://www.dfid.gov.uk/news/files/Speeches/dsa-connect-pandp.asp.

Tobias, Andrew. 2006. Speech to InterAction, April 10. United States Agency for International Development. http://www.usaid.gov/press/speeches/2006/sp060410.html.

PART ONE

THE COSTS OF TERRORISM

ONE

Economic Consequences of Terrorism in Developed and Developing Countries

An Overview

Todd Sandler and Walter Enders

Terrorism is the premeditated use or threat of use of violence by individuals or subnational groups to obtain a political or social objective through the intimidation of a large audience, beyond that of the immediate victim.[1] Although the motives of terrorists may differ, their actions follow a standard pattern, with terrorist incidents assuming a variety of forms: airplane hijackings, kidnappings, assassinations, threats, bombings, and suicide attacks. Terrorist attacks are intended to apply sufficient pressures on a government so that it grants political concessions. If a besieged government views the anticipated costs of future terrorist actions as greater than the costs of conceding to terrorist demands, then the government will grant some accommodation. Thus, a rational terrorist organization can, in principle, achieve some of its goals more quickly if it is able to augment the consequences of its campaign. These consequences can assume many forms, including casualties, destroyed buildings, a heightened anxiety level, and myriad economic costs. Clearly, the attacks on September 11, 2001, (henceforth, 9/11) had significant costs that have been estimated to be in the range of $80 to $90 billion when subsequent economic losses in lost wages, workman's compensation, and reduced commerce are included (Kunreuther et al. 2003). The cumulative costs of 9/11 were a small percentage of U.S. gross domestic product (GDP), which exceeded $10 trillion.

---

[1] This short definition reflects 25 years of debate among terrorist experts. It identifies the perpetrators (subnational groups or individuals), the audience (as being beyond the immediate victims), and necessity of political demands or objectives. Thus, an alternative definition – e.g., terrorism is the intentional targeting of civilians – is inadequate because it encompasses criminal acts with no political objective. Our short definition is the basis for which datasets (see the next section) are constructed. We exclude state, but not state-sponsored, terrorism because datasets used in economic studies of terrorism ignore state terror. The economic effect of state terror is very difficult to measure because the counterfactual is very hard to construct.

Terrorism can impose costs on a targeted country through a number of avenues. Terrorist incidents have economic consequences by diverting foreign direct investment (FDI), destroying infrastructure, redirecting public investment funds to security, or limiting trade. If a developing country loses enough FDI, which is an important source of savings, then it may also experience reduced economic growth. Just as capital may take flight from a country plagued by a civil war (see Collier et al. 2003), a sufficiently intense terrorist campaign may greatly reduce capital inflows (Enders and Sandler 1996; Enders et al. 2006). Terrorism, like civil conflicts, may cause spillover costs among neighboring countries as a terrorist campaign in a neighbor discourages capital inflows or a regional multiplier causes lost economic activity in the terrorism-ridden country to resonate throughout the region.[2] In some instances, terrorism may affect specific industries, as 9/11 did on airlines and tourism (Drakos 2004; Ito and Lee 2004). Another cost is the expensive security measures that must be instituted following large attacks – for example, the massive homeland security outlays since 9/11 (Enders and Sandler 2006a, chap. 10). Terrorism also raises the costs of doing business in terms of higher insurance premiums, expensive security precautions, and larger salaries to at-risk employees.

The size in terms of GDP *and* the diversity of an economy have much to do with the ability of a country to withstand terrorist attacks without showing significant economic effects. Yemen's shipping industry suffered greatly after the terrorist attacks on the USS *Cole* and the *Limburg*; half of Yemen's port activities diverted to competitive facilities in Djibouti and Oman due to a 300 percent increase in insurance premiums (U.S. Department of State Fact Sheet 2002). This diversion resulted in a loss of $3.8 million per month to Yemen's shipping industry. Such losses have a greater potential economic effect in a country with a smaller GDP because they represent a greater share of GDP. Although the same number of people may lose jobs, the percentage of the work force affected is greater for smaller less-developed than for larger developed countries. The degree of diversification of the affected economy also matters. In a more diversified and developed economy, such shipping losses may have a temporary influence as resources (capital and labor) are reallocated to other industries (including those in the export sector) or better security measures are deployed to allay concerns. When a small developing country's export sector is tied to a few activities (e.g., shipping), an attack

---

[2] For civil conflicts, these spatial spillovers are measured by Murdoch and Sandler (2002, 2004).

that affects one of these activities will have a significant effect on the country's foreign exchange earnings. The ability of released resources to bolster other exporting activities is limited if there are few alternatives.

This chapter has four purposes. First and most important, it takes stock of the literature on the economic consequences of terrorism and evaluates the methodology used to date. The literature dates back to the early 1990s, with most of the contributions coming after 9/11. Second, macroeconomic influences of terrorism are distinguished from microeconomic sector- or industry-specific effects. Third, terrorism effects in developed countries are contrasted with those in developing countries. Fourth, we indicate how researchers can better account for economic consequences in developing countries.

The remainder of the chapter contains seven sections. Section 1 reviews concepts and definitions that are necessary for understanding the economic consequences of terrorism. In Section 2, we investigate how the United States, representative of other developed nations, cushioned the blow and sped recovery from the unprecedented attacks of 9/11 through monetary, fiscal, and other policies. Section 3 reviews and evaluates some macroeconomic studies of the effect of terrorism, whereas Section 4 contrasts anticipated differences between how terrorism affects developing and developed countries. In Section 5, we review and analyze past microeconomic studies of the economic fallout from terrorism. Section 6 discusses past methodologies. Section 7 provides future directions and conclusions.

1. Essential Concepts

Studies over the last decade have established that internal conflicts can have significant economic consequences in terms of reduced growth within a conflict-ridden country (e.g., Collier and Hoeffler 2004; Collier and Sambanis 2002; Collier et al. 2003) and in neighboring countries (Murdoch and Sandler 2002, 2004). A civil war is a broader conflict than terrorism because the former usually involves a minimum of one thousand deaths and may result in tens of thousands of casualties, while a terrorist incident results, on average, in a single death (Sandler 2003). Thus, a country may be plagued with at least one terrorist incident in, say, ten of ten years but experience relatively few deaths and modest property damage. Terrorism is a tactic that may or may not be associated with a civil war, insurrection, or other form of political violence. As such, terrorism typically involves little loss of life and property. Naturally, there are exceptions, such as the March 11, 2004,

Madrid train bombings or the December 21, 1988, downing of Pan Am flight 107, where two to three hundred people perished, respectively. But even in these cases, the loss of life, though tragic, is small compared with most internal conflicts so that the likely macroeconomic effect of terrorist events is not anticipated to rival civil wars.

This prediction may change under a few scenarios: a large-scale attack like 9/11, a protracted terrorist campaign with many deadly incidents, or some devastating attack on a developing country's export sector (recall the Yemen shipping example). One should not expect that a modest number of terrorist incidents in most countries will greatly affect the countries' income growth. Sector-specific microeconomic influences are often the most likely consequences from terrorism.

1.1. Cost Distinction

Numerous cost distinctions could be drawn regarding terrorism losses. Direct costs, for example, involve the immediate losses associated with a terrorist attack or campaign and include damaged goods, the value of lives lost, the costs associated with injuries (including lost wages), destroyed structures, damaged infrastructure, and reduced short-term commerce. In contrast, indirect or secondary costs concern attack-related subsequent losses, such as higher insurance premiums, increased security costs, greater compensation to those at high-risk locations, and costs tied to attack-induced long-run changes in commerce. Indirect costs may surface as reduced growth in GDP, lost FDI, changes in inflation, or increased unemployment. A judgment must be made as to how to distinguish between direct and indirect costs, in which any distinction would strike some researchers as arbitrary.

Fortunately, this distinction is not really necessary to characterize the economic effect of terrorism, which can be represented in terms of some well-defined macroeconomic (e.g., real per capita GDP growth) or microeconomic variable (e.g., reduced tourist receipts). These variables then represent the consequences of terrorism in terms of aggregate or sectoral activity. If lost output, casualties, and damaged infrastructure are sufficiently large, then they will affect the economy's productive capacity with macroeconomic or microeconomic repercussions. The identification of these effects is of greater importance than the mere tally of losses if policy is to ameliorate the economic ramifications of terrorism. Thus, we concentrate on relating terrorism to macroeconomic and microeconomic variables that policy can be designed to bolster.

1.2. Domestic Versus Transnational Terrorism

Terrorism comes in two essential types: domestic and transnational. Domestic terrorism is homegrown and affects the host country most: its institutions, citizens, property, and policies. In a domestic terrorist incident both the victim and perpetrators are from the host country. The Oklahoma City bombing on April 19, 1995, was a domestic terrorist event as was the kidnapping of members of Parliament by Colombian terrorists. Many ethno-nationalist conflicts (e.g., the Tamils of Sri Lanka) are associated with mostly domestic terrorism, unless the rebels desire to target citizens from other countries to publicize their cause to the world. Domestic events outnumber transnational terrorist events about eight to one (Enders and Sandler 2006a).

In contrast, transnational terrorism involves more than one country. This international aspect can stem from the victims, targets, institutions, supporters, terrorists, and transnational consequences. For example, 9/11 is a transnational terrorist event because the victims were from many different countries, the mission was financed and planned from abroad, the terrorists were foreigners, and the implications of the events (e.g., financial and security) were transnational. Transnational terrorist attacks often entail transboundary externalities: actions or authorities in one country impose uncompensated consequences on persons or property in another country. Thus, spillover costs can result so that the economic effect of a terrorist event transcends the host country. The toppling of the World Trade Center towers on 9/11 killed many British nationals and had ramifications for British financial institutions. Chen and Siems (2004, Tab. 2, Figs. 2–3) showed that 9/11 negatively influenced average returns on stock markets globally. In fact, the 11-day cumulative average abnormal returns were larger on the London, Frankfurt, Paris, Toronto, Amsterdam, Switzerland, Italy, and Hong Kong stock markets than on the New York Stock Exchange following 9/11. The four blasts on 9/11 reverberated on capital markets worldwide.

The distinction between domestic and transnational terrorism is of utmost importance when determining the right data for calculating the economic consequences of terrorism. Suppose that we want to relate the growth in real per capita GDP to a country's *level of terrorism*. For a country plagued by both domestic and transnational terrorism, *all* terrorist events must be included if the estimated coefficient on the terrorist term is to be properly interpreted. If, for example a country has just one transnational terrorist event but twenty domestic terrorist incidents, and if, moreover, *only* transnational terrorist events are included, then the terrorism coefficient is going to attribute its effect to one event when there are twenty-one events. When, instead, a country has no transnational terrorism but is plagued by domestic terrorism, a drop in growth will be attributed to nonterrorism causes, even though domestic terrorism may be the culprit. The argument that transnational terrorism can serve as a proxy for all terrorism is not necessarily valid because no one really knows whether the two types of terrorism are correlated. Moreover, the magnitude of the correlation is unknown and may not be constant over time and space. There are countries (e.g., Sri Lanka) with lots of domestic terrorism and little transnational terrorism and other countries with lots of transnational terrorism and little domestic terrorism. Even if the two types of terrorism were perfectly correlated, the magnitude of the terrorism coefficient must be interpreted with care. Additionally, the potential correlation between domestic terrorist incidents and other independent variables remains a concern. The exclusion of domestic terrorism is an issue for cross-section and country-specific studies of the consequences of terrorism on macroeconomic variables.

This problem can be partly circumvented if an internal conflict measure is introduced as an independent variable (see Blomberg, Hess, and Orphanides 2004), because domestic terrorism is anticipated to be somewhat correlated with internal conflict. The latter can then control for the influence of domestic terrorism. The terrorism coefficient would thus reflect the effect of transnational terrorism and not terrorism per se.

In the case of net foreign direct investment (NFDI), transnational terrorism is the appropriate terrorism variable when terrorist attacks have been directed at foreign investments or their personnel and little or no domestic terrorism exists (Enders and Sandler 1996). In a recent cross-sectional study, Enders et al. (2006) used transnational terrorist events to gauge the effect on the stock of FDI in targeted countries. Such events are appropriate because attacks against U.S. interests in host countries are transnational by definition and should have a greater effect than domestic incidents in reducing U.S. foreign investments in these countries. If foreign tourism is being investigated, then transnational terrorist attacks are appropriate when such attacks are against tourist venues or infrastructure serving tourism. Moreover, any domestic terrorism must be far from these tourists so that they do not feel threatened.

1.3. On Terrorism Data

To date, much of the literature has relied on the *International Terrorism: Attributes of Terrorist Events* (ITERATE) dataset (Mickolus et al. 2004) of transnational terrorist events. Based on newspaper and media accounts,

ITERATE records many variables (e.g., incident date, incident location by country, type of event, number killed, groups claiming responsibility, and demands made) for transnational terrorist events from 1968 through 2004. ITERATE does not classify terrorism incidents that relate to declared wars or major military interventions by governments or guerrilla attacks on military targets conducted as internationally recognized acts of belligerency. However, ITERATE classifies attacks against civilians or the dependents of military personnel as terrorist acts when such attacks are intended to create an atmosphere of fear *to foster political objectives*. ITERATE allows a researcher to match terrorist incidents with countries so as to compute losses from transnational terrorist campaigns. These losses would have to be inferred from macroeconomic and microeconomic data drawn from other sources.

The International Policy Institute for Counterterrorism (IPIC 2003) maintains an online dataset. IPIC describes its 1,427 terrorist incidents for 1987–2001 as "selected" transnational terrorist incidents. The data source does not, however, give its criteria for classifying an incident as a transnational terrorist event. Moreover, IPIC does *not* provide its selection criterion; ITERATE records many times the number of incidents during the same period. The IPIC selection criterion is particularly important for judging potential bias. When sampling the incidents, we found many incidents that would not have satisfied ITERATE's transnational criterion – for example, some Palestinian incidents in Israel. In fact, IPIC data include a disproportionate number of incidents from the Middle East. This is not surprising because IPIC is put together by the Interdisciplinary Center Herziliya in Israel (http://www.ict.org.il).

The National Memorial Institute for the Prevention of Terrorism (MIPT 2005) also maintains an online dataset on terrorism. From 1968 through 1997, the data consists of transnational terrorism. Thereafter, MIPT tallies both domestic and transnational terrorist events. The Web site makes it easy to make graphs and other displays. A researcher must expend much effort to put the data in a form that would relate incidents by countries so that statistical analysis on the economic consequences of terrorism can be accomplished. The addition of domestic events is very useful but there are only seven years of data.

Figure 1.1 displays a comparison of yearly ITERATE and MIPT incident totals from 1968 through 2005. Until the start of 1996, ITERATE used the Foreign Broadcast Information Service (FBIS) *Daily Reports* as one of its information sources. With the dropping of the FBIS *Daily Reports*, ITERATE totals beginning in 1996 may not be directly comparable with those of earlier years. Omitted incidents after 1995 are apt to be threats and hoaxes that

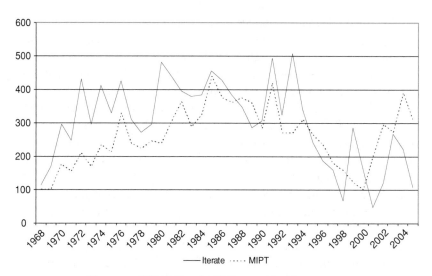

Figure 1.1. ITERATE and MIPT annual incident counts.

have little newsworthiness. To make the ITERATE data more consistent throughout the period, we purged threats and hoaxes for all years displayed by the unbroken time series.

The general shape of the two time-series plots in Figure 1.1 are reasonably similar until 2004. Both series rose from slightly more than one hundred annual incidents in 1968 and 1969 and reached their highest sustained levels in the 1980s. In the early 1990s, both series began a steady decline, which stopped in 1998 for ITERATE and in 2000 for MIPT. The number of incidents in ITERATE generally exceeded those in the MIPT data until 1995. Subsequently, the MIPT incidents generally exceeded those in ITERATE. The larger ITERATE totals for 1998 and 1999 are due to MIPT not collecting data for these years and having to do so a number of years later. There are sufficient differences between the series that the results of an empirical study might hinge on which of the datasets is used. The difference remains sizable even if threats and hoaxes are added back to the ITERATE data.

Most of the recent differences between ITERATE and MIPT are attributable to the Iraq War and its aftermath. As shown in Figure 1.1, ITERATE report 222 incidents in 2004 and 108 in 2005. MIPT report 398 and 303, respectively, for these same years. To explain this discrepancy, we note that MIPT reports a transnational terrorist incident on January 1, 2005, when the bodies of two Iraqi drivers working for U.S. forces were found in Baghdad. The weapons used in the attack and the group responsible for the killing are unknown. This same event is not included in ITERATE. Because the cause of death and the attackers are unknown, it is not clear that this is a terrorist act. Even if the attackers were terrorists, it is not clear that this is a transnational terrorist incident because the drivers were Iraqis. Moreover, some researchers may argue that attacks against persons employed by the U.S. military in Iraq are attacks against an occupying force that are excluded by ITERATE and other data sources (e.g., U.S. Department of State). The simple correlation coefficient between ITERATE and MIPT data series is 0.69 through 2000. The correlation coefficient falls to 0.53 using the dataset through 2005, so that discrepancies grew in recent years.

There are a few datasets available for conducting specific country studies – see Abadie and Gardeazabal (2003) on Spain and Eckstein and Tsiddon (2004) on Israel. In the latter case, the Israeli terrorism data came from IPIC. Country-level data are also available for Colombia and a few other countries.

1.4. Causality

A final preliminary concerns the causal nature between terrorism and the macroeconomic variable that proxies the consequences of terrorism. If economic downturns can create grievances that result in terrorism, then economic conditions may be both a root cause of terrorism and a consequence of terrorism. Recently, researchers have established with panel estimates that economic conditions, particularly downturns, can generate transnational terrorist attacks.[3] Given this evidence, a researcher must be prudent to test and/or correct for a potential endogeneity bias.

2. Macroeconomic Effects of Terrorism

An economy as rich and diverse as that of the United States is anticipated to withstand most terrorist events with few macroeconomic consequences. During most years, the United States experienced few terrorist events on its own soil – for example, in 1998, 2000, and the years following 2001, no terrorist events occurred in the United States (Sandler and Enders 2004; U.S. Department of State 1999–2004). Moreover, the breadth of U.S. economic activities is sufficiently diverse to absorb the effect of an attack by shifting

---

[3] Studies include Blomberg, Hess, and Orphanides (2004), Blomberg, Hess, and Weerapana (2004), Li (2005), and Li and Schaub (2004). These studies investigated causes beyond economic conditions – e.g., globalization, democracy, and government restraint.

activities to unaffected sectors. A mature market economy generates signals (i.e., prices and profits) to direct resources to where returns are the greatest. These signals also help channel resources to where rebuilding and other responses are required. If an affected sector has a slow recovery, then some resources will leave for better short-term prospects and will return when prospects improve.

The immediate costs of typical terrorist acts, such as kidnappings, assassinations, or bombings, are localized, not unlike ordinary crimes. Currently, crimes such as identity theft have far greater potential economic consequences for developed countries than terrorism. In most developed countries, terrorism generally causes a substitution from sectors vulnerable to terrorism into relatively safe areas and, thus, does not affect the entire macroeconomy.[4] If airlines become risky, factors of production will shift from the airline sector to other relatively safer sectors. Of course, a terrorist act of the magnitude of 9/11 can shake confidence and influence sufficiently many sectors to have macroeconomics repercussions. But as we show later in this chapter, developed countries are positioned to take actions to limit these effects.

This representation is in marked contrast to small economies in which terrorism is prevalent and affects daily activities, as in Colombia, Israel, and the Basque region of Spain. For these economies, terrorism can reduce GDP and curb development, especially during prolonged campaigns (e.g., Israel since September 27, 2000). Protracted terrorism leads to the anticipation of future events, which create risk premiums that limit activities in terrorism-prone sectors. Investors, both at home and abroad, may decide to direct their assets to safer activities in other countries. If terrorists succeed in scaring away investments, they may be emboldened to take further actions to cause economic losses.

2.1. U.S. Experience in Light of 9/11

Figure 1.2 provides strong evidence for the view that the U.S. economy quickly rebounded from 9/11. The vertical line in the center of each panel of Figure 1.2 represents the third quarter of 2001 (i.e., 2001:Q3) corresponding to 9/11. Panel 1 shows that real GDP was virtually unchanged throughout 2000 and fell slightly in the first and third quarters of 2001. The key feature is that real GDP began to grow sharply beginning in the fourth quarter of 2001 following 9/11. Panel 2 shows that the Conference Board's measure of

---

[4] On terrorism-induced substitution, see Enders and Sandler (1993, 2004, 2006b).

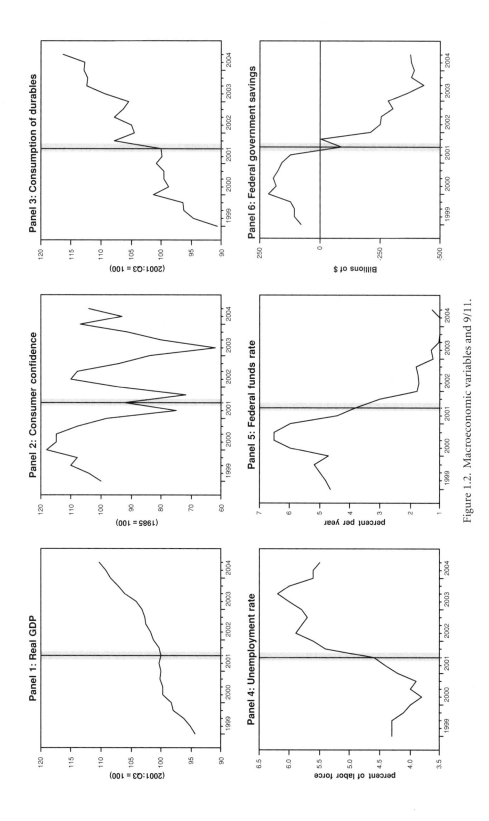

Figure 1.2. Macroeconomic variables and 9/11.

consumer confidence plummeted right before the onset of the 2001 recession; however, immediately following 9/11, confidence actually soared. Some of this increase might be attributed to the patriotism of the American public. As displayed in Panel 3, the rebound in economic activity was buoyed by strong consumer demand for durables. These "big-ticket" items are the most volatile component of total consumption, which jumped in the fourth quarter of 2001. Panel 4 indicates that the unemployment rate was rising prior to 9/11 and rose dramatically after the attack. Because the unemployment rate is a lagging indicator of economic activity, this rate would likely have increased even without 9/11. Thus, we must wonder what would have happened to unemployment in the absence of 9/11 – that is, the unemployment rate *may* have risen even faster.

There is a consensus that well-orchestrated macroeconomic policy making cushioned the shock from 9/11 in the United States. The financial markets were in disarray as bond market trading was suspended for a day and stock market trading did not resume until the following week. During uncertain times, risk-averse asset holders increase the proportion of highly liquid assets in their portfolios. As shown in Panel 5, the Federal Reserve reacted to this surge in liquidity demand by sharply cutting the Federal Funds rate, thereby keeping funds available for investment and other needs. Fiscal policy also performed a supportive role. The first tax cut since 1985 was signed into law in May 2001, months before 9/11. As a direct reaction to 9/11, the U.S. Congress approved a $40 billion supplemental appropriation for emergency spending for such items as search and rescue efforts at the four crash sites and tightened security at U.S. airports and other venues. In addition to the needed disaster relief, this surge in government spending acted as a powerful stimulus to aggregate demand. Starting on October 7, 2001, the war in Afghanistan also bolstered government spending. As shown in Panel 6, government saving (i.e., the negative of what many call the federal government's budget deficit) plummeted from uncharacteristic surpluses to record deficits. Although the government budget deficit can have some long-term undesirable influences, U.S. fiscal and monetary policies appear to have played an essential role in restoring consumer and business confidence.

3. Review of Macroeconomic Literature on Terrorism Effects

The literature on the macroeconomic consequences of terrorism only began in 2003 and involves only a handful of studies. One set of studies examines the influence of various terrorist variables on real per capita GDP growth, whereas a second set of studies consists of case studies of a country experiencing a long-term terrorist campaign. Two basic findings derive from these studies: (1) the effects of terrorism on reduced growth is on average, quite small, and (2) countries with sustained terrorist campaigns may lose over 10 percent of their GDP.

Blomberg, Hess, and Orphanides (henceforth, BHO) (2004) examined a pooled cross-section of 177 countries from 1968 to 2000. Their estimating equation is:

$$\Delta y_i = \beta_0 + \beta_1 COM_i + \beta_2 AFRICA + \beta_3 \ln y_{0i} + \beta_4 I/Y_i + \beta_5 T_i$$
$$+ \beta_6 I_i + \beta_7 E_i + \varepsilon_i, \tag{1}$$

where Δy_i is country i's average per capita GDP growth rate; βs are coefficients; COM is a dummy variable for non-oil commodity exporters; AFRICA is a dummy for African countries; y_{0i} is country i's initial income; I/Y_i is country i's investment rate over the full sample; T_i is a transnational terrorism indicator (e.g., a dummy for terrorism occurring in a given year); I_i denotes the presence of an internal conflict in i; E_i indicates i's involvement in an external conflict; and ε_i is the error term. Their baseline regression indicated that non-oil commodity exporters and African nations had lower average per capita GDP growth of 1.2 percent and 1.36 percent, respectively. We are primarily interested in BHO's terrorism variable's effect on economic growth. BHO found that if a country experienced transnational terrorist incidents on its soil in *each* year of the sample period, then per capita income growth fell by 1.587 percentage points over the *entire* sample period. Given the definition of T_i, each year of terrorism led on average to a fall in growth of only 0.048 percent ($= 1.587/33$). BHO's initial terrorism measure treated a year with fifty deadly incidents the same as a year with a single nonfatal incident. As such, this measure does not indicate the growth effect of either the level or intensity (i.e., how deadly is the campaign) of terrorism; thus, the effect of an average terrorist incident on growth cannot be ascertained from this specification. Moreover, these authors used *just transnational terrorism incidents* drawn from the ITERATE dataset. Some sample countries would have experienced a far greater amount of domestic terrorism, which was not directly controlled in the study. BHO, were, however, careful to control for internal and external conflict: internal conflict had a significant negative effect on growth for some empirical specifications, whereas external conflict did not have a significant influence. The internal conflict measure should be picking up some of the effects of domestic terrorism because the latter is anticipated to be correlated with such conflicts.

BHO's study controlled for some endogeneity bias. An especially inter-esting part of their study is their panel estimates for nondemocratic coun-tries, OECD countries, African countries, the Middle Eastern countries, and Asian countries. The panel estimates altered some right-hand side variables compared with the cross-sectional regressions – for example, COM_i was dropped and trade openness was added along with lagged per capita growth. Except for the African panel, BHO's terrorism indicator was not significant, which is a cause of concern. As a geographical area, Africa displayed the least amount of terrorism in an average year (see BHO 2004, Tab. 1; Enders and Sandler 2006b, Figs. 5–6), yet Africa was the only panel where the esti-mated terrorism coefficient was significant. This rather surprising finding is consistent with less diversified economies experiencing a larger effect from terrorism. However, there are many undiversified economies in the Middle East and nondemocratic samples that did not display the same influence. The full panel estimates gave a much greater effect of terrorism on growth – that is, terrorism in a single year reduced per capita GDP growth by *over a half a percent* – compared with the cross-sectional estimates. No explana-tion was offered for this huge difference in the consequences of terrorism between the two estimating procedures. It is curious that terrorism's average influence on growth for the entire sample is not reflected in *any* of the panels where terrorism is the greatest concern. Moreover, their large cross-section analysis did not discriminate between different time periods where terror-ism changed in character – for example, from left-wing to fundamentalist groups. Previous studies showed that terrorism became more deadly with the rise of fundamentalist terrorism in the 1980s and beyond (Enders and Sandler 2000). As a consequence, the increased intensity of an "average" terrorist incident may have a greater economic effect in the latter half of the sample period.

In another set of panel estimates, BHO (2004) changed their terrorism indicator to terrorist incidents per capita. This new measure indicates the prevalence of terrorism in terms of the likelihood that incidents will affect someone in the population. The per capita measure also accounts for the level of terrorism. This change gives a significant terrorism effect on per capita GDP growth for the full sample, the nondemocratic panel, the OECD panel, and the African panel. Moreover, the effect of terrorism *varies widely* between the full sample and the smaller cohort panels, leading one to conclude that the full sample "average" picture may not be representative of how smaller cohorts or individual countries respond to terrorism.

Toward the end of the paper, BHO (2004) performed some panel estimates regarding terrorism's influence of the share investment to GDP and the share of government spending to GDP. These estimates are quite useful because they establish the pathway by which terrorism affects economic growth. BHO found that terrorism increased the government-spending share, while it decreased the investment share. This reallocation can affect growth by diverting government activities away from more productive activities to security. Moreover, reduced investment will limit growth directly.

A second cross-sectional study, by Tavares (2004), examined the cost of terrorism in terms of reduced per capita GDP growth. His sample period was 1987–2001 for a large unspecified sample of countries. The estimating equation is:

$$\text{Growth } GDPpc_{it} = \beta_0 + \beta_1 \text{ Growth} GDPpc_{i,t-1} + \beta_2 GDPpc_{it}$$
$$+ \beta_3 \text{ Terrorism}_{it} + \beta_4 \text{ Natural Disaster}_{it}$$
$$+ \beta_5 \text{ Currency Crisis}_{it} + \text{Additional Controls} + \varepsilon_{it},$$

$$(2)$$

where GrowthGDP_{pc} is per capita GDP growth. On the right-hand side of (2), there is lagged per capita GDP growth, per capita GDP, a terrorism measure, a natural disaster index, a currency index, additional controls, and an error term. The terrorism measure is either the total number of attacks per capita or the total number of casualties per capita. Tavares (2004) drew his terrorism variable from data provided by the IPIC (2003) for the 1987–2001 period.

Using instrumental variables to address the potential endogeneity between terrorism and real per capita GDP growth, Tavares found that the terrorism variable had a small but significant negative effect on GDP growth of 0.038 percent (Tavares 2004, Tab. 4), on par with BHO's (2004) initial set of estimates. Once additional determinants of growth (e.g., an education variable, trade openness, primary goods exports, and the inflation rate) were introduced into the estimating equation, *terrorism was no longer a significant* or *negative influence on economic growth*. This raises a concern because many of these additional variables are in standard analyses of growth, so that Tavares' earlier findings about the consequences of terrorism must be questioned. The absence of key growth variables in his earlier equations suggests that they were misspecified.

Tavares (2004) went on to compare the costs of terrorism in democratic versus nondemocratic countries. For our purposes, the key part of his regression equation is:

$$\Delta y_{it} = 0.261 \Delta y_{it-1} - 0.029 T_{it} + 0.121 \left(T_{it} \times R_{it} \right)$$
$$+ \text{ other explanatory variables,} \qquad (3)$$

where Δy_{it} is country i's growth of per capita GDP in year t, Δy_{it-1} is country i's growth of per capita GDP in year $t - 1$, T_{it} is the number of terrorist attacks in country i in year t, and R_{it} is a measure of political rights in country i in year t. This last variable increases when the level of political freedom rises.

Equation (3) is a dynamic specification for which current period growth is affected by growth in the previous period. In contrast to Tavares' original specification that ignored political rights, all of the coefficients reported in (3) are statistically significant. The coefficient on T_{it} indicates that a single terrorist incident in country i in year t reduces annual growth for that year by 0.029 percent. Because the model is dynamic, this growth effect has some persistence. An interesting finding involves the positive coefficient on the interaction term $T_{it} \times R_{it}$, for which the effect of a typical terrorist attack decreases as the level of political freedom increases. That is, democracies are better able to withstand terrorist attacks than other types of governments with less flexible institutions. Yet another interpretation is that democracies are better prepared to weather attacks because they rely on markets to allocate resources. By not including R_{it} as an additional argument in (3), the coefficient of the interaction term is probably biased in an upward fashion.

3.1. Case Studies

To date, there are two macroeconomic case studies on specific terrorism-ridden economies. Both studies are careful and utilize methodologies that could be applied to other countries – for example, Colombia – that have experienced a prolonged campaign of terrorism. For the Basque region, Abadie and Gardeazabal (2003) estimated the per capita GDP losses attributable to a 20-year terrorist campaign. Because the Basque region differs from other regions in Spain, the authors had to construct a "synthetic" comparison region by taking a weighted average combination of other Spanish regions. The weights were chosen to yield the values to key growth variables – for example, real per capita GDP, investment share of GDP, population density, and human capital measures – that are nearly identical to those of the Basque region *prior* to its terrorism. Their synthetic region is required to provide a counterfactual "Basque region," whose growth in the absence of terrorism can be compared with the growth in the Basque region in the presence of terrorism. The authors demonstrated that the Basque and synthetic regions displayed similar per capita GDP values prior to 1975 and the start of the terror campaign. Thereafter, a GDP gap opened that averaged 10 percent over the next 20 years. During high-terrorism episodes, the gap equaled 12 percent, whereas during low-terrorism episodes, the gap closed to 8–9 percent.

To address a possible "placebo" influence, the authors also investigated the growth of another Spanish region – that is, Catalonia – that was similar to the Basque region but did not experience terrorism. A synthetic region was also constructed for Catalonia. The authors then showed that there was little gap in real per capita GDP over time for Catalonia and its synthetic region, both of which had no terrorism. The Abadie and Gardeazabal (2003) methodology is very clever and could be applied to a country study, *provided* that a synthetic country can be constructed. Their exercise is probably easier within a country than for an entire country.

Eckstein and Tsiddon (2004) applied a vector autoregression (VAR) methodology to investigate the effects of terrorism on the macroeconomy of Israel. These authors used quarterly data from 1980 through 2003 to analyze the effects of terrorism on real GDP, investment, exports, and nondurable consumer goods. Each of these variables served as a dependent variable in their four-equation VAR system. Their measure of terrorism was a weighted average of the number of Israeli fatalities, injuries, and noncasuality incidents. Their terrorism data included domestic and transnational attacks in Israel. They found that the initial effect of terrorism on economic activity was as short as a single quarter. Moreover, terrorism's influence on exports and investment was three times larger than on nondurable consumption and two times larger than on GDP.

Eckstein and Tsiddon (2004) also employed their VAR estimates to calculate the economic consequences of the Intifada. They used their data to estimate the VAR through 2000:Q3 (the beginning of the Intifada) and forecasted real GDP for quarters 2000:Q4 through 2003:Q4. Forecasts were conducted assuming either no subsequent terrorism or terrorism at the levels that actually prevailed for these three years. The differences in forecasts translated into a *per capita GDP loss of about 10 percent* for terrorism continuing at its prevailing elevated level.

The four key macroeconomic studies are summarized in Table 1.1 for ready reference. The first column indicates the study and its basic methodology,[5] while the second column provides a short description of the study. In the right-hand column, some key findings are indicated.

---

[5] Some studies utilized additional methodologies. For example, BHO (2004) also presented a VAR analysis. Abadie and Gardeazabal (2003) did an event study of abnormal returns of two portfolios of stocks: one for firms with business interests in the Basque region and one for firms with business interests elsewhere. The performance of the former portfolio was tied to terrorist events in the Basque region.

Table 1.1. *Macroeconomic studies of the effect of terrorism*

Study and method	Description	Findings
BHO (2004) *Cross-section and panel*	Growth in per capita income as a function of conflict, terrorism, and standard growth variables. Some runs control for endogeneity concerns. Entire sample and select cohorts are analyzed.	Terrorism has a small effect on per capita income growth for entire sample but not for most cohorts. Terrorism reduces I/Y, while it increases G/Y.
Tavares (2004) *Cross-section and panel*	Growth in real per capita GDP is a function of logged growth in real per capita GDP, terrorism, other crises, and growth variables. Some runs account for simultaneity bias. Introduces an interactive term between terrorism and political rights as a determinant of growth in per capita GDP.	Terrorism has a small effect on growth on par with that of BHO when standard growth variables are left out. When these variables are included, terrorism has no influence. Evidence is provided that countries with well-developed democratic institutions can withstand terrorism attacks.
Abadie and Gardeazabal (2003) *Case study for Spain*	Contrast the Basque region with terrorism and a "synthetic" region without terrorism. The latter is based on a weighted composite of other peaceful regions in Spain.	Finds a 10% average gap in per capita GDP that they attribute to terrorism over a 20-year period.
Eckstein and Tsiddon (2004) *VAR for Israel[a]*	The four interactive time series include per capita GDP, investment, exports, and nondurable consumption.	Terrorism has a significant negative effect on per capita GDP, investment, and exports. Terrorism's influence on investment and exports is two times its effect on per capita GDP. Counterfactual exercise shows that the high recent levels of terrorism resulted in a 10% annual decline in per capita GDP.

[a] *VAR* denotes vector autoregression.

4. Developed and Developing Countries Contrasts

Past macroeconomic studies have given limited insight on how developing countries' economies have weathered terrorist attacks. The two case studies have been for small *high-income* countries. The precise sample of the Tavares (2004) study was never made clear but included developed and developing countries; hence, terrorism's effect on developing countries was not isolated. BHO (2004) provided some insights for developing countries owing to their African and nondemocratic panels, where many countries are less developed. For Africa, there is evidence – significant at just the .10 level – that the presence of terrorism (i.e., one or more attacks in a year) reduced per capita growth. This evidence is much stronger for Africa when terrorist incidents per capita are used. A concern, however, arises because the -3.856 coefficient is rather large given the average growth level of African countries. Moreover, this coefficient also exceeds that for internal conflicts. In BHO's base runs, the nondemocratic countries displayed no terrorism effect on per capita growth, but this was not the case for terrorist incidents per capita.

To better quantify the influence of terrorism on the economies of developing countries, we suggest two approaches. First, the Abadie and Gardeazabal (2003) and Eckstein and Tsiddon (2004) methods should be applied to specific developing countries. Other appropriate case-study methods should be engineered. Second, cross-section and panel analysis, along the lines of BHO (2004), should be used on a cohort of developing countries. A broad sample of developing countries should first be assembled for a set of estimates. Next, some cohorts can be examined that experienced similar terrorist campaigns. Regional groupings of developing countries represent other appropriate cohorts.

There are a number of anticipated differences between how developed and developing countries are able to weather terrorism. Developed countries possess more capable governmental institutions that can apply monetary, fiscal, and other policies to recover from either a large-scale attack or a prolonged campaign. The United States case, discussed earlier in this chapter, is instructive. Debt also hinders many developed countries from applying monetary policy to cushion the consequence of a large-scale terrorist attack. Markets in developed countries are better able to respond to terrorism-induced changes in risk. Developed countries are also better equipped than developing countries to monitor their economies to determine the need for monetary or fiscal stimuli following terrorist attacks. In addition, developed countries can take decisive and effective security measures to restore confidence. Many less-developed countries lack this capacity.

Such security measures can speed recovery. Because developing countries are more dependent on the rest of the world for demand for their products and services, these countries are more vulnerable than richer countries to terrorism shocks in neighbors and important trading partners. Compared with their richer counterparts, developing countries are less diversified and more apt to experience a larger effect from a sector-specific attack. The earlier Yemen shipping example illustrates this insight. Finally, the presence of internal conflicts in many developing countries compromises their ability to address terrorist attacks, which may resonate with other forms of internal strife. To address this resonance, an interactive term between terrorism and internal conflict is needed in future empirical studies.

5. Microeconomic Consequences of Terrorism

Studies dating back to the early 1990s have investigated the microeconomic consequences of sector-specific attacks. In particular, studies have covered tourism, trade, and financial sectors. Because many of these studies are country specific, methods other than cross-section estimates have been used.[6]

5.1. Tourism

Attacks against tourist venues (e.g., airports, hotels, or attractions) or tourist modes of transportation (e.g., airplanes) make a tourist reconsider the risks of their vacation plans. Even a single heinous act at a popular terrorist venue can cause tourists to alter plans by either vacationing at home or else going to a terrorism-free country. Time-series analysis has been used in a number of tourism studies to gauge the effect of terrorism in the target country or region. A *transfer function* analysis is particularly suited to estimate the short- and long-run effects of a terrorist attack on a country's tourist industry. A very simple transfer function for, say, the effect of terrorism on Spanish tourism is:

$$y_t = a_0 + b_1 y_{t-1} + c_0 x_t + \varepsilon_t, \qquad (4)$$

where y_t is the number of tourists visiting Spain in period t, x_t is the number of terrorist incidents in Spain in period t, and ε_t is the error term. This

---

[6] A recent exception is the cross-sectional study of U.S. FDI by Enders et al. (2006). These authors found that terrorist attacks against U.S. interests had a significant, but small, effect on the stock of U.S. FDI in Organization of Economic Cooperation and Development (OECD) countries. Greece and Turkey displayed the largest declines – 5.7% and 6.5% of their average U.S. FDI stocks.

equation reflects that the number of tourists visiting Spain in any period is affected by its own past, y_{t-1}, as well as the number of terrorist events in Spain. Because periods with high versus low levels of tourism tend to cluster, we expect b_1 to be positive; a large y_t tends to follow a large y_{t-1}. In (4), c_0 measures the contemporaneous effect of a terrorist incident on tourism; a negative c_0 means that terrorism negatively effects tourism.

Equation (4) can be used to estimate the indirect effects on terrorism. To perform the desired counterfactual analysis, a researcher estimates (4) to obtain the magnitudes of a_0, b_1, and c_0 for a particular country. Once these values are ascertained, what each value of y_t would have been in the absence of terrorism (i.e., $x_t = 0$) can be calculated. The difference between this counterfactual and the actual value of y_t is then due to the effect of terrorism. This analysis can be generalized to permit terrorism to affect tourism and vice versa, so that a VAR methodology applies.

Enders and Sandler (1991) applied a VAR methodology to Spain for the 1970–91 period, during which Euzkadi ta Askatasuna (ETA) and other groups had terrorist campaigns. During 1985–87, ETA *directed* its bombs and threats against the Spanish tourist trade and even sent letters of warning to travel agents in Europe. Using monthly data, we showed that the causation was unidirectional: terrorism affected tourism but not the reverse. Each transnational terrorist incident was estimated to dissuade more than 140,000 tourists after all monthly effects were included. This can translate into a sizable amount of lost revenue when multiplied by the average spending per tourist. Transnational terrorist attacks denote the appropriate terrorism measure because much of the ETA terrorist campaign was transnational attacks to chase away foreign tourists and FDI. Domestic terrorist attacks were performed with precision and away from tourist venues.

In a follow-up study, Enders et al. (1992) used an autoregressive integrated moving average (ARIMA) analysis with a transfer function to investigate the effect of transnational terrorism on tourism for 1974–88 in Austria, Greece, and Italy – three countries with highly visible transnational terrorist attacks against foreign tourists during this period. The dependent variable was the country's share of tourist receipts from the region. These authors found that terrorism had a significant negative lagged influence on these tourism shares that varied by country: two quarters for Italy, three quarters for Greece, and seven quarters for Austria. Because it takes time for tourists to revise plans, the lags are understandable. Losses varied by country: Austria lost 3.37 billion special drawing rights (SDRs); Italy lost 861 million SDRs; and Greece lost 472 million SDRs. The authors also showed that some of the lost revenues left a sample of European countries for safer venues in North America.

Drakos and Kutan (2003) applied the Enders-Sandler-Parise methodology to Greece, Israel, and Turkey for 1991–2000 based on monthly transnational terrorism data drawn from ITERATE. In addition to the home-country effects, Drakos and Kutan were interested in cross-country or "spillover" effects – both positive and negative – that may arise if, say, a transnational attack in Israel shifts would-be Israeli tourists to safer venues in Italy, Greece, or elsewhere. Their ARIMA model with a transfer function had an equation for each country's tourist share, where, say, the share of tourism in Greece depends on: past tourist shares in Greece, current and past terrorist attacks in Greece, current and past terrorist attacks in Israel, and current and past terrorist attacks in Turkey. There was also an equation for tourist shares of Italy, which was a relatively safe haven. Based on transnational terrorist attacks,[7] these authors calculated that Greece lost 9 percent of its tourism market share; Turkey lost more than 5 percent of its tourism market share; and Israel lost less than 1 percent of its tourism market. Close to 89 percent of lost tourism due to terrorism in Europe flowed to safer tourist venues in other countries.[8] Drakos and Kutan also uncovered significant spillover effects – low-intensity terrorist attacks in Israel reduced Greek tourism revenues.

5.2. Net Foreign Direct Investment (NFDI)

Foreign investors must be aware of all kinds of risks, including those posed by terrorism. This risk is especially germane when a terrorist campaign specifically targets NFDI. Terrorist risks raise the costs of doing business as expensive security measures must be deployed and personnel must be duly compensated, both of which reduce the returns to NFDI. As these risks rise, investors will redirect their investments to safer countries. Enders and Sandler (1996) provided estimates of the effects of terrorism on NDFI in two relatively small European countries – Greece and Spain. Large countries – for example, France, Germany, and the United Kingdom – draw their foreign capital inflows from many sources and appeared to endure attacks without a measurable aggregate diversion of inflows. Large countries are also better equipped to take defensive measures to restore confidence after an attack. Greece and Spain were selected as case studies insofar as both experienced

[7] In the case of Israel, the exclusion of domestic terrorism presents a potential bias because domestic terrorist attacks would surely influence tourism to Israel.
[8] Sloboda (2003) also used a transfer function to analyze the effects of terrorism on tourism revenues for the United States following the Gulf War of 1991.

numerous transnational terrorist attacks aimed at foreign commercial interests during the 1968–91 sample period.

For Spain, we applied an ARIMA model with a transfer function that associated NFDI to its past values and to terrorist attacks; for Greece, we applied a VAR model that related NFDI to its past values and to terrorist attacks. Once again, we modeled a counterfactual exercise, analogous to those for tourism, to compute the terrorism-induced losses in NFDI in these two economies. For Spain, there was a long delay of eleven quarters between the advent of a terrorist incident and the response in NFDI. A typical transnational terrorist incident in Spain was estimated to reduce NFDI by $23.8 million. On average, transnational terrorism reduced *annual* NFDI in Spain by 13.5 percent. For Greece, the story was similar; transnational terrorism curbed annual NFDI by 11.9 percent. These are sizable losses for two small economies that were heavily dependent on NFDI as a source of savings during the sample period.

5.3. Trade Influence

In a recent contribution, Nitsch and Schumacher (2004) estimated the effects of transnational terrorism on bilateral trade flows using a standard trade-gravity model. In their model, trade flows between trading partners depended on terrorist attacks, the distance between the two countries, an income variable, an income per capita variable, and a host of dummy variables. They formally estimated the effects of terrorism within each country on all of the nation's trading partners. The dataset consists of 217 countries and territories over the 1968–79 period. Their terrorism data were drawn from ITERATE and only included transnational attacks, even though domestic terrorism would have also affected trade flows. The authors found that the first transnational terrorist attack reduced bilateral trade by almost 10 percent, which is a very sizable influence that may be picking up the effect of domestic terrorism. Nitsch and Schumacher also found that a doubling of the number of terrorist incidents reduced bilateral trade by 4 percent; hence, high-terrorism nations had a substantially reduced trade volume. Although more recent terrorism data are available, the authors only examined this historical period, which is not reflective of current-day terrorism.

5.4. Financial Markets

Chen and Siems (2004) applied an event-study methodology to investigate changes in average returns of stock exchange indices to fourteen terrorist and military attacks that dated back to 1915. An event study computes abnormal returns – negative or positive – following some shock or occurrence, such as the downing of Pan Am flight 103 or 9/11. These authors showed that the influence of terrorist events on major stock exchanges, if any, is very transitory, lasting just one to three days for most major incidents. The sole exception is 9/11 where the Dow Jones Industrial Average took forty days to return to normal. These authors also showed that this return period varied according to the stock exchange – exchanges in Norway, Jakarta, Kuala Lampur, and Johannesburg took longer to rebound, while those in London, Helsinki, Tokyo, and elsewhere took less time to rebound. Most terrorist events had little or no effect on major stock exchanges.

Eldor and Melnick (2004) applied time-series methods to ascertain the influence of the Israeli terror campaign following September 27, 2000, on the Tel Aviv 100 Stock Index (TA 100). Given the continual nature of these terrorist attacks, the time-series method is clearly appropriate. Analogous to the other time-series studies, they performed a counterfactual exercise to determine losses to the value of the TA 100 index by using the *estimated* time-series equation for returns but substituting a zero value in for terrorist attacks. Their analysis estimated that the TA 100 was 30 percent lower on June 30, 2003, owing to the terrorist campaign. When these authors investigated specific types of terrorist attacks, they found that only suicide attacks had a significant effect. Their article also related the Israeli terrorist campaign to exchange rate fluctuations.

By way of summary, Table 1.2 indicates the microeconomic studies, their methods, study description, and major findings.

6. Methodology Discussion

To date, two basic methodologies have been applied to estimate macroeconomic and microeconomic consequences of terrorism: panel estimates with large cross-sections of countries and time-series estimates with one or more equations. Each methodology has its advantages and disadvantages as displayed in Table 1.3. The appropriate method depends on the question at hand and data availability.

Time-series methods have been effectively used for microeconomic estimates of tourism losses, NFDI losses, and stock market declines. The Eckstein and Tsiddon (2004) study of Israel also illustrates that the same method can be employed to estimate the within-country consequences of terrorism on macroeconomic variables such as consumption per capita and GDP per capita. Not only can a time-series analysis lend itself to counterfactual

Table 1.2. *Microeconomic studies of the effect of terrorism*

Study and method	Description	Findings
Enders and Sandler (1991) *VAR*	Using monthly data for 1970–99, the study relates terrorism and tourism for Spain. A causality test establishes that terrorism affects tourism but not the reverse.	A typical terrorist incident is estimated to scare away just more than 140,000 tourists when all monthly effects are combined.
Enders et al. (1992) *ARIMA with a transfer function*	Relates share of tourist receipts to lagged shares of tourist receipts and lagged terrorist attacks. Focuses on Austria, Spain, and Italy for 1974–88. Other continental countries included to investigate out-of-region losses.	During sample period, tourist losses varied: Austria lost 3.37 billion SDRs, Italy lost 861 million SDRs, and Greece lost 472 million SDRs. The sample of European countries lost 12.6 billion SDRs of tourist receipts to North America.
Drakos and Kutan (2003) *ARIMA with a transfer function*	Using monthly data for 1991–2000, the study relates a country's share of tourist receipts to terrorism. Focuses on Greece, Israel, and Turkey. Allows for terrorist-induced substitutions within and among regions.	Greece lost about 9% of its tourism market shares due to terrorism; Israel lost less than 1% of its tourism market share due to terrorism; and Turkey lost just over 5% of its tourism market share due to terrorism. About 89% of lost European tourism flowed to safer regions.
Enders and Sandler (1996) *ARIMA with transfer function for Spain, VAR for Greece*	Employs time-series methods to ascertain losses in net foreign direct investment (NFDI) due to terrorism. The sample period is 1968–91.	On average, terrorism reduced annual NFDI in Spain by 13.5%, while it lowered annual NFDI in Greece by 11.9%. There was a long lag between an incident and its effect on NFDI. Large rich countries weathered terrorism without displaying a loss in NFDI.
Nitsch and Schumacher (2004) *Trade-gravity model*	Terror attacks are added to a gravity model to ascertain their effect on bilateral trades for more than 200 countries for 1968–79. Independent variables include a language dummy, a colonizer dummy, common border, and other controls.	Terrorist incidents in a trading partner reduce bilateral trade by almost 10%, compared with terrorism-free trading partners.

(*continued*)

Table 1.2 *(continued)*

Study and method	Description	Findings
Chen and Siems (2004) *Events-study methodology*	This study applies the events-study methodology to uncover how many days are required for stock markets to recover their value after a large-scale terrorist attack.	For the Dow, market value is recovered in one to a few days following large-scale terrorist attacks. For 9/11, the Dow recovered in 40 days. Major conflicts are associated with long recovery periods.
Eldor and Melnick (2004) *Time-series methods*	Relies on time-series methods to display the influence of terrorist attacks on the Israeli stock market. Daily observations are used.	The terrorist campaign beginning on September 27, 2000, lowered stock values on the Tel Aviv exchange by 30%. Only suicide attacks had a significant influence. The size of the attack in terms of casualties was a significant determinant of financial market losses.

exercises, but it can also be used for forecasting purposes. Although most time-series estimates do not have antecedent behavioral models, the Eckstein and Tsiddon (2004) article indicates that this need not be the case because their estimating equations stemmed from a dynamic theoretical model. By incorporating a VAR analysis with multiple equations (i.e., one for each country), a researcher can examine cross-border spillovers, as in Drakos and Kutan (2003).

Panel studies also have advantages and disadvantages as indicated in the bottom half of Table 1.3. A crucial variable (e.g., real per capita GDP growth) may display little variation for a country so that identification becomes a problem. To circumvent this difficulty, cross-section and panel estimates introduce sufficient variation to enhance identification. Hence, such estimates have a real role to play in identifying the effect of terrorism on various GDP growth measures. To limit extreme heterogeneity that may arise from diverse samples, cohorts can be constructed. Moreover, independent variables can control for some heterogeneity – for example, democratic institutions or stage of development. If, however, the sample is too heterogeneous, then the "average" picture provided by the coefficient estimates may not be descriptive of the experience of many sample countries. Even some dynamic factors can be introduced by lagging a variable; however,

Table 1.3. *Measurement of economic consequences of terrorism: panel versus time series*

Time-series estimation
- *Advantages*
  - There is no need to construct a behavioral model with explicit exogenous and endogenous variables.
  - Dynamic processes can be readily identified; i.e., can evaluate shocks and the pattern of adjustment over time.
  - Forecasts can be provided.
  - Microeconomic effects can be readily identified.
  - Cross-border spillovers can be estimated.
- *Disadvantages*
  - The estimated model may be atheoretical with no antecedent behavioral model.
  - The number of countries examined is severely limited.
  - A large number of observations are required.
  - A generalized picture across nations is not given.

Panel estimation
- *Advantages*
  - A wide variety of countries can be considered.
  - Variation in key variables (e.g., per capita GDP growth) is larger; hence, identification is enhanced.
  - Degrees of freedom are large.
  - The influence of terrorism on cohorts can be compared and contrasted.
- *Disadvantages*
  - The estimation's average picture may not be descriptive of many sample countries, especially when the panel includes vastly diverse countries. This heterogeneity is a problem when it is not controlled.
  - Data problems may arise from using different sources.
  - The dynamic effect of terrorism on key variables is often not displayed.
  - Cross-border spillovers are difficult to identify.

---

the amount of dynamic interaction is limited compared with time-series estimates.

Alternative studies have used different measures of terrorism. A dummy for the presence of terrorism in a given year may be appropriate if terrorist campaigns differ greatly among sample countries and outlier problems are to be avoided. Incidents per capita captures the prevalence of terrorism relative to the population base, thereby indicating the likelihood that an attack will affect individuals. The number of incidents indicates the extent of the campaign and may be particularly appropriate for a country study. If the intensity of terrorism is to be captured, then the number of incidents with casualties (i.e., a death or injury) is a useful measure. For time-series studies, the time dimension of the incident series (i.e., daily, monthly, quarterly, or annual) is an important consideration. For example, researchers often rely on quarterly totals to eliminate zero or near-zero observations that violate the underlying normal distribution assumption associated with many time-series methods. Because time-series techniques require many data points, monthly or daily incident series maintains a large number of observations. If zero values then become a concern, estimates can be based on a discrete Poisson distribution.

Some studies use more than one terrorism measure (e.g., BHO 2004; Tavares 2004). For these studies, the robustness of the economic consequences to alternative measures becomes a relevant consideration.

7. Concluding Remarks and Future Directions

Table 1.4 lists some of the main principles that we have gleaned regarding the economic consequences of terrorism. A few of these principles are worth highlighting. Given the low intensity of most terrorist campaigns, the macroeconomic consequences of terrorism are generally modest and short-lived. Terrorism is not on par with civil or guerilla wars and, in general, should have very localized economic effects. The likely candidate countries for noticeable macroeconomic effects are either developing or small

Table 1.4. *Economic effect of terrorism: Summarizing principles*

- For most economies, the macroeconomic consequences of terrorism are generally modest and of short-term nature.
- Large diversified economies are able to withstand terrorism and not display adverse macroeconomic influences. Recovery is rapid even from a large-scale terrorist attack.
- Developed countries can use monetary and fiscal policies to offset adverse economic effects of large-scale attacks. Well-developed institutions also cushion the consequences.
- The immediate costs of most terrorist attacks are localized, thereby causing a substitution of economic activity away from a vulnerable sector to relatively safe areas. Prices can then reallocate capital and labor quickly.
- Terrorism can cause a reallocation from investment to government spending.
- The effects of terrorism on key economic variables – e.g., net foreign direct investment – are anticipated to be greatest in small economies confronted with a sustained terrorist campaign.
- Some terrorist-prone sectors – e.g., tourism – have displayed substantial losses following terrorist attacks. In the absence of further attacks, these sectors rebound rather quickly.
- Small countries, plagued with significant terrorist campaigns, display macroeconomic consequences in terms of losses in GDP per capita.

countries that experience a protracted terrorist campaign. In general, the economic influence of terrorism is anticipated to surface in specific sectors that face an enhanced terrorism risk, such as the tourist industry or foreign direct investment.

Both macroeconomic case studies applied clever methods to display substantial economic losses – in the range of 10 percent of GDP per capita – stemming from protracted terrorist campaigns. Cross-section and panel estimates have shown modest effects of terrorism on per capita GDP growth. These studies should incorporate both domestic and transnational terrorism data to better gauge the effect of terrorism for some cohorts that include just developing countries. There is also a need for additional case studies, especially of developing countries. VAR analysis can be applied to a few countries confronting terrorist campaigns in the same region to capture cross-border influences. In addition, spatial econometrics can identify the dispersion of economic consequences. Microeconomic estimates of terrorism consequences have been informative. The associated methodology can be extended to other countries, especially developed countries, as case studies and small panels. More effort should be expended to identify sector-specific, cross-border spillovers – for example, in the case of FDI. These methods can also be applied to vulnerable sectors previously unexamined. The effect of terrorism on trade needs to be reexamined for a more current period after 1980 when the nature of transnational terrorism changed. This proposed study should possess cohorts of countries so as to distinguish terrorism effect on trade in less-developed countries from that in developed countries.

Measures of diversity and development should be introduced in large cross-sectional estimates to quantify how well such characteristics can insulate an economy from the harmful economic consequences of terrorism. Such factors can be introduced in the same manner that political rights have been introduced in past studies. Finally, empirical studies need to identify not only the effect of terrorism on an economy but also the longevity of this effect, similar to measurements event studies of stock exchanges provide.

References

Abadie, Alberto, and Javier Gardeazabal. 2003. "The Economic Cost of Conflict: A Case Study of the Basque Country." *American Economic Review* 93:113–32.

Blomberg, S. Brock, Gregory D. Hess, and Athanasios Orphanides. 2004. "The Macroeconomic Consequences of Terrorism." *Journal of Monetary Economics* 51:1007–32.

Chen, Andrew H., and Thomas F. Siems. 2004. "The Effects of Terrorism on Global Capital Markets." *European Journal of Political Economy* 20:249–66.

Collier, Paul, V. L. Elliott, Håvard Hegre, Anke Hoeffler, Marta Reynal-Querol, and Nicholas Sambanis. 2003. *Breaking the Conflict Trap: Civil War and Development Policy.* Washington, DC: World Bank and Oxford University Press.

Collier, Paul, and Anke Hoeffler. 2004. "Greed and Grievance in Civil War." *Oxford Economic Papers* 56:563–95.

Collier, Paul, and Nicholas Sambanis. 2002. "Understanding Civil Wars: A New Agenda." *Journal of Conflict Resolution* 46:3–12.

Drakos, Konstantinos. 2004. "Terrorism-Induced Structural Shifts in Financial Risk: Airline Stocks in the Aftermath of the September 11th Terror Attacks." *European Journal of Political Economy* 20:436–46.

Drakos, Konstantinos, and Ali M. Kutan. 2003. "Regional Effects of Terrorism on Tourism in Three Mediterranean Countries." *Journal of Conflict Resolution* 47:621–41.

Eckstein, Zvi, and Daniel Tsiddon. 2004. "Macroeconomic Consequences of Terror: Theory and the Case of Israel." *Journal of Monetary Economics* 51:971–1002.

Eldor, Rafi and Rafi Melnick. 2004. "Financial Markets and Terrorism." *European Journal of Political Economy* 20:367–86.

Enders, Walter, and Todd Sandler. 1991. "Causality between Transnational Terrorism and Tourism: The Case of Spain." *Terrorism* 14:49–58.

———. 1993. "The Effectiveness of Anti-Terrorism Policies: A Vector-Autoregression-Intervention Analysis." *American Political Science Review* 87:829–44.

———. 1996. "Terrorism and Foreign Direct Investment in Spain and Greece." *Kyklos* 49:331–52.

———. 2000. "Is Transnational Terrorism Becoming More Threatening? A Time-Series Investigation." *Journal of Conflict Resolution* 44:307–32.

———. 2004. "What Do We Know About the Substitution Effect in Transnational Terrorism?" In *Research on Terrorism: Trends, Achievements and Failures*, ed. Andrew Silke, 119–37. London: Frank Cass.

———. 2006a. *The Political Economy of Terrorism.* Cambridge: Cambridge University Press.

———. 2006b. "Distribution of Transnational Terrorism among Countries by Income Class and Geography after 9/11." *International Studies Quarterly* 50:367–93.

Enders, Walter, Adolfo Sachsida, and Todd Sandler. 2006. "The Impact of Transnational Terrorism on U.S. Foreign Direct Investment." *Political Research Quarterly* 59:517–31.

Enders, Walter, Todd Sandler, and Gerald F. Parise. 1992. "An Econometric Analysis of the Impact of Terrorism on Tourism." *Kyklos* 45:531–54.

International Policy Institute for Counterterrorism. 2003. Terrorism Database, http://ict.org.il, accessed May 19, 2005.

Ito, Harumi, and Darin Lee. 2004. "Assessing the Impact of the September 11 Terrorist Attacks on U.S. Airline Demand." *Journal of Economics and Business* 57:1, 79–95.

Kunreuther, Howard, Erwann Michel-Kerjan, and Beverly Porter. 2003. "*Assessing, Managing and Financing Extreme Events: Dealing with Terrorism*," Working Paper 10179, National Bureau of Economic Research, Cambridge, MA.

Li, Quan. 2005. "Does Democracy Promote Transnational Terrorist Incidents?" *Journal of Conflict Resolution* 49:278–97.

Li, Quan, and Drew Schaub. 2004. "Economic Globalization and Transnational Terrorism," *Journal of Conflict Resolution* 48:230–58.

Mickolus, Edward F., Todd Sandler, Jean M. Murdock, and Peter Flemming. 2004. *International Terrorism: Attributes of Terrorist Events, 1968–2003 (ITERATE)*. Dunn Loring, VA: Vinyard Software.

Murdoch, James C., and Todd Sandler. 2002. "Economic Growth, Civil Wars, and Spatial Spillovers." *Journal of Conflict Resolution* 46:91–110.

_____. 2004. "Civil Wars and Economic Growth: Spatial Spillovers." *American Journal of Political Science* 48:138–51.

National Memorial Institute for the Prevention of Terrorism. 2005. *MIPT Terrorism Database*, http://www.mipt.org, accessed May 19, 2005.

Nitsch, Volker, and Dieter Schumacher. 2004. "Terrorism and International Trade: An Empirical Investigation." *European Journal of Political Economy* 20:423–33.

Sandler, Todd. 2003. "Collective Action and Transnational Terrorism." *World Economy* 26:779–802.

Sandler, Todd, and Walter Enders. 2004. "An Economic Perspective on Transnational Terrorism." *European Journal of Political Economy* 20:301–16.

Sloboda, Brian W. 2003. "Assessing the Effects of Terrorism on Tourism by the Use of Time-Series Methods." *Tourism Economics* 9:179–90.

Tavares, Jose. 2004. "The Open Society Assesses its Enemies: Shocks, Disasters and Terrorist Attacks." *Journal of Monetary Economics* 51:1039–70.

United States Department of State. 1999–2004. *Patterns of Global Terrorism*. Washington, DC: U.S. Department of State.

United States Department of State Fact Sheet. 2002. "Yemen: The Economic Cost of Terrorism," http://www.state.gov/s/ct/rls/fs/2002/15028.htm, accessed December 12, 2004.

TWO

The Costs of Responding to the Terrorist Threats

The U.S. Case

Gregory F. Treverton, Justin L. Adams, James Dertouzos, Arindam
Dutta, Susan S. Everingham, Eric V. Larson

1. Introduction

The end of the cold war and the rise of international terrorism have dramatically changed perceptions of national security. Where nations once saw
threats emanating primarily from state actors located abroad, they now look
also at nonstate entities acting both at home and abroad, as well as to failed
states. Threats from nonstate actors have become a more significant issue
for both rich and poor states. Table 2.1 displays those changes in perception
of the threat, using the United States as an example.

A full analysis of the costs of terrorism would include the costs to rich
and poor states, including those costs of rich country efforts to defend
against terrorist threats imposed on the poor. This chapter takes a first
step by examining the costs to the rich states of addressing the terrorism
threat, *not* the costs of terrorism itself or of the immediate responses to
an attack.[1] In that sense, the costs might be thought of as the "secondary"
cost of countering terrorism, rather than the "proximate" costs of terrorism.
Understandably, the latter have received more attention than the former.[2]
However, some sense of where the money is going is necessary to identify
possible trade-offs and ask whether the current portfolio of expenditures is
the most sensible one. Table 2.2 summarizes the various distinctions and
their implications for cost.

---

[1] This larger research project from which this chapter was drawn was conducted for the
World Bank, under the auspices of International Programs at the RAND Corporation.
International Programs conducts research on regionally and internationally focused topics
for a wide range of U.S. as well as international clients, including governments, foundations,
and corporations.

[2] Enders and Sandler (2006) provide a broad analysis of terrorism, using economic and other
tools. Their assessment of the economic cost of terrorism focuses on the proximate costs
of terrorism itself, as does most of the literature.

Table 2.1. *Changing U.S. perceptions of "security"*

	Cold war definition	Current definition
What is the threat?	Primarily states	Primarily nonstates or failed states but also "threats" from disease, financial contagion
Where is the threat?	Abroad	Abroad and at home
What is the ranking of threats?	WMD (Weapons of mass destruction) in hands of states, major conventional warfare between East and West	WMD in hands of nonstates and states, other forms of terror, but also global pandemic
What policy instruments are available?	Primarily military	Military, homeland security, diplomacy, international assistance, and engagement of various sorts
How important are allies and partners?	NATO and Warsaw Pact but much of policy was unilateral (U.S., USSR)	Inherently multilateral, well beyond military alliances
How much are ordinary citizens affected?	Not much. Paid taxes, felt "nuclear threat," but security was business of the military	Much more. Citizens affected through security measures (airport screening, etc.) Many levels of government involved, also business and civil society

Table 2.2. *Defining terms*

Conceptual distinction		Cost distinction	
Action	Response	*Proximate* costs of terror acts	*Secondary* costs of counterterrorism
Government	Private	*Budgetary* costs of all branches of government	*Private* firms' and individuals' costs
Direct	Indirect	*Monetary* costs spent by governments and by private firms	*Nonmonetary costs* (or their monetary valuations) imposed by homeland security actions on firms and individuals

Several points should be emphasized at the outset:

- The data are primarily from the United States, with some additional material from Britain. Quantifying expenditures is not easy, however, and using the United States as the primary example makes sense not only because it is at the center of the campaign against terrorism, but it also spends considerably more than any other nation.
- The costs are incremental. They are estimates of costs incurred that would not have been incurred had it not been for fears of terrorism, particularly the fears stemming from the attacks of 9/11.
- Costs are both direct and indirect, as Table 2.2 indicates. Direct costs, primarily public costs, are those spent for security activities. Indirect costs, mainly private, are those incurred by changes made to increase security – for instance, the effect on business of diminished travel and increased inspection of goods.
- Akin to indirect costs are opportunity costs, costs of shifting resources from activities in which they would have been used, absent terrorism.
- The analysis distinguishes between U.S. actions at home, most of them nonmilitary, and actions abroad, most of them military. The longer RAND report provides detail on costs borne by states and localities and by the private sector, but those are only summarized here as a point of comparison.

This chapter first provides context for the more specific discussion to follow by laying out the full range of costs and benefits, then discusses the methodological challenges of identifying *incremental* costs, of deciding which categories of cost to include and of how to value those incremental costs. The second section describes the security activities the United States has undertaken. Section three estimates the costs of those activities, looking at pre- and post-9/11 trends in security spending by the U.S. federal government, with some British data as a comparison. It concludes with a brief summary of the larger project's findings on state and local governments and the private sector. Section four makes concluding observations, including comments on benefits relative to costs.

Our analysis of expenditures leads to two main conclusions about the U.S. response to terrorism. First, *excluding* the expenditures on the wars in Iraq and Afghanistan, expenditures in response to terrorism grew only modestly following 9/11, by around a half percent of GDP. Second, again discounting expenditures on the wars in Iraq and Afghanistan, the expenditures are significantly tilted to homeland security, such as border, port, and airport security, which account for nearly 40 percent of the federal nondefense spending response to terrorism. On the other hand, expenditures that might potentially defuse the sources of terrorism, principally economic assistance, account for only between an eighth and a quarter of nondefense spending. Finally, and obviously, if the military expenditures in Iraq and Afghanistan are *included*, total expenditures double, to between a percent and a percent and a quarter of GDP, and the emphasis on security rather than developmental expenditures is strongly accentuated.

1.1. Flows of Costs and Benefits

In thinking about trade-offs among possible expenditures to prepare for the terrorist threat, the United States and other countries confront that threat by, in effect, setting up a layered defense, ranging from increases in development assistance to minimize conflict within developing countries and thus the likelihood that terrorists will be spawned or harbored; to law enforcement and intelligence cooperation abroad; to military actions to root out terrorist threats; to policies to control international flows of people, finance, and trade with the purpose of inhibiting international terrorism; to homeland security activities to protect critical infrastructures and provide emergency response to potential terrorist attacks.

These policies impose direct costs on (and generate benefits for) the United States and also for the developing countries toward which some of them are targeted. Direct costs are visible in the resources to fund security activities or in the effect on developing countries of military interventions there. Opportunity costs arise when people and resources are transferred to address the terrorism threat from other activities they were or might be doing. And U.S. policies can also have indirect costs. For example, tightened border controls in the United States and other countries impose direct costs on them (as well as conveying benefits), but the costs for poor countries of those actions would be indirect in the form of diminished business travel, migration, and the like. Understanding all costs, both direct and indirect as well as where they occur, is necessary in designing a sensible portfolio of security policies.

Although this chapter focuses on reckoning the costs, plainly, whatever the numbers for costs, those numbers cannot be assessed without some sense of the benefits. Accordingly, we make some comments about benefits in the concluding section. The benefits of U.S. or other country actions are measured by the reduction in the level of the perceived security threat. Military operations, for example, may root out terrorists and criminal activity and, in so doing, reduce the likelihood of a terrorist attack in the future. Similarly,

Table 2.3. *Some previous estimates of the higher security costs*

Type of cost[a]	Value	Time period	Source
U.S. response, private, direct action & U.S. response, private, indirect[b]	$151 billion	2001–02	Bernasek 2002
	0.25% of nominal GDP[c] in 2001 ($25–27 billion)	Annual	IMF (WEO 2001, 19)
U.S. response, private, direct[d]	$39.1 billion	Annual	UBS Warburg 2001
U.S. response, private, indirect	$8–32 billion (delays at airports)	Annual	Navarro and Spencer 2001
U.S. response, government, direct[e]	$9.45 billion ("microeconomic terrorism tax")	Annual	Navarro and Spencer 2001
U.S. response, private, indirect	$11 billion (delays at airports)	Annual	Becker and Murphy 2001
action, private, indirect[f]	0.2% of GDP in 2001 ($20–21 billion)	Annual	Becker and Murphy 2001

Notes:

[a] For a review of such estimates and a discussion of measurement issues, see "The Economic Costs of Terrorism," Joint Economic Committee, U.S. Congress, April 2002.

[b] These costs are assigned to "directly affected" industries such as airlines, hotels, and the leisure industry that suffer a 10% decline in short-term business as a result of increased terrorism risk.

[c] The figure for nominal U.S. GDP in 2001 used in this table is in the range $9.96–10.7 trillion (Source: IMF, World Economic Outlook, 2001).

[d] This figure comprises higher security costs at $1.6 billion per year, the extra financing burden of carrying 10% higher inventories at $7.5 billion per year, and an increase in commercial insurance premiums of 20% at about $30 billion per year (UBS Warburg 2001).

[e] These costs consist of Sky Marshals (direct incremental cost), the additional cost of using government TSA agents at airports, the cost of retrofitting aircraft with antiterrorism devices and other technology fixes (Navarro and Spencer 2001).

[f] Costs of capital go up, which leads to a 0.2% of GDP cost imposed on the U.S. economy (Becker and Murphy 2001).

homeland security actions help deter terrorist attacks from abroad. And foreign assistance may help foster economic development and other state-building activities in developing countries.

The task of estimating costs, let alone benefits, is daunting, and the uncertainties remain large. Yet, given how scattered the available estimates are, it seemed more than worth trying to be as systematic as possible. Table 2.3 displays some previous estimates of cost, derived in a variety of ways, as an illustration.

1.2. Estimating – and Valuing – "Incremental" Changes in Spending

Attributing "incremental costs" to changed security perceptions after 9/11 is no mean feat, and various approaches have their strengths and weaknesses. For instance, picking a pre-9/11 baseline year and comparing it with a post-9/11 year would be simplest but would not allow for the possibility that policy makers intended to raise spending in relevant accounts even before 9/11. To account for that, the future spending plan described in the President's Budget could be used as the baseline, and differences in spending in any given year between the preexisting spending plan and the revised plan would be attributed to post-9/11 policy responses.[3] But spending plans are wishes more than plans, and the gap between them and actual appropriations or expenditures often is a yawning one.

Instead, we compare trend lines before and after 9/11 in order to compare the difference between actual spending and what would have occurred if the preexisting trend were extrapolated into future years. We look at the few years before 9/11 and several years afterward to try to establish an equilibrium level of spending before and after 9/11. That enables us to identify spikes after 9/11, then discern whether those spikes were ephemeral, became the new level at which equilibrium seems to have stabilized by 2004 or so, or seemed the beginning of a continuing upward trend. Ideally, we would test any differences with formal statistical techniques. Unfortunately, the time series before and after are too short to make that testing sensible, but the magnitudes of most differences are big enough so that they are not likely to be spurious.

A second challenge is deciding which categories of incremental costs to include. If the costs of concern are the incremental costs that arise because of the terrorist *threat* – that is, costs for measures designed to prevent or limit the damage associated with terrorist acts – that definition is less clear than it might appear, a challenge that particularly afflicts the private sector costings. For instance, it seemed appropriate to include the cost of insurance, but insurance is not really a preventive measure but rather a way of protecting against losses if and when they occur. So, too, we included, as costs, reduced consumer demand for air travel, which could be seen as a reaction to terrorism itself, not just to the inconvenience of preparations for it. In general, we included costs when those (a) were additional to costs before 9/11 and (b) resulted from needs driven by perceptions of the terrorist threat. We

---

[3] For examples, see Daggett (1994) and the year-to-year comparisons of defense spending plans in Larson, Orletsky, and Leuschner (2001).

have tried, though, to be transparent in these and other judgments so that readers with other perspectives or values could use the framework to reach their own estimates.

Third, these incremental costs no doubt understate the total costs because they do not capture the opportunity costs of public agencies (and private institutions) changing their mix of activities. Although the public agencies received additional funding for increased homeland security activities, many of them also switched personnel to those activities from something else. They did more "homeland security" at the cost of doing less of something else. That opportunity cost of switching was vivid in the case of state and local authorities – which generally were sharply limited in the amount of new funding they could generate – but it surely was important at the federal level as well. The Federal Bureau of Investigation, for instance, shifted 480 agents to the counterterrorism mission after 9/11 from anticrime work, especially countering white-collar crime and illegal drugs (Mueller 2002).

How to measure the opportunity costs is debatable. In the very short run, society's resources are finite, and money spent by the government for one purpose cannot be spent for another. The *opportunity cost* of the spending is the other opportunity foregone. Yet society's resources grow over time; tomorrow's country will have more technology and more wealth than today's. For this reason, economists use discount rates in thinking about cost (and benefit) streams over time.

Different judgments about these issues naturally lead to different estimates of the "real" cost of the increments. For instance, a very conservative approach might assume that the federal government achieved higher security spending without foregoing any nonsecurity-related activities; instead it used its ability to finance programs through running deficits and accumulating debt. By that line of reasoning, the opportunity cost for homeland security programs would be their relevant share of interest payments. That seems too conservative, for though any given increment in deficits may "cost" only its share of interest, overall deficits eventually have to be "repaid" in higher taxes, higher interest rates, a cheaper currency, or some combination of the three.

Another approach would compare the growth in federal spending on homeland security programs to the average growth of nonsecurity-related programs over time. That assumes that any "above average" increase going to homeland security is funding that could have been used for other priorities. Again, different people will reach different conclusions, and we lay out the various numbers.

How to value these increments in spending takes the analysis into complicated issues of welfare. In principle, for instance, if there were considerable slack in the economy, resources devoted to homeland security might previously have simply been idle. In that case, the indirect or opportunity cost of employing them would approach zero. That, though, was not the case for the United States as it moved out of the recession of the early 2000s.

By contrast, both the direct and indirect costs as estimated might significantly understate the welfare losses associated with the terrorism threat. To capture the basic idea, imagine that there are two goods, "security" and all other goods and services. "Security" does *not* mean expenditures on security activities but rather is the threat level that is actually experienced, which is, in part, influenced by expenditures to combat the threat. Assume that neither 9/11 nor the attacks in Spain and Britain changed rich country preferences for security. Rather, they can be thought of as either a real or perceived increase in the resources required to purchase given levels of safety. In effect, the *price* of acquiring security went up.

When it becomes more difficult or costly to achieve a given level of security, less security is likely to be purchased. However, unless there are very good substitutes, the higher "price" would also imply that more is spent on security, and at the same time, less is available to spend on all other goods. Simply looking at the incremental expenditures ignores the fact that welfare takes a double hit – more spent on security (for less) and less for consumption of other kinds of goods as well.

How big a hit depends on many factors, not all of them knowable. What does the welfare function look like? Is security a "normal" good, one that is "consumed" more as incomes rise? In an illustrative simulation, the welfare cost of an increased threat turned out to be more than double the cost of increased expenditures on security. For the sake of simplicity, we focused on the total increments in spending attributable to the campaign against terrorism, while recognizing that those increments probably understate the true welfare costs.

2. Cataloging Security Activities

Using the United States as an example, this section categorizes the major actions that countries have taken in response to the terrorist threat to safeguard homeland security. As a first approach, it distinguishes between security activities that are primarily – though not exclusively – carried out inside rich countries and those that primarily take place outside of them.

This categorization is convenient not only as an organizing device, but also because it corresponds to how U.S. federal spending is tracked.

2.1. Activities Primarily Inside Countries

This framework of security activities builds off a process used by the U.S. federal government, particularly the U.S. Office of Management and Budget (OMB), to track federal and federally supported security efforts. The six categories are set out in U.S. Office of Homeland Security (2002).

- **Intelligence and warning** involves detecting terrorist activity before it manifests itself as an attack so that proper preemptive, preventative, and protective action can be taken. Specifically, this area consists of efforts to identify, collect, analyze, and distribute source intelligence information or the resultant warnings from intelligence analysis.
- **Border and transportation security** focuses on programs to promote the efficient and reliable flow of people, goods, and services across borders, while preventing terrorists from using transportation conveyances or systems as weapons or to deliver implements of destruction. Transportation systems include seaports, airports, highways, pipelines, railroads, and waterways.
- **Domestic counterterrorism** involves law enforcement programs that investigate and prosecute criminal activity to prevent and interdict terrorist activity domestically. It includes all homeland security programs that identify, halt, prevent, and prosecute terrorists domestically. It also includes pursuit of their sources of funding and organizational support.
- **Protecting critical infrastructure and key assets** involves programs that improve the protection of the individual pieces and interconnecting systems making up critical infrastructure, including both physical and cybersecurity. It also includes the protection of key assets – that is, unique facilities, sites, and structures whose disruption or destruction could have significant consequences.
- **Defending against catastrophic threats** includes programs that involve protecting against, detecting, deterring, or mitigating the terrorist use of weapons of mass destruction, including understanding terrorists' efforts to gain access to the expertise, technology, and materials needed to build chemical, biological, radiological, and nuclear weapons. It also includes efforts or planning to decontaminate buildings, facilities, or geographic areas after a catastrophic event.

- **Emergency preparedness and response** involves programs that prepare to minimize the damage and recover from any future terrorist attacks that may occur. It includes programs that help to plan, equip, train, and practice the skills of first responder units such as police officers, firefighters, emergency medical providers, and emergency management officials. It also includes response plans and activities to build a national system for incident management.

2.2. Activities Outside Rich Countries

The security categories just discussed include actions that are primarily, but not exclusively, taken within countries. Two other categories, military actions and preparation and international assistance, take place primarily, but not exclusively, outside those countries:

- **Military activities** include the cost of (a) specific military operations, both abroad and at home, intended to support the campaign against terror; and (b) other military activities on the home front that are specifically intended to support homeland security. For the United States, these estimates include the incremental cost of the war in Iraq. Critics, including some of the authors, would argue that the war in Iraq is a diversion from the campaign against terror rather than a contribution to it.[4] Again, our estimates are transparent, and the Iraq-related costs could simply be subtracted.
- **International assistance** is defined according to categories used in the U.S. federal budget. These categories are general enough to span the actions of other countries, rather than being so tailored as to only include actions by the United States. Most foreign assistance programs are grouped into three broad areas:

---

[4] Here, the challenge is deciding what to include as incremental. Popular estimates for the cost to the United States of homeland security often include the entire defense budget. That plainly is too inclusive, as the United States would have had a large defense budget had 9/11 never occurred. The salaries and compensation of serving military personnel, for instance, would be incremental in wartime only to the extent of added military bonuses, risk-related pay, and the salaries of reservists and new recruits that were added to the force after 9/11. A second approach would be to attribute the entire increase in defense spending since 9/ll to homeland security, but that, too, seems too inclusive. Much of that increase has gone to fund deferred improvements and weapons modernization that have little to do with the campaign against terror.

1. **International security assistance** involves military assistance including financing, training, and nonproliferation activities. It also includes peacekeeping operations.
2. **International development and humanitarian assistance** involve activities pertaining to combating poverty and diseases such as AIDS. It also includes elements such as disaster recovery funding, debt restructuring, and contributions to development banks and similar international institutions.
3. **International financial programs** include activities such as contributions to the International Monetary Fund.

The categories are meant to be inclusive, if not comprehensive, of the major actions taken by the United States (and other countries) in preparation for terrorism. The list of activities could be refined, but it seems unlikely to exclude activity categories that involve major costs. The one exception is increases in intelligence activities against terrorism by U.S. *foreign* intelligence agencies, like the Central Intelligence Agency or the National Security Agency, whose budgets are classified. In the immediate aftermath of 9/11, they, like the FBI (Federal Bureau of Investigation), experienced mostly opportunity costs as they shifted people to counterterrorism from other missions. But they also grew rapidly after 9/11, if probably not so rapidly as the FBI, whose budget increased by 80 percent between 2001 and 2006 (from $3.2 to $5.8 billion). By contrast, over the same time period other Department of Justice components grew by an average of 15 percent. Some new intelligence units were created, such as the Director of National Intelligence and the National Counterterrrorism Center, and existing agencies grew; the CIA committed, for instance, to doubling both its analyst and operator cadres. As for other agencies, not all that growth addressed the terrorism threat, but terrorism was the main justification.

3. Estimating Rich-Country Security Costs

This section presents several approaches to estimating the costs of the activities described in the previous section, starting with direct *federal expenditures at home*. It concludes with a summary analysis of costs borne by *states and localities*, and *the private sector*. In principle, the increments in U.S. federal government spending on homeland security across the eight mission areas of section two would include new programs and activities that did not exist before 9/11 and growth above and beyond what pre-9/11 trends would have indicated. Assessing the first type of increment, new programs, is relatively easy. For instance, BioShield – a federal effort to develop and make available drugs and vaccines to protect against attacks by biological weapons, chemical weapons, or other dangerous pathogens, with a budget of $5.6 billion (over nine years) – is a clear response to the changed security circumstances.[5]

However, spending also increased beyond the prior trend in activities that had pre-9/11 counterparts. Not only is the actual increment hard to measure because the trends are difficult to measure, as discussed earlier, but also the organizations and categories have themselves changed since 9/11. For the United States, the biggest organizational change is the creation of the Department of Homeland Security (DHS) out of twenty-nine constituent agencies. Because of the difficulty in separating out budgetary headings, the spending against some threats to "homeland security" that have little connection to terrorism – such as preparation for pandemics and national emergencies, or foreign assistance that is essentially humanitarian in nature, not political or strategic – may still be included in our calculations despite our efforts to exclude them.

Next we describe two approaches to estimating the increments for nondefense spending at the federal level, given the complication of organizational change. The first is a back-of-the-envelope calculation that extrapolates from trends before and after 9/11 in the broad "parent" programs of the more specific homeland security activities. The second traces budget authorizations back using budget accounts of several of the activities that are now subsumed under DHS and activities of independent agencies. This information is presented graphically so that the "prior trend" can be roughly identified. Fortunately, the two approaches produce very similar results.

3.1. Nondefense Costs, Approach 1: Extrapolations from Broad Trends

Reports by the U.S. Office of Management and Budget (OMB) provide figures on spending on U.S. homeland security programs by agency. In particular, OMB (2005a, 2005b) categorizes agency and program spending on specific homeland security activities by mission area. Note that OMB figures represent the level of spending that Congress authorizes agencies to spend during the fiscal year – budget authority (BA) – instead of actual outlays (i.e., expenditures). We assumed that homeland security expenditures for FY 2004 reached the levels of the budget authority and then adjusted these

---

[5] Unless otherwise noted, all costs in this section are given in 2005 dollars.

Table 2.4. *U.S. federal government estimated security costs, FY 2004*

Mission area	Total FY 2004 (billions)	Total FY 2005 (billions)	Request FY 2006 (billions)
Border and transportation security	$16.9 (38.3%)	$17.6 (36.3%)	$19.3 (38.7%)
Protecting critical infrastructure and key assets	$13.0 (29.5%)	$14.9 (30.7%)	$15.6 (31.3%)
Emergency preparedness and response	$6.4 (14.5%)	$5.8 (12.0%)	$6.1 (12.2%)
Domestic counterterrorism	$3.6 (8.2%)	$3.9 (8.0%)	$4.5 (9.0%)
Defending against catastrophic threats	$3.1 (7.0%)	$3.4 (7.0%)	$3.9 (7.8%)
Other activities[a]	$0.9 (2.0%)	$2.6 (5.4%)	$0.1 (0.2%)
Intelligence and warning	$0.3 (0.7%)	$0.3 (0.6%)	$0.4 (0.8%)
Total	$44.1 (100.0%)	$48.5 (100.0%)	$49.9 (100.0%)

Note:

[a] Includes BioShield. Figure in brackets is the percentage of total security-related spending in the U.S. in that FY.

Source: "Appendix – Homeland Security Mission Funding by Agency and Budget Account," FY 2006 Budget, OMB, 2005b.

figures for inflation.[6] Table 2.4 presents estimates of the U.S. federal government expenditures on homeland security, across the six mission areas pertaining to homeland security.

The table makes clear that the bulk of spending on homeland security activities was devoted to two areas in FY 2004 – border and transportation security and protecting critical infrastructure and key assets. Together these two areas accounted for nearly $30 billion (67.8%) of the $44.1 billion the federal government spent on homeland security. The next largest area was emergency preparedness and response at $6.4 billion (14.5%). The remainder consisted of domestic counterterrorism at $3.6 billion (8.2%), defending against catastrophic threats at $3.1 billion (7.0%), intelligence and warning activities at $300 million (0.7%), and other activities at $900 million (2.0%).

OMB did not track spending on these homeland security activities prior to 2002. Thus it is not possible to use OMB figures to measure the growth in federal homeland security spending relative to a pre-9/11 baseline. However, historical data do exist for the federal programs of which these activities are

[6] To adjust figures for inflation, we use the U.S. Bureau of Labor Statistics' inflation calculator. The inflation calculator is based on the average Consumer Price Index (CPI) for a given year.

components. These data allow us to obtain a rough gauge of homeland security spending over time.

Between FY 1998 and FY 2004, federal programs devoted to national and homeland security – including *the entire U.S. defense budge* – grew from $464 billion to $752 billion in current prices, or an increase of 62.1 percent over that period. By contrast, inflation as measured by the Consumer Price Index (CPI) rose by only 15.9 percent over that same span, indicating a real growth rate of 46.2 percent. Assuming that homeland security activities between FY 1998 and FY 2004 grew at rates commensurate with this aggregate, then this would suggest that spending on homeland security activities totaled only $30.2 billion in real terms in FY 1998. Thus the real increase of $13.9 billion (from $30.2 billion to the $44.1 billion spent in 2004) can directly be attributed to the stepped-up campaign against terrorism.

3.2. Considering Opportunity Costs

Presumably, some portion of the $13.9 billion might have been spent on other priorities, such as low-income housing assistance or environmental protection. In other words, it represents spending that was forgone to fund homeland security activities. Estimating the opportunity costs of the $13.9 billion is a speculative exercise because we can never know what might have occurred in the absence of the campaign against terrorism.

We attempt to do so, however, by comparing the growth in federal spending on homeland security programs to the average growth of nonsecurity-related programs over time (the second approach described earlier).

In real terms, spending on all nonsecurity programs (all programs except for homeland security, defense, and foreign assistance programs) grew by an average of 12.3 percent between FY 1998 and FY 2004; by comparison, spending on homeland security programs grew by 46.2 percent over the same period. Assuming that spending on homeland security activities had grown by only 12.3 percent from its (estimated) FY 1998 base of $30.2 billion, it would have totaled $33.9 billion in FY 2004. Instead, $44.1 billion was actually spent on homeland security activities. This suggests that the difference between actual and estimated spending, $10.2 billion, might have been used for purposes other than homeland security.

3.3. Nondefense Costs, Approach 2: Building from Agency Programs

A second approach to measuring the incremental costs is to disaggregate to budget components, before and after 9/11. OMB (2003) first defined

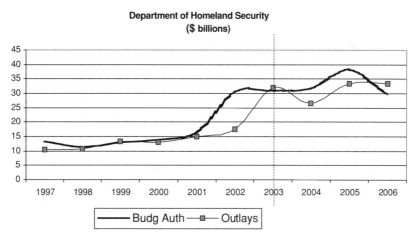

Figure 2.1. Trend in Department of Homeland Security funding.

the six mission areas in 2003 and has provided data by mission area going back to FY 2001. That prevents a real "before and after 9/11" analysis of the increase in security spending, although FY 2001 for practical purposes approximates "pre-9/11" spending because FY 2001 ended on September 30, 2001. A fuller before and after estimate can be assembled by disaggregating to track specific budget accounts, for which data are available on budget authority (from 1976) and actual outlays (from 1962).

When the Department of Homeland Security (DHS) was created in 2003, it incorporated more than thirty programs from other agencies (and even entire agencies, such as FEMA). These programs were then rearranged within DHS under its six directorates (Border and Transportation Security; Emergency Preparedness and Response; Science and Technology, Informa-tion Analysis and Infrastructure Protection; U.S. Coast Guard; and U.S. Secret Service). Whereas DHS did not exist before 2003, individual pro-grams and agencies did, so it is possible to track well-known programs or pre-DHS agencies for before-after comparisons around 9/11.

Figure 2.1 starts by assembling a phantom DHS incorporating all the directorates and incorporated programs (previously under a variety of fed-eral departments and agencies), and portraying total aggregate spending for these programs from the 1997 actuals through the 2005–2006 estimates. The large spike in DHS-related activities (before 2003 housed in various other agencies and independent programs) can be seen immediately after 2001. The size of the increment is nearly 100 percent, from about $15 billion in 2001 to more than $30 billion in 2003. Since 2003, the growth in the agency's spending has slowed.

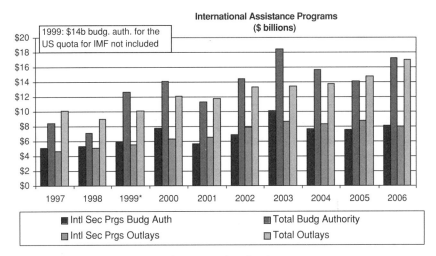

Figure 2.2. Trend in international assistance programs.

By disaggregating, this crude estimate of the increment in homeland security spending can be tested, and it can be discerned whether the real growth in homeland security spending has been in the traditional areas of customs, borders, and transport security; or in some new bins, such as preparedness and local grants or foreign aid; or even accounts unrelated to security such as disaster responses for hurricanes, floods, and forest fires.

Foreign aid is one example (see Fig. 2.2). In the figure, the line items "international assistance programs," and the subcategory "international security assistance," are of interest; the latter is a major part of the nonmilitary spending of the campaign against terrorism. The figure shows a sharp increase in expenditures (including payments to the IMF) since 2002, compared to its plateau in 2000–2001. More specifically, International Security program assistance has been maintained at around the $8 billion mark for the entire 2002–2005 period, compared with the $5–6 billion mark over 1999–2001, suggesting an increase of $2–3 billion in the equilibrium level of spending. Moreover, the graphical depiction can form a basis in what follows for an intuitive understanding of where, among the six mission areas, major changes in the equilibrium level of spending have been situated.

Customs and INS were moved from the Department of Treasury and the Department of Justice, respectively. Figure 2.3 recreates these programs from subfunctions of the DHS that are tracked back over time in the budget data. Spending again shows a huge spike after 2001 – from $4 billion to about $8 billion in outlays – then flattened after the creation of DHS in 2003. The spike stands out from the trend in the years 1997–2001, clearly suggesting a change in perceptions of the security environment.

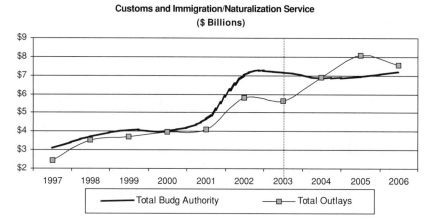

Figure 2.3. Trend in DHS components – Customs and INS.

As another example, in Figure 2.4, the core transportation security programs that were inherited from the Department of Transportation (DOT) are, like Customs and INS, part of DHS's Border and Transportation Security directorate. These programs have also seen tremendous growth since 2001, with a similar flattening after 2003. The growth from FY 2000 to recent FY 2006 in budget authority is more than double. The total transportation security related costs are close to 48 percent of DHS outlays (and approximately 41 percent of budget authority) for FY 2004.

Other DHS components, Secret Service and the Coast Guard, show increases, though not as sharp as that for the components of the B&TS

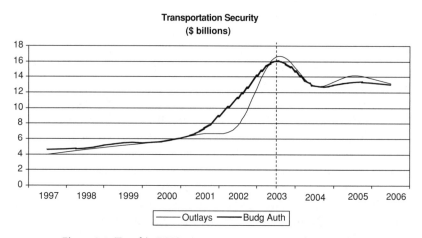

Figure 2.4. Trend in DHS components – transportation security.

Table 2.5. *Summary of nondefense costs*

Method of estimating	Estimated increment (billions)	Illustrative opportunity costs – above "normal" increases (billions)
Increment in DHS spending	15	
Approach 1: Extrapolating from broad trends	14	10
Approach 2: Disaggregating by program	13–14	

directorate. The DHS directorate, Emergency Preparedness and Response, has subfunctions grouped under the title "Disaster relief and insurance," which could be conceived as being inherited from the Federal Emergency Management Agency (FEMA). While growth after 2001 looks greater than the trend beforehand, the data are harder to read because so much of the spending is not terrorism related but instead is driven by natural disasters occurring in the fiscal year for which emergency funds are released, and hence there is also a disconnect between actual outlays and budget authority figures. We have excluded this increment in spending, on the argument that it is virtually all response, not preparation – and, with the big exception of the 9/11 attacks, responses to natural disasters, not terrorism.

Summing up these expenses across components – with the exception of the disaster relief and insurance spending – would produce a total in the range of $13–14 billion. Reassuringly, that is the same range as both the increment in the official number for DHS spending and the estimate of the increment produced by extrapolating from broader budget trends. Table 2.5 summarizes the results for nondefense spending.

3.4. Federal Expenditures Primarily Outside: Defense

On the defense side for the United States, the major military operations supporting the campaign against terror have been two abroad – Operation Enduring Freedom (OEF) in Afghanistan and Operation Iraqi Freedom (OIF) in Iraq – and one at home, Operation Noble Eagle (ONE),[7] along with other enhanced security and military activities on the home front. Evaluating the incremental costs of these activities carries its own difficulties and uncertainties.[8] The U.S. Congress' research and analytic organizations

---

[7] Operation Noble Eagle includes such activities as combat air patrols over major metropolitan areas and other DoD activities in response to the events of September 11, 2001.

[8] On the difficulties of compiling complete data on the costs of military activities since 9/11, see Donnelly 2003. One can find data on the costs of selected DoD campaigns

have compiled official data that provide a starting point for estimating these costs, and these can be supplemented with the most recent available data to produce what appears to be a relatively complete picture of U.S. Department of Defense (DoD) spending on the campaign against terrorism.

The available estimates include both funds authorized and appropriated by Congress for military operations and other counterterrorism activities, and incremental obligations – that is, actual outlays or costs.[9] The appropriated funding came through a combination of regular appropriations and emergency supplemental appropriations that, taken together, totaled nearly $275 billion by 2005, about $245 billion of which was spent in direct support of U.S. military operations, with the remaining $30 billion attributable to DoD activities funded by campaign against terror-related appropriations that were not directly supporting military operations.[10]

The Congressional Research Service has estimated that from September 11, 2001, through March 2005, the Congress appropriated and authorized $201 billion for the campaign against terror,[11] including OEF, OIF, and enhanced security and other operations at home, including Operation Noble Eagle (ONE).[12] The DoD FY 2005 emergency supplemental that was passed after CRS released its report (Public Law 109–13) boosted the total

against terror-related activities in Congressional appropriation and authorization bills and documentation associated with the President's Budget, the DoD budget, supplemental requests, the Emergency Response Fund (ERF), the Overseas Contingency and Transfer Fund (OCOTF), and so on, but these data provide only a somewhat piecemeal picture.

[9] Discretionary spending limits for DoD are established in a Defense appropriation bill, one of thirteen separate appropriations bills originating in House and Senate Appropriations Committees. An Authorization is substantive legislation that provides the authority for an agency to carry out a particular program, and may be annual, for a specified number of years, or of indefinite duration. Outlays, or expenditures, are the liquidation of the government's obligations, and generally represent cash payments. There also are estimates of the costs of individual operations.

[10] For example, $16.6 billion was earmarked for procurement and RDT&E. See DoD, FY 2005 Supplemental Request for Operation Iraqi Freedom (OIF), Operation Enduring Freedom (OEF), and Operation Unified Assistance, Washington, DC, February 2005, 3–4, 7.

[11] Belasco 2005.

[12] A June 2004 Congressional Budget Office report estimated DoD obligations for Operation Noble Eagle (ONE), which, as follows: $5.7 billion in FY 2002, $6.3 billion in FY 2003, and $4 billion in FY 2004. See CBO, Estimated Costs of Continuing Operations in Iraq and Other Operations of the Global Campaign against Terrorism, Washington, DC, June 25, 2004, Tab. 1.3. Rather than being covered under contingency costs, it also appears that some homeland security costs are being absorbed by the services themselves. On this point, see Colarusso and Bloker (2005).

Table 2.6. *Funding for Iraq, Afghanistan, and enhanced security, FY 2001–2005 in $billions*

Fiscal year	Afghan.	Iraq	Enhanced security & other	Total
2001	11.9	–	4.6	16.5
2002	12.5	–	1.5	14
2003	18.1	48.5	9.6	76.2
2004	7.8	54.7	7.1	69.5
Subtotal FY01–04	47.1	105.4	17.8	170.3
2005, of which:				
PL 108–287	3.5	21.5	–	25
PL 109–13	4.2	67.2	–	71.4
Total, FY01–05	58	192	23	274[a]

Note:

[a] Assumes that the $1 billion that Congress added to the president's initial request was entirely in support of the campaign against terror.

Source: Derived from Amy Belasco, *The Cost of Operations in Iraq, Afghanistan, and Enhanced Security,* Washington, DC: Congressional Research Service, RS21644, March 14, 2005, tab. 2, p. 4; U.S. Senate Committee on Appropriations, "Senate and House Conferees Agree to FY 2005 Supplemental," news release, May 3, 2005.

estimated funding for the campaign against terror from 9/11 through the end of FY 2005 to about $275 billion.[13] The total and a breakdown are displayed in Table 2.6.[14]

[13] The Congressional Research Service estimated that the president's emergency supplemental of $74.9 billion would mean that DoD's total costs through 2005 might total "about $192 billion for Iraq, about $58 billion for Afghanistan, and about $20 billion for enhanced security by the end of FY 2005," and concluded that "If Congress approves this amount [$75 billion], DoD's funding through FY 2005 for these missions will exceed $275 billion." Ibid, 1. On May 3, 2005, the Senate and House agreed to an $82 billion FY 2005 Emergency Supplemental bill, with approximately $75.9 billion going to defense-related appropriations or about $1 billion more than the president had requested. On May 11, 2005, the president signed into law Public Law 109–13, the "Emergency Supplemental Appropriations Act for Defense, the Global Campaign against Terror , and Tsunami Relief." See U.S. Senate Committee on Appropriations, "Senate and House Conferees Agree to FY 2005 Supplemental," news release, May 3, 2005, and White House, "Statement on H. R. 1268, the 'Emergency Supplemental Appropriations Act for Defense, the Global Campaign against Terror, and Tsunami Relief, 2005,'" May 11, 2005. For our calculations, we simply assumed that the total of $22.7 billion for enhanced security through March 2005 would not actually drop to $20 billion as might be inferred from CRS' language, and that the $1 billion that was added to the president's original request would be used entirely to support the campaign against terror, yielding a total of about $274 billion.

[14] Wallsten and Kosec (2005) reach a higher estimate of the war's cost to the United States, $255 billion from March 2003 to August 2005. Their estimates include monetized figures

Table 2.7. *DoD obligations of funds for Iraq, Afghanistan, and enhanced security, FY 2001–2004 ($billions)*

Fiscal year	Afghan.	Iraq	Enhanced security & other	Total
2001	0.4	0.0	0.1	0.5
2002	19.5	0.0	7.5	27.0
2003	16.2	44.1	6.3	66.6
2004	11.0	61.3	3.9	76.2
Subtotal FY01–04	47.1	105.5	17.8	170.4
2005, of which:			6.9^a	6.9^a
PL 108–287	2.4	20.7	–	23.1^b
PL 109–13	9.4	35.5	–	44.9^b
Total, FY01–05	58.9	161.6	24.7	245.2

Note:

[a] Assumes that spending on Operation Noble Eagle and enhanced security and other homeland security activities in FY 2005 was roughly the same as in FY 2004, or about $4 billion.

[b] Includes costs for military operations in Iraq and Afghanistan only.

Source: Derived from Amy Belasco, *The Cost of Operations in Iraq, Afghanistan, and Enhanced Security*, Washington, DC: Congressional Research Service, RS21644, March 14, 2005, tab. 3, 6; DoD, *FY 2005 Supplemental Request for Operation Iraqi Freedom (OIF), Operation Enduring Freedom (OEF), and Operation Unified Assistance*, Washington, DC, February 2005, 3–4, and authors' estimates.

Making pre- and post-9/11 comparisons on a yearly basis is much harder here than for homeland security activities inside the country because so much depends on the spending on single operations, especially Iraq.

Comparing 2001 with 2003 and 2004 would suggest a yearly increment in the range of $50–60 billion. Comparing 2001 with 2005 would suggest that the increment was even larger, again largely because of spending on Iraq.

While DoD does not track actual spending (outlays) on contingency operations, it is possible to make good estimates from a variety of other data. Table 2.7 presents CRS' estimate of DoD obligations for the campaign against terror-related activities since 9/11, supplemented by more recent data and estimates. The table suggests that DoD had obligated a total of about $170 billion for the campaign against terrorism-related operations through FY 2004. If we use DoD's estimate that $23.1 billion of its regular FY 2005 appropriation (Public Law 108–287) and $44.9 billion of its FY 2005

for deaths and injuries, as well as lost wages of reservists. They also estimate costs avoided by the war, principally those of enforcing sanctions and "no fly" zones, as well as monetized costs for people murdered by the previous regime.

supplemental (Public Law 109–13) were obligated to supporting counter-terror operations abroad in FY 2005,[15] and assume that DoD spending on ONE and other homeland security operations remained what it was in FY 2004 (about $6.9 billion),[16] that would suggest that DoD obligated a total of about $75 billion in support of the campaign against terror in FY 2005, for a total of about $245 billion since 9/11.

Thus, the estimated incremental costs of the campaign against terrorism-related military operations from 9/11 through FY 2005 would appear to be around $245 billion, accounting for all but about $30 billion (12 percent) of the funding Congress has approved for the campaign against terror through its regular and supplemental appropriations since 9/11. The per year comparisons remain elusive, but, not surprisingly, would be in the same $50–75 billion range. Again, however, Iraq is far and away the largest item, and so deciding whether to include or exclude it as part of countering the terrorist threat makes a big difference.

3.5. Federal Expenditures Primarily Outside: Foreign Assistance

For these purposes, U.S. federal spending on foreign assistance includes outlays for all federal programs related to international security assistance and international development and humanitarian assistance for FY 2004 (OMB 2005c). We omit federal spending on international financial programs because the nature of these programs precludes easy calculations of federal contributions.[17]

Excluding international financial programs and adjusting for inflation, federal spending on foreign assistance totaled $22.8 billion in FY 2004. Of this amount, $14.2 billion (62 percent) went toward international development and humanitarian assistance. Responsibility for these programs is spread across the federal budget; many of these programs fall under the

---

[15] DoD's supplemental request requested $35.5 billion for operations in Iraq and $9.4 billion for operations in Afghanistan, for a total of $44.9 billion. See DoD, FY 2005 Supplemental Request for Operation Iraqi Freedom (OIF), Operation Enduring Freedom (OEF), and Operation Unified Assistance, Washington, DC, February 2005, 4.

[16] DoD, FY 2005 Supplemental Request for Operation Iraqi Freedom (OIF), Operation Enduring Freedom (OEF), and Operation Unified Assistance, Washington, DC, February 2005, 40.

[17] U.S. spending on international financial programs involves funding primarily for two revolving funds – the International Monetary Fund and the U.S. Export-Import Bank. These funds make loans and loan guarantees from contributions to the funds, loan repayments, and/or interest earned. Because new contributions to the funds are sporadic and, by convention, are not always accounted for in the budget, annual outlays for these programs do not necessarily capture all of their actual activities.

Table 2.8. *Ten largest foreign assistance activities (excluding international financing), by FY 2004 outlays*

Activity	Agency	Area	FY 2004 cost (billions)
Foreign military financing program	International Assistance Programs	Security assistance	$5.456
Iraq relief and reconstruction fund	Executive Office of the President	Development and humanitarian assistance	$3.094
Economic support fund	International Assistance Programs	Security assistance	$2.936
Foreign agricultural service	Department of Agriculture	Development and humanitarian assistance	$1.864
Child survival and disease programs	U.S. Agency for International Development	Development and humanitarian assistance	$1.693
Sustainable development assistance program	U.S. Agency for International Development	Development and humanitarian assistance	$1.379
Contribution to International Development Association	International Assistance Programs	Development and humanitarian assistance	$1.371
Migration and refugee assistance	Department of State	Development and humanitarian assistance	$0.855
Operating expenses	U.S. Agency for International Development	Development and humanitarian assistance	$0.636
Andean counterdrug initiative	Department of State	Development and humanitarian assistance	$0.632

Source: Public Budget Database, Budget of the United States Government, Fiscal Year 2006, OMB, 2005c.

U.S. Agency for International Development (USAID), but others fall under agencies such as the State Department, the Department of Agriculture, the Department of Defense, the Treasury Department, and the Peace Corps. The remaining $8.6 billion (38 percent) spent on foreign assistance in FY 2004 went toward international security assistance. Almost all of these programs are classified as International Assistance Programs in the federal budget.

For illustrative purposes, Table 2.8 displays the largest foreign assistance activities (excluding international financial programs) by level of spending.

Calculating the precise influence of the campaign against terrorism on the growth in foreign assistance spending is tricky at best. Some newer activities can (arguably) be directly tied to the campaign against terrorism, such as funding for relief and reconstruction in Iraq. But other activities have less clear connections. Disaster relief for a developing country, for example, can both alleviate suffering *and* improve the standing of the United States in the eyes of the world; both can be useful in the campaign against terrorism.[18] Because assistance activities can serve multiple goals, a full accounting of the effect of the campaign against terrorism would require a complete understanding of the motivations of policy makers, which is impossible.

In light of these caveats, we use two approaches to estimate the increase in foreign assistance spending directly attributable to the campaign against terrorism: we identify the programs that are clearly tied to the campaign against terrorism and calculate their total spending, and we analyze the growth in foreign assistance spending over time. With respect to the first approach, we identified three programs in the federal budget explicitly pertaining to Iraqi relief and reconstruction and to the operating expenses of the Coalition Provisional Authority for FY 2004. These programs, all operated by the Department of Defense, totaled $3.7 billion in inflation-adjusted dollars. (Again, if Iraq were judged unrelated to preparing for the terrorism threat, these expenditures could be subtracted.) With respect to the second approach, OMB (2005c) provides historical data on these programs as well as current data that enable us to compare post-9/11 spending to a pre-9/11 baseline. Between FY 1998 and FY 2004, total outlays on international security assistance and international development and humanitarian assistance increased by $10.2 billion, from an inflation-adjusted $12.6 billion to $22.8 billion. This increase is illustrated in Figure 2.5. Consequently, the annual increase in foreign assistance spending (broken down by area) is estimated to be in the range of $1.7 billion to $3.7 billion.

As with homeland security spending, we also estimate the opportunity costs that could be associated with the growth in foreign assistance spending due to the campaign against terror. Comparing the growth in foreign assistance to the average growth of nonsecurity-related programs over time identifies above-average increases going to foreign assistance. As mentioned, real

---

[18] Polling by the Pew Research Center's Global Attitudes Project in May 2005, for example, shows that the image of the U.S. had improved markedly in Indonesia and other countries affected by the December 2004 tsunami, and anti-Americanism had shown modest signs of abating elsewhere. For example, 79% of Indonesian respondents said that they had a much more favorable view of the United States as a result of the relief efforts. See Pew Research Center, *American Character Gets Mixed Reviews: U.S. Image Up Slightly, but Still Negative*, Washington, DC, June 23, 2005.

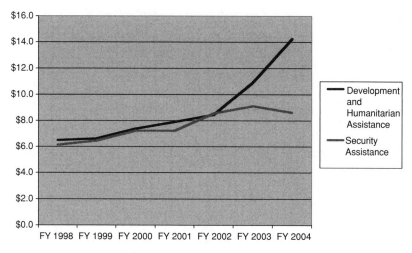

Figure 2.5. Real foreign assistance outlays (excluding international financing), FY 1998 to FY 2004 (in billions).[19]

spending on all nonsecurity programs (all programs except for homeland security, defense, and foreign assistance programs) grew by 12.3 percent between FY 1998 and FY 2004, whereas real spending on foreign assistance programs grew by 81.0 percent over the same period. Had real spending on foreign assistance programs increased by only 12.3 percent, it would have totaled $14.1 billion in FY 2004 rather than $22.8 billion. The difference suggests that $8.7 billion total, or $1.5 billion annually, could have gone to other, nonterrorism-related priorities.

3.6. Other Countries' Expenditures: Britain

Some comparative flavor can be gained by looking at Britain, another front-line state in the campaign against terrorism (see Tab. 2.9). As shown in the table, aggregate spending on security is much lower for Britain than the

---

[19] The total burden imposed on a rich society by preparations taken in response to the terrorist threat includes not only those increases in spending but also the indirect costs imposed on the private sector and on individuals as a result of their own actions to defend against terrorism – the subject of the next section. In this chapter, we use "homeland security" and "counterterrorism" nearly interchangeably to include the portfolio of actions intended to protect against and, ideally, prevent a terrorist attack. Because of the difficulty in separating out budgetary headings, the spending against some threats to "homeland security" that have little connection to terrorism – such as preparation for pandemics and national emergencies, or foreign assistance that is essentially humanitarian in nature, not political or strategic – may be included in our calculations.

Table 2.9. *British budget allocations for counterterrorism and domestic security*

Pre 9/11 (2000–01)	2001–02	2002–03	2004–05	2007–08
< $1.8 billion/year	~$ 3.5 billion		~$ 2.7 billion	> $ 3.7 billion/year
< £ 1 billion/year	~£ 1.91 billion		~ £ 1.5 billion	> £ 2.1 billion/year

Split by heads of spending (projected, $ Million)

	2006–07	2007–08
Intelligence[a]	220	346
Emergency Planning[b]	36	36
Counterterrorism[c]	558	630
Totals	814	1012

Note:
[a] Total DEL. Full resource budgeting basis, net of depreciation.
[b] Provided as increase to Formula Spending Share for local authorities through the EPCS (Environmental Protective and Cultural Services) block.
[c] Resource DEL plus Capital DEL. Indicative additional provision across a range of departments. Subject to final internal departmental allocations. Figures not available on Total DEL basis as they depend on final allocation decisions.
Source: HM Government of UK, HM Treasury Spending Report 2004.

United States, a fact that is not surprising given that Britain has a much smaller population and GNP. For FY 2001–2002 there was a special provision from the British Reserve of $1.395 billion[20] (£ 775m) for spending more than 2001–2002 and 2002–2003 under the headings of "Counterterrorism and Domestic Security." Budget 2002 allocated a further $110 million (£ 61m) and Budget 2003 a further $598 million (£ 332 m) from the Capital Modernization Fund. Additional resources were made available, totaling $814 million (£ 452m) in 2006–2007 and $1.01 billion (£ 562m) in 2007–2008, to enable departments to improve Counterterrorism and Resilience capabilities. By 2007–2008, Britain's planned investment in this area will be over $3.6 billion (over £2 billion), more than double the pre-9/11 levels.

We have two main pieces of data on British spending on military operations:

- Between 2001–2002 and 2004–2005 Britain spent $7.92 billion (£4.4 billion) to meet the *extra* costs of the military deployments in Iraq, Afghanistan, and other international obligations.

---

[20] Exchange rate used is an average of approximately US$1.8/GBP.

Table 2.10. *Federal grants to states and localities*

Grant program	2003 (Parts I + II)	2004
HSGP[#]	2.066	2.22
Locality-based funding*	0.73	0.796
Total	2.8	3.016

Source: Department of Homeland Security.

[#]: HSGP: Since 2004, it is constituted of SHSGP (State HS Grant Programs), LETPP (Law Enforcement Terrorism Prevention Programs), and CC (Citizen Corps).

*This includes: UASI (Urban Area Security Initiative) + Mass Transit grants + Port Security grants (2004 data unavailable for Port Security grants. 2003 data used for 2004 as well).

- Announced: $ 940m (£ 520m) more funding in 2005 for operations in Iraq/Afghanistan, bringing the total outlay to *$8.9 billion (∼£ 5 billion) so far.*[21]

Thus, post-9/11 security spending by Britain appears to have been substantially smaller than that by the United States. We would conjecture that other rich countries probably have spent even less.

3.7. Points of Comparison: State and Local Costs and Private Costs

The costs to states and localities are among the hardest costs to measure, for they are dispersed across 18,000 different units of government in the United States. The costs funded from federal grants are easy to measure – and those expenditures are included in the federal spending analyzed earlier – but not so the opportunity costs. Reports from large cities, like New York, suggested as much as half the money they spent on homeland security after 9/11 came from their own resources and thus reflected *opportunity costs*; they did more in the realm of homeland security at the price of doing less in other areas. By contrast, smaller jurisdictions may have spent only federal grant money (and perhaps spent some of that for other than "homeland security" purposes).

Given this variation, we started with the federal grants program, which is summarized in Table 2.10. We then constructed a "grant source percentage (GPF)" by state, as a function of size and exposure to terrorism risk based on past reported threats directed at the state, the presence of sensitive

---

[21] Source: "Britain ups funding for Iraq, Afghanistan forces," *Agence France Presse*, London, December 1, 2004.

Table 2.11. *Summary of private costs of antiterrorism*

Cost category	Annual value ($ billions)
Investments in security	$5.2
Terrorism risk insurance premiums	$3.6
Airport screening opportunity costs	$9.4
Declines in airline travel demand	$5.9
Consumer welfare losses	$24.1

infrastructure or military assets in the state, number and locations of high population density areas, and the like. Improving these estimates is an area for further work, and RAND's Center for Terrorism Risk Management Policy is making efforts to calculate risk at the city level (especially, Willis et al. 2005). The GPFs ranged from .55 for New York and California, to .90 for Alaska. Not surprisingly, New York and California were in a class by themselves, given size and risk. Put together, the numbers suggested that state and localities provided about $1.2 billion per year in their own funding to the campaign against terror – a lower estimate than many others. In FY 2006, total grant-based funding went up 40 percent on the FY 2004 base, but this increase may substitute for local own source funding, such that own source funding may stagnate at about $1.2 billion or even reduce.

For the private sector, the first costs of interest are the direct costs of security investments to prevent incidents and limit their damage, then direct investments in insurance against the risk of terrorism and finally an estimate of the opportunity cost of time spent waiting in lines for airport screening. We then estimated a variety of indirect costs, including the reduction in air transportation demand and consumer welfare reductions that followed 9/11. We concluded by considering some of the broader financial and macroeconomic consequences of private responses to terrorism.

The results are summarized in Table 2.11. The estimates are rough-and-ready ones, based on sparse information. For instance, the estimate for investments in security started with estimates of how many additional private sector guards were hired after 9/11 in critical sectors – banking, chemical, transportation, and energy. The incremental cost on guards was then adjusted upward to account for additional security measures, by a factor based on the past experience of security investments made by a set of high technology hardware companies. The airport screening opportunity cost began with U.S. Transportation Security Administration (TSA) numbers that indicated average delays had increased by 19.5 minutes. In 2004, passengers took 785 million domestic one-way flights. This implies that passengers spent over 255 million hours waiting to pass through screening.

Surveys suggest that passengers value their time at about $37 per hour on average. In other words, the value of time lost due to screening can be valued at $9.4 billion.

Finally, many of the costs, delays, and inconveniences will result in declines in the quantities of goods and services provided to consumers in affected markets. Firms will attempt to recapture some of the lost profits by increasing their prices, especially in cases where the magnitude of cost increases vary with the quantity of output. The resulting price increases will cause consumers to reduce purchases of goods and services, resulting in an efficiency loss that can be quite significant. Indeed, it is reasonable to assume that, under a variety of circumstances, this "consumer surplus" loss can be greater than the initial change in cost or demand that lead to the decline in quantity.[22] Thus, the private losses associated with antiterrorism responses are probably at least double the direct cost increases.

That excludes still more diffuse macroeconomic effects, like effects on property values or the stock market, business location decisions or consumer spending. For instance, Hubbard and Deal (2004) simulated the broader effect of effectively doubling the insurance premium for terrorism insurance (currently totaling about $3.6 billion). They concluded that this was equivalent to a $107 billion reduction in property values, resulting in more than $5 billion annual declines in consumer spending. Based on a macroeconomic model, Gross Domestic Product would fall by $53 billion and more than 300,000 jobs would be lost. Although we have not tried to repeat this exercise for the other private costs of antiterrorism, it is clear that they could add up to be quite substantial.

4. Concluding Observations

As is plain, estimates of the total incremental costs of post-9/11 responses to the greater threat depend very much on what is included and what is excluded and on views about opportunity cost and welfare losses. The total increment ranges from slightly over a half percent of GDP to a percent and an eighth of GDP, depending on whether the expenditures for the wars in Afghanistan and Iraq are excluded or included. Table 2.12 summarizes the estimates of

---

[22] Dertouzos, Larson, and Ebener (1999) provided a range of plausible estimates for the value of consumer welfare lost as a result of firm responses to high technology hardware theft. They demonstrated that these losses, depending on market circumstances, easily exceed direct losses by a factor of 2 or 3. For current purposes, we performed simulations of losses caused by a 7.4% decline in demand. Under a variety of assumptions, consumer welfare losses due to output declines exceeded profit losses incurred by firms.

Table 2.12. *Total post-9/11 equilibrium for incremental spending on Homeland Security by the United States, annual in $billions*

Category	Amount
Public	
Federal nondefense	13–14
(Estimated from broad departmental trends)	(14)
(Disaggregated by program)	(13–14)
Federal defense	
Enhanced security, primarily at home	4–8
Major operations abroad, primarily Afghanistan, Iraq	50–70
Federal economic assistance abroad	2–4
State and local own spending	1–2
Private	
Direct	
Security enhancements and other protection	5
Insurance	5
Indirect	
Opportunity cost to airline passengers for waiting	9
Decline in airline travel demand	6
Losses in consumer welfare	24
Total	119–147

the total incremental costs for the United States, by the major categories we have used in this chapter; it also illustrates the sensitivities of the totals to what is included.

There is no need to repeat all the caveats: the numbers are rough estimates. Subtracting the war in Iraq as unrelated to the terrorism threat would reduce the total by a third or more. Applying an opportunity cost adjustment to the federal spending might reduce those numbers. It would do so somewhat if it were assumed that the increments were only those above and beyond the more general increase in federal spending during the period before and after 9/11. The effect would be more dramatic if it were assumed that the increment carried no opportunity costs other than the increase in the service on the federal debt occasioned by the spending.

On the other hand, the numbers for private spending could well be under-stated, in particular the losses in consumer welfare, which could vary sharply with different assumptions. Nevertheless, if the orders of magnitude are roughly right, the incremental cost of homeland security for the United States, as an example, is in the range of $100–200 billion. The first observation is that the number is not all that large, some 1 to 2 percent of a gross domestic product (GDP) of $12 trillion.

Second, spending by the federal government accounts for more than half the total spending. If only *direct* costs were included, then more than four-fifths of the total spending would be by the federal government. Third, and perhaps most striking, a very large fraction of the total incremental spending, about half in our estimates (two-thirds if only direct increments were tallied), is accounted for by the big military operations abroad, especially Iraq, and so how the spending is evaluated turns very much on how those operations are assessed.

The fourth observation is that, those big military operations aside, most of the U.S. spending on homeland security is at home; framed in terms of the layered defense analogy, the inner layers get most of the attention. Border, port, and airport security account for nearly two-fifths of federal nondefense spending, with protecting critical infrastructure and other sites taking almost a third; virtually all the direct private spending goes for site protection, and the indirect cost of airport security is at least as large as the direct cost. That conclusion might be softened somewhat, though not changed, if estimates for increased counterterrorism intelligence abroad by the CIA, NSA, and other secret intelligence agencies were included.

These may or may not be wise allocations, but in terms of the layered defense logic, they are very skewed. The large spending on airport security plainly was a political response to the 9/11 attack, reflecting the fact that public and private leaders feel very personally the vulnerability of airplane travel. Still more important, while judgments pro or con on the Iraq War depend on a host of factors, its price tag in both lives and money seems very large *in terms of its specific contribution to countering terrorism*. It is hard not to suspect that money (not to mention lives) would have greater payoff if spread more evenly across the layers of defense against terrorism.

In any event, that leads directly to the final observation – the desirability of extending the estimates to costs for the developing countries and to benefits for both rich and developing countries. Absent some sense for relative benefits, qualitatively if not quantitatively, it is hard to judge either the total spent on homeland security or the allocations across categories. Whether the total increment for the United States – between a half percent and one and an eighth percent of GDP – is judged small or large depends on perspective. The upper estimate for the total increment is still less than the increase in U.S. defense spending before and after 9/11, yet the lower estimate is still equal to the defense spending of Britain and Germany combined. What we can say is that the increment in spending on homeland security now mostly goes for specific military operations abroad and for protective measures at home.

References

Becker, Gary, and Kevin Murphy. 2001. "Prosperity Will Rise Out of the Ashes," *Wall Street Journal*, October 29, p. A22.

Belasco, Amy. 2005. *The Cost of Operations in Iraq, Afghanistan, and Enhanced Security*. Washington, DC: Congressional Research Service, RS21644.

Bernasek, Anna. 2002. "The Friction Economy." *Fortune*. 145: 4 (February 2).

Colarusso, Laura M. and Ben Bloker. 2005. "Paying for Protection; Homeland Defense Flights Take $1.1B Bite from 2005 Budget." *Air Force Times*. February 21, 2005.

Congressional Budget Office. 2004. *Estimated Costs of Continuing Operations in Iraq and Other Operations of the Global Campaign against Terrorism*. Letter to Senator Kent Conrad. http://www.cbo.gov/ftpdocs/55xx/doc5587/Cost_of_Iraq.pdf.

———. 2005. *An Alternative Budget Path Assuming Continued Spending for Military Operations in Iraq and Afghanistan and in Support of the Global Campaign against Terrorism*. http://www.cbo.gov/ftpdocs/60xx/doc6067/02-01-WarSpending.pdf.

Daggett, Stephen. 1994. *A Comparison of Clinton Administration and Bush Administration Long-Term Defense Budget Plans for FY 1994–99*. Washington, DC: Congressional Research Service Report 95–20F.

Department of Defense. 2005. *FY 2005 Supplemental Request for Operation Iraqi Freedom (OIF), Operation Enduring Freedom (OEF), and Operation Unified Assistance*. Washington, DC:

Dertouzos, James N., Patricia A. Ebener, and Eric V. Larson (1999). *The Economic Costs and Implications of High-Technology Hardware Theft*. Santa Monica: RAND Corporation.

Donnelly, John M. 2003. "Key Details Lacking on Post-9/11 Billions." *Defense Week*. http://www.kingpublishing.com/publications/dw/dw05122003_article1.htm.

Enders, Walter, and Todd Sandler. 2006. *The Political Economy of Terrorism*. Cambridge: Cambridge University Press.

HM Government of UK. *HM Treasury Spending Report 2004*.

International Monetary Fund, Chapter II. 2001. "How Has September 11 Influenced the Global Economy?" In *World Economic Outlook: The Global Economy After September 11, pp. 14–33*. Washington: International Monetary Fund.

Joint Economic Committee. 2002. "The Economic Costs of Terrorism." Report prepared by Dr. Robert Keleher, Chief Macroeconomist.Washington, DC: U.S. Congress.

Larson, Eric V., David Orletsky, and Kristin Leuschner. 2001. *Defense Planning in a Decade of Change*, MR-1387-AF. Santa Monica, CA: RAND Corporation.

Mueller, Robert S. III. 2002. "A New FBI Focus." *Testimony Before the Subcommittee for the Departments of Commerce, Justice, and State, the Judiciary, and Related Agencies, House Committee on Appropriations*. http://www.fbi.gov/congress/congress02/mueller062102.htm.

Navarro, Peter, and Aaron Spencer. 2001. "September 11, 2001: Assessing the Costs of Terrorism." *The Milken Institute Review*. Fourth Quarter: 16–31.

Office of Homeland Security. 2002. *National Strategy for Homeland Security*. http://www.whitehouse.gov/homeland/book/nat_strat_hls.pdf.

Office of Management and Budget. 2003. *Report to Congress on Combating Terrorism*. http://www.whitehouse.gov/omb/legislative/2003_combat_terr.pdf.

———. 2005a. *Analytical Perspectives, Budget of the United States Government, Fiscal Year 2006*. http://www.whitehouse.gov/omb/budget/fy2006/pdf/spec.pdf.

————. 2005b. *Appendix – Homeland Security Mission Funding by Agency and Budget Account, Budget of the United States Government, Fiscal Year 2006.*

————. 2005c. *Public Budget Database, Budget of the United States Government, Fiscal Year 2006.* http://www.whitehouse.gov/omb/budget/fy2006/sheets/outlays.xls.

————. "Report on Expenditures from the Emergency Response Fund: Tenth Quarterly Report (Amounts as of February 28, 2005) – 6/21/05." http://www.whitehouse.gov/omb/legislative/erfreports/.

Parfomak, Paul, Willis, Henry H., Andrew R. Morral, Terence K. Kelly, and Jamison Jo Medby. 2005. *Estimating Terrorism Risk*, MG-388-RC. Santa Monica, CA: RAND Corporation.

UBS Warburg. 2001. *Global Economic Strategy Research.*

Wallsten, Scott, and Katrina Kosec. 2005. "The Economic Costs of the War in Iraq." AEI-Brookings Joint Center Working Paper. http://aei-brookings.org/publications/abstract.php?pid=988.

PART TWO

DEVELOPMENT, DEMOCRACY, AND
THE ORIGINS OF TERRORISM

THREE

From (No) Butter to Guns? Understanding the Economic Role in Transnational Terrorism

S. Brock Blomberg and Gregory D. Hess

This chapter provides a comprehensive study of the economic determinants of transnational terrorism and the role that development plays in fostering a more peaceful world. We analyze models of conflict resolution to investigate the relative importance of economic development on domestic and transnational terrorism. We construct an original database from 1968 to 2003 for 179 countries in order to examine which economic factors influence the propensity to be affected by transnational terrorist activities. We also compare these results to a subsample from 1998 to 2003 on domestic terrorism. We find that economic development is associated with higher incidents of transnational terrorism, especially in higher income countries. However, when considering lower income countries, economic progress is actually negatively related to transnational terrorism.

1. Introduction

We live in the Age of Terrorism. Since the prominent incidents in high-income cities such as New York, Madrid, and London, and persistent terrorism in Middle Eastern countries such as Israel and Iraq, both academia and the media have become involved in a careful examination of the causes of terrorism. Terrorism is, however, neither new nor novel – indeed the very origin of the term dating back to the late 1700s[1] points to a long history. Given its long history, we know surprisingly little about it. The purpose of this chapter is to begin to unravel the important linkages between economic development and the incidence of terrorism.

---

[1] The word "terrorism" apparently first appeared in the English language in reference to the "Reign of Terror" associated with the rule of France by the Jacobins from 1793 to 1794. The first incident was actually reported in first century BC when Jewish terrorists, Zealots-Sicarri, incited a riot that led to a mass insurrection against the Roman Empire. See Laqueur 1977, 7–8.

Political scientists have long emphasized that terrorism has been a constant source of worldwide tension through much of the post-World War II era. In her seminal contribution on the causes of terrorism, Crenshaw (1981) identifies modernization, "social facilitation" and the spread of revolutionary ideologies as important factors that drive terrorism. This paradigm serves as a useful point of departure for empirical investigations of terrorism. Modernization can isolate certain groups while at the same time provide more cost-effective ways of equipping these same groups. Such a view of modernization suggests that terrorism may be more prevalent in more developed countries (i.e., OECD countries) that tend to experience higher rates of technological progress.[2] Social facilitation or "social habits and historical traditions that sanction the use of violence against the government" (382) is synonymous with the view that internal violence begets violence.[3]

Though terrorism has been present for longer than one might realize, its nature has clearly evolved over time. Indeed, with respect to the spread of revolutionary ideologies, there appears to be a potential change in the motive of many terrorists since the November 1979 takeover of the U.S. embassy in Tehran. Until that point, revolutionary and separatist ideologies had primarily motivated terrorism (see Wilkinson [2001]). Since then, the driving force appears to be more of a religious-based fundamentalism. The percent of terrorist organizations that are religious-based grew from 4 percent to more than 50 percent by 1995 (see Hoffman 1997). This shift points to the importance of considering the political motivation of terrorist groups when examining terrorism. In fact, in a more recent discussion, Crenshaw (2001) argues, "Terrorism should be seen as a strategic reaction to American power in the context of a globalized civil war. Extremist religious beliefs play a role in motivating terrorism, but they also display an instrumental logic." This points to the importance of considering theories of civil conflict as one assesses the relative significance of development, democratization, and globalization in determining terror.

This also suggests that domestic and transnational terrorism might be distinct phenomena. One might argue that transnational terrorism is more closely linked to external conflict between two countries whereas domestic terrorism is more akin to civil war or insurrection. Another might go a step further and conjecture that certain factors, say social facilitation, are

---

[2] See also Krueger and Maleckova (2002) for analysis that is consistent with this view.
[3] In our empirical analysis, we include variables such as religious and linguistic fractionalization to control for biases due to such social and historical traditions.

influential in civil conflict whereas others, say modernization, are determinants of external violence. While plausible, the empirical evidence strongly suggests that each of these factors is important to explaining both internal and external conflict. Researchers have shown that treating these factors as having distinct influences in only internal or external violence would bias the results. Blomberg and Hess (2002) and Blomberg, Hess, and Thacker (2006) are two recent papers that demonstrate the joint causal relationship between a host of factors, for example, modernization and social facilitation and both internal and external conflict. For this reason, we take a relatively agnostic view in differentiating between transnational terrorism and domestic terrorism.[4]

Operationally, how does one quantify these political motivations for terrorism? Interestingly, radicalism, separatism, and other ideological motivations for terrorism that appear to be intrinsically noneconomic may actually stem from underlying economic conditions. Marxist and Leftist separatist movements that dominated the terrorist landscape during the 1960s and 1970s were deeply rooted in economics. North/South inequality was a key factor in political movements that might on the surface appear to be motivated by injustice or the Cold War.

Similarly, radical religious movements often appeal to economic conditions as motivation for an attack. Even Osama Bin Laden advances a public finance argument to explain terrorism: "The ordinary man knows that [Saudi Arabia] is the largest oil producer in the world, yet at the same time he is suffering from taxes and bad services. Now the people understand the speeches of the ulemas in the mosques – that our country has become an American colony. They act decisively with every action to kick the Americans out of Saudi Arabia. What happened in Riyadh and [Dhahran] when 24 Americans were killed in two bombings is clear evidence of the huge anger of Saudi people against America. The Saudis now know their real enemy is America."[5] In summary, economic shortfalls can amplify many of these seemingly noneconomic motivations as sources of terrorist recruitment.[6]

---

[4] For our main results, we concentrate on using the richest data source available that only documents transnational events. However, we do investigate analogous empirical relationships using only domestic terrorism data, albeit over a shorter time sample. We find, not surprisingly given the literature, that the factors that influence transnational terrorism are also those that influence domestic terrorism.

[5] *The Washington Post*, 8/23/98.

[6] Still, it is important to consider these noneconomic factors in the empirical analysis, which we do.

Economic factors and levels of development may also directly have an effect on a country's likelihood of being affected by violent conflict.[7] Grossman (1991) provides the seminal economics paper investigating the integral linkages between civil conflict and the economy. This paper presents a general equilibrium model that treats insurrection and the suppression of insurrection as economic activities willingly undertaken by the participants. The ruler trades off higher taxes not only with the lower tax revenue that comes about when people devote less time to productive activities but also with the added cost of having to hire soldiering services to suppress insurrection. Grossman finds that economies in which the soldiering technology is effective can move themselves to no-conflict equilibria by devoting some resources to soldiering and maintaining a low tax rate environment.

With respect to the link between terrorism and the economic environment, Blomberg, Hess, and Weerapana (2004a) present a model that describe how one factor – the state of the economy – can lead groups to resort to terrorist attacks.[8] Other authors such as Bernholz (2003) and Wintrobe (2002) have studied the important influences of increased fundamentalism and group solidarity in driving terrorist activity. However, it is important to note that economic conditions are important to consider when identifying the underlying determinants of conflict and terrorist activity.[9] Blomberg, Hess,

---

[7] There also exists a longer standing literature analyzing the economic effect of terrorism versus other forms of violence. Blomberg, Hess, and Orphanides (2004) investigate the effect of various forms of conflict such as terrorism, internal wars, and external wars on a country's economic growth. They find that, on average, the incidence of international terrorism may have an economically significant negative effect on growth, albeit one that is considerably smaller and less persistent than that associated with either external wars or internal conflict. Terrorism is associated with a redirection of economic activity away from investment spending and toward government spending. They also find that the effects are largest in Africa and among nondemocratic states. Eckstein and Tsiddon (2004) provide an analysis of the macroeconomic consequences of terrorism in Israel. They find a large effect of domestic terrorism on economic activity in Israel. Using bilateral trade data, Blomberg and Hess (2006a) establish that terrorism has a diminishing effect on international trade and Blomberg and Mody (2005) demonstrate that violence also has a negative influence on foreign direct investment. Glick and Taylor (2004) provide an interesting complementary analysis of external conflict on international trade over a longer historical period.

[8] The work is in the spirit of Hirshleifer's (1994) view of how economists model conflict. The formulation of the paper, however, is closer to Tornell (1998) who presents a dynamic model in which organized groups extract rents from the economy, eventually depleting the resources to a point where a group not in power decides to abandon this status quo in an attempt to consolidate their own power and deprive the other group(s) of the access to resources. Tornell's model analyzes the question of why economic reforms come from within.

[9] An existing literature also analyzes how economics influences conflict in general. However, most of the analysis to this point has considered the effect on conflicts such as war

and Weerapana (2004b) provide an analysis of the relationship between economic growth fazes (e.g., expansions and contractions) and transitions into and out of terrorism incidents.

From a public policy perspective, the thrust of these papers is that development plays an important role in deterring costly terrorism. Rich countries may be more apt to experience terrorism, but they are also more insulated from the damaging effects from it. As a consequence, once a country reaches a certain stage in the development process, terrorism loses much of its capability to economically harm an economy.[10] Still, the existing literature has yet to definitively rule on the significance of the effect of development on terrorism. The economic literature has reinforced the political science literature by stressing terrorism's important link to institutions and pointing to the possible economic consequences of these factors. Drawing on this earlier literature, in our investigation of the economic causes of terrorism, we attempt to control several of these factors and parse the results by income. This is a central contribution of our work.

Our chapter introduces several important differences across income, trade, and terrorism that affect the relationship between economic development and terrorism. First, countries are more likely to experience terrorism as they develop, though the effect is largest in higher-income countries. Second, openness can help mitigate this effect, though once again, the effect is largely seen for higher-income countries.

The results are markedly different when considering low-income countries. In this case, income per-capita is negatively related to terrorism and openness is positively related to terrorism. Reconciling the positive

without considering alternative types of conflict such as terrorism. For example, Hess and Orphanides (1995, 2001a, 2001b) estimate that the probability of conflict doubles for the United States when the economy has recently been in a recession and the president is running for reelection. More broadly, Blomberg, Hess, and Thacker (2006) and Blomberg and Hess (2002) find some evidence for a relationship between the state of the economy and internal and external conflicts once the region and initial conditions are taken into account.

[10] Some evidence also exists on the empirical effect of public policies more specifically targeted toward preventing terrorism. Enders, Sandler, and Cauley (1990) have developed a model to assess the effectiveness of terrorist-thwarting policies on terrorism. Unfortunately, they find little evidence for legislative activity in preventing terrorism. They find that installing metal detectors in airports helped reduce the incidence of skyjackings while enhancing security in embassies helped increase the safety of U.S. diplomats albeit with the unintended consequence of decreasing the safety of nondiplomatic individuals. O'Brien (1996) looks at whether international superpowers use terrorism as a foreign policy tool: he shows that authoritarian regimes are more likely to sponsor terrorist attacks following setbacks in the foreign policy arena.

relationship between international terrorist incidents and levels of income for higher-income countries, with the subsequent negative relationship between international terrorist incidents and income for lower-income countries cannot be directly addressed in this chapter but is analyzed in our companion piece, Blomberg and Hess (2007). Finally, we find that for both high-and low-income countries, domestic terrorism falls as economies develop.

2. The Data and Empirical Regularities

In this section, we describe our data sources and examine some of its basic empirical regularities. In constructing the dataset, our goal is to combine terrorism data with the most standardized and broadly accepted international economic data source – namely, the Penn World Table data (Summers and Heston 1991).[11] This has certain implications for the organization of our data. Importantly, because our benchmark is given as a country-year panel, we convert data on the incidence of terrorism (and other variables) accordingly. Our intent is to examine the effects of the economy on the incidence of terrorism, controlling for a myriad of other factors that could also affect incidence of terrorism.

To measure terrorist activities, we employ the latest update of the "International Terrorism: Attributes of Terrorist Events" (ITERATE) dataset from Mickolus et al. (2002). In all, the resulting dataset covers 179 countries over 35 years providing an unbalanced panel dataset of over 4,000 observations.

Of course, the ITERATE dataset is certainly not the only dataset available, though we believe it is the most extensive and reliable. So, before describing our dataset, we begin with a brief description of other datasets available. For instance, recently the U.S. State Department's terrorism data have received much attention in the popular press. The State Department issues its annual report "Patterns of Global Terrorism report," which contains information on the number and location of international terrorist events. However, the 2003 report has come under heavy scrutiny (see Krueger and Laitin 2004). Due to these detailed criticisms, we choose not to employ the State Department data directly in our analysis, although we do examine it as a robustness check for our results.

Another widely used though less controversial source for terrorism data is given in Engene's (2004) book, the TWEED (Terrorism in Western Europe)

---

[11] We also considered matching our data with other types of data such as tourism, etc. However, the availability of the data limited our ability to investigate the issue on a large scale.

dataset. TWEED catalogs all terrorist events, including domestic and international events, in Western Europe since 1950. Unfortunately, the entire focus of the dataset is on Western Europe and so only eighteen countries are examined. Hence, because of the limited coverage of countries, we did not adopt the TWEED data for our analysis.

Tavares (2004) also provides an alternative dataset for terrorism from the International Policy Institute for Counter-Terrorism (IPIC 2003). The organization may be viewed as less political than the State Department and therefore the data may be more reliable. However, the number of years covered is significantly smaller than in both the State Department and ITERATE datasets. Notably, the IPIC dataset begins systematizing the data in 1987. Ultimately, for this reason, we declined to use the IPIC dataset.

Another well-known chronology of terrorist events is the RAND-St Andrew's Chronology of International Terrorist Incidents (henceforth, RAND). It includes a computerized database of worldwide international terrorist incidents since 1968. Although the database coverage is quite extensive, it generally excludes violence terrorists carried out within their own country against their own nationals and terrorism governments perpetrate against their own citizens (even if located abroad). The data coverage is quite extensive and is closer in spirit to ITERATE.[12] On the plus side, however, the RAND database is the only dataset available that does have some limited data on domestic terrorism. As such, we will employ the domestic data as a robustness check for our results on transnational terrorism. The time span for domestic terrorism is shorter, however, and only covers the years 1998–2003.

This leads us to the ITERATE dataset, which has larger country and temporal coverage than many of the other datasets. The one downside to employing this data is that it emphasizes the border-transcending character of terrorism. However, because the purpose of this project is to investigate terrorism and its relationship to development, democratization and globalization, ITERATE is the most well-suited data for our project.

The ITERATE dataset attempts to standardize and quantify the activities of transnational terrorist events. An international terrorist event is defined as:

the use, or threat of use, of anxiety-inducing, extra-normal violence for political purposes by any individual or group, whether acting for or in opposition to established governmental authority, when such action is intended to influence the attitudes and

---

[12] A future avenue of research would be to conduct the exercises employed in this chapter using the RAND database to examine the importance that development, democratization, and globalization play in determining state-sponsored terrorism.

behavior of a target group wider than the immediate victims and when, through the nationality or foreign ties of its perpetrators, its location, the nature of its institutional or human victims, or the mechanics of its resolution, its ramifications transcend national boundaries. (Mickolus et al. 2002, 2)

In short, a terrorist event is defined as having a political purpose, to influence a wider target group on an international scale. This means that events such as September 11, 2001, are included in this dataset but other terrorism events, such as the Oklahoma City bombing, are not deemed to meet all the relevant criteria.

ITERATE provides a rich microlevel dataset of more than 16,000 incidents of terrorism across 179 countries from 1968 to 2003; country summaries of the data are presented in Table 3.6. The raw data is grouped into four broad categories. First, there are incident characteristics related to the timing of each event. Second, there are terrorist characteristics that yield information about the number, makeup, and groups involved in the incidents. Third, victim characteristics describe analogous information on the victims involved in the attacks. Finally, life and property loss characteristics are given to quantify the damage of the attack. Unfortunately, the information across many of these categories is not provided in a consistent manner, as the original source material comes from news organizations that may fail to report a particular factor, such as the number of victims. Because of this limitation, we focus our attention on the number of terrorist incidents reported, which is the most consistent measure reported in the ITERATE dataset.[13] As an alternative, we also report results using the number of incidents-per-capita in a given year as a measure of the incidence of terrorism.

Before we leave this issue, it is useful to note that in aggregate, the dynamics across the major datasets are roughly similar. Table 3.1 reports the total number of incidents reported by the State Department, ITERATE and RAND datasets. In each dataset, the number of events increases during the period 1969 to 1987. The State Department and ITERATE estimate a similar steady increase from approximately 100 to 200 incidents per year, up to 500 to 600 incidents per year. RAND estimates a similar trend, though the levels are smaller (from a base of approximately 100 incidents per year). Likely, the

[13] Still, certain instances of the coding may seem arbitrary. On the coding of "transnationality," e.g., certain separatist movements such as in Puerto Rico and Corsica are included whereas others such as the Oklahoma City bombing are not. A larger issue may be trying to define the point at which terrorism stops and a civil war starts, as in Iraq. This distinction may not be a serious concern when evaluating results, however, see Blomberg, Hess, and Orphanides (2004).

Table 3.1. *Measures of international terrorism: 1968–2003*

Year	ITERATE data		State Dept. data		RAND data
	Number of incidents	Violent incidents	Number of incidents	Death/ incident	Number of incidents
1968	123	123	125	0.27	106
1969	181	181	193	0.29	103
1970	344	344	309	0.41	181
1971	301	301	264	0.14	157
1972	480	480	558	0.27	210
1973	341	341	345	0.35	176
1974	426	426	394	0.79	237
1975	342	342	382	0.70	215
1976	455	455	457	0.89	330
1977	341	341	419	0.55	240
1978	290	284	530	0.82	227
1979	336	319	434	1.61	248
1980	525	522	499	1.02	241
1981	469	469	489	0.34	306
1982	423	421	487	0.26	368
1983	428	295	497	1.28	299
1984	473	355	565	0.55	330
1985	525	364	635	1.30	450
1986	538	360	612	0.99	383
1987	504	504	665	0.92	369
1988	417	318	605	0.67	387
1989	359	281	375	0.51	364
1990	371	371	437	0.46	293
1991	578	578	565	0.18	427
1992	359	359	363	0.26	276
1993	554	554	431	0.25	274
1994	377	377	322	0.98	316
1995	315	315	440	0.37	272
1996	223	223	296	1.06	246
1997	189	189	304	0.73	183
1998	96	96	274	2.70	162
1999	295	295	395	0.59	125
2000	167	167	426	0.95	103
2001	52	52	355	9.28	205
2002	130	130	202	3.59	293
2003	275	275	208	3.00	273
Total	12,602	11,807	14,857	0.83	9,375

Note: See text for a full description of the data sources.

difference in the levels of terrorism in these datasets is because RAND does not include terrorism from state actor to nonstate actor within a country and so systematically underestimates the number of attacks.

Also, the results demonstrated in Table 3.1 indicate that from the time period 1987 to 1998 all the datasets demonstrate a steady decline of terrorist events, to about 100 to 200 incidents per year. Since then, however, the number of estimated incidents differs significantly. Data from the ITERATE and State datasets both indicate a smaller number of incidents than at the peak in the late 1980s, approximately 200 to 400 incidents per year. RAND, on the other hand, reports a larger jump in incidents since 2000. Therefore, as a first pass, the ITERATE data appear to share many of the same features as other datasets on terrorist incidents. As such, by employing the ITERATE dataset, we are likely to be capturing important and representative aspects of the determinants of terrorism.

Identifying terrorist incidents according to the country being targeted seems appropriate if we are to compare our results to the existing literature. If, in contrast, we identified terrorist incidents according to the nationality of the terrorist, we would be unable to see to what extent our data comoves with RAND or State. We do believe investigating the importance of terrorism at the source level would be interesting, for example to examine to what extent source-level ideologies, such as religion, influence terrorism. Such an investigation is beyond the scope of this chapter, but we investigate this issue in our companion chapter, Blomberg and Hess (2007).

2.1. The Trends in Terrorism

As discussed earlier, since 1968 (the first year that the ITERATE data are available), the number of terrorist incidents steadily increased year after year until peaking in the mid- to late 1980s, – see Table 3.1. For several years thereafter, the worldwide intensity of transnational violence – violence motivated by international political considerations – fell steadily. In the late 1980s, according to the ITERATE dataset, approximately one-and one-half transnational violent events occurred every day. This frequency declined to less than one-half of an event a day by 2000. The decline also indirectly implies that the number of countries affected by a violent event fell over that period.[14] This trend to a more peaceful world may be linked to the

---

[14] Other measures of violence also ebbed during the 1990s. For example, the threat of nuclear holocaust, as defined by the Doomsday Clock, fell sharply in 1991 with the signing of the Strategic Arms Reduction Treaty between the United States and the Soviet Union. The Doomsday Clock is calculated by the Bulletin of the Atomic Scientists

upswing in democratization and globalization.[15] The direct relationship among globalization, democratization, and terrorism is investigated in our companion chapter, Blomberg and Hess (2007).

The dynamics of terrorism are obviously more complicated than is suggested in the previous paragraph. A careful examination of Table 3.1 demonstrates five facts about the trend of terrorism.

First, the number of terrorist incidents has fallen since peaking in the late 1980s. Terrorism was halved from approximately 500–600 incidents per year in 1991 to 200–300 in 2003. On a per capita basis, the trend away from terrorism is even larger. The number of incidents per million was .43 during the 1970s, .46 during the 1980s, .28 during the 1990s, and .12 beyond. This point has been more seriously addressed in Enders and Sandler (2005) who demonstrate that there has been no increase in violence from terrorism since 9/11. They show, if anything, that terrorism has fallen. Second, however, over the same time period in question, the violence terrorists create may have increased – particularly since 9/11. The average number of deaths per incident was 0.83 from 1968 to 1993. In seven of the next ten years, the number of deaths per incident was higher than that. Table 3.1 calculates that over the entire sample (1968–2003) there has been about one death per incident, and since 2001, the average has been five times that rate.

Third, the recent drop in terrorism is systematic across regions, governments, income classes, and degrees of openness. Tables 3.2–3.4 provide a breakdown of the data decade by decade, parsed by region, governance, and geography. In each and every case, there was an increase in terrorist incidence per capita during the 1970s and 1980s and a subsequent fall in the 2000s. During the 1970s and 1980s, rich countries saw both the number of terrorist incidents and the number of incidents per capita rise.[16] Since then, rich countries have seen a successive 50 percent drop in terrorism per capita in the 1990s and 2000s. The drop in terrorism follows a similar path in poorer countries. Tables 3.2 and 3.3 also report the different terrorism trends partitioned by form of government – democratic or nondemocratic, and by integration – globalized and nonglobalized.

(www.thebulletin.org/clock.html). Russett and Slemrod (1993) demonstrate the Doomsday Clock has a significant impact on savings.

[15] For example, the early 1990s also mark the point of a decisive break in global foreign investment. A sharp increase occurred in the ratio of Foreign Direct Investment (FDI) to global investment for the rest of the decade. Though the run-up of FDI in the 1990s, especially in the second half of that decade, has several explanations, the correlation with a decline in worldwide violence is striking. Since 1991, the simple correlation coefficient between violence and FDI is -0.91.

[16] A rich or developed country is defined as a high-income country by the World Bank. See www.worldbank.org for more details.

Table 3.2. *Terrorism by development and governance*

Years	All		Developed		Developing		Democracies		Nondemocracies	
	T	T/N	T	T/N	T	T/N	T	T/N	T	T/N
1960s	0.72	0.20	2.47	3.56	0.41	0.14	2.53	2.13	0.76	0.39
1970s	1.72	0.43	6.09	8.32	0.96	0.29	5.59	3.73	1.18	0.53
1980s	2.20	0.46	6.56	8.38	1.45	0.36	5.38	2.65	1.42	0.55
1990s	1.57	0.28	3.24	3.87	1.28	0.27	2.30	0.75	1.40	0.56
2000s	0.73	0.12	1.25	1.42	0.64	0.12	0.70	0.26	0.60	0.32
Total	6.94	1.49	19.61	25.54	4.74	1.19	16.49	9.53	5.36	2.34

Note: T/N is the number of terrorist incidents in a given country per year, per million. A country is developed if the World Bank identifies it as a high-income country in the World Development Indicators database. A country is labeled as a democracy if the variable polity is greater than 7 or the executive plus legislative index of political competitiveness equals 14. Terrorism is the number of incidents in a given time period as reported in ITERATE. Each time period is denoted by the decadal averages except that 1960s refer to 1968–1969 and 2000s refer to 2000–2003.

Fourth, the hot spots for terrorism, as measured by incidence per-capita, appear to be richer democracies, economies more open to trade and Middle Eastern countries. Though the globalizers/nonglobalizers and democracies/nondemocracies saw declines in terrorism and terrorism per capita in the more recent periods, globalizers and democracies saw the sharpest declines.[17] On a per capita basis, terrorism is about one-tenth the size during the 2000s as it was in the 1980s for globalizers and democracies. Table 3.2 demonstrates that both the number of incidents and incidents per capita were larger in the high-income sample.[18] Table 3.2 also demonstrates that democracies have been more susceptible to terrorism.

Tables 3.3 and 3.4 continue the data description exercise and parse the data by region and the extent to which a country is open to trade. Over the entire sample, globalized economies appear to have about eight times the incidence of terrorism per capita than nonglobalizers. Interestingly, as Eastern European countries became more open since 1990, the rate of terrorism per capita began to rise and approach the rate of Western Europe. Note that the Middle East has experienced significantly higher rates of terrorism per capita than any other region examined. For example, during the 2000s,

[17] A country is labeled as Globalized (Non-Globalized) if trade as a percent of GDP is greater than (less than or equal to) 50%. Examples of such countries in this category are: Chile, Singapore, and Taiwan. A country is labeled as a democracy if the variable polity is greater than 7 or the executive plus legislative index of political competitiveness is greater than 14. Examples of such countries in this category are the United States, France, and South Korea.

[18] Note that, for comparison, these decadal breakdowns are given as yearly averages.

Table 3.3. *Terrorism by globalization and region*

Years	All T	All T/N	Globalized T	Globalized T/N	Nonglobalized T	Nonglobalized T/N	sub-Sah Africa T	sub-Sah Africa T/N	Mid East T	Mid East T/N
1960s	0.72	0.20	0.62	3.79	0.74	0.22	0.12	0.44	1.67	12.95
1970s	1.72	0.43	1.46	3.53	1.84	0.51	0.31	0.95	3.63	23.93
1980s	2.20	0.46	1.59	2.31	1.00	0.24	0.76	1.79	7.25	35.60
1990s	1.57	0.28	1.08	0.68	2.33	0.58	1.04	1.85	3.89	14.75
2000s	0.73	0.12	0.71	0.25	0.75	0.23	0.47	0.70	2.85	9.39
Total	6.94	1.49	5.47	10.56	6.66	1.78	2.69	5.73	19.29	96.62

Note: See Table 3.2 for definitions. A country is denoted as globalized if trade as a percent of GDP > 50 percent.

the Middle East had four times the rate of terrorism per capita in Western Europe and ten times the rate in Asia, Latin America, and sub-Saharan Africa.

Finally, there appears to be a significant change in the incidence of terrorism since the 1980s. The gap between democracies versus nondemocracies and globalizers versus nonglobalizers has disappeared. In fact, since the 2000s, nondemocracies and nonglobalizers have had higher incidence of terrorism per capita. This issue is explored in greater detail in the companion chapter, Blomberg and Hess (2007).

2.2. The Geography of Terrorist Incidents

As a starting point, we provide a summary of the incidence of terrorism using a map of the world (Figure 3.1a). Each country has a graduated color

Table 3.4. *Terrorism by region*

Years	All T	All T/N	W Europe T	W Europe T/N	E Europe T	E Europe T/N	Lat Amer T	Lat Amer T/N	Asia T	Asia T/N
1960s	0.72	0.20	1.17	3.40	0.08	0.25	1.00	3.82	0.25	0.15
1970s	1.72	0.43	5.56	15.63	0.09	0.29	3.14	10.30	1.76	0.90
1980s	2.20	0.46	6.32	17.19	0.14	0.41	3.45	9.05	2.19	0.92
1990s	1.57	0.28	3.48	9.12	0.77	2.16	2.38	5.19	2.50	0.88
2000s	0.73	0.12	0.94	2.40	0.22	0.65	0.63	1.23	1.80	0.58
Total	6.94	1.49	17.47	47.74	1.31	3.75	10.59	29.59	8.50	3.42

Note: See Tables 3.2 and 3.3.

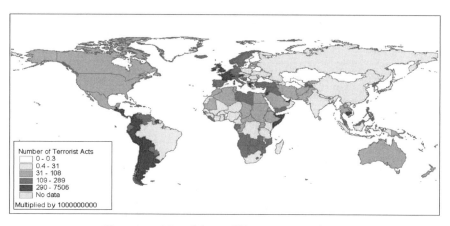

Figure 3.1a. Map of the world by terrorist incidents.

with the darkest representing the countries with the most terrorist events and the lightest representing the countries with the least.[19] The areas of the world that appear to have the most terrorism are the Americas and Europe, while there appears to be far less terrorism in Africa.

From Figure 3.1a one might conclude that terrorism is an unfortunate consequence of economic development and political freedom. For example, after Lebanon, with 24.4 terrorist events per year, the United States experiences the second highest terrorist incidence, with an average of about 19.6 terrorist events a year, followed closely by Germany and France at 18.4 and 17.9, respectively. However, neighboring countries with similar income and political systems often do not suffer from terrorism. Countries such as Canada at 1.4 incidents per year and the Nordic countries such as Sweden (1.5), Norway (0.5), and Finland (0.0) do not have such problems.

To understand some of the difficulties associated with interpreting the incidence of terrorism, consider the following fact from two of the high-incidence countries mentioned earlier – the United States and France. During the 1960s, 1970s, and part of the 1980s, the main perpetrator in each country came from a single organization. In the United States, the main culprit was the FALN (Armed Front for National Liberation), a Puerto Rican separatist group. In France, the main instigator was the Corsican National Liberation Front (CNLF). Yet, in both cases, during the latter part of the 1980s and 1990s, both the FALN and CNLF became virtually nonexistent.

---

[19] Recall that these are graphs of international terrorism that take place in a given country. That is, an international terrorist incident that takes place in Africa but that targets U.S. interests would be viewed as an incident in Africa not in the U.S.

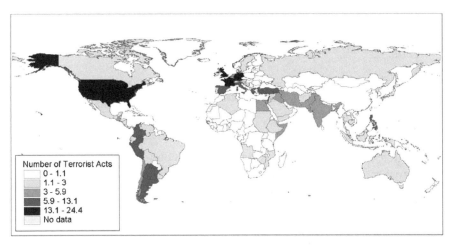

Figure 3.1b. Map of world by terrorist incidents per capita.

Such anecdotal evidence is suggestive of many complicating factors facing researchers dealing with these data. For instance, some statistics may be unduly influenced by one interest group, region, or country and may be quite hard to generalize going forward.[20]

If we considered the prevalence of terrorism on a per-capita basis, the relationship between governance, income, and terrorism is somewhat diminished. While a simple Spearman rank correlation shows that the correlation between the country rankings of average incidence of terrorism and the country rankings of average terrorism per capita is .60, countries with large populations such as the United States drop in world rankings. For example, the three countries mentioned previously – France, Germany, and the United States – rank 41, 51, and 87 out of 210 countries when using incidence per capita as the measure for terrorism.

Indeed, as one might suspect, countries in the Middle East tend to be countries with higher rates of terrorist incidents per capita. This is best seen in Figure 3.1b, which plots a summary of incidence on a per capita basis. Indeed, the Middle East comprises seven of the top ten terrorism per-capita countries in the world.

In summary, the past two subsections point out that when considering the economic causes of terrorism, terrorism varies systematically across time,

[20] Indeed, Enders and Sander (2005) catalog the types of terrorism over time to highlight the importance of such idiosyncrasies. From the early 1960s to the late 1980s, nationalism, separatism, and other more radical considerations predominantly motivate terrorism. Since the 1990s, however, religion appears to have played a larger role.

region, and income. As such, these factors must be controlled to understand the incidence of terrorism. We pursue this issue in the following section.

3. Econometric Evidence

The purpose of this section is twofold. First, we want to examine our results within the context of long-horizon, cross-sectional regressions. Second, we wish to reexamine these results in panel regressions controlling for specific country and year effects. Finally, we extend our analysis for international terrorism to domestic terrorism.

3.1. Cross-country Regressions

We begin these exercises by constructing a baseline model from the literature on economic growth. As one of our basic questions is whether the level of economic development affects terrorism incidence, we believe that the economics literature that considers the cross-country determinants of economic growth is a useful starting point for thinking about the cross-country determinants of terrorism. The workhorse model employed in the literature is cross-country regressions (e.g., see Levine and Renelt 1992), where a country's economic growth is explained by exogenous (or, at least, predetermined) factors such as past levels of income, human capital (i.e., education), and so forth.

From the economic growth literature, our baseline cross-country regression model includes as control variables measures of development, governance, and openness. All variables are 35-year averages for each country from 1968 to 2003. We proxy for economic size and level of development by including in our specification the following variables: the natural logs of real GDP [LN(GDP)] and real GDP per capita [LN(GDP/N)]. Furthermore, our measure of openness is the ratio of exports plus imports to GDP, trade/GDP [LN(OPEN)]. Finally, to proxy for political governance, we construct measures of governance from the POLITY IV database (Marshall et al. 2004) and from the Database of Political Institutions (Beck et al. 2001): namely, our measure of democracy is DEM, a dummy variable that is equal to 1 if Polity is greater than 7 or the executive plus legislative index of political competitiveness is equal to 14, or 0 if it is less.[21]

---

[21] Both measures are conventional measures of democracy – polity is a 1–10 scale of democracy from the POLITY IV database and the executive+legislative index is a 2–14 scale of electoral rules from the Beck, et al. (2001) database.

In addition, our empirical specification allows for measures of modernization that researchers have pointed to as important factors in terrorism, namely the amount of language fractionalization (LANG), amount of religious fractionalization (REL), and literacy rate (EDUC). We also include dummies for sub-Saharan Africa (AFRICA) and Asia (ASIA), which researchers have consistently identified as important, both in economic and statistical terms. Starting from this baseline model, and in line with earlier work in this literature, we examined other policy, regional, or institutional variables that might be important in explaining economic growth.

Equation (1) specifies a simple empirical regression for the cross-sectional determinants of terrorism for country i, T_i as

$$T_i = \beta_0 + \beta_1 LN(GDP) + \beta_2 LN(GDP/N)_i + \beta_3 LN(OPEN)_i + \beta_4 DEM_i \\ + \beta_5 LANG_i + \beta_6 REL_i + \beta_7 EDUC_i + \beta_8 AFRICA_i + \beta_9 ASIA_i + \varepsilon_i$$

$$(1)$$

Our findings shown in Table 3.5 are broadly consistent with the early research – most institutional, geographical, or policy variables tended to be fragile in their ability to statistically influence terrorism, specially when considered across income class.

Before discussing the results from this regression, Figures 3.2a–3.2b graphically demonstrate that terrorism is generally associated with higher levels of development, democracy, and openness. These bar charts – partitioned by income, democracy, and globalization quintile on the horizontal axis – demonstrate the rise in terrorism associated with increases in each. Figure 3.2a uses the number of incidents as its measure of terrorism while Figure 3.2b uses the number of incidents in per-capita terms.

Figure 3.2b shows that in per-capita terms, terrorism rises as countries move up the income, democracy, and openness scale. Figure 3.2a shows a similar result, though the effect due to openness appears to move in the opposite direction. This is likely because openness is highly correlated with country size.

Table 3.5 provides statistical evidence supporting Figures 3.2a–3.2b. In this case, we estimate the pure cross-sectional relative effects of development, democracy, and globalization on terrorism. Table 3.5 provides several key results. First, development has a positive effect on terrorism incidents that is statistically robust across all and higher-income countries. Second, openness has a negative effect on terrorism that is significant for the entire sample and when we exclude low-income countries. Finally, democracy has little effect on terrorism in the pure cross-section. These results persist if we focus only on violent incidents of terror, as in the panel analysis in the next section.

Table 3.5. *International terrorist incidents cross-country regressions: 1968–2003*

	All			Low income			Not low income		
	Base 1	MOD 2	REG 3	Base 4	MOD 5	REG 6	Base 7	MOD 8	REG 9
LN(GDP)	0.348**	0.330*	0.378**	0.545	0.787***	0.822***	0.246	0.124	0.083
	[0.171]	[0.185]	[0.177]	[0.338]	[0.301]	[0.277]	[0.184]	[0.158]	[0.145]
LN(GDP/N)	0.413**	0.438**	0.538**	-0.727*	-0.952**	-0.996***	0.564**	0.632***	0.910***
	[0.196]	[0.221]	[0.246]	[0.388]	[0.386]	[0.367]	[0.243]	[0.240]	[0.289]
LN(OPEN)	-1.743**	-1.426**	-1.386**	0.198	1.688**	1.595**	-2.556***	-2.457***	-2.574***
	[0.686]	[0.670]	[0.641]	[0.664]	[0.733]	[0.649]	[0.885]	[0.861]	[0.728]
DEM	0.031	0.412	0.494	-0.8	0.291	0.043	0.28	0.683	0.62
	[0.938]	[0.919]	[0.926]	[1.490]	[1.261]	[1.499]	[0.950]	[1.174]	[1.145]
EDU		-0.016	-0.011		-0.045***	-0.043***		-0.013	-0.009
		[0.015]	[0.017]		[0.015]	[0.015]		[0.024]	[0.022]
LANG		-0.32	-0.815		-1.668	-1.637		0.522	-0.446
		[0.998]	[0.940]		[1.016]	[1.009]		[1.242]	[1.131]
REL		-1.241	-1.863		0.604	0.464		-2.033	-3.071**
		[0.945]	[1.160]		[1.149]	[1.347]		[1.282]	[1.397]
ASIA			0.606			-0.457			1.745**
			[0.591]			[0.803]			[0.774]
AFRICA			1.178*			-0.206			1.600*
			[0.626]			[0.939]			[0.866]
Observations	114	109	108	41	39	39	73	70	69

Note: Clustered standard errors by region are presented in parentheses. ***, **, and * represent statistical significance at the .01, .05, and .10 levels, respectively. Each column is the basic model estimated over full country sample 1968–2003. Columns 1–9 were estimated using the Tobit Method to allow for a substantial number of zero value observations. Columns 1, 4, 7 are the basic model, columns 2, 5, 8 are Modernization models [MOD], and columns 3, 6, and 9 are Regional models [REG]. Columns 1–3 are estimated over the entire sample of countries. Columns 4–6 are estimated for low-income sample, and columns 7–9 are estimated for "not low" income sample. Included in the regression are: Logs of Real GDP [LN(GDP)] and Real GDP per capita [LN(GDP/N)] and trade/GDP [LN(OPEN)], amount of language fractionalization (LANG), amount of religious fractionalization (REL), literacy rate (EDUC), and measure of democracy (DEM is dummy variable which is 1 if polity > 7 or executive + legislative veto points = 14, 0 otherwise) and dummy variables for Asia [ASIA] and sub-Saharan Africa [AFRICA].

$T_i = \beta_0 + \beta_1 LN(GDP)_i + \beta_2 LN(GDP/N)_i + \beta_3 LN(OPEN)_i + \beta_4 DEM_i + \beta_5 LANG_i + \beta_6 REL_i + \beta_7 EDUC_i + \beta_8 AFRICA_i + \beta_9 ASIA_i + \varepsilon_i$

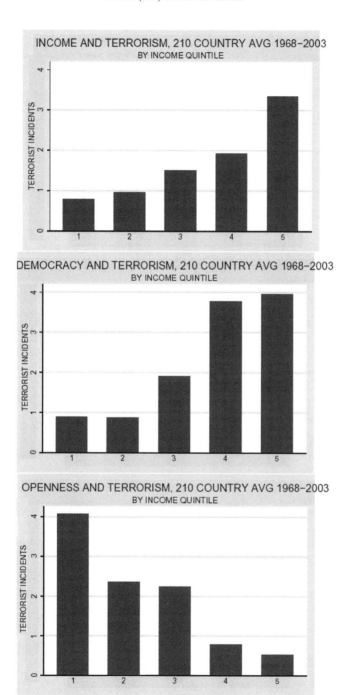

Figure 3.2a. Terrorist incidents by development, democracy, and globalization.

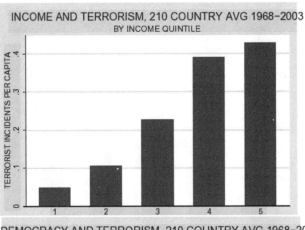

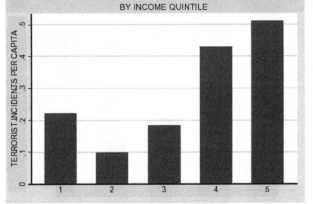

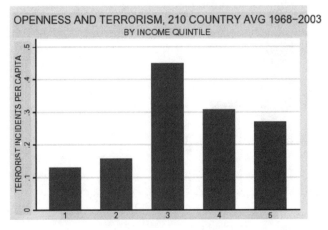

Figure 3.2b. Terrorist incidents per capita by development, democracy, and globalization.

Interestingly, the results are markedly different when considering low-income countries. In this case, income per capita is negatively related to terrorism and openness is positively related to terrorism. There are two possible explanations for the difference across income levels. First, there may be a nonlinear or "take-off" effect, in which good policies that encourage higher income, governance, and openness deter terrorism for the most disadvantaged. However, as countries develop, terrorism becomes a "luxury good" employed by dissident groups for political purposes. This point is discussed in Blomberg, Hess, and Weerapana (2004b) and is addressed in our companion chapter, Blomberg and Hess (2007).

3.1. Panel Regressions

In this section, we extend the model so that we can examine short-run effects on terrorism and add observations over time from 1968 to 2003. In addition, we consider two extensions over the cross-section by including two different measures of terrorism. First, we examine a measure of the intensity of terrorism so that we include only violent incidents of terror. Second, we investigate only domestic incidents using the RAND dataset. As mentioned earlier, the series is of shorter duration so we are only able to estimate the influences on domestic terrorism from 1998 to 2003.

The results from the panel estimation, as demonstrated in Tables 3.6–3.8, continue to support the cross-sectional findings with a few notable caveats. Greater levels of development and democracy are actually positively related to terrorism in the full sample, while openness has a mitigating influence. For developing countries, however, higher income continues to discourage terrorism. The caveats are as follows: when considering violent incidents or domestic incidents, higher income is negatively associated with terrorism across all subsamples. Moreover, not surprisingly, openness has little influence on domestic terrorism.

The regression results in Tables 3.6–3.8 are similar to that employed earlier with a time subscript added to each variable; namely, terrorism for country i in year t is determined as follows:

$$
\begin{aligned}
T_{it} = {} & \beta_0 + \beta_1 LN(GDP)_{it} + \beta_2 LN(GDP/N)_{it} + \beta_3 LN(OPEN)_{it} \\
& + \beta_4 DEM_{it} + \beta_5 LANG_{it} + \beta_6 REL_{it} + \beta_7 EDUC_{it} + \beta_8 AFRICA_{it} \\
& + \beta_9 ASIA_{it} + \varepsilon_{it}
\end{aligned} \tag{2}
$$

Table 3.6 reports the results from the basic panel model. These results continue to support the earlier findings. Most interestingly, we find that

Table 3.6. *International terrorist incidents panel regressions: 1968–2003 full country sample*

	All				Low income				Not low income				
	Base	MOD	REG	Base	MOD	REG	POISSON	IV	Base	MOD	REG	POISSON	IV
	1	2	3	4	5	6	7	8	9	10	11	12	13
LN(GDP)	1.437***	1.103***	1.178***	1.180***	1.236***	1.292***	0.496***	2.167***	1.385***	0.970***	0.984***	0.183***	0.885**
	[0.197]	[0.182]	[0.199]	[0.181]	[0.212]	[0.225]	[0.045]	[0.352]	[0.229]	[0.216]	[0.229]	[0.018]	[0.393]
LN(GDP/N)	0.499***	0.298	0.012	−0.674*	−1.371***	−1.744***	−0.834***	−6.008***	0.426*	0.656***	0.643**	0.134***	0.969
	[0.179]	[0.208]	[0.251]	[0.402]	[0.509]	[0.511]	[0.108]	[1.329]	[0.242]	[0.250]	[0.294]	[0.029]	[1.006]
LN(OPEN)	−2.248***	−2.495***	−2.376***	−0.677	−0.798	−0.862*	0.077	1.213	−2.726***	−2.911***	−2.898***	−0.621***	−3.064***
	[0.423]	[0.448]	[0.441]	[0.451]	[0.530]	[0.520]	[0.110]	[0.800]	[0.529]	[0.535]	[0.540]	[0.039]	[0.983]
DEM	1.253***	0.910**	0.904**	0.617	0.232	−0.075	−0.113	−0.356	1.316***	1.104**	1.079**	0.259***	1.196**
	[0.394]	[0.393]	[0.392]	[0.495]	[0.488]	[0.478]	[0.104]	[0.597]	[0.480]	[0.522]	[0.522]	[0.044]	[0.547]
EDU		0.035***	0.034***		0.007	−0.001	−0.006**	0.005		0.038***	0.038**	0.014***	0.045**
		[0.010]	[0.011]		[0.011]	[0.012]	[0.003]	[0.014]		[0.015]	[0.016]	[0.002]	[0.018]
LANG		1.765**	2.409***		−3.172***	−1.912*	−0.816***	−3.859***		3.171***	3.168***	0.808***	3.198***
		[0.746]	[0.816]		[1.051]	[1.068]	[0.201]	[1.343]		[0.963]	[1.024]	[0.094]	[1.126]
REL		−7.688**	−7.379***		−0.247	0.622	−0.35	0.912		−10.821***	−10.879***	−2.091***	−11.364***
		[1.098]	[1.153]		[0.956]	[1.072]	[0.285]	[1.452]		[1.591]	[1.668]	[0.114]	[1.452]
ASIA			−1.437**			−3.166***	−1.270***	−5.536***			−0.1	−0.026	0.006
			[0.680]			[0.982]	[0.177]	[1.181]			[0.868]	[0.084]	[1.755]
AFRICA			−1.037			−3.368***	−1.153***	−4.466***			0.035	−0.449***	0.455
			[0.703]			[0.916]	[0.217]	[1.135]			[1.007]	[0.146]	[1.301]
Observations	2966	2842	2841	1008	942	942	942	872	1958	1900	1899	1899	1773

Note: Clustered standard errors by region are presented in parentheses. ***, **, and * represent statistical significance at the .01, .05, and .10 levels, respectively. See Table 3.5 for details. Columns 7 and 12 estimate REG model using Poisson estimation. Columns 8 and 13 estimate REG model using IV estimation with IMF and WTO participation rates as instruments for LN(GDP/N).

$T_{it} = \beta_0 + \beta_1 LN(GDP)_{it} + \beta_2 LN(GDP/N)_{it} + \beta_3 LN(OPEN)_{it} + \beta_4 DEM_{it} + \beta_5 LANG_{it} + \beta_6 REL_{it} + \beta_7 EDUC_{it} + \beta_8 AFRICA_{it} + \beta_9 ASIA_{it} + \varepsilon_{it}$

Table 3.7. *International violent terrorist incidents panel regressions: 1968–2003*

	All			Low income			Not low income		
	Base 1	MOD 2	REG 3	Base 4	MOD 5	REG 6	Base 7	MOD 8	REG 9
LN(GDP)	28.053***	25.073***	25.458***	32.908***	34.597***	37.140***	26.892***	23.331***	22.821***
	[3.862]	[4.049]	[4.098]	[5.086]	[7.659]	[8.104]	[4.644]	[4.954]	[4.869]
LN(GDP/N)	−3.93	−4.787	−8.418*	−13.855	−31.039**	−42.768***	−3.191	0.112	0.822
	[3.418]	[4.206]	[4.605]	[11.266]	[15.577]	[14.496]	[4.453]	[5.112]	[5.369]
LN(OPEN)	−12.548**	−14.171**	−12.984**	−18.858	−25.601	−28.089*	−9.557	−10.767	−11.429
	[6.034]	[6.236]	[6.168]	[12.741]	[16.611]	[16.811]	[7.007]	[7.277]	[7.104]
DEM	14.295**	12.558**	12.626**	7.176	−2.1	−11.457	14.796**	15.701**	16.231**
	[5.703]	[5.868]	[5.865]	[13.998]	[13.508]	[14.627]	[6.494]	[6.795]	[6.783]
EDU		0.243*	0.189		0.34	0.081		0.223	0.163
		[0.144]	[0.157]		[0.274]	[0.332]		[0.189]	[0.203]
LANG		25.953*	37.284**		−70.914*	−32.671		41.107**	40.215**
		[14.321]	[15.431]		[37.316]	[29.362]		[16.545]	[18.861]
REL		−89.630***	−79.118***		1.197	27.379		−118.671***	−116.112***
		[15.393]	[16.528]		[26.432]	[36.796]		[20.001]	[21.168]
ASIA			−17.813			−97.207**			3.816
			[12.057]			[39.232]			[15.886]
AFRICA			−23.121*			−100.570**			−8.279
			[12.936]			[44.819]			[14.827]
Observations	2966	2842	2841	1008	942	942	1958	1900	1899

Note: Clustered standard errors are presented in parentheses. ***, **, and * represent statistical significance at the .01, .05, and .10 levels, respectively. See Table 3.5 for details. The dependent variable is modified from the earlier results in that we use only terrorist incidents in which there are fatalities.

$$T_{it} = \beta_0 + \beta_1 LN(GDP)_{it} + \beta_2 LN(GDP/N)_{it} + \beta_3 LN(OPEN)_{it} + \beta_4 DEM_{it} + \beta_5 LANG_{it} + \beta_6 REL_{it} + \beta_7 EDUC_{it} + \beta_8 AFRICA_{it} + \beta_9 ASIA_{it} + \varepsilon_{it}$$

Table 3.8. *Domestic terrorist incidents panel regressions: 1998–2003 full country sample*

	All			Low income			Not low income		
	Base 1	MOD 2	REG 3	Base 4	MOD 5	REG 6	Base 7	MOD 8	REG 9
LN(GDP)	25.573***	25.212***	24.935***	60.124***	44.127**	38.474*	16.056***	22.067***	26.315***
	[5.974]	[6.227]	[5.802]	[21.697]	[22.069]	[19.897]	[2.852]	[5.031]	[6.119]
LN(GDP/N)	−23.752***	−25.456***	−25.732***	−43.374**	−57.675**	−47.415**	−21.749***	−21.205***	−28.079***
	[7.013]	[8.152]	[7.855]	[22.022]	[28.655]	[23.963]	[4.630]	[7.721]	[9.686]
LN(OPEN)	4.005	−12.731	−14.494	17.561	5.728	0.773	−4.414	−11.717	−1.982
	[6.154]	[9.280]	[10.588]	[18.986]	[16.286]	[17.090]	[7.369]	[11.078]	[11.453]
DEM	25.588***	33.808***	31.786***	−12.638	−14.904	−32.828*	31.951***	48.203***	47.760***
	[8.896]	[10.845]	[10.272]	[15.200]	[14.958]	[18.117]	[9.152]	[15.255]	[14.994]
EDU		1.097***	0.880**		0.829	−0.329		1.689***	1.936***
		[0.324]	[0.343]		[0.596]	[0.428]		[0.556]	[0.646]
LANG		29.017	38.211*		40.609	93.082		35.004**	40.099*
		[18.331]	[23.072]		[41.931]	[58.938]		[17.826]	[21.205]
REL		−93.577***	−76.879***		−156.056*	−50.453		−86.531***	−105.310***
		[25.690]	[27.599]		[80.866]	[50.851]		[28.980]	[38.819]
ASIA			−7.79			−33.641			−34.971**
			[12.311]			[23.384]			[16.029]
AFRICA			−25.803			−115.317**			21.961
			[21.480]			[52.930]			[31.093]
Observations	779	455	454	253	168	168	526	287	286

Note: Clustered standard errors are presented in parentheses. ***, **, and * represent statistical significance at the .01, .05, and .10 levels, respectively. See Table 3.5 for details. The dependent variable is modified from the earlier result in that we only use data on domestic terrorism available from the RAND database.

$T_{it} = \beta_0 + \beta_1 \, LN(GDP)_{it} + \beta_2 LN(GDP/N)_{it} + \beta_3 LN(OPEN)_{it} + \beta_4 \, DEM_{it} + \beta_5 \, LANG_{it} + \beta_6 \, REL_{it} + \beta_7 \, EDUC_{it} + \beta_8 \, AFRICA_{it} + \beta_9 \, ASIA_{it} + \varepsilon_{it}$

higher income leads to more terrorism for richer countries but less terrorism for poorer countries.

There are a couple of econometric issues that one can explore using the larger panel dataset. First, considering a different econometric technique that would take into account the count nature of the dependent variable can strengthen the results. To do this, we estimate the full models in both the low-income and high-income cases using a Poisson-regression. These results are included as columns 7 and 12 in Table 3.6. Second, the results can be reexamined regarding the possibility of reverse causality (i.e., terrorism may cause poverty, rather than stem from it). To consider this, we estimate the full models in both the low-income and high-income cases using a Tobit instrumental variables regression assuming that participation in the WTO or an IMF program are appropriate instruments for LN(GDP/N).[22] These results are included as columns 8 and 13 in Table 3.6. In each of these cases, the results are qualitatively similar to the other columns implying that the results are not sensitive to endogeneity bias or the econometric technique employed.

One concern from this analysis is that these results do not consider the intensity of the violent attacks. In other words, perhaps all terrorist incidents are more or less associated with development but may not actually have large negative consequences. To address this issue, Table 3.7 reestimates the model in equation (2) except we replace our left-hand side variable with all violent terrorist incidents. The results from this robustness check continue to support our earlier findings: namely, higher income is negatively related to terrorism in poor countries and is positively related to terrorism in higher-income countries.

As a final robustness check, Table 3.8 reports our estimate of the model in equation (2) using domestic terrorist incidents as the variable of interest. Domestic terrorist events occur at a much greater frequency, but we were only able to obtain data from 1998 to 2003. The results continue to support our earlier findings, although there are two interesting differences. First, openness seems to have little statistical effect on domestic acts of terrorism in contrast to international. Second, and most important, higher income discourages terrorism in both poor and rich countries. These effects are both economically and statistically more significant than in the earlier

---

[22] We found evidence that our instruments were "strong" in the sense that they were significant at the 0.0000 level in the first stage. Our instruments also passed tests of our exclusion restrictions. For examples, the p-value associated with the chi-squared test in the last column is 0.48.

tables. Though we note these statistical differences between domestic and international terrorism, given the short time period for the former dataset, we will have to leave the interpretation of these differences to future research.

4. Conclusion

In this chapter, we investigate the effect of development on terrorism. We began by considering the large volume of work that has yet to conclusively rule on the issue. By parsing the data into income classes, we were able to see why. Transnational terrorism incidents tend to be associated with higher-income countries. However, we find that for low-income countries, development tends be associated with declines in the likelihood of a terrorist attack. This is borne out when we consider only domestic terrorist attacks, which appear to be negatively correlated with income across all income groups.

This result has strong implications for policy. Our chapter documents the need for policies that encourage income growth in poorer regions to encourage peace. We show that this is true for both transnational and domestic terrorism and especially true for the more violent acts of terror. In our companion paper, Blomberg and Hess (2007), we provide bilateral evidence on the role of development in affecting which countries are targets of international terrorism and which are sources of international terrorism. Our companion paper turns out to be helpful for reconciling the differential relationships between income and terrorism across high- and low-income countries that are prominent in this chapter.

Table 3.9. *Terrorism in country, annual average 1968–2003*

Country	T	T/N	GDP/N	Trade/GDP	Polity	LIEC	EIEC	Tensys
Aruba	0.00	0.00		234.03				
Andorra	0.00	0.00						
Afghanistan	2.08	0.59	129.43	36.61	−7.11	1.75	1.54	3.04
Angola	2.42	2.67	774.38	111.63	−6.37	3.33	3.52	8.19
Albania	0.31	0.99	1030.81	48.36	−4.97	4.57	4.57	16.86
N. Antilles	0.00	0.00						
U.A.E.	0.61	5.52	31423.48	111.31	−8.00	1.61	2.00	17.50
Argentina	10.81	4.19	6979.50	17.28	1.16	5.50	5.75	7.64
Armenia	0.03	0.08	586.58	85.22	3.22	6.58	6.25	5.58
American Samoa	0.00	0.00						
Antigua and Barbuda	0.03	4.42	6991.49	158.83				
Australia	1.25	0.84	15548.48	33.97		7.00	7.00	58.50
Austria	2.53	3.32	17498.93	74.31	10.00	7.00	7.00	34.50
Azerbaijan	0.19	0.26	738.01	96.99	−4.44	6.59	5.77	5.18
Burundi	0.56	0.93	123.74	30.89	−6.54	3.36	2.43	4.75
Belgium	3.47	3.51	16671.30	129.02	10.00	7.00	7.00	58.50
Benin	0.00	0.00	321.05	45.80	−2.90	4.36	4.07	9.04
Burkina Faso	0.06	0.07	197.34	34.38	−4.65	3.21	2.68	3.68
Bangladesh	0.39	0.04	277.47	22.53	−0.79	5.02	5.30	3.71
Bulgaria	0.14	0.16	1569.26	91.02	−2.28	5.00	4.71	17.82
Bahrain	0.58	11.03	10455.00	177.50	−9.52	1.11	2.00	14.50
Bahamas, The	0.08	4.17	14051.35	129.62		6.82	6.75	16.50
Bosnia and Her.	1.36	2.60	991.48	92.38		6.00	6.00	1.00
Belarus	0.00	0.00	1218.58	121.40	0.00	4.09	5.18	3.82
Belize	0.00	0.00	2193.02	117.38		6.76	6.76	11.00
Bermuda	0.00	0.00						
Bolivia	2.25	4.46	975.45	49.53	2.31	5.50	4.96	6.61
Brazil	2.25	0.20	2973.20	18.30	0.69	7.00	6.93	15.50
Barbados	0.14	5.65	7732.95	119.41		6.79	6.79	23.50
Brunei	0.00	0.00				2.00	2.00	17.50
Bhutan	0.00	0.00	456.83	68.94	−8.00	4.00	2.00	18.50
Botswana	0.19	1.87	1828.13	110.41	8.81	6.29	6.29	23.50
C.A.R.	0.08	0.33	295.59	50.96	−4.09	3.61	3.61	5.93
Canada	1.36	0.55	17819.31	57.14	10.00	7.00	7.00	58.50
Switzerland	2.22	3.43	29748.33	67.55	10.00	7.00	7.00	58.50
Channel Islands	0.00	0.00						
Chile	4.44	3.66	3124.35	50.29	0.50	3.79	4.32	8.07
China	0.56	0.00	379.41	26.66	−7.28	3.00	3.00	7.11
Cote d'Ivoire	0.19	0.20	797.33	70.52	−8.26	4.93	4.36	16.36
Cameroon	0.08	0.08	614.05	48.89	−6.84	4.86	4.36	9.79

S. Brock Blomberg and Gregory D. Hess

Table 3.9. *Continued*

Country	T	T/N	GDP/N	Trade/ GDP	Polity	LIEC	EIEC	Tensys
Congo, Rep.	0.19	0.65	977.61	107.88	−5.35	3.25	2.46	5.04
Colombia	13.14	3.85	1684.04	32.17	7.81	7.00	7.00	15.50
Comoros	0.00	0.00	412.68	56.60	−1.92	4.94	4.22	6.00
Cape Verde	0.00	0.00	956.44	72.95		5.04	3.78	7.11
Costa Rica	1.75	7.36	3266.82	74.97	10.00	7.00	7.00	40.50
Cuba	0.64	0.63		32.67	−7.00	3.39	3.00	28.93
Cayman Islands	0.00	0.00						
Cyprus	3.81	58.04	7943.14	104.63	9.41	6.96	6.75	28.50
Czech Republic	0.00	0.00	5164.87	112.53	−1.71	7.00	7.00	6.50
Germany	18.44	2.32	17923.82	48.81	10.00	7.00	7.00	40.50
Germany, F.R.	0.00	0.00		51.40				
Djibouti	0.22	7.14	1061.39	103.53	−7.09	4.52	4.44	7.24
Dominica	0.00	0.00	2879.35	114.78				
Denmark	1.06	2.07	23308.77	65.99	10.00	7.00	7.00	58.50
Dominican Republic	0.83	1.68	1613.59	63.26	3.38	6.86	6.39	23.50
Algeria	2.50	0.95	1708.84	55.04	−7.19	4.46	3.82	6.54
Ecuador	1.47	1.92	1248.92	53.18	4.94	5.93	6.11	10.32
Egypt, Arab Rep.	4.50	0.88	1074.00	50.28	−5.13	5.96	5.96	12.93
Eritrea	0.19	0.70	166.65	99.86	−6.00	2.00	2.00	5.00
Spain	8.28	2.19	10040.41	38.74	5.76	6.46	6.46	11.75
Estonia	0.06	0.37	3639.32	151.40	6.00	7.00	7.00	5.50
Ethiopia	2.33	0.59	96.52	32.05	−6.22	2.89	3.00	5.32
Finland	0.00	0.00	16997.04	57.27	10.00	7.00	7.00	58.50
Fiji	0.14	1.92	1867.81	104.47	6.50	5.71	5.93	5.14
France	17.92	3.29	17232.41	42.06	8.34	7.00	7.00	58.50
Faeroe Islands	0.00	0.00						
Micronesia	0.00	0.00	1962.76	87.70				
Gabon	0.14	1.54	4295.06	97.00	−7.55	5.05	4.29	13.14
United Kingdom	17.75	3.11	18094.81	52.34	10.00	7.00	7.00	20.50
Georgia	0.50	0.94	1154.97	79.24	4.56	6.85	5.70	3.40
Ghana	0.11	0.09	240.58	47.37	−3.21	3.36	4.14	5.11
Guinea	0.08	0.12	386.99	51.34	−6.81	3.14	3.96	10.89
Gambia, The	0.00	0.00	314.79	102.59	5.13	4.75	6.50	8.36
Guinea-Bissau	0.00	0.00	171.40	51.98	−5.08	3.18	3.18	5.57
Equatorial Guinea	0.06	1.35	1524.21	112.86	−6.19	3.39	2.46	11.46
Greece	11.50	11.84	8436.38	43.30	6.00	7.00	7.00	24.50
Grenada	0.03	3.10	2787.47	114.24		5.14	5.46	10.11
Greenland	0.00	0.00						
Guatemala	5.08	7.01	1534.21	41.07	0.58	6.36	6.46	12.00
Guam	0.00	0.00						
Guyana	0.06	0.74	788.68	161.48	−0.81	6.57	6.57	16.50
Hong Kong, China	0.39	0.77	15331.19	222.35				
Honduras	2.33	5.86	887.67	72.99	3.13	5.50	5.75	8.79

Table 3.9. *Continued*

Country	T	T/N	GDP/N	Trade/GDP	Polity	LIEC	EIEC	Tensys
Croatia	0.28	0.60	3885.36	102.81	−4.00	7.00	7.00	5.50
Haiti	0.86	1.44	673.87	39.39	−5.13	4.77	3.36	5.86
Hungary	0.22	0.21	3684.35	86.82	−1.35	5.29	4.71	16.11
Indonesia	2.14	0.12	482.43	49.80	−6.50	6.57	2.43	16.96
Isle of Man	0.00	0.00						
India	5.36	0.08	295.44	16.65	8.31	6.93	6.93	71.50
Ireland	2.97	9.06	13213.86	114.08	10.00	7.00	7.00	14.50
Iran	3.69	0.90	1451.29	38.86	−6.59	4.61	3.86	11.64
Iraq	3.39	1.82			−8.13	3.75	2.00	11.46
Iceland	0.06	2.32	22417.94	72.38	10.00	7.00	7.00	14.50
Israel	8.03	20.81	13658.71	88.16	9.03	7.00	7.00	86.50
Italy	10.83	1.94	14251.69	42.98	10.00	6.96	6.96	68.50
Jamaica	0.44	2.19	3042.16	91.77	9.78	6.05	6.05	24.68
Jordan	3.00	12.77	1753.43	119.70	−7.09	3.71	2.00	30.57
Japan	1.67	0.14	27922.16	21.32	10.00	6.96	6.96	30.50
Kazakhstan	0.00	0.00	1265.16	89.90	−3.44	5.64	3.00	6.00
Kenya	0.61	0.28	338.32	59.96	−5.84	5.36	4.07	7.64
Kyrgyz Republic	0.17	0.34	327.83	81.86	3.89	5.50	6.27	3.82
Cambodia	2.92	2.89	259.65	61.37	−3.53	4.21	3.29	6.21
Kiribati	0.00	0.00	640.84	118.69				
St. Kitts and Nevis	0.00	0.00	5103.48	132.16				
Korea, Rep.	0.00	0.00	5715.60	60.82	−0.68	6.82	6.50	9.04
Kuwait	1.89	11.36	23260.43	98.45	−8.45	3.04	2.00	12.79
Lao PDR	0.33	0.86	262.56	48.30	−7.04	3.19	2.59	4.19
Lebanon	24.36	75.06	3435.22	72.50	4.14	4.21	3.54	4.39
Liberia	0.69	2.73	483.28		−5.44	3.61	3.07	3.43
Libya	0.53	1.66		75.29	−7.00	1.93	2.07	19.50
St. Lucia	0.00	0.00	3520.27	140.43		6.83	6.83	12.00
Liechtenstein	0.00	0.00						
Sri Lanka	0.97	0.60	564.60	69.39	6.03	6.57	7.00	39.50
Lesotho	0.19	1.48	340.84	124.10	−3.63	2.96	3.29	8.89
Lithuania	0.03	0.08	3262.03	104.45	10.00	7.00	6.80	5.50
Luxembourg	0.14	3.78	26797.98	205.86	10.00	7.00	7.00	24.50
Latvia	0.11	0.44	3025.18	104.87	7.89	7.00	6.27	4.36
Macao, China	0.00	0.00	13193.97	157.31				
Morocco	0.86	0.39	990.55	53.84	−7.97	6.36	2.00	23.43
Monaco	0.00	0.00						
Moldova	0.03	0.06	566.30	122.45	6.44	6.09	6.45	6.00
Madagascar	0.03	0.02	302.78	41.81	−1.35	5.07	5.30	8.19
Maldives	0.00	0.00	2156.14	116.25		4.00	3.00	13.93
Mexico	2.69	0.43	4813.69	34.45	−1.78	6.75	6.71	49.50
Marshall Islands	0.00	0.00	2045.95					

Table 3.9. *Continued*

Country	T	T/N	GDP/N	Trade/ GDP	Polity	LIEC	EIEC	Tensys
Macedonia, FYR	0.11	0.55	1716.01	87.20	6.00	7.00	6.41	6.00
Mali	0.03	0.03	208.74	48.48	−3.55	4.25	4.04	11.11
Malta	0.31	8.57	5572.17	172.24		7.00	7.00	24.50
Myanmar	0.00	0.00		11.46	−7.00	2.25	2.50	7.32
Mongolia	0.00	0.00	483.37	120.46	−2.31	4.43	4.29	5.50
N. Mariana Is.	0.00	0.00						
Mozambique	1.92	1.44	168.36	44.21	−4.20	4.37	3.78	5.11
Mauritania	0.06	0.37	328.28	101.09	−6.72	3.39	3.89	6.18
Mauritius	0.00	0.00	2719.27	117.42	9.56	6.89	6.96	24.50
Malawi	0.03	0.04	147.39	61.97	−5.97	4.75	3.43	15.93
Malaysia	2.14	1.70	2363.38	132.13	3.88	6.57	6.57	22.50
Mayotte	0.00	0.00						
Namibia	0.39	2.39	1769.47	115.37	7.80	7.00	6.33	6.50
New Caledonia	0.00	0.00	11246.77	45.08				
Niger	0.19	0.24	228.08	42.87	−4.61	3.07	3.75	5.61
Nigeria	0.94	0.08	343.49	54.58	−3.93	2.71	3.25	3.86
Nicaragua	1.22	3.94	1062.50	62.58	−1.27	5.89	5.84	7.18
Netherlands	4.67	3.38	17359.28	103.85	10.00	7.00	7.00	25.50
Norway	0.50	1.21	26985.38	73.90	10.00	7.00	7.00	17.50
Nepal	0.33	0.18	178.77	34.74	−2.63	5.18	4.75	4.50
New Zealand	0.14	0.47	15326.22	57.19	10.00	7.00	7.00	86.50
Oman	0.03	0.28	6457.46	94.36	−9.72	1.39	2.00	18.50
Pakistan	5.86	0.58	400.39	33.17	1.61	4.32	4.43	8.88
Panama	1.69	7.56	3309.54	155.29	−1.44	5.93	5.64	7.79
Peru	7.81	3.99	2056.89	33.50	0.73	5.93	5.93	9.82
Philippines	8.83	1.60	899.12	62.60	−0.03	5.71	5.18	11.50
Palau	0.00	0.00	6061.08	81.58				
Papua New Guinea	0.17	0.41	656.31	88.92	10.00	6.86	6.86	14.50
Poland	0.44	0.12	3683.58	51.86	−1.81	5.39	4.71	6.39
Puerto Rico	1.22	4.03	10397.36	139.52				
Korea, Dem. Rep.	2.22	1.15			−9.00	3.00	3.00	28.07
Portugal	2.11	2.16	7081.89	60.88	6.00	6.78	6.81	13.07
Paraguay	0.42	1.13	1350.37	52.32	−3.38	7.00	6.46	32.50
French Polynesia	0.00	0.00	11911.62	29.11				
Qatar	0.03	1.02		80.45	−10.00	1.00	2.00	10.75
Romania	0.28	0.12	1872.10	60.57	−3.16	5.29	4.61	11.93
Russian Federation	2.39	0.17	1944.46	56.73	4.38	6.64	7.00	6.00
Rwanda	0.17	0.26	242.57	31.24	−6.42	2.79	2.57	9.07
Saudi Arabia	1.39	0.85	10931.46	76.21	−10.00	1.32	2.00	8.89

Table 3.9. *Continued*

Country	T	T/N	GDP/N	Trade/ GDP	Polity	LIEC	EIEC	Tensys
Sudan	1.92	0.81	307.64	27.96	−5.07	3.14	3.25	7.82
Senegal	0.11	0.15	439.24	67.28	−2.84	6.14	6.07	13.07
Singapore	0.36	1.29	12474.80		−2.00	6.00	6.00	20.50
Solomon Islands	0.11	2.75	662.69	126.76		6.88	6.88	12.50
Sierra Leone	1.06	2.24	236.33	47.23	−5.52	4.43	3.64	5.54
El Salvador	5.31	11.37	1908.01	58.11	3.26	6.09	6.09	7.43
San Marino	0.00	0.00						
Somalia	4.19	5.51		57.15	−6.39	2.41	2.71	14.00
Sao Tome & Pr.	0.00	0.00	326.33	82.87				
Suriname	0.19	4.90	2133.25	90.33		5.56	5.19	3.70
Slovak Republic	0.00	0.00	3532.72	114.71	7.43	7.00	7.00	5.50
Slovenia	0.00	0.00	8527.48	118.47	10.00	7.00	7.00	5.50
Sweden	1.50	1.79	20970.47	62.63	10.00	7.00	7.00	58.50
Swaziland	0.81	12.08	1112.25	157.60	−8.22	2.07	2.00	8.39
Seychelles	0.03	4.22	4932.81	137.04				
Syrian Arab Republic	1.28	1.45	939.12	54.64	−8.88	6.21	3.00	15.43
Chad	0.28	0.57	196.26	45.22	−6.25	1.84	3.18	3.93
Togo	0.22	0.67	312.55	87.23	−5.83	3.93	3.96	11.21
Thailand	1.81	0.35	1220.07	66.74	3.07	6.02	6.09	5.04
Tajikistan	1.14	1.94	304.56	120.32	−4.33	6.81	7.00	4.11
Turkmenistan	0.00	0.00	768.04	98.14	−8.78	5.00	3.00	6.00
Timor-Leste	0.00	0.00	435.85					
Tonga	0.00	0.00	1358.50	87.54				
Trinidad & Tobago	0.25	2.33	5563.23	84.38	8.53	6.82	6.82	22.50
Tunisia	0.64	0.84	1445.27	76.25	−6.72	4.86	2.50	15.43
Turkey	9.11	1.91	2263.38	30.65	6.22	6.36	6.29	7.11
Taiwan, China	0.69	0.36	7093.99	90.75	−2.56	3.79	3.86	5.64
Tanzania	0.25	0.13	265.07	48.10	−5.97	3.82	4.00	10.04
Uganda	0.89	0.57	204.36	32.05	−4.30	3.86	3.96	4.75
Ukraine	0.11	0.02	928.77	82.84	6.33	7.00	7.00	6.00
Uruguay	1.47	5.13	4846.29	37.84	2.67	5.21	5.54	7.75
United States	19.56	0.88	25808.69	18.79	10.00	7.00	7.00	32.50
Uzbekistan	0.00	0.00	584.39	58.11	−9.00	4.00	4.09	6.00
St. Vincent & Gren.	0.00	0.00	2110.01	134.43				
Venezuela, RB	2.92	1.77	5639.01	47.01	8.66	7.00	6.93	36.50
Virgin Islands (U.S.)	0.00	0.00						
Vietnam	0.06	0.01	297.72	78.55	−7.03	3.36	3.36	4.61
Vanuatu	0.00	0.00	1165.17	103.97		6.86	6.86	11.50
West Bank and Gaza	0.00	0.00	1330.75	78.99				
Samoa	0.00	0.00	1201.62	92.77		6.14	6.14	8.36
Yemen, Rep.	2.61	1.77	487.25	77.15	−2.00	4.05	4.13	6.14
Serbia and Mont.	0.00	0.00	894.45	61.45	−6.09			
South Africa	0.89	0.28	3094.27	50.48	5.07	6.64	6.64	14.50
Congo, Dem. Rep.	0.31	0.10	217.88	38.63	−8.92	2.86	2.64	17.57
Zambia	0.67	1.08	438.99	74.01	−4.28	4.82	4.64	13.89
Zimbabwe	1.25	1.68	571.43	54.01	−0.79	6.25	6.21	11.57

Note: Data are defined in the text.

References

Beck, Thorsten, George Clarke, Alberto Groff, Philip Keefer, and Patrick Walsh. 2001. "New Tools in Comparative Political Economy: The Database of Political Institutions." *World Bank Economic Review* 15(1): 165–176.

Bernholz P. 2003. Supreme Values as the Basis for Terror. Unpublished paper, University of Basel, Switzerland.

Blomberg, S. Brock, and Gregory D. Hess. 2002. "The Temporal Links Between Conflict and Economic Activity." *Journal of Conflict Resolution* 46(1): 74–90.

———. 2007. "How Much Does Violence Tax Trade?" *Review of Economics and Statistics* 88(4): 599–612 (October).

———. 2007. "The Lexus and the Olive Branch," this volume.

Blomberg, S. Brock, and Ashoka Mody. 2005. "How Severely Does Violence Deter International Investment?", mimeo.

Blomberg, S. Brock, Gregory D. Hess, and Athansios Orphanides. 2004. "The Macroeconomic Consequences of Terrorism." *Journal of Monetary Economics* 51(5): 1007–1052.

Blomberg, S. Brock, Gregory D. Hess, and Akila Weerapana. 2004a. "An Economic Model of Terrorism." *Conflict Management and Peace Science* 21(1):17–28.

———. 2004b (Spring). "Economic Conditions and Terrorism." *European Journal of Political Economy*.

Blomberg, S. Brock, Gregory D. Hess, and Siddharth Thacker. 2006. "On the Conflict-Poverty Nexus." *Economics and Politics* 18(3): 237–267.

Crenshaw, Martha. 1981. "The Causes of Terrorism." *Comparative Politics* 13(4): 379–399.

———. 2001. "Why America? The Globalization of Civil War." *Current History* 100(650): 425–433.

Eckstein, Zvi, and Daniel Tsiddon. 2004. "Macroeconomic Consequences of Terror: Theory and the Case of Israel." *Journal of Monetary Economics* 51(5): 971–1002.

Engene, Jan Oskar. 2004. *Terrorism in Western Europe: Explaining the Trends Since 1950.* Elgar: North Hampton, MA.

Enders, Walter, and Todd Sandler. 2005. "After 9–11: Is It All So Different Now?" *Journal of Conflict Resolution* 49(2): 259–277.

Enders, Walter, Todd Sandler, and Jon Cauley. 1990. "Assessing the Impact of Terrorist-Thwarting Policies: An Intervention Time Series Approach." *Defence Economics* 2(1), 1–18.

Glick, Reuven, and Alan Taylor. 2004. "Collateral Damage: The Economic Impact of War," mimeo.

Grossman, Herschel I. 1991. "A General Equilibrium Model of Insurrections." *The American Economic Review* 81(4) 912–921.

Hess, Gregory D., and Athanasios Orphanides. 1995. "War Politics: An Economic, Rational-Voter Framework." *American Economic Review* 85(4): 828–846.

Hess, Gregory D., and Athanasios Orphanides. 2001a. "Economic Conditions, Elections, and the Magnitude of Foreign Conflicts." *Journal of Public Economics* 80(1): 121–140.

Hess, Gregory D., and Athanasios Orphanides. 2001b. "War and Democracy." *The Journal of Political Economy* 109(4): 776–810.

Hirshleifer, J. 1994. The Dark Side of the Force. *Economic Inquiry* (January): 1–10.

Hoffman, Bruce. 1997. "The Confluence of International and Domestic Trends in Terrorism." *Terrorism and Political Violence* 9(1): 1–15.

Krueger, Alan, and David Laitin. 2004. "Misunderestimating Terrorism." *Foreign Affairs* 83(5): 8–13 (October).

Krueger, Alan, and Jitka Maleckova. 2002. "Education, Poverty, Political Violence and Terrorism: Is There a Causal Connection?" NBER Working Paper 9072, July.

Laqueur, Walter. 1977. *Terrorism.* London: Weidenfeld and Nicolson.

Levine, Ross, and David Renelt. 1992. "A Sensitivity Analysis of Cross-Country Growth Regressions." *American Economic Review* 82(4): 942–63.

Marshall, Monty, Keith Jaggers, and Ted Gurr. 2004. Polity IV: Political Regime Characteristics and Transitions, 1800–2004. College Park: University of Maryland, Center for International Development and Conflict Management.

Mickolus, Edward, Todd Sandler, Jean Murdock, and Peter Flemming. 2002. "International Terrorism: Attributes of Terrorist Events (ITERATE)." Vinyard Software, code-book.

O'Brien, Sean P. 1996. "Foreign Policy Crises and the Resort to Terrorism: A Time Series Analysis of Conflict Linkages." *The Journal of Conflict Resolution,* 40(2): 320–335.

Russett, Bruce, and Joel Slemrod. 1993. "Diminished Expectations of Nuclear War and Increased Personal Savings: Evidence from Individual Survey Data." *American Economic Review* 83(4): 1022–33.

Summers, Robert, and Alan Heston. 1991. "The Penn World Table (Mark 5): An Expanded Set of International Comparisons." *Quarterly Journal of Economics* 106(2): 327–368.

Tavares, J. 2004. "The Open Society Assesses its Enemies: Shocks, Disasters, and Terrorist Attacks." *Journal of Monetary Economics* 51(5): 1039–1070.

Tornell, A. 1998. Reform from Within. Working Paper 6497, NBER, Cambridge, MA.

Wilkinson, Paul. 2001. *Terrorism versus Democracy: The Liberal State Response.* London: Frank Cass.

Wintrobe, R. 2002. Can Suicide Bombers be Rational? Unpublished paper, University of Western Ontario, Canada.

FOUR

The Lexus and the Olive Branch

Globalization, Democratization, and Terrorism

S. Brock Blomberg and Gregory D. Hess

This chapter provides an original study into how democratization and globalization influence terrorism, examining the motives of terrorists and how democratic institutions and international integration influence nonstate economic actors. We employ a gravity model to investigate the relative importance of globalization and democratization on transnational terrorism. We construct an original database of more than 200,000 observations from 1968 to 2003 for 179 countries to examine the extent to which economic, political, and historical factors influence the likelihood of citizens from one country to engage in terrorist activities against another. We find that the advent of democratic institutions, high income, and more openness in a source country significantly reduce terrorism. However, the advent of these same positive developments in targeted countries actually increases terrorism. *Ceteris paribus*, the effect of being a democracy or participating in the WTO for a source country decreases the number of transnational terrorist strikes by about two to three per year, which is more than two standard deviations greater than the average number of strikes between any two countries in a given year.

1. Introduction

World foreign direct investment flows (FDI), which amounted to less than $13 billion in 1970, quadrupled every ten years, reaching $54 billion in 1980 and $209 billion in 1990. During the last half of the 1990s, however, FDI practically exploded, reaching a peak of $1.4 trillion in 2000. Worldwide trade also increased dramatically over the same time period. Trade as a percent of GDP grew from 27 percent in 1970 to 38 percent by 1980 to 45 percent by the year 2000.

During the same time period in question, democratization across the globe has increased. The percent of countries that are nondemocracies, as calculated by Freedom House, starts at 46 percent in 1972. The percent falls to 35 percent by 1980 and steadily declines to 25 percent by the year 2000. These democracy and FDI trends are often used to demonstrate the extent to which the world is democratized and economically integrated or globalized.

Although the runup of FDI, trade, and democracy in the 1990s, and especially in the second half of that decade, has several explanations, it is strikingly correlated with a decline in worldwide violence during that period. In the late 1980s and early 1990s, approximately 1.5 transnational terrorist events occurred every day. As globalization and democratization grew at an ever-faster rate, the frequency of terrorist events declined sharply, reaching fewer than 0.5 events a day by 2000. Did this shift toward a more integrated and democratic world contribute to the large increase in peace during that same period? And, if the world has since become less peaceful in the wake of 9/11, can the dropoff in FDI and the painful process of democratization be blamed?

One view is that violence harms the real economy in the same manner as any trade cost. In this case, external conflict, internal conflict, or an international terrorist attack leads to a fall in trade and, in turn, a decline in aggregate economic activity. Put differently, an increase in terrorism in country A increases the cost to doing business with country A so that country B will either purchase goods or services domestically or from another more peaceful country. Thus, violence acts as a distorting tax or tariff that limits the attainment of the benefits from free trade.

Anderson and Marcouiller (2002) have pursued this angle employing corruption and imperfect contract enforcement as impediments to international trade. They find that omitting indexes of institutional quality obscures the negative relationship between per capita income and the share of total expenditure devoted to traded goods. Their chapter, however, does not consider direct measures of conflict.[1] Blomberg and Hess (2006a) calculate that, for a given country year, the combined presence of terrorism, as well as internal and external conflict is equivalent to as much as a 30 percent tariff on trade. This is larger than estimated tariff-equivalent costs of border and language barriers and tariff-equivalent reduction through Generalized Systems of Preference and World and World Trade Organization participation. In a complementary study, Glick and Taylor (2004) consider the

---

[1] Nitsch and Schumacher (2004) also analyze some aspects of conflict's affect on trade but over a significantly shorter time horizon.

direct effect of very large external wars on trade from a broader historical perspective. To estimate the quantitative implications of violence and globalization on international investment, Blomberg and Mody (2005) use a gravity model of bilateral FDI flows. Three findings emerge from Blomberg and Mody's (2005) analysis. First, violence at home tends to move investment abroad. Second, violence in the host country deters both trade and FDI flows. Host-country violence hurts inflows of investment with particular force in developing countries. Finally, they find a strong positive influence of WTO membership on bilateral FDI flows. Taken together, these results suggest that while violence raises political risk and discourages investment flows, WTO membership acts as a commitment device that, by limiting the possibility of arbitrary policy changes, lowers country risk. These results are robust across a variety of specifications.

While these papers provide important evidence of violence's influence on globalization, they fail to consider the opposite effect – namely globalization's influence on terrorism. Moreover, they also do not formally examine the effect of democratization. The central contribution of our chapter is to do just that.

Other papers do examine the role of globalization and democratization in terrorism. Li and Schaub (2004) employ a sample of 112 countries from 1975 to 1997 and find that neither trade nor investment has a positive effect on terrorism. Li (2005) uses the same data to analyze the effect of democracy on terrorism. He finds that democracy can reduce terrorism.

This line of research has serious limitations. In particular, by using standard panel estimation in the analysis, these papers are unable to separate globalization or democratization's effect on terrorism from the host and the source-country perspective. For example, suppose increased economic integration has the consequence of harming individuals in import-competing industries. Further, suppose these individuals join forces with a terrorist organization and express their displeasure through a terrorist attack on a trading partner. This attack on the host country from a neighboring source country will not be appropriately taken into account in estimations that only control for host-country trade values. In fact, to truly understand the impetus for any transnational event, one must understand the motivation from the point of view of both the host of the attack and the source of the attack. The standard treatment of the data is unable to address this crucial issue.

How then can we possibly make sense of these conflicting theoretical claims, and the even less satisfying empirical record? Here we make use of the concept of the "directed dyad" that differentiates explicitly between the characteristics of the state that is the source of the terrorist activity and the state that is the target. By separating out the effects of democracy and globalization on the source and target states, we generate clearer and more precise hypotheses and results than are available using standard panel regression techniques.

We start by focusing our attention on "transnational terrorism," recognizing that this type of terrorism is fundamentally dyadic in nature. Hence it is amenable to investigation using an approach similar to the gravity of model of international trade.

Our focus is on the determinants of transnational terrorism. Following the definition Mickolus et al. (2002) adopted, a transnational terrorist event is defined as:

the use, or threat of use, of anxiety-inducing, extra-normal violence for political purposes, by any individual or group, whether acting for or in opposition to established government authority, when such action is intended to influence the attitudes and behavior of a target group wider than the immediate victims and when, through the nationality or foreign ties of its perpetrators, its location, the nature of its institutional or human victims, or the mechanics of its resolution, its ramifications transcend national boundaries. (2)

Transnational terrorism requires, therefore, a flow of resources across international borders – whether it is foreign terrorists attacking domestic (and other foreign) targets or domestic nationals attacking the property and lives of foreign nationals on domestic soil. As a result, it seems appropriate in any investigation of the determinants of transnational terrorism to consider the characteristics of both the source and target countries. Moreover, the characteristics of a country that might make it a likely target country may indeed be very different from the characteristics that make a country a likely source of international terrorism. The features of the polity that make a country a terrorist producer may be different from the political structures, institutions, and environment that make a state a terrorist target.

To analyze the importance of both democratization and globalization in determining terrorism, we embed the analysis in the workhorse model of trade and finance – the gravity model. The gravity model is useful because it allows researchers to examine the net flow of activity among countries while netting out domestic terrorist activities. Netting out is useful because there is no comprehensive dataset that includes country-level measures of domestic terrorism over a long time horizon. In its simplest form, a gravity model postulates that bilateral activity, usually trade or investment, is positively related to the size of the two economies and negatively influenced by the distance between them. We extend this analysis by considering terrorism as the bilateral activity between each country-year-pair. In addition to including the size and distance variables in basic gravity equations, our baseline specification includes other control variables commonly used. Importantly, they rely on estimates that include bilateral country-pair dummies, which control not only for distance but also for all unobserved common relationships between the countries.

The purpose of estimating a gravity equation for terrorism is to estimate the importance of democratization and globalization on terrorism and to compare these relative magnitudes with other factors previously highlighted as relevant in explaining terrorism, for example, GDP or GDP per capita. In this way, we begin with a baseline terrorism model in which development is the main engine in determining terrorism. Then we add measures of globalization and democratization to determine the significance of each. In addition, we add new variables and consider specifications suggested by recent advances in the interpretation of gravity models.[2]

Our approach allows us to examine the following hypotheses:

H1: The effects of democracy and globalization on terrorism differ for source and target countries
H2: Terrorism falls with democracy and globalization in the source countries
H3: Terrorism rises with democracy and globalization in the target countries.

We find that differences in income, democracy, and openness go a long way toward explaining transnational terrorism. We find that the presence of democratic institutions in a source country significantly reduces terrorism. However, the presence of these same institutions in host countries actually increases terrorism, providing more support for our earlier conjecture.

We also find that source-country openness has a negative and statistically significant effect on terrorism. Once again, however, host-country openness often has a positive and statistically significant on terrorism. Ceteris paribus, the effect of being a democracy or participating in the WTO for a source country, decreases the number of terrorist strikes by about two to three,

---

[2] For examples in the trade literature, see among others, Anderson (1979) who championed use of the gravity equation in structural trade models. Blomberg and Hess (2006a) focus on trade, especially on comparing the costs of conflict with measures for trade promotion. Alternatively, Blomberg, Hess, and Orphanides (2004) investigate the effect of various forms of conflict such as terrorism, internal wars, and external wars on a country's economic growth.

which is more than two standard deviations greater than the average number of strikes between any two countries in a given year.

2. The Data and Empirical Regularities

In this section, we describe our data sources and examine some basic empirical regularities of the resulting dataset. This issue is described in greater detail in our companion chapter. Hence, we refer the reader to Blomberg and Hess (2007) for a more detailed account. Terrorism is adopted from the ITERATE dataset (see Mickolus et al. [1993]). The ITERATE project began as an attempt to quantify characteristics, activities, and effects of transnational terrorist groups. The dataset is grouped into four categories. First, incident characteristics code the timing of each event. Second, the terrorist characteristics yield information about the number, makeup, and groups involved in the incidents. Third, victim characteristics describe analogous information on the victims involved in the attacks. Finally, life and property losses attempt to quantify the damage of the attack.

A central contribution of our chapter is to employ the data in a different manner than has been previously employed in the literature. Overall, the variables we construct measure the net effect of terrorism between countries. We consider several bilateral definitions of terrorism. First, we define terrorism, T, as the number of events in a host country, h, from attackers who are nationals of source country, s. To check robustness, we also measure T as the number of victims rather than number of incidents in a given year. Second, we define terrorism as the number of events perpetrated on individuals from host country, h, from attackers who are nationals of source country, s.

Before proceeding, several caveats are in order. First, one may be concerned that the nationality of the source attacker may not represent the views of the country for which he is associated. While a possibility, this problem is no less severe than what we encounter when we try to measure any international variable. For example, how do we properly account for the nation of origin of a Mercedes-Benz manufactured in Alabama using parts imports from Asia? Second, one may be concerned that there could be more than one nationality included in the attacking force, making the source country of the terrorist incident hard to determine. This concern turns out to be less of an issue in practice for the following reason: 98 percent of attacks are reported with only one source country.[3] Finally, one may be concerned

---

[3] Experimenting with different classification for source country had no discernable effect on the results. Hence, we did not include source countries for multiple country attacks.

that we could be undercounting the number of incidents because not all attacks are identified with a particular group. Even so, the vast majority of attacks do have an identified source country, amounting to more than 8,000 incidents. It is also likely that incidents that are reported without association to any particular group are unsuccessful terrorist attacks and are less likely to be economically significant. As the definition of terrorism in ITERATE requires knowledge of a political agenda, the events without associated countries are unlikely to have any direct effect on the relationship between any two countries in particular.

2.1. Globalization, Democratization, and Terrorism

As shown in our companion piece, Blomberg and Hess (2007), rich countries have had approximately four times as many incidents and incidents per capita as poor countries, and democracies have also had approximately four times as many incidents per capita as nondemocratic regimes. Why might this be so?[4]

Krug and Reinmoeller (2004) argue that globalization is an important determinant of terrorism. In their paper, they build a model to explain the internationalization of terrorism as a natural response to a globalizing economy. As countries become more economically integrated and market oriented, there is no discrimination between what certain terrorist groups might see as "bad" products and "good" products or investments. Moreover, the same advances in technology that allow for easy access of goods and services also allow for easy access to military hardware and technology.

In the short run, globalization may have the consequence of creating a series of winners and losers. These same losers will have easier access to weapons of retaliation in response to their losses, thereby multiplying the effect of globalization on terrorism.

An alternative view put forth by Crenshaw (2001) is that it is naive to believe that globalization is encouraging international terrorism. Although globalization and terrorism may be seemingly affecting one another, something more complicated is at work. Globalization does not necessarily drive the latest wave of terrorism. Instead, she argues that this wave should be seen as a series of civil wars that may be motivated by a strategically unified reaction to American power rather than by globalization.

---

[4] One possibility not explored here is that there may be underreporting of terrorist events in nondemocratic regimes due to the lack of freedom of the press.

It is an empirical matter to determine which hypothesis the existing evidence supports. Tables 4.1 and 4.2 report the total number of terrorist incidents and incidents per capita parsed by globalization, democratization, and growth.[5] If globalization, democratization, or growth are the culprits, then we would expect terrorism to be greater in liberalizing or growing economies. Tables 4.1 and 4.2 provide little evidence to support this. During the 1960s and 1970s, high globalizing and democratizing economies were more likely to be targeted by terrorism. In the 1970s; for example, democratizers had eight times the rate of terrorism per capita than nondemocratizers. There has been an interesting twist in the dynamic since the 1980s, the period of greatest peace, democratization, and globalization: namely, terror is less likely to hit high growth, democratizing, or globalizing countries. In each comparison group during the 1990s and 2000s, less-democratic, less-open, and lower-growth countries experienced more terrorism per capita. This point can be made stronger by examining Table 4.3. These columns parse the data by considering globalized versus nonglobalized democracies. Note that globalizers continue to experience higher rates of terrorism per capita than nonglobalizers, on the order of 100 to 300 percent more. Moreover, democratizers tend to experience more terrorism, although the difference between terrorist incidents per capita (T/N) for nonglobalized democracies and nonglobalized nondemocracies is quite small.

Interestingly, the gap between globalizers/nonglobalizers and democracies/nondemocracies has fallen during the period of greatest democratization and globalization. For example, during the 2000s (albeit for a short time period) there is no significant difference between nonglobalized nondemocracies (NOGLOB & NODEM) and globalized democracies (GLOB & DEM).[6]

---

[5] Our definitions for high or low globalization, democratization, and growth are standard measures. High (low) growth is defined as average growth per capita $>$ ($<$)1.5 percent per year; high (low) democratic is defined for countries with polity $>$ ($<$)7 and/or the executive plus legislative index of political competitiveness $>$ ($<$)14; high (low) globalized is defined as countries with trade as a percentage of GDP $>$ ($<$)30 percent. The general qualitative results are not sensitive to changes in these cutoff values.

[6] To see this in a different way, a working paper version of this chapter reports the total number of terrorist incidents, incidents per capita, democracy, and GDP per capita of the source countries. This allows us to directly examine the motivation of the terrorist-originating countries and provides two interesting facts. First, there is little correlation among measures of globalization, democracy, development, and terrorism among the twelve countries that are the source of the most terrorist incidents per capita. These high incidence source countries are not particularly democratic/nondemocratic, developed/developing or open/closed. For example, for these twelve countries, six have higher than average incomes and six have higher than average incomes; six have lower than average openness and six have lower than average values.

Table 4.1. *Terrorism by growth and governance: 189 country sample*

Years	All T	All T/N	High growth T	High growth T/N	Low growth T	Low growth T/N	More democratization T	More democratization T/N	Less democratization T	Less democratization T/N
1960s	0.72	0.20	0.77	0.29	0.48	0.51	2.21	1.78	0.76	0.40
1970s	1.72	0.43	1.47	0.52	2.60	2.17	5.29	3.27	0.99	0.47
1980s	2.20	0.46	2.07	0.57	2.42	2.16	4.41	1.92	1.50	0.64
1990s	1.57	0.28	1.29	0.32	1.99	1.25	2.09	0.60	1.45	0.69
2000s	0.73	0.12	0.69	0.15	0.80	0.57	0.67	0.22	0.61	0.43
Total	6.94	1.49	6.28	1.84	8.30	6.66	14.67	7.79	5.31	2.63

Note: T/N is the number of terrorist incidents in a given country per year, per million. A country is high growth if growth per capita > 1.5 percent in a country year. Otherwise, the country is a low-growth country. A country experiences more democratization if polity > 5 and/or the executive plus legislative index of political competitiveness > 10. Otherwise a country experiences less democratization.
Source: ITERATE, Penn World Data, Beck et al. (2001).

Table 4.2. *Terrorism by globalization: 189 countries*

Years	All T	All T/N	More globalized T	More globalized T/N	Less globalized T	Less globalized T/N
1960s	0.72	0.20	0.68	1.23	0.74	0.24
1970s	1.72	0.43	2.08	1.91	1.40	0.48
1980s	2.20	0.46	2.48	1.60	1.78	0.55
1990s	1.57	0.28	1.66	0.44	1.24	0.68
2000s	0.73	0.12	0.80	0.17	0.53	0.39
Total	6.94	1.49	7.71	5.34	5.68	2.34

Note: T/N is the number of terrorist incidents in a given country per year, per million. See Table 4.1. A country is determined to be more globalized if trade as a percentage of GDP > 30 percent.

Table 4.3. *Terrorism by globalization and democratization: 210 countries*

Years	GLOB & DEM T	GLOB & DEM T/N	NOGLOB & DEM T	NOGLOB & DEM T/N	GLOB & NODEM T	GLOB & NODEM T/N	NOGLOB & NODEM T	NOGLOB & NODEM T/N
1960s	1.73	9.48	0.61	0.18	0.00	0.00	1.03	0.56
1970s	4.48	10.51	1.22	0.34	0.74	2.92	1.38	0.69
1980s	5.15	7.31	1.37	0.34	1.02	2.44	1.70	0.78
1990s	2.23	1.51	1.11	0.27	1.16	1.48	1.75	1.01
2000s	0.70	0.42	0.74	0.17	0.73	0.92	0.40	0.36
Total	14.30	29.23	5.06	1.29	3.65	7.75	6.25	3.41

Note: See Tables 4.1–4.2.

In summary, to best assess the influence of globalization, democratization, and development on terrorism, researchers must not only account for the changes in these variables but must also account for the relative size of these variables. Hence, a bilateral model, which allows for cross-country comparisons, may best help to understand the economic motives of terrorist groups. This can be seen in the gravity model described in the following section.

3. The Gravity Model

For several decades, the most frequently used empirical specification for linking trade volumes with underlying economic conditions is known as the gravity model, an analogy borrowed from physics. It has long been understood that gravitational force between two bodies depends on the mass of the two bodies and the distance between them. From international trade theory, the volume of trade between two countries depends on the size of their economies and physical distance between them. More refined specifications add variables such as income per capita, language differences, and the regime types of the two countries. In this chapter, we claim that the flow of transnational terrorism between states similarly depends on the incomes of the two countries, the distance between them, language differences, the regime types of the two states, and a number of other variables that describe the underlying economic and political conditions of both states.

We adopt an explicitly dyadic approach and we follow the insights drawn from international economics. A country's willingness to engage in international trade – to import and export – depends on key features of both the underlying economies. Following Heckscher-Ohlin, a country's trading patterns (whether it is an importer or exporter of a particular good) depends crucially on its factor endowments, relative to its trading partner. A country relatively well endowed with a particular factor will export goods that use that factor intensively. We draw the obvious analogy when considering transnational terrorism – what matters are the underlying political conditions present in both the sending and receiving country, not just in the country in which the event took place.

The notion of considering the importance of both sources of and targets for transnational terrorism is gaining popularity in economics and political science. For example, Laitin and Shapiro (2007) in this volume provide a very nice review of the microfoundations for source and targets of terror.

A central contribution of our chapter is to introduce terrorism, T, as the dependent variable into these various gravity models. To include T in the aforementioned approaches, consider the following gravity equation for log trade x_{hst} for country pair h, s at time t and its determinants:

$$x_{hst} = f(y_{hst}, Y_{hst}, Z_{hst}, p_{hst}) \qquad (1)$$

where y is log of real GDP per capita, Y is log of real GDP, Z is a vector of observables to include trade costs τ (e.g., distance and language barriers), and p are multilateral resistance terms such as prices that refer to the bilateral barrier between countries relative to the average trade barrier each country faces with all trading partners.[7] These multilateral resistance terms may be thought of as product price variables that may create wedges to trade.

For traditional trade gravity models, one representation of equation (1) is:

$$x_{hst} = \alpha_0 + \alpha_{1Y_{ht}} + \alpha_{2Y_{st}} + \alpha_3 Y_{ht} + \alpha_4 Y_{st} + \delta\, Z_{hst} + \varepsilon_{hst} \qquad (2)$$

We employ measures of Z such as distance (both physical and technological measures), and language barriers and the error may be specified to control for random or time/country fixed effects. We modify equation (2) by specifying Z and redefining the left-hand-side variable as T, so that we have:

$$
\begin{aligned}
T_{hst} = {} & \alpha_0 + \alpha_1 \cdot y_{ht} + \alpha_2 \cdot y_{st} + \alpha_3 \cdot Y_{ht} + \alpha_4 \cdot Y_{st} + \alpha_5 \cdot \log distance_{hs} \\
& + \alpha_6 \cdot + Comlang_{hs} + \alpha_7 \cdot area_{hs} + \alpha_8 \cdot REL_h + \alpha_9 \cdot REL_s \\
& + \alpha_{10} DEM_{ht} + \alpha_{11} \cdot DEM_{st} + \alpha_{12} \cdot GLO_{ht} + \alpha_{13} \cdot GLO_{st} + \varepsilon_{ijt}
\end{aligned}
\qquad (3)
$$

where h, s denote countries, t denotes time, and the variables are defined as: T is the number of a terrorist attacks on country h from "a" group representing country s, Y is log of real Gross Domestic Product, y is the log of real GDP per capita, distance is the natural log of distance between two countries, Comlang is a dummy variable that is one if countries have a common language and zero otherwise, area is the natural log of the product of the size of the countries, REL is a zero to one index of religious fractionalization of a country, DEM is defined both as an index of democratization from the Polity dataset and as a dummy variable if the country exhibits competitive elections. The globalization variables, GLO, are defined both as trade/GDP and an index of integration such as trade or participation in the WTO.[8]

---

[7] For convenience, we have written the variable for a country pair as Y_{hs}, but we switch to Y_h and Y_s to refer to an individual country.

[8] We also considered measures of imports/GDP with little qualitative change in the results.

The purpose of estimating the gravity equation would be to consider the importance of DEM and GLO in affecting the likelihood of terrorism and to compare the relative magnitude to other factors highlighted in Blomberg and Hess (2007) as relevant in explaining terrorism, for example, GDP per capita.[9]

Although, we include many of the usual suspects that may influence T, to consider all possible covariates in a regression is impossible. Throughout, we include specifications that include time dummies to control for global shifts in terrorism trends. But, in addition, we present specifications that control for country-pair random effects. An important advantage of the country-pair model is that it accounts also for so-called multilateral resistance, that is, the relationship between the two countries and the rest of the world. The alternative approach of including host or source-country dummies is a special case of the country-pair dummy approach.

It is also worthwhile to note that many of the bilateral terrorist observations are zero. To correctly estimate the elasticities, then, it is necessary to consider the bias due to censoring. We employ the Tobit model that estimates the coefficients through a maximum likelihood procedure.

4. Empirical Results

4.1. Cross-Country Empirical Motivation

We motivate our discussion by considering the link between terrorism that occurs within county h by outsiders from country s and terrorism that occurs by country h's citizens in other countries. Crudely speaking, what we are doing is examining bilateral terrorist net imports. The purpose of this preliminary exercise is to see if the same countries that experience significant international terrorism are those whose citizens are terrorizing other countries abroad. This is useful because it sheds light on the causes of terror: whether terrorism is driven by civil strife between countries who may have been given arbitrary borders by colonial powers; whether terrorism is linked to particular countries such as the United States that may have very strong or polarizing international policies; whether terrorism is due to globalization/democratization/development such that those countries are more apt to be net importers of terrorism rather than net exporters.

---

[9] All data reported are taken from sources in Blomberg and Hess (2007). A detailed discussion is provided therein.

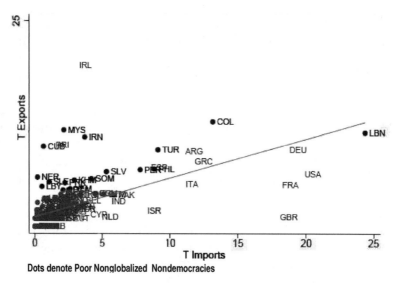

Figure 4.1a. 1968–2003 T imports and T exports.

Figure 4.1a plots countries by the number of terrorist exports versus the number of terrorist imports and a line of best fit. If countries import and export the same amount of terrorism, we would expect the data to fall along the 45-degree line. In fact, the line of best fit is measured at 43 degrees consistent with such a hypothesis. This result merely demonstrates an identity – in equilibrium, net exports, and net imports must be equated in total, though obviously not for a given country pair.

However, there are several important differences. First, there are notable net importers of terrorism – they include Israel, the United States, France, and Great Britain. There are also several notable net exporters of terrorism – Ireland, Iran, and Cuba. Though many factors may shift countries away from the diagonal line, it is interesting to note that, in general, the net importers mentioned are more democratic and wealthier than the net exporters. We denote the least democratic/wealthy/open countries with dots. Most appear to be net exporters of terrorism. Hence, when developing our gravity model, it would appear that the traditional variables included in gravity models would also apply to terrorism – namely income, trade, and institutions.

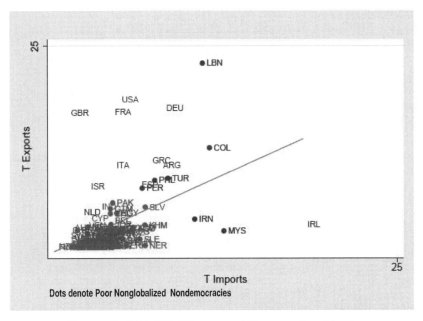

Figure 4.1b. 1968–2003 T imports and T exports: Conditional.

A different way to see this is to repeat the experiment, this time controlling for democracy, openness, and income. In this case, there does not appear to be such a difference in estimated imports or exports from terrorism. Figure 4.1b plots this conditional regression. Notice that in this case there are just as many dots below and above the estimated line.

However, while these figures may be illuminating, they do not provide any direct evidence regarding the relationship among globalization, democratization, and terrorism. The purpose of the next subsection is to address these issues.

4.2. Baseline Results

We begin by explaining the estimation results from the gravity model (3). In Table 4.4, the estimates reported in columns 1–7 include variables that do not change over time. These include distance, land mass, as well as dummy variables for language. Columns 2–7 report estimates of different subsamples – those in which either source or host country are democratic (DEM), members of the WTO or GATT (GLO), or both. Column 8 estimates

Table 4.4. Gravity model for terrorist incidents by location: 1968–2003 full country sample$_h$

	1 Base	2 DEM	3 DEM	4 GLO	5 GLO	6 DEM&GLO	7 DEM&GLO	8 F.E.	9 R.E.
Y$_h$	0.999***	0.752***	0.721***	1.267***	0.922***	1.071***	0.684***	0.400**	0.949***
	[0.235]	[0.223]	[0.200]	[0.292]	[0.225]	[0.294]	[0.198]	[0.158]	[0.149]
Y$_s$	−1.790***	−1.725***	−1.711***	−2.033***	−1.702***	−2.107***	−1.675***	−1.904***	−1.323***
	[0.329]	[0.330]	[0.323]	[0.393]	[0.317]	[0.426]	[0.318]	[0.292]	[0.161]
Y$_h$	2.559***	2.746***	2.646***	2.419***	2.524***	2.554***	2.621***	2.677***	1.322***
	[0.499]	[0.550]	[0.518]	[0.478]	[0.494]	[0.521]	[0.515]	[0.416]	[0.154]
Y$_s$	1.018***	0.999***	1.176***	1.165***	1.065***	1.266***	1.201***	1.314***	0.873***
	[0.201]	[0.212]	[0.231]	[0.239]	[0.212]	[0.277]	[0.239]	[0.215]	[0.133]
Distance	−3.532***	−3.200***	−3.231***	−3.281***	−3.483***	−3.029***	−3.215***	−3.226***	−2.497***
	[0.683]	[0.637]	[0.637]	[0.642]	[0.678]	[0.608]	[0.637]	[0.510]	[0.194]
Comlang	3.019***	3.076***	3.179***	3.014***	3.075***	3.096***	3.245***	3.068***	1.914***
	[0.719]	[0.768]	[0.755]	[0.736]	[0.727]	[0.787]	[0.764]	[0.605]	[0.340]
Border	1.332**	1.910***	1.878***	1.682**	1.417***	2.174***	1.906***	1.973***	0.664
	[0.610]	[0.724]	[0.688]	[0.672]	[0.619]	[0.781]	[0.691]	[0.615]	[0.515]
Area	−0.028	−0.325***	−0.243**	−0.507***	−0.02	−0.670***	−0.231**	−0.344***	0.184**
	[0.069]	[0.121]	[0.095]	[0.136]	[0.070]	[0.182]	[0.097]	[0.099]	[0.082]
REL$_h$	0.155	0.376	0.071	0.6	−0.142	0.9	−0.115	−0.284	
	[0.724]	[0.859]	[0.751]	[0.772]	[0.704]	[0.920]	[0.734]	[0.678]	
REL$_s$	−7.609***	−8.496***	−7.857***	−8.137***	−7.321***	−9.083***	−7.568***	−7.837***	
	[1.644]	[1.878]	[1.706]	[1.777]	[1.607]	[2.018]	[1.664]	[1.394]	
Polity$_h$		0.128***				0.108**			
		[0.049]				[0.043]			

	(1)	(2)	(3)	(4)	(5)	(6)	(7)	(8)	(9)
Polity$_s$		−0.045***				−0.046***			
		[0.013]				[0.013]			
DEM$_h$			2.131***				1.864***	2.907***	0.356
			[0.550]				[0.549]	[0.584]	[0.228]
DEM$_s$			−1.914***				−1.505***	−1.103***	−1.357***
			[0.507]				[0.467]	[0.410]	[0.284]
OPEN$_h$				−0.039***		−0.032***			
				[0.009]		[0.011]			
OPEN$_s$				−0.023***		−0.006			
				[0.006]		[0.006]			
GLO$_h$					1.872***		1.428**	1.468***	0.514*
					[0.545]		[0.555]	[0.510]	[0.290]
GLO$_s$					−1.611***		−1.390***	−1.434***	−0.982***
					[0.461]		[0.448]	[0.420]	[0.338]
Observations	208613	136962	182794	190812	208613	129542	182794	182794	183275

Note: Clustered standard errors by income per capita are presented in parentheses. ***, **, and * represent statistical significance at the .01, .05, and .10 levels, respectively. Each column is the basic gravity model estimated over full country sample 1968–2003. Columns 1–9 were estimated using the Tobit method to allow for zero value observations. Column 8 includes year fixed effects. Column 9 estimates the model using random effects by country-pair year income. Included in the regression are: Real GDP Y_i and Real GDP per capita y_i for host $i = h$, and source $i = s$ countries, log physical distance (distance), log physical area (area), dummy variable for language (Comlang), dummy variable for border (border), measures of religious fractionalization (REL), and measures of democracy (polity is index of democracy on 0–10 scale with 10 being most democratic) (DEM is dummy variable which is 1 if polity > 7 or executive + legislative veto points from Beck et al. (2001) > 14, 0 otherwise) and measures of globalization (OPEN is total trade / GDP) (GLO is dummy variable, which is 1 if member of WTO/GATT, 0 otherwise.

the model to include controls for time and country fixed effects. Column 9 estimates the model to control for random effects by country-pair. Each of these models are estimated using the Tobit estimator with standard errors clustered by the income per capita group of each country-pair.

Consider, first, the traditional gravity variables. Greater distance between the source and host countries reduces terrorism (as has been well documented for trade and FDI). Traditional barriers to trade such as borders and language also appear to increase terrorism. In this sense, terrorism appears to be more of a regional threat than a global one. Further, larger country size typified by higher GDP increases terrorism. One way to interpret this result is that larger means more of everything – including terrorism. Even so, terrorism is significantly more responsive to country size at the host rather than from the source perspective.

Religious fractionalization tends to decrease source-country terrorism with little effect on host-country violence. Low fractionalized countries such as Iran (.11) are associated with more source terrorism than high-fractionalized countries such as the UK (.66). This result supports the view that radicalism, at least at the source level, is a determinant in provoking violence.

Perhaps the most interesting and robust result is when analyzing differences in income. Richer host countries (higher per capita GDP) generate more terrorism whereas richer source countries generate less terrorism. This result is consistent across each specification, with the effect from source income being slightly greater in magnitude than the effect from host income. Taken literally, the estimation results from Table 4.4 imply that a one percentage point increase in a source country's income should decrease the number of terrorist events by two per year. A one percentage point increase in a host country's income would invite about one more terrorist event per year.[10]

This finding provides a segue into the thrust of our chapter's main question. This result could indicate that terrorism is the unfortunate consequence of a widening divide between rich and poor countries. During a process of

---

[10] Because we have already controlled for size of the host and source countries by including their respective GDP, one interpretation for the sign of the coefficients associated with per capita GDP is that small (in population) host countries are less likely to experience terrorist attacks and large (in population) source countries are more likely to supply nationals who undertake terrorist acts. Still, it is worthwhile to note that the coefficients associated with per capita GDP remain the same sign and significance even when GDP is omitted in the regression.

sweeping change over the past twenty years as countries have become more globalized and democratized, some countries have been "left behind" while others have flourished. Perhaps, terrorists in these "left behind" economies have chosen to strike against those countries that have become more advantaged during the period in question.

We directly address this point as we consider the effect of these dynamic forces – globalization and democratization – on terrorism. There are two main results from this estimation. First, the advent of democratic institutions in a source country significantly reduces terrorism. However, the advent of these same institutions in host countries actually increases terrorism, providing more support for our earlier conjecture.

Second, source-country openness has a negative and statistically significant effect on terrorism. Once again, however, host-country openness often has a positive and statistically significant effect on terrorism. Ceteris paribus, the effect of being a democracy or participating in the WTO for a source country, decreases the number of terrorist strikes by about one to two events, which is more than two standard deviations greater than the average number of strikes between any two countries in a given year.

How should one interpret our findings? Do the forces of modernization (democracy, globalization, and growth) lead terrorists to attack other countries, or do terrorists from poor countries attack rich neighbors because it's a low-cost method of voicing their discontent?

Democracy's effect on a country's likelihood of being a source for transnational terrorism is not firmly established. Nondemocracies create fewer outlets for political grievances to be addressed, making violent means of political action more likely. This might lead to increased domestic terrorism but doesn't speak to the country as a source of transnational terrorism. When the autocratic government is perceived to have its authority bolstered by its foreign relations with democracies however, we might expect that the terrorist group advocating the removal of the illegitimate autocrat might indeed target its foreign allies, some of whom might be democracies. One would expect, therefore, that the presence of a nondemocracy abroad could increase transnational terrorism at home.

As to what makes a country a source of terrorists, we are unable to make strong assertions. Discussion in this regard has rarely distinguished between domestic and transnational terrorism. Where political conflict is domestic, the lack of outlets for political discontent makes violent means of protest more likely. Where a wider variety of groups get to participate in the political process, nonviolent means likely predominate first. Others have argued that in a more democratic regime more political action of all kinds, violent and nonviolent alike, is likely. Overall, the lack of clarity on the issue stems, in our view, from treating the source and target countries in the same manner; when the effects of democracy are permitted to differ conditionally on whether the observation is a source or target, this allows a more precise view on the determinants of transnational terrorism.

Globalization also affects the costs, benefits, and resources available for terrorist activities. First, if terrorism emerges from a sense of relative deprivation, then globalization, insofar as it encourages economic growth, may mitigate terrorist tendencies. On the other hand, if globalization is associated with increased inequality across countries and groups, then we might expect globalization to lead to more violence. On the costs side of the equation, the lowered barriers to the flows of goods, money, people, and ideas makes the networks of terrorist operations cheaper to operate. Terrorist themselves find it easier to move across increasingly permeable borders; resource flows across borders necessary to finance terrorist operations become more difficult to monitor by authorities overwhelmed by the growth of the international financial system. Norms of privacy in international banking make information about these resource flows scarce. The fact that customs agents inspect only a small fraction of goods imported makes the smuggling of terrorist material cheaper, while the freer flow of information makes the knowledge and techniques of terrorist action more easily transferred. Globalization, like democracy, affects the costs, benefits, and resources constraints of terrorists in many ways. The literature has focused on some of these mechanisms and the evidence has been substantially inconclusive.

The popular discourse seems to put some of the blame for transnational terrorism on "globalization" – this increased flow of goods, services, ideas, people, and culture across international borders. The *Economist* suggests that the relative ease with which resources and people move around the world increases the risks associated with transnational terrorism, while Paul Martin (2002), as Canadian Finance Minister, claimed that the terrorists themselves are hostile to the process of globalization, witnessed by the choice of target by the 9/11 hijackers – a center of world trade and finance.

Others argue that globalization encourages terrorism for yet further reasons. If globalization increases world inequality, then it will increase feelings of relative deprivation. These feelings produce political action, some of it violent. Or merely, globalization results in a kind of cultural imperialization significantly reducing the quality of life of people committed to a particular set of norms governing social behavior, norms that foreign influences break.

Our chapter cannot hope to disentangle each of these issues. Rather, it is the first to document three phenomena:

- The effects of democracy and globalization on terrorism differ for source and target countries
- Terrorism falls with democracy and globalization in the source countries
- Terrorism rises with democracy and globalization in the target countries.

Moreover, as the results in Table 4.5 demonstrate, our baseline estimates of the traditional gravity specification in equation (3) reported in Table 4.4 are generally robust across modifications to take into account region, time, and income class. The estimates reported in columns 1 through 6 of Table 4.5 are for the results from a gravity specification where we include measures of globalization and democratization in each specification.[11]

Greater distance, borders, and language appear to have similar statistically significant effects in Table 4.5 as in Table 4.4. Larger country size continues to increase terrorism. Richer host countries continue to generate more terrorism in each case except when only rich countries are considered.[12] Poorer source countries continue to generate more terrorism.[13]

Finally, and most importantly, the influence on globalization and democratization are similar across the subsamples. As can be seen from the appropriate rows of the table, the estimate associated with host democracy is statistically significant at below the .01 level in most cases, and the coefficient estimates are positive in each case (except in Latin America), varying between 1.5 in Asia income countries to 0.5 in the Middle East and North Africa. The estimate associated with source democracy is statistically significant at below the .01 level in most cases, and the coefficient estimates vary between −.1 in Latin America income countries to −1.5 in the Middle East and North Africa.

The estimates associated with globalization continue to be positive for host countries, ranging from 0.5 in sub-Saharan Africa to 1.3 in Latin America. They are statistically significant at below the 0.01 level in each case but

---

[11] The regions we consider are, respectively, South East Asia, East Asia, the Middle East, North Africa, Latin America and the Caribbean, and High and Low Income countries. The latter classification is from Rose (2004) and is obtained from the World Bank Development Indicators.

[12] This may be because rich countries are less likely to commit terrorist acts.

[13] Again, except for the low-income sample, which may be less likely to strike against its poor counterparts.

Table 4.5. *Robustness checks: Gravity model for terrorist incidents: 1968–2003 full country sample*

	1 Asia	2 ssafr	3 menaf	4 latca	5 highi	6 lowin	7 1968–85	8 1986–2003
y_h	0.475**	0.568**	0.394***	0.371**	−0.561**	0.696***	0.568**	0.615***
	[0.197]	[0.221]	[0.120]	[0.180]	[0.237]	[0.163]	[0.250]	[0.229]
Y_s	−0.505***	−0.064	−1.185***	−0.680***	−4.364***	−0.335***	−1.904***	−1.866***
	[0.161]	[0.205]	[0.180]	[0.221]	[0.328]	[0.128]	[0.290]	[0.238]
Y_h	0.645***	0.881***	1.121***	0.792***	3.386***	0.727***	3.227***	2.310***
	[0.146]	[0.212]	[0.144]	[0.132]	[0.233]	[0.108]	[0.250]	[0.191]
Y_s	0.676***	0.465**	1.232***	0.614***	0.299	0.644***	0.925***	1.458***
	[0.157]	[0.192]	[0.173]	[0.149]	[0.211]	[0.112]	[0.216]	[0.195]
Distance	−1.529***	−2.386***	−1.455***	−1.196***	−4.168***	−1.856***	−2.516***	−3.785***
	[0.313]	[0.522]	[0.208]	[0.209]	[0.331]	[0.278]	[0.318]	[0.328]
Comlang	1.575***	1.566***	0.289	0.848***	4.227***	1.907***	2.184***	4.188***
	[0.381]	[0.453]	[0.315]	[0.328]	[0.595]	[0.325]	[0.585]	[0.490]
Border	1.436**	−0.326	1.250***	1.883***	−1.255	1.260***	1.275	1.904***
	[0.662]	[0.658]	[0.399]	[0.413]	[0.937]	[0.468]	[0.869]	[0.684]
Area	0.159	0.027	−0.169*	−0.12	0.129	0.160*	−0.585***	−0.008
	[0.110]	[0.112]	[0.094]	[0.078]	[0.133]	[0.089]	[0.139]	[0.133]
REL_h	−1.452*	0.043	−1.940***	0.027	−0.444	−1.041*	−0.876	−0.727
	[0.783]	[0.817]	[0.593]	[0.724]	[1.131]	[0.585]	[1.195]	[0.944]

RELs	−0.546	0.824	−1.254*	−1.474**	−5.657***	−0.562	−5.915***	−8.594***
	[0.827]	[0.848]	[0.696]	[0.688]	[1.257]	[0.592]	[1.266]	[1.049]
DEM$_h$	0.629*	0.473	1.145***	1.256***	3.206***	0.895***	2.410***	2.376***
	[0.353]	[0.413]	[0.274]	[0.303]	[0.637]	[0.291]	[0.582]	[0.545]
DEMs	−0.252	−0.451	−0.785**	−0.673**	−0.209	−0.459	−1.178*	−1.275**
	[0.386]	[0.491]	[0.342]	[0.279]	[0.794]	[0.303]	[0.671]	[0.572]
GLO$_h$	1.403***	0.448	0.760**	−0.689**	3.040***	0.561	3.168***	0.15
	[0.524]	[0.619]	[0.299]	[0.274]	[0.913]	[0.352]	[0.777]	[0.599]
GLOs	−0.427	−1.555***	−1.631***	0.002	−2.708***	−0.141	−0.617	−2.190***
	[0.491]	[0.543]	[0.325]	[0.305]	[0.927]	[0.343]	[0.689]	[0.592]
Observations	44410	70575	28159	60120	91435	83911	67952	114842

Notes: Clustered standard errors are presented in parentheses. ***, **, and * represent statistical significance at the .01, .05, and .10 levels, respectively. Each column is the basic gravity model estimated over subsamples where either the host or source country is in the respective region: Asia, (sub-Saharan Africa) ssafr, (Middle East and North Africa) menaf, (Latin America and Caribbean) latca; income: highi, lowin; and time: 1968–1985, 1986–2003. See Table 4.4.

one, sub-Saharan Africa. The influence from source-country globalization remains positive, though less often statistically significant. All of these effects are more pronounced in high-income countries than in low-income countries. Columns 8 and 9 explore the effect when we split the sample in 1985. Interestingly, the estimated effect of the gap from globalization and democratization is much larger in absolute value in the source country, though still statistically significant, for the 1985–2003 subsample. The coefficient is two times larger in absolute value for the second half of the sample. This may be because despite the trends in globalization and democratization, the motives and technology available to terrorists may have changed.

4.3. Analyzing the Robustness Across Different Measures of Terrorism

In Table 4.6, we consider an alternative measure of terrorism. Rather than define the host as the nation where the terrorist attack occurred, we define it according to the nationality of the victim, no matter where the attack occurred. In national income accounting terms, we consider a GNP measure of host terrorism rather than the GDP measure of host terrorism described earlier. We employ the exact same specification as in Table 4.4. We find that in general, the coefficients have the same sign, of similar magnitude, and statistically significance as those in Table 4.4.

The remarkable similarity in results between Tables 4.4 and 4.6 also give us some information about possible measurement issues. As discussed in Section 3, there may be some concerns that we are unable to capture the intent of the terrorist given the inherent challenges to using media-based measures of terrorism. Yet, when we select a different way of measuring the target for terrorism, namely by the nationality of the victim, we get precisely the same results. Obviously, this cannot account for all the possible problems associated with measuring terrorism, but the similarity is noteworthy. Other possible measurement issues are analyzed in Tables 4.7 and 4.8.

In Table 4.7, we consider a different measure of terrorism to account for the intensity of the violence. In this case, we define terrorism as the number of victims rather than the number of incidents.[14] The advantage to considering this measure is that it may better account for the actual damage of each attack inflicted on its country. The disadvantage would be that often terrorists may be less interested in targeting victims than in getting a response from its target. At the very least, it provides a robustness check to our early results.

---

[14] For comparative purposes, we divide the left-hand-side variable by ten so that the coefficients are of similar magnitude to terrorism in Tables 4.4–4.6.

Table 4.6. Gravity model for terrorist incidents by nationality: 1968–2003 full country sample

	1 Base	2 DEM	3 DEM	4 GLO	5 GLO	6 DEM&GLO	7 DEM&GLO	8 F.E.	9 R.E.
Y_h	1.901*** [0.099]	1.809*** [0.116]	1.650*** [0.106]	2.080*** [0.111]	1.831*** [0.101]	2.060*** [0.133]	1.638*** [0.107]	1.198*** [0.107]	0.947*** [0.072]
Y_s	-1.713*** [0.097]	-1.660*** [0.114]	-1.678*** [0.104]	-1.794*** [0.119]	-1.669*** [0.097]	-1.712*** [0.138]	-1.654*** [0.104]	-1.461*** [0.107]	-1.092*** [0.085]
Y_h	2.373*** [0.083]	2.371*** [0.096]	2.349*** [0.087]	2.157*** [0.093]	2.336*** [0.083]	2.132*** [0.114]	2.333*** [0.087]	2.121*** [0.088]	0.447*** [0.063]
Y_s	0.465*** [0.071]	0.430*** [0.085]	0.508*** [0.077]	0.454*** [0.088]	0.421*** [0.074]	0.385*** [0.105]	0.475*** [0.079]	0.565*** [0.081]	1.199*** [0.059]
distance	-1.946*** [0.126]	-1.668*** [0.144]	-1.720*** [0.133]	-1.793*** [0.131]	-1.929*** [0.126]	-1.630*** [0.148]	-1.732*** [0.133]	-1.756*** [0.135]	-1.036*** [0.091]
comlang	2.898*** [0.213]	2.909*** [0.242]	2.948*** [0.220]	2.777*** [0.223]	2.883*** [0.213]	2.789*** [0.253]	2.942*** [0.220]	2.769*** [0.222]	2.027 [0.000]
border	1.389*** [0.338]	2.114*** [0.380]	1.813*** [0.352]	1.658*** [0.348]	1.417*** [0.338]	2.169*** [0.388]	1.801*** [0.352]	2.074*** [0.354]	1.285*** [0.233]
Area	0.406*** [0.046]	0.322*** [0.059]	0.314*** [0.052]	0.004 [0.056]	0.449*** [0.048]	0.03 [0.067]	0.346*** [0.054]	0.196*** [0.055]	0.207*** [0.048]
REL_h	2.674*** [0.418]	3.174*** [0.477]	2.649*** [0.433]	3.224*** [0.426]	2.283*** [0.423]	3.883*** [0.489]	2.438*** [0.438]	1.167*** [0.447]	
REL_s	-4.505*** [0.417]	-5.037*** [0.488]	-4.733*** [0.436]	-4.639*** [0.439]	-4.518*** [0.420]	-5.196*** [0.508]	-4.741*** [0.440]	-4.256*** [0.448]	

(continued)

Table 4.6 (continued)

	1 Base	2 DEM	3 DEM	4 GLO	5 GLO	6 DEM&GLO	7 DEM&GLO	8 F.E.	9 R.E.
$polity_h$		0.092*** [0.013]				0.078*** [0.013]			
$polity_s$		−0.025*** [0.007]				−0.022*** [0.007]			
DEM_h			2.194*** [0.245]				951*** [0.258]	1.831*** [0.264]	0.589*** [0.134]
DEM_s			−0.889*** [0.235]				−0.891*** [0.244]	−0.658*** [0.245]	−0.772*** [0.132]
$OPEN_h$				−0.036*** [0.004]		−0.033*** [0.005]			
$OPEN_s$				−0.027*** [0.004]		−0.023*** [0.005]			
GLO_h					1.520*** [0.279]		0.890*** [0.304]	0.855*** [0.304]	0.370** [0.173]
GLO_s					−0.236 [0.248]		−0.031 [0.267]	−0.17 [0.270]	−0.138 [0.166]
Observations	209471	137648	183563	191629	209471	130218	183563	183563	184044

Note: Clustered standard errors are presented in parentheses. ***, **, and represent * statistical significance at the .01, .05, and .10 levels, respectively. See Table 4.5. The data for terrorism in these results differ in this case because we determine the target based on the nationality of the victim.

Table 4.7. *Gravity model for victims of terrorism: 1968–2003 full country sample*

	1 Base	2 DEM	3 DEM	4 GLO	5 GLO	6 DEM&GLO	7 DEM&GLO	8 F.E.	9 R.E.
y_h	1.145***	0.924***	0.857***	1.413***	1.058***	1.286***	0.817***	0.420**	2.009***
	[0.173]	[0.196]	[0.179]	[0.190]	[0.174]	[0.221]	[0.181]	[0.169]	[0.217]
y_s	-2.047***	-1.984***	-1.920***	-2.177***	-1.940***	-2.248***	-1.879***	-2.105***	-2.454***
	[0.181]	[0.204]	[0.192]	[0.217]	[0.182]	[0.250]	[0.193]	[0.187]	[0.280]
Y_h	2.745***	2.965***	2.837***	2.477***	2.702***	2.631***	2.804***	2.735***	1.467***
	[0.158]	[0.182]	[0.166]	[0.166]	[0.159]	[0.200]	[0.167]	[0.158]	[0.208]
Y_s	1.120***	1.120***	1.303***	1.180***	1.182***	1.280***	1.331***	1.397***	2.344***
	[0.137]	[0.159]	[0.149]	[0.162]	[0.144]	[0.195]	[0.154]	[0.148]	[0.185]
distance	-3.736***	-3.379***	-3.375***	-3.314***	-3.662***	-3.110***	-3.343***	-3.122***	-4.572***
	[0.246]	[0.265]	[0.249]	[0.240]	[0.245]	[0.264]	[0.249]	[0.232]	[0.336]
comlang	2.982***	2.971***	3.106***	2.797***	3.030***	2.830***	3.172***	2.725***	4.029***
	[0.394]	[0.438]	[0.403]	[0.394]	[0.393]	[0.443]	[0.404]	[0.377]	[0.517]
border	0.835	1.371**	1.444**	1.150**	0.932	1.548**	1.475**	1.417**	1.502**
	[0.574]	[0.638]	[0.592]	[0.570]	[0.573]	[0.639]	[0.591]	[0.553]	[0.708]
Area	0.008	-0.304***	-0.228**	-0.543***	0.011	-0.698***	-0.216**	-0.348***	0.505***
	[0.088]	[0.110]	[0.099]	[0.105]	[0.091]	[0.127]	[0.102]	[0.097]	[0.135]
REL_h	-0.549	-0.424	-0.713	-0.028	-0.867	0.245	-0.921	-1.255*	
	[0.744]	[0.841]	[0.764]	[0.734]	[0.751]	[0.842]	[0.772]	[0.735]	
REL_s	-7.486***	-8.301***	-7.683***	-7.706***	-7.073***	-8.618***	-7.307***	-7.117***	
	[0.819]	[0.931]	[0.843]	[0.832]	[0.824]	[0.948]	[0.848]	[0.820]	
$polity_h$		0.125***				0.102***			
		[0.023]				[0.022]			

(continued)

141

Table 4.7 (continued)

	1 Base	2 DEM	3 DEM	4 GLO	5 GLO	6 DEM&GLO	7 DEM&GLO	8 F.E.	9 R.E.
$polity_s$		−0.054*** [0.011]				−0.052*** [0.011]			
DEM_h			2.180*** [0.402]				1.882*** [0.415]	3.102*** [0.410]	0.389 [0.404]
DEM_s			−2.368*** [0.438]				−1.882*** [0.461]	−1.194*** [0.432]	−2.456*** [0.497]
$OPEN_h$				−0.047*** [0.006]		−0.041*** [0.009]			
$OPEN_s$				−0.032*** [0.007]		−0.016* [0.008]			
GLO_h					1.943*** [0.467]		1.515*** [0.497]	1.572*** [0.466]	0.211 [0.499]
GLO_s					−1.974*** [0.440]		−1.627*** [0.477]	−1.653*** [0.445]	−1.824*** [0.567]
Observations	208613	136962	182794	190812	208613	129542	182794	182794	183275

Note: Clustered standard errors are presented in parentheses. ***, **, and * represent statistical significance at the .01, .05, and .10 levels, respectively. See Table 4.5. The data for terrorism in these results differ in this case because we determine the target based on the number of victims.

Table 4.8. *Gravity model for terrorist victims of U.S.: 1968–2003 full country sample*

	1 Base	2 DEM	3 DEM	4 GLO	5 GLO	6 DEM&GLO	7 DEM&GLO	8 F.E.	9 R.E.
y_h	0.921**	0.674	0.6	1.011**	0.810**	0.547	0.521	0.125	0.008***
	[0.403]	[0.487]	[0.421]	[0.435]	[0.403]	[0.535]	[0.424]	[0.403]	[0.003]
y_s	−1.821***	−1.441***	−1.504***	−1.619***	−1.680***	−1.155*	−1.522***	−1.833***	−0.023***
	[0.429]	[0.521]	[0.463]	[0.501]	[0.435]	[0.625]	[0.467]	[0.462]	[0.003]
Y_h	3.020***	3.601***	3.144***	2.844***	3.032***	3.640***	3.166***	3.165***	0.022***
	[0.378]	[0.482]	[0.401]	[0.399]	[0.383]	[0.548]	[0.407]	[0.395]	[0.002]
Y_s	1.277***	1.405***	1.611***	1.120***	1.472***	1.223*	1.737***	1.855***	0.018***
	[0.333]	[0.423]	[0.371]	[0.386]	[0.355]	[0.505]	[0.388]	[0.381]	[0.002]
distance	−3.688***	−3.289***	−3.207***	−3.176***	−3.567***	−2.823***	−3.123***	−2.988***	−0.010***
	[0.580]	[0.668]	[0.592]	[0.564]	[0.576]	[0.660]	[0.590]	[0.563]	[0.003]
comlang	3.576***	4.318***	3.679***	3.519***	3.568***	4.526***	3.752***	3.488***	−0.001
	[0.961]	[1.161]	[0.991]	[0.955]	[0.960]	[1.174]	[0.994]	[0.947]	[0.006]
border	−0.03	0.243	0.926	0.447	0.206	0.713	1.062	0.897	−0.006
	[1.467]	[1.792]	[1.520]	[1.437]	[1.457]	[1.778]	[1.516]	[1.442]	[0.009]
area	0.047	−0.424	−0.257	−0.563**	−0.017	−0.919***	−0.325	−0.455*	−0.001
	[0.211]	[0.282]	[0.237]	[0.248]	[0.216]	[0.325]	[0.247]	[0.242]	[0.002]
REL_h	−0.392	−0.114	−0.712	−0.157	−0.528	−0.279	−0.713	−0.947	
	[1.771]	[2.149]	[1.835]	[1.737]	[1.792]	[2.144]	[1.856]	[1.799]	

(*continued*)

143

Table 4.8 (*continued*)

	1 Base	2 DEM	3 DEM	4 GLO	5 GLO	6 DEM&GLO	7 DEM&GLO	8 F.E.	9 R.E.
REL_s	−8.385***	−10.211***	−8.458***	−8.675***	−7.502***	−10.664***	−7.799***	−7.698***	
	[2.008]	[2.528]	[2.078]	[2.041]	[2.012]	[2.592]	[2.088]	[2.056]	
$polity_h$		0.057				0.043			
		[0.045]				[0.042]			
$polity_s$		−0.075**				−0.074***			
		[0.029]				[0.028]			
DEM_h			2.922***				2.868***	3.965***	0.008
			[0.988]				[1.023]	[1.027]	[0.005]
DEM_s			−4.579***				−3.721***	−2.744**	−0.033***
			[1.116]				[1.165]	[1.094]	[0.006]
$OPEN_h$				−0.042**		−0.017			
				[0.015]		[0.020]			
$OPEN_s$				−0.051***		−0.048**			
				[0.018]		[0.024]			
GLO_h					1.46		0.54	0.807	0.002
					[1.076]		[1.154]	[1.108]	[0.005]
GLO_s					−3.637***		−2.662**	−2.896**	−0.024***
					[1.090]		[1.187]	[1.132]	[0.006]
Observations	208613	136962	182794	190812	208613	129542	182794	182794	183275

Note: Clustered standard errors are presented in parentheses. ***, **, and * represent statistical significance at the .01, .05, and .10 levels, respectively. See Table 4.5. The data for terrorism in these results differ in this case because we determine the target based on the number of U.S. victims.

144

The results in Table 4.7 continue to support the earlier findings. The sign and statistical significance of each relevant coefficient is similar to those discussed earlier. However, the magnitude of the coefficients associated with income per capita, globalization, and democratization are slightly larger – on the order of 10 percent greater. Because the left-hand-side variables in both Tables 4.6 and 4.7 have been scaled to be of similar magnitude, one can only conclude that the effect of these variables is greater on the number of victims than it is on the number of incidents.

To place some perspective on the magnitude of these results, a one-percentage point increase in income in a host country causes the number of victims to rise by about one. A one-percentage point increase in the income of the source country causes the number of victims to fall twofold or by about two. The advent of a democracy or participation in the WTO in a host country causes the number of victims to rise twofold or by about two. Participation in the WTO in a source country causes the number of victims to fall twofold or by about two.

Finally, Table 4.8 considers the same measure as the number of victims but does this only for victims who are U.S. citizens. This provides a final robustness check as the United States may be the most likely target country for terrorism and the media may be exceptionally likely to report terrorist attacks that affect U.S. citizens. The results in Table 4.7 mirror our earlier findings, but the magnitudes are different. It appears that being a democracy for the source country is greater than in the full sample. The magnitude of the democratization effect is much larger when the sample is restricted to U.S. victims of terrorism. Finally, it appears that openness provides a greater hedge to terrorist attacks from source countries than in the previous regressions.

5. Conclusion

Thomas Friedman (2000) has been influential in understanding how the forces of globalization are helping to shape the evolution of world events. He writes:

on October 11, 1998, at the height of the global economic crisis, Merrill Lynch ran full-page ads in major newspapers through America to drive this point home. The ads read:

The World Is 10 Years Old

It was born when the Wall fell in 1989. It's no surprise that the world's youngest economy – the global economy – is still finding its bearings. The intricate checks and balances that stabilize economies are only incorporated with time. Many world markets are only recently freed, governed for the first time by the emotions of the people rather than the fists of the state. From where we sit, none of this diminishes the promise offered a decade ago by the demise of the walled-off world.... The spread of free markets and democracy around the world is permitting more people everywhere to turn their aspirations into achievements. And technology, properly harnessed and liberally distributed, has the power to erase not just geographical borders but also human ones. It seems to us that, for a 10-year-old, the world continues to hold great promise. In the meantime, no one ever said growing up was easy. (*Lexus and the Olive Tree*, 1)

Do these "growing pains" imply that we should observe more conflict around the globe, and in particular, terrorist attacks, as a consequence? Our chapter seeks to answer this question. We construct a new database on bilateral conflict and estimate a gravity model for terrorism. We find that development, democracy, and openness are each positive influences in creating a more peaceful environment for countries that are a source of terrorism. We also find that these same factors make a country more likely to be a target for terrorism.

What do these results mean for policy makers? Our chapter is one of the first of its kind to document the need for development, democracy, and openness in encouraging peace for terrorist nations. This means that policies that can encourage more liberal institutions to facilitate political and economic freedom will have a pacifying influence on a terrorist state. As such, these factors can help to reduce the supply of terrorist activity.

References

Anderson, J. 1979. "A Theoretical Foundation for the Gravity Equation." *American Economic Review* 69(1): 106–116.

Anderson, J., and Marcouiller, D. 2002. "Insecurity and the Pattern of Trade: An Empirical Investigation." *Review of Economics and Statistics* 84(2): 342–352.

Beck, Thorsten, George Clarke, Alberto Groff, Philip Keefer, and Patrick Walsh. 2001. "New Tools in Comparative Political Economy: The Database of Political Institutions." *World Bank Economic Review* 15(1): 165–176.

Blomberg, S. Brock, and Gregory D. Hess. 2007. "How Much Does Violence Tax Trade?" *Review of Economics and Statistics* 88(4): 599–612 (October).

———. 2007. "From (No) Guns to Butter." This volume.

Blomberg, S. Brock, and Ashoka Mody. 2005. "How Severely Does Violence Deter International Investment?", mimeo.

Blomberg, S. Brock, Gregory D. Hess, and Athansios Orphanides. 2004. "The Macroeconomic Consequences of Terrorism." *Journal of Monetary Economics* 51(5): 1007–1052.

Crenshaw, Martha. 1981. "The Causes of Terrorism." *Comparative Politics* 13(4): 379–399.

————. 2001. "Why America? The Globalization of Civil War." *Current History* 100(650): 425–433.

Friedman, Thomas. 2000. *The Lexus and the Olive Tree*. New York: Anchor Books.

Glick, Reuven, and Alan Taylor. 2004. "Collateral Damage: The Economic Impact of War," mimeo.

Krug, Barbara, and Patrick Reinmoeller. 2004. "The Hidden Cost of Ubiquity: Globalisation and Terrorism," mimeo, October.

Laitin, David, and Jacob Shapiro. 2007. "The Political, Economic and Organizational Sources of Terrorism." This volume.

Li, Quan. 2005. "Does Democracy Promote or Reduce Transnational Terrorist Incidents?" *Journal of Conflict Resolution* 49(2): 278–297.

Li, Quan, and Drew Schaub. 2004. "Economic Globalization and Transnational Terrorist Incidents: A Pooled Time Series Cross-Sectional Analysis." *Journal of Conflict Resolution* 48(2): 230–258.

Mickolus, Edward F., Todd Sandler, Jean M. Murdock, and Peter Fleming. 1993. *International Terrorism: Attributes of Terrorist Events*, 1988–1991 (ITERATE 4). Dunn Loring, VA: Vinyard Software.

————. 2002. "International Terrorism: Attributes of Terrorist Events (ITERATE)." Vinyard Software, codebook.

Nitsch, Volber, and Dieter Schumacher. 2004. "Terrorism and International Trade: An Empirical Investigation," *European Journal of Political Economy* 20:423–433.

Rose, Andrew. 2004. "Do We Really Know that the WTO Increases Trade?" *American Economic Review* 94(1): 98–114.

FIVE

Kto Kogo?: A Cross-country Study of the Origins and Targets of Terrorism

Alan B. Krueger and David D. Laitin

1. Introduction

Popular wisdom in the burgeoning literature on terrorism focuses on the economic motivations of terrorists. "We fight against poverty," President George W. Bush explained in Monterrey, Mexico, on March 23, 2002, "because hope is an answer to terror." Stern (2003) also draws a direct connection between poverty and terrorism. Though poverty is an attractive answer to the question of "why terrorism?", the data do not lend much support for it. Macroeconomic shifts generally fail to map on to changes in terrorist activity. For example, in the late 1990s and 2000, when terrorism reached new heights against Israeli citizens, the typical Palestinian was reporting a rosier economic forecast and unemployment was declining. Using a longer time series, Berrebi (2003) finds little correlation between economic conditions in the West Bank and Gaza Strip and the number of terrorist incidents against Israel. An even more perplexing problem for the poverty thesis arises on the microlevel. Several studies at the individual level of analysis have failed to find any direct connection between education, poverty, and the propensity to participate in terrorism (Russell and Miller 1983; Taylor 1988; Hudson 1999; Krueger and Maleckova 2003; Berrebi 2003; Atran 2003). If anything, those who participate in terrorism tend to come from the ranks of the better off in society.

Those who claim a connection between poverty and terrorism could respond that at least on the microlevel, well-to-do citizens become terrorists out of public spiritedness for their impoverished fellow citizens, and organizations choose them to perform these tasks because of their reliability and skill. Consider the anecdotal findings of Nasra Hassan (2001), for example. She interviewed 250 militants and their associates involved in the Palestinian cause from 1996 to 1999. One Hamas leader told her, "Our biggest problem is the hordes of young men who beat on our doors, clamoring to be sent [on suicide missions]. It is difficult to select only a few." And whom did they choose from these hordes? She reports that" "none of them were uneducated, desperately poor, simple minded or depressed. Many were middle class and, unless they were fugitives, held paying jobs." She also found, "two were the sons of millionaires." Thus a "Robin Hood" connection might be made linking poverty to terrorism. Individuals can become terrorists because of poverty in their country, even if they are themselves not impoverished.

Moreover, the fact that terrorist organizations actively screen and recruit members, perhaps choosing the elite from a long queue of applicants, may mask the role that individuals' personal economic circumstances play in the supply of terrorists (see Bueno de Mesquita 2003). That is, poverty may induce the poor to supply their services as terrorists, but the organizations may not select them. If this is the case, then the available microevidence, which reflects both supply *and* demand factors, may paint a misleading picture of the role of economic factors on the supply of terrorists.

Cross-national studies of terrorism have begun to address this question of whether poverty induces terrorism, allowing researchers to identify the effect of national economic conditions on terrorism, reflecting both the role of supply-side factors (i.e., determinants of who volunteers) and demand-side factors (i.e., terrorist organizations recruiting and screening participants). These studies are most relevant to the question of how the equilibrium differs under different economic conditions. A modest literature has examined the correlates of participation in terrorism at the national level, either using the country of origin of the terrorists (Krueger and Maleckova 2003) or the country where the event occurred (Piazza 2003) as the unit of observation. Both types of studies have found little correlation between economic factors, such as GDP per capita or GDP growth, and the incidence of terrorism. Similarly, Abadie (2004) examines the effect of terrorism risk from insurance ratings, including both domestic and international terrorism. He finds that a country's income per capita is unrelated to terrorism risk, while political rights have a nonmonotonic relationship with terrorism risk. Countries with a high level of political rights or authoritarian rule had the lowest risk of terrorism in his data.

Other studies provide suggestive but inconclusive results in regard to the economic foundations of terrorism. Burgoon (2006) finds that welfare spending relative to GDP is inversely related to the number of terrorist incidents occurring in a cross-section of countries and in a panel of countries over time. His model also controls for government capacity, however, which is a composite measure that largely reflects GDP per capita. Government capacity is positively related to the number of terrorist incidents. Trade open-ness is unrelated to the number of terrorist incidents. Li and Schaub (2004) estimate a similar model and control for economic development. They inter-pret their estimates as indicating that economic development discourages terrorism, but they also control for government capabilities, which has a sizable positive effect on terrorism that likely offsets their claimed nega-tive effect of economic development. Their model is also hard to interpret because they control for lagged terrorist incidents. Because most of the vari-ability in income is cross-sectional and long-lasting, controlling for lagged incidents clouds the interpretation of income on terrorist incidents.

In this chapter, we extend the previous literature by linking both the country of origin *and* the target country of the terrorist event. As Lenin often reminded those who briefed him on revolutionary affairs, the key pair of questions to ask is: "*Kto kogo?*", or "Who, to whom?" Relying on our coding of the U.S. State Department's data on international terrorism and a new dataset on suicide attacks, we look not only at the attacker but also at the target. We find that controlling for political regime, there is little economic foundation for terrorist national origins (the *kto*). Rather, the economic story for terrorism is in the characteristics of the target (the *kogo*). The data suggest that the national origins of terrorism are in countries that suffer from political oppression; the targets are countries that enjoy a measure of economic success.

2. Datasets and Description of Terrorist Events

2.1. The Dataset on International Terrorist Incidents

We rely on two distinct datasets. The first is on international terrorism. In its annual report, *Patterns of Global Terrorism*, the U.S. State Department tracks terrorist incidents. According to the State Department, 9,737 international terrorist events took place since 1981, with 1,953 of them occurring from 1997 through 2002.[1] Specific information is provided on 781 "significant" events from 1997 to 2002; the other events in that period are judged to be insignificant.[2] To qualify as "significant," an event must be judged by the U.S. Government's Incident Review Panel to result "in loss of life or serious injury to persons, abduction or kidnapping of persons, major property damage, and/or [be] an act or attempted act that could reasonably be expected to

[1] Descriptive statistics are available at their Web site: http://www.state.gov/s/ct/rls/pgtrpt/2002/html/19997.htm.
[2] There were actually 785 events, but 4 were excluded from our analysis because of missing information on the suspected origins of the perpetrators.

create the conditions noted." We have coded the 781 significant events into a dataset on the national origins and targets of terrorist attacks.

To define terrorism, the State Department reports that it relies on guidance from Title 22 of the United States Code, Section 2656f(d), which it claims defines terrorism as "premeditated, politically motivated violence perpetrated against noncombatant targets by subnational groups or clandestine agents, usually intended to influence an audience."[3] The State Department further restricts its statistical efforts toward the identification of "international terrorism," which means terrorism involving citizens or the territory of more than one country.

Yet international terrorism is a tricky concept to define. The State Department's *Global Terrorism* report recognizes some of these problems. For example, in its early years of reporting, Palestinians were defined as stateless people, and therefore their attacks on other Palestinians in the territories occupied by Israel were counted as international terrorism; but in later years, consistent with criteria for civil war violence, these events were recoded as domestic terrorism and were, therefore, retroactively deleted from the earlier annual reports.

Several additional coding problems are not acknowledged. Colombia since 1997 has had the second highest exposure to international terrorism according to the State Department data. However, some of these events appear from their description in the State Department files as tactics to control drug traffic rather than "politically motivated violence" to "influence an audience." A different problem arises with India, the country with the largest number of incidents since 1997. Ninety percent of these incidents are connected with an insurgency in Jammu and Kashmir against Indian claims to sovereignty. To code these incidents as international terrorist events implies (without full justification) that the perpetrators are from Pakistan.[4] Most are surely from Jammu and Kashmir, which the international community recognizes as India, and thus these events do not quite properly fit into a dataset on *international* terrorism. A third problem arises in West Africa. The longstanding civil wars in Sierra Leone and Liberia have spilled over borders, especially into Guinea and into Ivory Coast as well. Attacks by armed bands from one of these countries, terrorizing villagers from another, is rarely counted as international terrorism by the State Department. If they were counted as assiduously as are FARC atrocities against (white) foreigners in

---

[3] Interestingly, the code itself does not include the phrase, "usually intended to influence an audience."
[4] It is also possible (but not noted in the descriptions) that non-Indians were injured in the attacks, which would qualify them as international terrorism.

Colombia, the regional breakdown of terrorism (and perhaps UN budgets seeking its eradication) likely would be quite different.[5]

The data clearly have their limits.[6] Nevertheless, we have some reasons to be confident in our results. For one, these data correlate well with an independent data source, Todd Sandler's ITERATE dataset. The correlation between our dataset and the ITERATE dataset aggregated to the level of the country where the event took place is 0.52. The largest outlier is that the State Department codes many Indian events as international, while Sandler's dataset does not. Excluding India (which we will do as part of our robustness tests), the State Department data and Sandler's correlate at .90 at the level of the place of the attacks, and at 0.89 at the country of origin. However, our reading of the State Department vignettes and assigning a nationality to the target correlates only at .41 with Sandler's place-based data.[7] The latter correlation suggests the importance of disaggregating by target as well as national origin. Nonetheless, the general similarity of the two independently collected datasets gives some confidence in their external validity. Second, to address the questions of "*Kto, kogo?*" (and not only the question of which regions are most susceptible to terrorism), we see no obvious systematic biases in the State Department dataset and feel confident in relying on it to capture the differences between the perpetrators and targets of terrorism.

We consequently rely on the U.S. State Department dataset to analyze the "Who, whom?" of international terrorism. Specifically, for each event, we coded the country of origin of the terrorists, the name of the organization (if any) involved, the country where the event occurred, the country of the primary target, whether the event involved a suicide attack, and whether multiple perpetrators were involved.[8] Thus, at the most basic level, the unit of observation is a terrorist event, but we can aggregate the data to the country of origin level, to the country of target level, or the cross-tabulation between all potential origin and target countries. For example, the terrorist attacks of September 11, 2001, were coded as four separate events that occurred in

---

[5] For three examples of these African events – only one of which is counted as international terrorism in the U.S. Department of State dataset – see U.S. Committee for Refugees, September 13, 2000, at http://www.reliefweb.int/w/rwb.nsf/0/e59f7718ab26c29785256959006 ccc16 (downloaded October 30, 2003).

[6] Another limitation is that state-sponsored terrorism is excluded from the State Department data. Although we do not deny the existence of state-sponsored terrorism, we do not consider this a major limitation because modeling state-sponsored terrorism would require a different methodological approach than what we use in this chapter.

[7] This correlation is for a sample that excludes India. If India is included, the correlation falls to 0.23.

[8] We infer the target from the primary country of the victims. For 187 events, we also collected information on the "secondary target," defined as the country of the second largest number of victims, but we do not analyze those data here.

the United States, that were carried out mostly by Saudis, and that targeted Americans.[9] We added to the dataset several variables describing the country, such as GDP per capita, GDP growth, and measures of terrain, religious affiliation, and literacy. These variables can be attached to the dataset based on either the country of origin or target country.

Table 5.1 summarizes the State Department data, aggregated to the suspected country of origin of the perpetrators. The data are presented in order of the total number of events perpetrated by terrorists from each country. The number of events per population in the origin country is also provided. (Most events involved multiple perpetrators, but we do not take that into account in this table.) Many countries are not associated with international terrorist events in this period, and they are not shown in the table. India clearly has the largest number of events, but on a per capita basis, India is close to the mean, which is 0.26 per million people. Israel, Sierra Leone, and Angola are associated with the largest number of per capita terrorist attacks.

In 87 percent of incidents, the country where the event took place was also the suspected country of origin of the perpetrators. In only 46 percent of cases, however, were the origin and the target countries the same, and in only 52 percent of cases were the target country and the country where the event took place the same. In 44 percent of cases, the target, place, and origin were all the same. (By definition, one might think this should be zero, but the largest group affected by a terrorist attack may be the natives of the country where the attack occurred, even though a foreigner was also a victim. In addition, the State Department describes Kashmir attacks as perpetrated by Indians, taking place in India, and targeting Indians; similarly, attacks by Palestinians against Israelis are coded as originating in and targeting Israel.) Thus, perpetrators of international terrorism tend to stay local, finding targets from foreign countries close to home. Events like September 11 are the exception, not the rule; the murder of *Wall Street Journal* reporter Daniel Pearl in February 2002 perpetrated in Pakistan or the suicide attacks on foreign housing in Riyadh, Saudi Arabia, on May 13, 2003, are more typical of the terrorist incidents in our database. A focus on international terrorism, where origin and target countries are distinct, provides a valuable perspective on the who and whom of terrorism.

---

[9] We attributed three of the events to Saudi Arabia and one to the United Arab Emirates, because it is believed that fifteen of the hijackers were from Saudi Arabia, two were from the United Arab Emirates, one was from Egypt, and one from Lebanon. Attributing one of the events to people from the UAE was a judgment call that could be disputed, but we tried to adhere to a rule that assigned responsibility based on the country of origin of those directly involved in carrying out the attack. In the suicide database, the events of September 11 were coded as one attack originating from Saudi Arabia because *al Qaeda* is mainly a Saudi-run terrorist organization.

Table 5.1. *Number of Terrorist Events Originating from Each Country and Events per Million People*

Country	Events	Events/Mil	Country	Events	Events/Mil
Azerbaijan	1	0.13	Somalia	4	0.49
Belgium	1	0.10	South Africa	4	0.10
Cuba	1	0.09	Sudan	4	0.13
Germany	1	0.01	United Kingdom	4	0.68
Guinea	1	0.14	Ecuador	5	0.41
Morocco	1	0.04	Iran	5	0.08
Nicaragua	1	0.21	Italy	5	0.09
Senegal	1	0.11	Jordan	5	1.09
Thailand	1	0.02	Spain	5	0.13
Tunisia	1	0.11	Algeria	6	0.20
United Arab Emirates	1	0.37	Ethiopia	7	0.11
Zambia	1	0.10	Rwanda	7	0.86
Bahrain	2	3.11	Sri Lanka	7	0.37
Bangladesh	2	0.02	Yugoslavia	7	0.66
Chad	2	0.27	Georgia	9	1.65
Chile	2	0.13	Saudi Arabia	9	0.46
El Salvador	2	0.33	Burundi	10	1.53
France	2	0.03	Uganda	10	0.48
Kuwait	2	1.07	Greece	11	1.05
Liberia	2	0.67	Indonesia	11	0.05
Macedonia	2	0.99	Tajikistan	11	1.79
Myanmar	2	0.04	Russia	15	0.10
Peru	2	0.08	Philippines	18	0.25
Tanzania	2	0.06	Sierra Leone	21	4.35
Uzbekistan	2	0.08	Pakistan	24	0.18
Democratic Republic of Congo	3	0.06	Turkey	24	0.38
Egypt	3	0.05	Nigeria	26	0.21
Iraq	3	0.13	Israel	30	5.03
Afghanistan	4	0.16	Angola	41	3.31
Bosnia	4	1.06	Angola	41	3.31
Cambodia	4	0.35	Yemen	49	2.95
			Columbia	97	2.38

2.2. Suicide Attack Dataset

The second dataset is exclusively on suicide attacks from 1980 to 2002. A suicide attack is a tactic in which the perpetrator of the attack will die with a probability of one if the attack is a success (Berman and Laitin 2005). In this chapter, to produce a broad set of cases that qualify as suicide attacks, we merge two suicide datasets. The first is from Pape (2003, 357–60). The second is from the International Policy Institute for Counter-Terrorism (ICT) at the Interdisciplinary Center Herzliya. In the combined dataset, there are 236 recorded suicide attacks in 11 countries.[10]

As with the case of the State Department data archive on international terrorism, this dataset is not without coding issues. Consider the case of Palestinian attacks on Israelis, amounting to 42 percent of the events. Most datasets (including the State Department's) classify the perpetrators as coming from "the West Bank." However, the Palestinians are under the *de facto* control of Israel and are fighting an insurgency either to take control over all of Palestine (capture the center) or to build a Palestinian state on some portion of current-day Israel. Suicide bombing is a tactic in the pursuance of one of these goals, and the Palestinian attackers are therefore coded as having Israel as their country of origin. Israel is also the country in which these events have taken place and the target. This decision seems well justified though not unambiguous (as it is possible to view the suicide attackers coming from the incompletely sovereign Palestinian Authority).

However, unlike terrorism in general, which is often mired in ambiguities, suicide attacks are rather simple to code, without much disagreement as to whether a particular incident qualifies. Though many could debate whether FARC kidnappings of Italian businessmen or Liberian gangs shooting up Sierra Leonian villagers constitute international terror, there is no dispute that FARC and the gangs associated with Charles Taylor have not perpetrated suicide attacks.

For purposes of our "*Kto, kogo?*" questions the two datasets focus on somewhat different contexts but nonetheless complement each other. By definition, the dataset on international terrorism will have an individual or group (the "who") from one political unit attacking a target (the "whom") from another political unit. By contrast, in the suicide attack dataset nearly all (187 out of 210) events involve a perpetrator and target from the same country. In these cases, the relevant differences are in the ethnicity or religion of the attackers as compared with the targets.

2.3. Brief Description of Events

Of the 781 terrorist events and the 236 suicide attacks in the two datasets, several patterns are worth noting (see Table 5.2). First, as shown in row 1,

---

[10] This is available on the Web at: http://www.ict.org.il/. The version we use was downloaded Sept. 12, 2003. For coding rules that went into the construction of this combined dataset, see Berman and Laitin 2005.

Table 5.2. *Description of events*

	All international terrorist events	Suicide attacks
Organizations claim responsibility or suspected	74%	95%
Attacks on embassies	3.3%	2.6%
Attacks on international organizations	7%	0%
U.S. buildings or citizens as targets (direct or indirect)	14%	4.6%
Religious difference between perpetrator and principal target	57.8%	89.9%
Five most common countries of origin of perpetrators (number of events)	India (227) Colombia (97) Yemen (49) Angola (41) Israel (30)	Israel (100) Sri Lanka (75) Lebanon (30) Turkey (13) Saudi Arabia (8)

terrorism and suicide attacks are both mainly the product of organizational strategy rather than the efforts of individual zealots or lone madmen.[11] Therefore, explanations for terrorism cannot be adequate without an account of why leaders in a hierarchy would send their cadres on such missions. Organizations staff terrorist events and seek to accomplish their goals through the use of high-quality cadres, who would be more reliable to carry out the planned missions than less-skilled cadres. They are able to recruit even suicide missionaries successfully, and here the explanation is consistent with Emile Durkheim's classic study of suicide, in religious organizations and armies, that is in places where "social integration is too strong." The result is what Durkheim calls "altruistic" suicide. People prone to suicide are a constant across societies. Suicide rates vary, however, based on both a social condition of low network solidarity (anomic suicide) and one of high network solidarity (altruistic suicide). In this latter case, with socially dense networks, all too many volunteer to give up their lives for the glory of their organizations.[12]

Second, as shown in rows 2 and 3, symbolic attacks on foreign property (embassies or international organizations) are not everyday occurrences, nor

[11] See Kydd and Walter (2002), Gupta and Mundra (2003), and Berrebi and Klor (2003) for empirical and theoretical analyses of suicide bombings as strategic behavior on the part of Palestinian terrorist organizations.

[12] Emile Durkheim, [1897 (1951)], *Suicide* (New York: The Free Press), Book 2, chap. 4. See Azam (2003) for a recent attempt to model suicide bombers as being motivated by intergenerational altruism. See Wintrobe (2006) for an alternative explanation, where attackers are not altruistic but consuming solidarity.

are they rare. It is interesting to speculate as to why (at least up until 2003 in Baghdad) suicide missions had not been directed at international organizations at all while these organizations are subject to a significant number of terrorist events. We suggest that because international organizations are immensely "soft" targets, along lines suggested by Berman and Laitin (2005), it is not necessary to sacrifice the life of a cadre in order to "hit" them.

Third, as indicated on row 5, the probability that the perpetrator and target will be from different religious groups is clearly different for international terrorism than it is for suicide bombing. Taking a rough estimate of the world population for the world's four major religions (Muslim, Christian, Hindu, and Buddhist) and a single category of Other (that includes nearly all Chinese and all Jews), the probability that any two randomly selected individuals in the world (with replacement) will be from different religions is 77.2 percent. Therefore, other things being equal, international terrorism about twenty percentage points more likely to involve intrareligious parties than if it were randomly determined throughout the world.[13] By contrast – but consistent with Berman and Laitin (2005) – suicide attacks are more likely to be interreligious than would be expected from random selection of pairs from the world's population. Because suicide attacks in our dataset often involve people from the same country, arguably a better benchmark might be to compute the chance of two randomly selected people *within each* country being from different religions. In the average country in the world, 27.3 percent of any pair of people are from different religions, so suicide attacks are far more likely to involve parties from different religions than would be expected from randomness.[14] This does not mean, however, that religious differences are necessarily a motivation for suicide attacks.

Finally, as illustrated on row 6, the origin countries for terrorism and suicide attacks are different, with only Israel in the top five of both datasets. The suicide national origin countries are richer. The mean log GDP per capita for the five leading terrorist sources in 1980 was 7.56; and for the five leading suicide sources, it was 8.40.[15] An examination of the top five origin countries suggest a great amount of concentration and low level of diffusion

---

[13] The State Department dataset contains 28 suicide attacks. All of these involved religious differences between the parties. Therefore, eliminating suicide attacks would make the data show even higher rates of intrareligious killing than would be expected if it were random.

[14] Table 5.5 later also shows a different pattern for ethnolinguistic fractionalization, with lower fractionalization associated with more suicide attacks in either origin or target countries, but with such a small number of countries involved in suicide attacks, we do not emphasize this relationship.

[15] Compare this with 7.0 for the mean logged GDP per capita in 1985 dollars (lagged by one year) for all countries that had a civil war onset. See Fearon and Laitin (2003), replication dataset.

to other insurgencies of these tactics of warfare. The top five origin countries account for 57 percent of the total cases in the terrorist dataset; they account for 96 percent of the cases in the suicide dataset.

As to questions of "*Kto, kogo?*", in the international terrorism dataset, as noted earlier, in less than half of the cases (44%) are the country of origin, the place of the attack, and the citizenship of the target the same. In less than half of the events as well, the citizenship of the perpetrator and that of the target are the same.

Suicide attacks have a different profile, at least in part because the international terrorist dataset purposefully excludes domestic terrorism. For the suicide attacks, in a full 90 percent of the cases, the country of the attack, the country of the attacker, and the country of the victims are the same. The perpetrators and the targets were of the same country in 90 percent of the suicide events; the target and the country of attack were the same in 92 percent of the events; and the perpetrator performed the suicide mission in his or her own country in 95 percent of the cases.

3. Country-level Analyses

In this section, we analyze terrorism using the country of origin of the perpetrator, country of the target, or the country where the event took place as the unit of observation. This could be thought of as providing an analysis of the margins of the matrix describing the events: who, to whom, and *where*, or as Lenin might ask, *Kto? Kogo? Gde?* We defer an analysis of the joint probabilities – who, to whom – to section 4.

As an initial way to summarize the characteristics of the countries of those involved in terrorism, Table 5.3 assigns country-level attributes to each terrorist incident, and computes the average across incidents, using the country of origin, country of the primary target, or country where the event occurred to merge on the country attributes. For example, in column 2 we merged data based on the country of origin and computed the mean across incidents. This amounts to a weighted average of characteristics – such as GDP per capita, illiteracy, ethnic fractionalization, and political and civil rights – across countries, where the weights are the number of international terrorist incidents attributed to citizens of each country. Column 3 presents the same statistics excluding incidents originating in India and Colombia from the sample. Column 4 presents results based on the target country of the attack and column 5 based on the country where the attack occurred. For a point of reference, column 1 presents the weighted mean of the country attributes, using as weights the population of the country.

Table 5.3. *All events: Sample means, depending on origin, target, or place of occurrence*

Characteristic	Pop-Wtd world mean	Perpetrator origin country	Origin w/o India & Colombia	Targeted country	Country of occurrence
GDP per capita ('97–01)	5,577	2,385	3,404	10,640	3,021
Poor	0.32	0.53	0.40	0.39	0.53
Lower middle	0.37	0.18	0.30	0.08	0.16
Upper middle	0.15	0.20	0.14	0.15	0.21
Rich	0.17	0.09	0.16	0.38	0.10
GDP growth '90–00	0.46	0.16	0.03	0.25	0.17
Male illiteracy rate	0.17	0.22	0.20	0.16	0.22
Female illiteracy rate	0.30	0.38	0.35	0.27	0.38
Total illiteracy rate	0.23	0.29	0.25	0.21	0.29
Infant mortality (/1000)	43.99	61.57	65.59	40.94	61.54
Population (mil.)	481	315	43	378	321
Freedom House low civil rights	4.34	4.37	4.88	3.12	4.18
Freedom House low political rights	4.04	3.64	4.49	2.25	3.45
Freedom House Index	2.06	2.02	2.28	1.49	1.93
Democ. Index (-10 to $+10$)	2.16	3.94	0.73	7.48	4.35
Instability dummy	0.07	0.13	0.23	0.06	0.12
Anocracy	0.13	0.28	0.49	0.11	0.28
Ethnic/linguistic fractionalization	0.46	0.62	0.49	0.57	0.63
Ethnic fractionalization	76.79	63.93	60.51	71.93	65.20
Religious fractionalization	0.29	0.33	0.38	0.36	0.35
Proportion Muslim	0.22	0.32	0.48	0.16	0.29
Proportion Christian	0.30	0.31	0.33	0.43	0.35
Proportion Buddhist	0.07	0.01	0.03	0.02	0.02
Proportion Hindu	0.15	0.24	0.00	0.27	0.24
Oil exporter (>1/3 exp rev)	0.09	0.20	0.35	0.08	0.20
Pct. mountainous terrain	21.95	22.86	24.80	18.29	21.64
Max. sample size	159	781	457	709	769

To more easily spot the discrepancies between terrorists and the world population, Figure 5.1 presents a "radar chart" depicting the ratio of the mean of the indicated variable for terrorists based on their country of origin and the weighted-average person in the world. Figure 5.2 presents the analogous ratio of the target country to the weighted-average world population. If the terrorists come from countries that are on average no different than the world population, the ratio would be one and the points would lie on the unit circle in Figure 5.1. If the country characteristics differ between

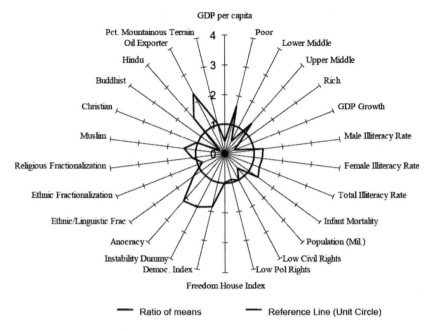

Figure 5.1. Radar plot for origin countries of terrorist relative to all countries.

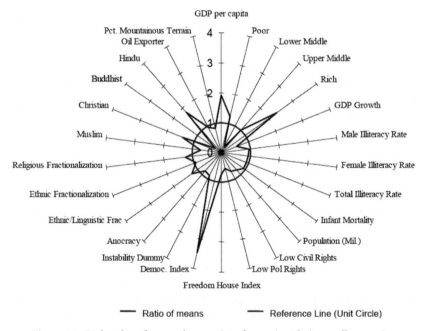

Figure 5.2. Radar plot of targeted countries of terrorist relative to all countries.

the terrorists' home and the world population, then the ratio will exceed one or be less than one. These radar plots are just meant to be descriptive: they clearly have analytical problems. For example, for some variables a ratio of 1.2 may indicate a more significant divergence than a ratio of 2.4 for other variables. More importantly, the charts and table break down the population on an endogenous variable – by conditioning on whether the individual was a terrorist, rather than on the country characteristic – so in a real sense these charts are equivalent to sampling on the dependent variable. Nevertheless, they still provide a vivid description of how terrorists differ from the world population, or of how the targets of terrorism differ from the world population, in terms of country-level characteristics.

Compared with the world population, the results indicate that terrorists are more likely to come from low-income countries with low GDP growth (from 1990 to 2000). The pattern is not monotonic in terms of income, however, as terrorists are overrepresented among the poorest quartile of countries and the third quartile of countries.[16] The terrorists are also more likely to come from countries characterized by anocracy and political instability.[17] Insofar as targets are concerned, the targeted individuals tend to live in wealthier countries that are more stable, less anocratic, and more democratic than the average person in the world. As for country of occurrence, it is a profile far closer to that of the perpetrator's country – poor, high illiteracy, and high infant mortality. In many cases (Kashmir and Jammu, Bosnia, Kosovo, West Bank and Gaza, and Afghanistan), the attacks occur against armies or army installations of what are perceived to be foreign or "occupying" powers. When in future work the attacks against American installations in Iraq starting in 2003 are analyzed, this pattern will be reinforced.

Table 5.4 and Figures 5.3 and 5.4 present the same information using data on suicide attacks. (Recall that the suicide attacks span a longer time period. Nevertheless, for comparison we have attached the same country characteristics used in Table 5.3.)[18] The figures for perpetrators and targets look remarkably similar because the target of most of the suicide attacks

[16] The quartile GDP per capita cutoffs were not weighted by population.
[17] Based on the coding of Fearon and Laitin (2003), using the Polity IV dataset, instability is a dummy variable that takes a value of one if the country had a three-or-greater change on the regime index in any of the three years prior to the country-year in question. Anocracy is another dummy variable that takes a value of one if the regime index for that year is between a −5 and a +5, on an index that spans from −10 (full autocracy) to +10 (full democracy).
[18] The dataset spans the period from 1980 to 2002, with the most recent suicide attack on November 22, 2002.

Table 5.4. *Suicide attacks: Sample means, depending on origin, target, or place of occurrence*

Characteristic	Pop-Wtd world mean	Perpetrator's origin countries	Targeted countries	Country of occurrence
GDP per capita ('97–01)	5,577	13,116	13,544	13,204
Poor	0.32	0.00	0.03	0.04
Lower middle	0.37	0.14	0.12	0.12
Upper middle	0.15	0.07	0.07	0.07
Rich	0.17	0.79	0.79	0.77
GDP growth '90–00	0.46	0.26	0.26	0.27
Male illiteracy rate	0.17	0.05	0.05	0.06
Female illiteracy rate	0.30	0.11	0.12	0.13
Total illiteracy rate	0.23	0.08	0.08	0.09
Infant mortality (/1000)	43.99	9.97	11.79	13.09
Population (mil.)	481	25	43	44
Freedom House low civil rights	4.34	3.44	3.29	3.34
Freedom House low political rights	4.04	1.78	1.59	1.65
Freedom House Index	2.06	1.31	1.24	1.27
Democ. index (−10 to +10)	2.16	7.36	7.92	7.89
Instability dummy	0.07	0.00	0.01	0.01
Anocracy	0.13	0.15	0.14	0.14
Ethnic/linguistic fractionalization	0.46	0.30	0.32	0.32
Ethnic fractionalization	76.79	43.84	41.65	41.83
Religious fractionalization	0.29	0.32	0.34	0.34
Proportion Muslim	0.22	0.21	0.19	0.21
Proportion Christian	0.30	0.04	0.05	0.05
Proportion Buddhist	0.07	0.09	0.07	0.07
Proportion Hindu	0.15	0.02	0.03	0.03
Oil exporter (>1/3 exp rev)	0.09	0.06	0.02	0.03
Pct. mountainous terrain	21.95	6.43	6.51	7.53
Max. sample size	159	107	107	107

resided in the same country as the perpetrator. The suicide attacks tend to involve (both as targets and origins) people from wealthier countries than the world average. In addition, people from stable, democratic countries are more likely to be represented in suicide attacks, either as target or perpetrator, than the average person in the world. Notice also that because Sri Lanka is primarily a Buddhist country, Buddhism is overrepresented among both the country of perpetrators and targets.

Table 5.5 summarizes the data in a more conventional way, broken down by country characteristics rather than the outcome variable. Specifically, using origin or target countries as the unit of analysis, we computed the average number of terrorists per person (in either the origin country or target

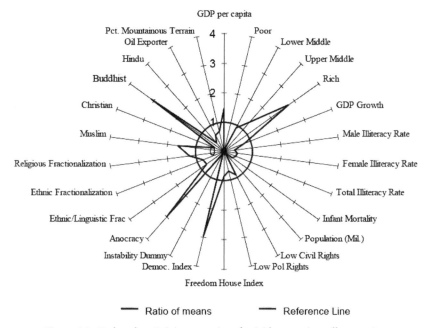

Figure 5.3. Radar plot: Origin countries of suicide terrorists, all countries.

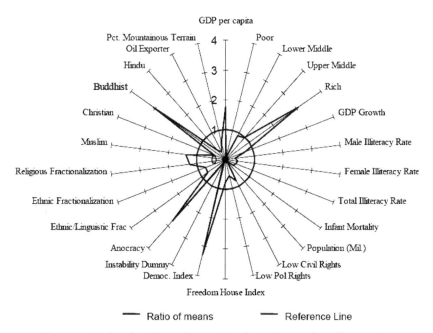

Figure 5.4. Radar plot: Targeted countries of suicide terrorists, all countries.

Table 5.5. *Terrorist attacks per million population (origin or target country) by country characteristics*

Country characteristic	All events		Suicide attacks	
	Origin	Target	Origin	Target
GDP per capita				
Quartile 1	0.37	0.11	0.00	0.00
Quartile 2	0.18	0.07	0.10	0.10
Quartile 3	0.17	0.30	0.19	0.11
Quartile 4	0.34	0.47	0.35	0.38
	[p = 0.45]	[p = 0.00]	[p = 0.01]	[p = 0.01]
GDP growth				
< Median	0.31	0.12	0.01	0.00
> Median	0.23	0.30	0.27	0.24
	[p = 0.44]	[p = 0.01]	[p = 0.01]	[p = 0.00]
Illiteracy rate				
< Median	0.27	0.26	0.22	0.23
> Median	0.18	0.19	0.11	0.07
	[p = 0.40]	[p = 0.01]	[p = 0.61]	[p = 0.26]
Civil liberties				
Low	0.42	0.19	0.12	0.07
Medium	0.27	0.38	0.31	0.33
High	0.02	0.12	0.00	0.00
	[p = 0.00]	[p = 0.00]	[p = 0.77]	[p = 0.00]
Political rights				
Low	0.39	0.11	0.11	0.07
Medium	0.30	0.14	0.14	0.14
High	0.13	0.38	0.19	0.20
	[p = 0.04]	[p = 0.00]	[p = 0.95]	[p = 0.65]
Political stability				
Stable	0.23	0.22	0.18	0.16
Instable	0.48	0.16	0.00	0.00
	[p = 0.15]	[p = 0.48]	[p = 0.03]	[p = 0.02]
Polity 2				
Totalitarian	0.22	0.04	0.01	0.02
Anocracy	0.50	0.14	0.10	0.10
Democracy	0.16	0.33	0.15	0.16
	[p = 0.03]	[p = 0.00]	[p = 0.35]	[p = 0.25]
Predominant religion				
Muslim	0.44	0.14	0.18	0.11
Christian	0.21	0.28	0.00	0.00
Buddhist	0.09	0.05	0.44	0.44

Country characteristic	All events		Suicide attacks	
	Origin	Target	Origin	Target
Hindu	0.06	0.06	0.00	0.00
Mixed/Other	0.31	0.32	0.61	0.65
	[p = 0.26]	[p = 0.01]	[p = 0.00]	[p = 0.00]
Mountainous terrain				
< Median	0.27	0.19	0.23	0.25
> Median	0.35	0.29	0.12	0.06
	[p = 0.41]	[p = 0.60]	[p = 0.61]	[p = 0.18]
Ethnolinguistic fractionalization				
< Median	0.22	0.21	0.30	0.26
> Median	0.31	0.23	0.00	0.01
	[p = 0.47]	[p = 0.52]	[p = 0.00]	[p = 0.00]
Religious fractionalization				
< Median	0.23	0.23	0.17	0.17
> Median	0.31	0.23	0.15	0.12
	[p = 0.52]	[p = 0.84]	[p = 0.96]	[p = 0.72]

Note: Sample sizes range from 135 to 159 depending on characteristic.
The brackets report the p-value for a chi-square test of the hypothesis that the groups have equal effects from a Negative Binomial regression of the number of events on indicators for the specified groups and log population, constraining the coefficient on population to equal 1.

country) by the indicated country characteristic. In addition, we report the p-value from a chi-square test of the null hypothesis that the characteristics are unrelated to participation in terrorism.[19] These results differ from the results underlying the radar charts in two important respects: first, it conditions on the explanatory variable; second, the unit of observation is a country, rather than a person.

The results often give a different picture than the radar charts. Consider results for all international terrorist events by country of origin. A country's GDP per capita is unrelated to the number of terrorists originating from that country. A country's degree of civil liberties, by contrast, is

---

[19] These tests require a word of explanation. Because the modal country has zero events, a conventional test of the equivalence of the means is inappropriate. Consequently, we computed each test by estimating a separate Negative Binomial regression, where the dependent variable was the number of incidents attributable to each country and the independent variables were dummies for the indicated categories and log population, constraining the coefficient on log population to equal one. Because the dependent variable in the Negative Binomial should be interpreted as the log of the number of events, these results do not correspond directly to the means reported in the table, but they do provide a valid test of the statistical significance of the characteristics.

associated with participation in terrorism: countries with a lower level of civil liberties have a higher participation rate in terrorism, on average. Thus, in contrast to the radar plots, low civil liberties are associated with greater participation in terrorism while economic factors are unrelated. If one is looking for country characteristics that are causal determinants of terrorism, we think the Table 5.5 results are more relevant, although it is of course possible that the associations revealed in the table do not represent causal relationships.

When the results are tabulated by the target country's characteristics, a different picture emerges. In column 2, we see that countries with higher GDP per capita are more likely to be the target of terrorism (on a per capita basis), and civil liberties in the target country do not bear a monotonic relationship with terrorism. In terms of political rights, the contrast is even greater: countries that afford a low level of political rights are more likely to be the springboards of terrorism and less likely to be the targets of terrorism. A country's terrain, ethnolinguistic fractionalization, religious fractionalization, and political stability are all unrelated to the incidence of terrorism per capita, either as a target or origin.

The right-hand section of Table 5.5 presents corresponding results for suicide attacks. Because suicide attacks originated in only 10 countries and targeted only 14 countries – in a sample of 159 countries – these results should be taken with a large grain of salt, and the results by origin and target hardly differ.[20] Nevertheless, the results provide a formal comparison of what is often compared informally. These results clearly indicate that wealthy countries are involved in suicide attacks, as either origins or targets. It is noteworthy that there are no countries involved in suicide attacks that are in the bottom quartile of countries for GDP per capita. This is powerful evidence that (as argued by Berman and Laitin 2005) suicide attacks have different sources than civil war onsets, which, as Fearon and Laitin (2003) show, are more common in countries with lower GDP per capita. By contrast, the origins of terrorism are more randomly distributed across the quartiles of GDP per capita. This suggests that terrorism as well differs from civil war insurgency, though less so than suicide attacks. Countries that are not likely targets of insurgencies (e.g., high-income countries) are likely targets of terrorism, however. The right side of Table 5.5 shows as well that fast-growing, stable countries are more likely to be the origin and target of suicide attacks.

---

[20] In addition, the chi-square tests in some instances are very sensitive. For example, the differences by civil liberties are very similar for origin and target countries, yet the chi-square tests are very different.

The influence of Sri Lanka, a majority Buddhist country, is again evidence on the results by religion. Similarly the influence of Israel, a majority Jewish country (classified here in Mixed/Other), has a high proportion of both origin and target. But as with Sri Lanka, the perpetrators are not of the same religion as the majority in the country. Religious fractionalization in a country, however, is unrelated to the incidence of suicide attacks, although, as noted, a high proportion of the suicide attacks involve perpetrators and victims from different religions.

Regression Models

We extended the bivariate comparisons in Table 5.5 by estimating a series of Negative Binomial regression models, simultaneously controlling for several possible determinants of terrorism. A sampling of our results is reported in Table 5.6. The dependent variable is the number of international terrorist events traceable to each country. The unit of observation is the country of origin in columns 1–2, the target country in columns 3–4, and the country where the event took place in columns 5–6. The explanatory variables in the first model are just log GDP per capita and log population; in the second model, we also include per capita GDP growth, the Freedom House Index of Civil Liberties, and the percent of the population belonging to each of the world's four largest religions. The explanatory variables correspond to the country that defines the unit of observation. We selected the variables shown in the table because, for the most part, other variables that we included in the model were insignificant or because there is particular interest in the relationship between these variables and terrorism. (We did not estimate corresponding models for suicide attacks because so few countries were involved in these attacks.)

The results have no surprises compared to the bivariate comparisons in Table 5.5. Quite sensibly, larger countries (in terms of population) are associated with more terrorism, at the origin, target, and place unit of analysis. At either the origin or place-of-occurrence levels, GDP per capita is insignificantly related to terrorism, but it is positively related to terrorism at the target-country level. A paucity of civil liberties, by contrast, is associated with more terrorism at the origin country and at the country where the event is perpetrated but not at the target-country level. In this sense, the results suggest that the genesis of terrorism involves political factors though the targets are more economic in nature. The disparate findings based on country of origin and target country illustrate the importance of aggregating separately by origin and target.

Table 5.6. *Negative binomial regressions with country-level data (Unit of observation is country of origin of terrorists, prime target of terrorists, or country where event occurred)*

Explanatory variable	Terrorist origin country		Prime target country		Country where occurred	
	(1)	(2)	(3)	(4)	(5)	(6)
Intercept	−9.65	−19.39	−14.21	−15.18	−8.28	−13.03
	(2.83)	(3.72)	(1.61)	(2.17)	(2.27)	(3.01)
Log Population	0.74*	0.94*	0.76*	0.73*	0.64*	0.70*
	(0.16)	(0.17)	(0.09)	(0.10)	(0.12)	(0.14)
Log GDP per capita	−0.17	0.23	0.33*	0.44*	−0.13	0.12
	(0.12)	(0.20)	0.08	(0.14)	(0.11)	(0.19)
GDP growth	–	−0.42	–	−0.24	–	−0.05
		(0.72)		(0.61)		0.68
Civil Liberties Index	–	0.80*	–	0.18	–	0.50*
[1 to 7 (low civil lib)]		(0.27)		(0.17)		(0.25)
Proportion Muslim	–	−0.35	–	−0.51	–	−0.52
		(0.76)		(0.52)		(0.70)
Proportion Buddhist	–	−1.25	–	−1.17	–	1.42
		(1.16)		(0.85)		(1.02)
Proportion Hindu	–	0.32	–	1.28	–	0.25
		(1.59)		(1.03)		(1.36)
Proportion Other	–	1.52	–	0.89	–	0.87
		(0.91)		(0.70)		(0.90)
P-value for 3 religions jointly equal 0	–	0.76	–	0.25	–	0.55
Pseudo-R-Square	0.05	0.09	0.13	0.13	0.05	0.07
Sample size	150	138	150	138	150	138

Note: Standard errors in parentheses. Dependent variable: Number of international terrorist events associated with each country, 1997–2002.

We cannot reject that the shares affiliated with the various religions jointly have no effect on terrorism at any of the levels of analyses. No religion appears to have a monopoly on terrorism; countries with very different religious faiths have all experienced terrorism, as targets, origins, and hosts.

An econometric issue of relevance for the estimates in Table 5.5 is whether the Negative Binomial specification is appropriate. In particular, with so many countries having a value of zero for the number of terrorist attacks (either in the origin or target equation), one could wonder whether the Negative Binomial specification fits the data well. An alternative specification is the zero-inflated negative binomial model, which allows for a different process to determine countries with a zero value of the dependent variable. Indeed, a Vuong test of the Negative Binomial versus the more general

zero-inflated negative binomial model raises questions about the specification: the p-value for the test is 0.13 in column 1 and .002 in column 2.
It is reassuring, however, that if we dichotomize the dependent variable by
setting it equal to one if the country was an origin of international terrorism and zero if not, and then estimate a logit model, our main conclusions regarding income and income growth are unaffected. In particular, if
we estimate such a model using the explanatory variables in column 2 of
Table 5.5, both GDP per capita and GDP growth have statistically insignificant and small effects. The civil liberties variable, however, is also statistically
insignificant in this logit specification.

4. *Kto, Kogo?* Characteristics of Origins and Targets

Our last set of analyses involves the matrix of who to whom: that is, we model
the cross-tabulation of the origins and targets of terrorism. Each country
is a potential origin country for perpetrators who can attack any country
in the world. Because we have a maximum of 159 countries in our sample,
and, without further structure, the full *Kto, kogo?* analysis would involve a
matrix with $159 \times 159 = 25,122$ cells, most of which would be empty, we
need to simplify the analysis. Here we focus on two important dimensions
of origin and target countries: their income and civil liberties.

First consider income. We divided the countries into income quartiles
based on GDP per capita. Specifically, we assigned all possible country pairs
to cells based on their GDP per capita as potential targets and potential
origins. Thus, instead of a 159×159 matrix, our data are reduced to a
4×4 matrix. In each cell, we tallied the number of incidents perpetrated
by people from a country in one income bracket against people from a
country of another income bracket. For every entry, we normalized the
counts by dividing by the geometric mean of the *total* population across
countries in the two income brackets. Note that this differs subtly from our
analysis in Table 5.5 and 5.6, where we weighted countries equally; here we
weight countries by a combination of their size and their potential target's
size. Conceptually, this formulation makes sense if the characteristics of the
countries (in this case, income) are relevant, but the borders are not relevant.
Mathematically, an entry in Table 5.7, P_{ij}, is given by:

$$P_{ij} = C_{ij}/(N_i * N_j)^{.5}$$

where C_{ij} is the number of incidents perpetrated by people from countries
with an income level falling in quartile "i" against people in countries with
income levels falling in quartile "j," and N_i and N_j represent the aggregate

Table 5.7. *Target country's GDP per capita quartile*

Origin country GDP quartile	1	2	3	4
1	0.145	0.001	0.008	0.062
2	0.003	0.022	0.015	0.029
3	0.003	0.001	0.084	0.088
4	0.002	0.002	0.002	0.065

Note: Entries are number incidents of international terrorism for the cell divided by the geometric mean of population (in millions) in the origin and target country quartiles.

number of people (in millions) in the origin and target quartiles, respectively.[21]

Table 5.8 provides the analogous matrix where the countries were cross-categorized into 3×3 cells based on their civil liberties index. That is, i refers to the civil liberties of the originating countries (low, medium, and high) and j refers to the civil liberties available in the target countries (low, medium, and high). Again, we pool all countries that fall in the same civil liberties category and normalize by the geometric mean of the total population in each category.

Despite the (somewhat) different weighting and the added feature of cross-classification, the results are similar to what we observed from Table 5.6. Terrorists from most countries are particularly likely to strike at others in countries with about the same income level, because a large number of the attacks target individuals in the country of origin. For this reason, the diagonals of Figure 5.7 have large entries. But terrorists who do not strike against targets in their own income brackets are much more likely to strike against targets from the highest-income countries than from low-income countries. Indeed, for terrorists from countries in the middle-income quartiles, targets in the highest-income quartile are more likely to be affected by their terrorist acts than are targets from countries in their own income quartile.

Although one might be tempted to interpret the evidence in Table 5.7 as supporting a relative-income hypothesis – that is, terrorists target countries that are richer than their country of origin – two considerations support more of an absolute-income hypothesis, with the wealthy countries more

---

[21] A reason for the multiplicative formulation of population is that if terrorism were just random – i.e., Brownian motion, ignoring distance – then the number of events involving peoples from quartiles i and j would be proportional to the product of their populations.

Table 5.8. *Target country civil liberties*

Origin country	Low	Medium	High
Low	0.036	0.018	0.073
Medium	0.004	0.154	0.060
High	0.001	0.001	0.021

Note: Entries are number of incidents of international terrorism for the cell divided by the geometric mean of population (in millions) in the origin and target country civil liberties categories.

likely to be targets *regardless* of the income in the country of origin of the terrorists. First, in Table 5.6, origin country GDP per capita is insignificant while target country GDP per capita is highly statistically significant. Second, Table 5.7 indicates that countries in the highest income quartile are more likely to be targets than are countries in the moderate income quartiles for events that terrorists from the lowest and second lowest quartile countries instigate. If all that mattered were relative income, we would expect the intervening income quartiles to be more frequent targets for events carried out by people from the bottom half of countries in terms of income.

Lastly, Table 5.8 shows that countries with a high degree of civil liberties are unlikely to be origin countries for terrorist acts. The lower- and (especially) middle-level countries in terms of civil liberties are more likely to be origin countries for terrorism. Compared with Table 5.5, the increase in source countries from those with a middle level of civil liberties is a result of the new aggregation (by countries within a civil liberties category) and the different scaling. Interestingly, countries with a high level of civil liberties appear to be somewhat more likely a target in these tabulations.

5. Conclusion

Nearly six months after he articulated a naïve economic explanation for terrorism and on the first anniversary of the al Qaeda attacks on American soil, President Bush provided a more nuanced view, closer to what the data reported in this chapter show. He wrote the following in *The New York Times* (Op-Ed, September 11, 2002): "Poverty does not transform poor people into terrorists and murderers. Yet poverty, corruption and repression are a toxic combination in many societies, leading to weak governments that are unable to enforce order or patrol their borders and are vulnerable to terrorist networks and drug cartels."

The most salient patterns in the data on global terrorism that we presented suggest that, at the country level, the sources of international terrorism have more to do with repression than with poverty. The regression analysis showed that neither country GDP nor illiteracy is a good predictor of terrorist national origins. Past work suggests that at the individual level, higher economic and social status lead to greater identification with terrorist goals. Therefore, the well-to-do represent a fount of supply. On the demand side, organizations (especially for attacks that require planning and coordination, with low chances for defection) will want to recruit disciplined cadres who will more likely succeed. Thus terrorist perpetrators are not necessarily poor. But those who are repressed politically tend to terrorize the rich, giving international terrorist events the feel of economic warfare.

Suicide attacks reveal much less on the interstate level. To be sure, in ten of the twenty-three cases where the targets were of a different country than the perpetrators, the targets were Americans, suggesting that when they do go international, suicide attackers go after the rich and the powerful. (India is the only target country suffering from an international suicide attack with a GDP per capita lower than the median, and this was a direct assault on its prime minister.) To the extent that we can eke out patterns from the marginals (where perpetrator and target are different) in the suicide dataset, we see as with international terrorism, the national origins are more likely to be in countries that deny civil liberties as compared with targets.

Several extensions of this research merit consideration. First, we need to dock the suicide data with that of international terrorism to have a general terrorism dataset. We then can construct a 150 × 150 matrix by country of origin and target, yielding a much more precise picture of who terrorizes whom. One can as well to link our findings with systematic data on countries that sponsor and/or harbor terrorist organizations. Finally, we have noted a relationship of political "occupation" and being a target for terrorist attacks. This relationship merits further scrutiny.

To sum up, our data analysis up until now confirms the lesson that President Bush has already learned, namely that the economic foundations of terrorism are at best only indirect. More specifically, we have shown that on the margin, the *kto* are those who are politically repressed, and the *kogo* are those who are wealthy. The *kto* is political; the *kogo* economic.

References

Abadie, Alberto. 2004. "Poverty, Political Freedom, and the Roots of Terrorism." National Bureau of Economic Research Working Paper 10859, Cambridge, MA.

Atran, Scott. 2003. "Genesis of Suicide Terrorism." *Science* 299: 1534–1539.

Azam, Jean-Paul. 2003. "Suicide-Bombing as Inter-Generational Investment." *Public Choice* 122(1): 177–198 (January).

Berman, Eli, and David D. Laitin. 2005. "Hard Targets: Theory and Evidence on Suicide Attacks." National Bureau of Economic Research Working Paper 11740, Cambridge, MA.

Berrebi, Claude. 2003. "Evidence About the Link Between Education, Poverty and Terrorism Among Palestinians." Princeton University Industrial Relations Section Working Paper No. 477 (September).

Berrebi, Claude, and Esteban Klor. 2003. "On Terrorism and Electoral Outcomes: Theory and Evidence from the Israeli-Palestinian Conflict," mimeo., Princeton University.

Bueno de Mesquita, Ethan. 2003. "The Quality of Terror," mimeo., Dept. of Political Science, Washington University, St. Louis, MO.

Burgoon, Brian. 2006. "On Welfare and Terror: Social Welfare Policies and Political-Economic Roots of Terrorism." *Journal of Conflict Resolution* 50(4): 176–203.

Bush, George, W. 2002. "Remarks by the President at United Nations Financing for Development Conference," Cintermex Convention Center, Monterrey, Mexico. March 22. http://www.whitehouse.gov/news/releases/2002/03/20020322-1.html.

Fearon, James, and David Laitin. 2003. "Ethnicity, Insurgency, and Civil War." *American Political Science Review* 97(1): 75–90.

Gupta, Dipak, and Kusum Mudra. 2005. "Suicide Bombing as a Strategic Instrument of Protest: An Empirical Investigation." *Terrorism and Political Violence* 17(4): 573–598.

Hassan, Nasra. 2001. "An Arsenal of Believers." *The New Yorker* (November 19): 36–41.

Hudson, Rex A. 1999. "The Sociology and Psychology of Terrorism: Who Becomes a Terrorist and Why?" Report prepared under Interagency Agreement by the Federal Research Division, Library of Congress, Washington, DC.

Krueger, Alan, and Jitka Maleckova. 2003. "Education, Poverty, and Terrorism: Is There a Causal Connection?" *Journal of Economic Perspectives* 17(4): 119–144 (Fall).

Kydd, Andrew, and Barbara Walter. 2002. "Sabotaging the Peace: The Politics of Extremist Violence." *International Organization* 56(2): 263–96.

Li, Quan, and Drew Schaub. 2004. "Economic Globalization and Transnational Terrorism: A Pooled Time-Series Analysis." *Journal of Conflict Resolution*, 48(4): 230–258.

Pape, Robert A. 2003. "The Strategic Logic of Suicide Terrorism." *American Political Science Review* 97(3): 343–61.

Piazza, James A. 2003. "Rooted in Poverty?: Terrorism, Poor Economic Development and Social Change," mimeo., Meredith College, Raleigh, North Carolina.

Russell, Charles, and Bowman Miller. 1983. "Profile of a Terrorist," reprinted in *Perspectives on Terrorism*, 45–60. Wilmington, DE: Scholarly Resources Inc.

Stern, Jessica. 2003. *Terror in the Name of God: Why Religious Militants Kill.* New York: Ecco-HarperCollins.

Taylor, Maxwell. 1988. *The Terrorist.* London: Brassey's Defence Publishers.

Wintrobe, Ronald. 2006. *Rational Extremism.* Cambridge: Cambridge University Press.

SIX

Terrorism and Civil War

Nicholas Sambanis

1. Introduction

Terrorism is an elusive concept. It is a violent strategy that can take place during wartime or peacetime. Terrorism is also thought of as a distinct form of violence with different causes than other forms of violence such as insurgencies or civil wars. In this chapter, I consider what linkages, if any, connect terrorism to civil war. If we consider terrorism as a strategy – a means to an end – then the links are obvious: civil wars create opportune environments for terror and terrorists. Indeed, as we shall see later, most terrorist events tend to take place in countries affected by civil war. I accept the identification of terror as a strategy, but I also consider whether near-exclusive use of this violent strategy constitutes a distinct *form* of violence, with separate causes than other forms. If so, then we can probe further to uncover differences and similarities between terrorism and civil war.

A way to approach the linkages between terrorism and civil war is to consider the conditions under which terrorism will lead to civil war and vice versa and to compare situations where terrorism takes place outside of the context of civil war to cases where there is civil war with or without terrorism. I provide such a comparison to illuminate the linkages between domestic terrorism and civil war. Both international and domestic terrorism can grow out of civil war or lead to it, but such a conflict transformation is more likely when terrorism is domestic. Domestic terrorism, like civil war, is "homegrown and home directed ... the perpetrators, victims, and audience are all from the host country."[1] I argue that there are important differences between the two phenomena and terrorism usually cannot evolve into civil war. But in some cases, the comparison breaks down: this is when terrorism

[1] Rosendorff and Sandler (2005, 172).

is in effect a proto-civil war and terrorist violence is a strategy used in the first stages of an insurgency.

The main goal of this chapter is to provide a conceptual discussion of differences and similarities between terrorism and civil war. Part of this discussion is informed by simple empirical tests that are merely suggestive rather than conclusive. The empirical analysis is also constrained by the practical difficulties of measuring terrorism and civil war accurately and cleanly separating domestic from international terrorism. I discuss limitations with the data before presenting the empirical analysis. I also propose a typology of political violence that distinguishes terrorism from civil war on the basis of differences in the set of attributes of violent events that we would classify as terrorism as opposed to civil war. The typology will be analytically useful if it identifies causally different, coherent forms of violence. To see if terrorism and civil war have causal coherence, I review some of the relevant literature and provide simple cross-national empirical comparisons of the characteristics of countries that are affected by those two forms of violence. Differences in the "structural" characteristics underlying terrorism and civil war would be consistent with a conceptual distinction of these two phenomena. My argument is that there is a form of violence that is typically associated with the strategy that we define as "terrorism" and that while civil wars can easily generate conditions that favor terrorism, the transition from terrorism to civil war is difficult. Groups using terrorism will usually be unable to transform the conflicts that they are engaged in into a civil war. In the conclusion, I consider the policy implications of this argument.

2. Definitions and Measurement

Civil war is usually defined as an armed conflict between the government of a sovereign state and domestic, politically organized groups that can mount effective resistance and engage the state in relatively continuous fighting that causes more than 1,000 deaths over a specified period.[2] Though there are variations of this basic definition, all definitions of civil war use some threshold of violence to distinguish civil war from lower-level internal armed conflict.

By contrast, the level of violence is not a defining feature of terrorism. Standard definitions of terrorism focus squarely on the purpose of

---

[2] See Sambanis (2004a) for a discussion and a more detailed version of this definition and for a list of civil wars from 1945 to 1999.

violence rather than on its magnitude.[3] A widely used definition is the State Department's, which defines terrorism as "premeditated, politically motivated violence perpetrated against noncombatant targets by subnational groups or clandestine agents, usually intended to influence an audience" (Krueger and Malecková 2003). Todd Sandler (2003, 780) defines terrorism as "the premeditated use, or threat of use, of extra-normal violence or brutality to gain a political objective through intimidation or fear of a targeted audience." Sandler's definition reflects a shared understanding of the concept of terrorism among scholars, so I use his definition as my reference point.[4]

Tilly (2004) tells us that the word "terror" entered the Western political vocabulary to characterize French revolutionaries' actions against their enemies in 1793–1794. Though terrorism originally referred to state violence, most modern definitions focus on nonstate violence (though Sandler's definition can accommodate both state and nonstate violence). Tilly (2004, 8) also reminds us that a useful definition should point to a "detectable" phenomenon with "some degree of causal coherence." But is terrorism a causally coherent social phenomenon? Government armies, militias, self-determination movements, ideological extremists, and a host of other actors can use terrorism to achieve political goals. Thus, if terrorism is conceptualized as a strategy that can be used by any actor in any number of contexts, then it becomes hard to find a coherent set of causes for it (Tilly 2004, 5–13).[5]

In light of this, to compare terrorism with civil war we must conceptualize terrorism as a distinct form of violence and not just as a strategy that can take place in the context of any other form of violence. The question then becomes under what conditions are we likely to see terrorism outside of the context of civil war?

To answer this question, we must first properly classify violent events into different forms. Yet, when we look at an event of political violence, it is often difficult to classify it as terrorism, civil war, or some other form without relying on *ad hoc* coding criteria. In the case of civil war, though

---

[3] Civil war definitions also require that the challengers have political goals (such as secession or capture of the political center) and large-scale political violence that does not involve the state is excluded. But the key distinction between civil war and other reciprocal political violence is the higher death threshold.

[4] The similarities between Sandler's definition and the State Department definition are also clear.

[5] On the same point, Walter Laqueur (2003, 22) writes, "Many terrorisms exist.... The endeavor to find a 'general theory' of terrorism, one overall explanation of its roots, is a futile and misguided enterprise."

there may exist a core set of "ideal" cases that everyone would consider as civil wars, too many cases are sufficiently ambiguous to tell when civil war starts and other violence ends. For example, does a coup that kills several hundred government agents and is immediately followed by widespread reprisals by the government constitute a civil war? Or should we think of these as two distinct events – a coup and politicide – that follow each other in close sequence? Does a genocide that kills thousands become a civil war if the targeted group is able to kill a couple of hundred agents of the state? Or is that an example of state terror? And what of conflicts in which both the state and its challengers use violence to terrorize each other's civilian support base? Should such "mutual terrorism" be considered a civil war? These questions point to conceptual ambiguity surrounding all forms of political violence. In addition, practical coding problems make matters worse.

A comparison of different lists of civil wars reveals extensive disagreement over when civil wars start or end or which internal armed conflicts should be classified as civil wars (Sambanis 2004a). The same violent event may be classified as terrorism in one database and civil war in another: if a civil war starts "slow" with a small band of guerillas targeting police, military, and civilian targets that are allied with the regime, it could be classified as terrorism in one dataset and civil war in another.[6] Regimes will often describe guerilla insurgencies as terrorism or banditry so as to downplay the extent of political opposition they face. But we usually think of terrorism as violence that falls "outside the forms of political struggle routinely operating within some current regime" (Tilly 2004). It follows that when regimes are in the midst of a civil war or at risk of state failure, violence will be used routinely. In such situations, we cannot easily distinguish terrorism from "routine" political violence, so reporting bias or coding confusion is likely to be widespread.[7] Thus, if what we want is to explain terrorism as a distinct phenomenon, we must exclude cases with civil war.

A second problem is that distinguishing domestic from transnational terrorism is often hard in practice. In some cases, the perpetrators are unknown; in others, violence targets domestic and international targets (civilians)

---

[6] Even large wars, such as the one in Angola that lasted for decades and killed tens of thousands of people, started very small, with UNITA reportedly starting as a band of two dozen fighters, hiding in the bush.

[7] Perhaps as a consequence of this, there seems to be serious underreporting of terrorist events in sub-Saharan Africa. In the Krueger and Laitin (2003) dataset that I use later in this chapter, only 29% of the countries with at least one terrorist incident from 1997 to 2002 were in sub-Saharan Africa whereas 42% of civil wars took place there. Africa has also had more coups and politicides than other regions, so the low incidence of terrorism is puzzling and could be due to reporting bias if small-scale violence goes unnoticed when larger problems plague those countries.

simultaneously; and in yet other cases it is difficult to sort out politically motivated violence against civilians from criminal violence. Usually, if the perpetrators commit violent acts in a country other than their country of origin, or if their targets are from a third country, this is considered transnational terrorism. However, domestic perpetrators often have connections to foreign groups or receive assistance from transnational terrorist networks. One might also argue that all governments have an incentive to prevent the use of private violence in their territory because it always affects the "host" country (there are economic costs from loss of tourism or investment and, more important, large-scale attacks can instill fear in the population regardless of the nationality of the target).

A third problem is the questionable reliability of reporting of terrorist attacks. Civil wars are harder to miss, given that large-scale violence is more likely to attract the attention of international media organizations. But, if terrorism takes place in the middle of a civil war, then reporting of it is less likely to be accurate because reporting from most war zones is typically not good. If terrorism takes place outside civil war, the risks of underreporting are also substantial. We may be more likely to see small terrorist attacks that challenge the state reported in democracies with substantial freedom of the press rather than in authoritarian regimes, which are likely to suppress such information.[8]

These conceptual and practical/measurement problems pose difficulties for any empirical analysis of the causes of civil war and terrorism. I do not resolve the measurement problems here but merely highlight them as more needs to be done to improve data quality in studies of terrorism. I focus instead on the conceptual issues that I have raised. In the next section, I propose a typology of political violence that can help us identify the main differences between "ideal cases" of terrorism and civil war. Such a typology can motivate an empirical investigation of whether or not civil war and terrorism have clear and distinct "natural histories."[9]

2.1. Terrorism and Civil War in a Typology of Political Violence

Different forms of violence may not be clearly distinct "species" with natural histories that set them apart from other forms of violence. This point has significant implications for the empirical analysis of civil war, terrorism, or

---

[8] For a discussion of reporting bias that is related to regime type, see Drakos and Gofas (2006).

[9] Tilly (2003, 14) argues that civil war and terrorism do not have distinct causal logics – they are both forms of "coordinated destruction."

other violence because the same causes underlying one form of violence may also underlie other forms.[10] A useful way to proceed is to establish an empirical typology of political violence based on the different "physical" attributes of violent events. We can then study the conditions under which forms of violence with different sets of attributes are likely to arise. This approach can get at the question of the causal coherence of different forms of violence.

There is no clear guide on how many attributes should go into such a typology. The following may be a reasonable list: (a) number and type of actors, (b) degree of organization of actors, (c) degree of public support for actors, (d) power balance among actors, (e) level of violence, (f) targets of violence, (g) declared purpose of violence.

We could add or subtract dimensions (or attributes) from this typology because not all dimensions are equally important. For example, Tilly's (2003) insightful typology privileges two dimensions: the level of violence and the degree of coordination among actors.[11] According to this typology, terrorism and civil war are both forms of *coordinated destruction*: they involve highly coordinated actors and damage/violence is salient. Tilly provides a fascinating discussion of violent forms, ranging from brawls to genocide, and shows that all forms share some common mechanisms. The implication of that argument is far reaching: if the same mechanisms underlie phenomena that we might call "civil war" and "terrorism," then those phenomena are not causally distinct. Historical contingency might explain which form of violence we are likely to see in different contexts and "civil war" and "terrorism" as labels are problematic because they do not point to detectable phenomena with some degree of causal coherence.

I want to push this logic a little further to consider if it holds as I add dimensions to Tilly's typology. Can we find some conceptual and empirical grounds to distinguish terrorism from civil war?

2.2. Toward a Typology of Political Violence

Who Are the Actors?
Actors participating in political violence can be state or nonstate, specialists in violence (military or police) or nonspecialists (civilians, militias), domestic or transnational, ethno-religious groups or social classes, ideological

---

[10] This argument may apply to all forms of contentious politics (McAdam, Tarrow, and Tilly 2001).
[11] Level of violence is conceptualized differently in Tilly's typology, which focuses on the "salience of short-run damage" and need not refer simply to a threshold of deaths.

extremists, nationalists, and so on. All of these actors can commit violent acts during civil war or as part of a campaign of terror. The state is by definition directly involved in violence during civil war but need not be directly involved in the case of terrorism (although it often indirectly involved either as the perpetrator of violence or as its target). Thus, this dimension does not distinguish civil war from terrorism sufficiently, though it does establish that terrorism can sometimes include violence strictly by nonstate groups. The type of actors is a dimension that separates civil war from other forms of nonstate violence, such as riots or intercommunal fighting, or from strictly interstate violence.

What Is the Degree of Organization of the Actors?

The degree of coordination or coherence of violent actors can distinguish terrorism from civil war. Terrorist groups are *on average* not as coherently organized as rebel armies. Most terrorist groups are based on the cell structure, which implies more decentralized decision making in the planning and execution of violent acts. The cell structure is a hierarchical command structure with little communication among cells and a small number of operatives in each cell. It is a versatile organizational structure that makes infiltration difficult and is therefore well suited for asymmetrical conflicts, where the weaker side needs to act with some degree of secrecy (Chai 1993, 102). It also has drawbacks in that decentralization makes factional splits easier as it encourages ideological autonomy. This creates barriers to the growth of terrorist organizations and to their transformation into a rebel army.[12]

By contrast, rebel armies can afford to organize more easily along the lines of traditional militaries by virtue of the fact that they control territory and have access to more resources and do not need to operate in as much secrecy as terrorist groups. Similar concerns with infiltration and organizational coherence may apply to rebel armies at the early stages of the violence. But, once rebels take control of territory, it should be the case that they can more easily recruit new members and obtain financing.[13]

Differences in the degree of organizational coherence of terrorist groups and rebel armies may also be due to the nature of targets. Targets of

[12] For other work that emphasizes the importance of organizational aspects of rebellion, see Merkl (1986).
[13] Territorial control may be the most important factor affecting recruitment. For evidence from Colombia, see Arjona and Kalyvas (2006).

terrorism are relatively disorganized because they do not know that they are being targeted. A cell structure can be effective against such "soft" targets, whereas it would be less effective if the aim was to acquire and hold territory.

What Is the Degree of Public Participation?

A major difference between civil war and terrorism is that terrorist groups have lower levels of active public support than do rebel armies. Terrorism is inherently a clandestine activity and does not require mass level support for the group's survival. By contrast, insurgents during a civil war require much more active support from civilians as the group needs a secure base from which to launch operations and extract resources. Thus, to explain differences in the causes of terrorism and civil war, we should focus on conditions that help transform minor violence into civil war by mobilizing mass-level support.[14]

What Is the Power Balance among Actors?

Terrorism and civil war differ significantly with respect to the degree of power symmetry between the actors. Power imbalance is a key element of terrorism. In civil wars, particularly those that last a long time because of a military stalemate, groups are roughly equal so that each can control some territory or challenge each other's ability to exercise control over its territory. But the degree of asymmetry is still lower than in one-sided violence, such as genocide. Violence can affect all parties in terrorist campaigns, just as in a civil war. This differentiates both terrorism and civil war from one-sided violence such as genocide.

What Is the Level of Violence?

The level of violence is perhaps the most important dimension that distinguishes civil wars from small-scale insurgencies, coups, and other political violence. Terrorist violence that escalates to a high level and which includes military targets and incites violent reprisals from the state would be classified as a civil war by many standard definitions. Thus, some "classic" cases of terrorism are "civil wars" for some scholars. For example, while Goodwin (2006) and Sandler (2003) consider the Irish Republican Army as a terrorist organization, others (Sambanis 2004a; Fearon and Laitin 2003) consider it as

---

[14] It follows that terrorism is not easily distinguishable from insurgency in its early stages when active public support for the insurgents is typically low.

a rebel organization engaged in a separatist civil war in the United Kingdom from 1971 until 1998.

The level of violence is not strictly a consequence of other dimensions of this typology: there is no a priori relationship between levels of violence and the number of actors, degree of organization, or the power balance. By contrast, the level of violence might explain to some degree the support for rebel organizations: if more people are forced to join rebel groups as violence engulfs more regions of a country, the level of active or tacit civilian support will grow. The purpose of violence (see later in this chapter) might also be related to violence levels, with conflicts over total goals (such as the annihilation of an ethnic group) typically leading to more deaths. But such extreme goals might also be achieved through other strategies, such as ethnic cleansing through mass expulsions, so there need not be an automatic link between the purpose and level of violence.

Military technology is a relevant intervening variable that affects the level of violence. In a given conflict, a technology "shock," such as new access to weapons of mass destruction, can lead to higher death tolls with no appreciable change in the purposes of violence, or in levels of public support.

Who Is the Target of Violence?

By most definitions, terrorist violence targets civilians with a view to influencing government policy indirectly. The forcible removal of a government typically goes far beyond the scope of most terrorist actions (assassinations of high-ranking officials share some of the scope of anti-government rebellion but are not similar in the magnitude of violence or the likelihood of success of political goals). The fact that civilians are targeted disproportionately more in terrorism, however, cannot distinguish terrorism from civil war since in modern civil wars civilians are far more likely to be targeted for violence than are military or police.[15]

Might more differences emerge if we look at the use of selective versus indiscriminate violence in civil war versus terrorism? Both forms of violence can involve both selective and indiscriminate violence. For civil war, Kalyvas (2006) shows that patterns of control determine whether violence will be selective or not. For terrorism, a relevant argument is made by Goodwin (2006), who separates "categorical" terrorism, defined as the indiscriminate targeting of a class or group of people where victims are anonymous,

---

[15] The distinction between civilian and military targets can also collapse in interstate wars. Carpet bombing or mutual assured destruction strategies affect government policy by holding civilians hostage.

from "individualized terrorism," where victims are known and targeted as individuals. Both can occur and an example of the former would be al Qaeda's attack of anonymous members of the American public during its September 11, 2001, attacks. An example of individualized terrorism would be the Greek November 17 organization, which targeted specific individuals for violence. Though civilians may also be selectively targeted for violence in civil war, the larger scale and scope of violence means that civilians are not targeted as individuals, but individual targets are exchangeable. This occurs more frequently in civil war than in terrorism, particularly in small-scale terrorism that takes place outside of the context of civil war and targets people as individuals.[16]

What Is the Purpose of Violence?

Finally, the intended aim of violence is often different in terrorism and civil war. Civil wars and terrorism both can be motivated by a desire to achieve national independence, overthrow the government, or affect specific government policies. In this regard, both terrorism and civil war can be distinguished from criminal violence. But the purpose of violence in civil war is linked directly to the achievement of these political goals, whereas terrorism is characterized by the indirectness of violence (violence is used to terrorize the public).[17] Violence during civil war need not be directed at instilling fear in the civilian population, though it will almost always have such an effect. If terrorism is a strategy of intimidation, then it is a subset of violent strategies that can be used during civil war.[18] The purpose of violence, therefore, is a dimension that highlights the narrower scope of terrorism and makes it hard to think of terrorism as a causally coherent, distinct phenomenon.

This typology establishes a number of differences between civil war and terrorism. Violent groups in civil wars are on average less unequal in terms of their capabilities; they are organized in more coherent, hierarchical structures; they have broader political goals and public support; and they

---

[16] There are exceptions to this argument about selective violence being used more often in domestic terrorism that takes place outside of civil war. The Oklahoma City bombings of 1995 in the United States are such an exception, where scores of civilians were killed as the result of a bombing of a government building.

[17] See, e.g., Crenshaw (1981), Sandler (2003), and Tilly (2004).

[18] Two countries with extremely high incidence of terrorism are India and Colombia, both of which have had civil wars. In Krueger and Laitin's data, only 5 out of the 33 countries with civil wars had no terrorist incidents (Central African Republic, Republic of the Congo, Guinea-Bissau, Nepal, Papua New Guinea).

can cause more destruction than violent groups engaged in terrorism. These differences place terrorism and civil war at different points in the multidimensional space that the variables in the typology define and suggest that the causes of "pure" terrorism – that is, terrorism that takes place outside of the context of civil war – should be different from the causes of civil war. I look more closely at this argument in the rest of the chapter.

3. The Causes of Terrorism and Civil War

To see if civil war and terrorism are different we could ask if a simple rationalist model of violence fits both phenomena roughly in the same way. Rationalist models of civil war draw on the economic logic of crime articulated by Becker (1957). Important contributions include Grossman's (1991, 1995) and Hirschleifer's (1995) models that explain violence as the product of "three interacting determinants: *preferences, opportunities,* and *perceptions*" (Hirschleifer 1995, 172). Divergent preferences reduce the size of the agreement zone in political bargains, as do subjective perceptions of each side's capacity to win more by fighting and violent conflict occurs when it is expected to be more profitable than peace.[19]

Two empirical studies that apply rationalist models to civil wars are Collier and Hoeffler (2004) and Fearon and Laitin (2003). Both explain the outbreak of civil war as a function of the opportunity to organize rebellion. For Collier and Hoeffler, the deciding factor is the economic opportunity cost of rebellion. Low costs imply high "labor supply" for insurgency. Supply will be high in poor countries, when education levels and job opportunities are low. For Fearon and Laitin (2003), the key is the state's ability to police its territory. Low state capacity facilitates the organization of insurgency.[20]

Other scholars focus more on the demand side, on the grievances that are due to different types of inequality or political injustice.[21] A prominent theory is Gurr's (1970) "relative deprivation," which posits that people rebel

---

[19] There are many variants of these theories. A useful collection of essays is in the December 2000 special issue of the *Journal of Conflict Resolution*, edited by Todd Sandler.

[20] For a similar argument, see Hobsbawm (1973) and Russell (1974).

[21] There is a large literature on the lack of political rights and revolution. There has also been substantial study of the link between interpersonal economic inequality and conflict, though there is not strong evidence in favor of a relationship to civil war. See, for example, Collier and Hoeffler (2004); Fearon and Laitin (2003). Evidence that a link does exist is provided by Nafziger and Auvinen (2002) who use Deininger and Squire's (1996) data and find that stagnation, decline in GDP, and income inequality are sources of humanitarian emergencies, but this is a broader category than civil war.

when they realize that there is a large discrepancy between their legitimate expectations of material rewards and their actual rewards.[22]

Results from empirical studies of civil war seem to support "supply-side" models. These studies control for a number of variables that measure grievances and opportunities for insurgency, such as the country's dependence on natural resources, the type of regime, the degree of social fractionalization, and so on. The key hypotheses are that the risk of an insurgency should be higher in countries with greater dependence on natural resources, low levels of democracy, and greater ethnic fragmentation. A number of other variables are also used as controls, though there is no consensus on what is the "right" model of civil war. There are many different ways in which these variables may be causally related to civil war, and I do not review those here.[23] I use these variables as controls to explore some of the ways in which civil war and terrorism might differ with respect to the role of income and democracy – the two most important variables in theoretical discussions of political violence.

The most robust empirical result in the civil war literature is a negative correlation between per capita income and civil war.[24] High rates of growth of per capita income are also associated with a lower risk of civil war onset.[25] The mean per capita GDP in countries affected by at least one civil war from 1960 to 1999 is less than half that of countries with no civil war and countries with no wars grow much faster than war-affected countries.[26] Several authors have found income to be negatively and significantly associated with

[22] These theories derive from a larger literature on the sociology of crime and violence. See Merton (1957), Braithwaite (1979), and Blau and Blau (1982), among others.
[23] See Sambanis (2002) for a review and Sambanis (2004b) for more on causal mechanisms in the civil war literature.
[24] This result is fairly robust to using different sets of countries, different time periods, different specifications, and different measures of civil war onset. But most of the evidence on the negative association between income and civil war is based on cross-country comparisons. There is less strong evidence from studies that analyze over-time differences in civil war and income within countries. There is no statistically significant effect of GDP in fixed effects models, except if we include the period from 1945 to 1959. In the post-1960 period, we do not find significance for the GDP variable in the standard economic models of civil war onset. See Sambanis (2005) for some results and more discussion. For robustness tests using different lists of civil war, see Sambanis (2004a). For robustness tests using different specifications of the civil war model, see Hegre and Sambanis (2006).
[25] See Collier and Hoeffler (2004) and Miguel et al. (2004) and, on the consequences of civil war for rates of economic growth, see Murdoch and Sandler (2004).
[26] Income average for 1960–1999 is $2,176 for civil war countries and $5,173 for no-war countries (Chain index, Penn World Tables data).

other forms of violence, such as coups and genocide.[27] Civil war countries also happen to be less democratic: the average democracy score for war-affected countries is 65 percent lower than that for no-war countries.[28] But the effects of income dwarf the effect of democracy on civil war (Fearon and Laitin 2003).

Recent quantitative studies of terrorism have pointed to a very different picture. They find per capita income not to be a significant determinant of terrorism, whereas measures of political rights are very significant (Krueger and Malecková 2003; Abadie 2004).[29] One complication may be that national-level income statistics used in cross-country studies do not always capture local-level economic conditions that influence the decision to join terrorist networks. For example, if we use Israeli national income data to analyze the risk of terrorism or civil war in Israel and consider the West Bank and Gaza as parts of Israel (as is conventionally done in quantitative studies), then we would not fully appreciate the economic effects of the second Intifada in the Palestinian territories. Although Israel has not been severely affected, the economic costs for West Bank and Gaza have been very large (about $5.4 billion) and more than half of the population was forced under the poverty threshold as a result of economic closings (World Bank 2003). Loss of economic opportunities for Palestinians is clearly correlated with spikes in violence in the second Intifada.

Although macrolevel data may sometimes make it hard to assess the link between income and terrorist violence, substantial microlevel evidence supports the view that income is not a critically important factor for terrorism. Interviews with failed suicide bombers revealed that they were not very poor and appeared to be average people with ordinary family backgrounds.[30] Krueger and Malecková (2003) found that perpetrators of terrorist acts are

[27] On the relationship between income and coup risk see, for example, Luttwak (1969), Finer (1962), Londregan and Poole (1990). On income and genocide risk, see Sambanis (2003a). Cases of civil war where politicide (one-sided state-sponsored violence) or genocide took place have a slightly lower GDP per capita ($1,338) than civil wars without genocide ($1,924).

[28] Using Polity IV data (Marshall and Jaggers 2000), the average polity score for war countries, coding periods of war and regime transitions as "0" on a -10 to 10 range, is -2.13, while the average for no-war countries is 1.36, showing a slightly more open polity.

[29] No clear evidence links income growth to terrorism or political assassinations. Krueger and Maleckova note that during the two bouts of insurgency associated with the Intifada in Israel, we observed one period of economic expansion and one economic contraction. Similarly, Horowitz (2001) surveys the literature on riots and finds no support for the common hypothesis that commodity shocks and slow growth increase the prevalence of riots.

[30] Nasra Hassan (2001).

more educated than the average person in the same countries.[31] This finding contradicts the economic opportunity logic of rationalist models of civil war, which would predict that educational attainment should be negatively associated with participation in violence because the economic opportunity costs of violence are higher for educated people.[32]

This brief review points to some empirical differences between terrorism and civil war. Whereas civil wars are affected more by economic factors, terrorism seems to be affected more by political factors. The fact that the logic underlying economic models of civil war does not fit terrorism very well indicates that the two phenomena might be causally distinct. In the next section, I look further into these differences by comparing the characteristics of countries that affect civil war and terrorism.

3.1. Comparing Terrorism to Civil War

Using civil war data from Sambanis (2004a) and terrorism data from Krueger and Laitin (2003), I compare the effect of income and democracy on terrorism and civil war. I focus on the period from 1997 to 2002, so my results may be slightly different in earlier periods.[33] My dependent variables are the incidence of civil war and the incidence of terrorism (both of them binary, coded 1 for any country that had at least one incident of terrorism or civil war in that period).[34] The Krueger and Laitin data include both domestic and transnational terrorist incidents. Given the difficulties in sorting out purely transnational events from domestic ones, I report results for all terrorism

[31] They found that more than 50% of the terrorists in their study have more than secondary education as compared with 15% for the general population. See, also, Berrebi (2003) and Kimhi and Even (2003).

[32] It would be interesting to see if the relationship between education and participation in political violence is different in different geographical regions and across forms of violence. For example, in nationalist conflict, mass literacy is almost always a necessity as national identities that drive such conflicts are cultivated by the national schooling system (see Darden 2004). Also, in countries where religious organizations are heavily involved in secondary schooling, it would not be unexpected to see schooling polarize the population rather than reduce social conflict. Studies that emphasize the role of education in reducing social conflict and violence include Huntington (1968), Hibbs (1973), Alesina and Perotti (1996).

[33] Krueger and Laitin's (2003) data, which I use, cover this period and no data on domestic terrorism are available before 1998 in any other database. The MIPT database, which I also use, begins to report domestic terrorist acts in 1998. The MIPT data can be accessed online at The National Memorial Institute for the Prevention of Terrorism (http://www.tkb.org/).

[34] Many countries have only one or a handful of terrorist events, especially if we exclude countries in the midst of a civil war. I also report results using the number of incidents as the dependent variable.

but also look separately at domestic terrorism by analyzing only events in which the place of the attack was the same as the country of origin of the perpetrator *and* at least one of the two countries that were most affected by the attack.[35] I also use data on domestic terrorism from the MIPT database for the period from 1998 to 2003 and report differences in footnotes.[36]

On the right-hand side of the regression equation, I include the main explanatory variables from rationalist models of civil war: income, democracy, population size, ethnic fractionalization, and a binary variable measuring dependence on oil exports.[37] These are all measured at the start of the period.

Previous studies have only looked at the direct effects of income and democracy by adding them separately in regressions. I focus on their combined effect drawing on Tilly (2003), who argues that the nature of contentious politics and the form of collective violence in each country is determined by the combination of regime type and regime capacity. Tilly (2003, 43–48) analyzes four regime type-capacity combinations: high-capacity democracies, low-capacity democracies, high-capacity autocracies, and low-capacity autocracies. Binary variables corresponding to each of these four types are created by interacting *Democracy* (a binary variable coded 1 if the country's polity score is greater than 5 on a scale from $^-10$ to 10 and 0 otherwise)[38] with *HighGDP* (a binary variable coded 1 for countries with per capita income above the median for the countries included in the analysis and 0 otherwise). Income is an imperfect measure of regime capacity, but it is the only measure used in cross-national studies of civil war (see Fearon and Laitin 2003).

Results are presented in Tables 6.1a, 6.1b, and 6.1c. In each column of Tables 6.1a and 6.1b, I present results from a model that controls for one of the four regime type/capacity combinations. In column 1, I compare high-income democracies to all other combinations. In column 2, I do the same for high-income nondemocracies; in column 3, for low-income

---

[35] There are 415 terrorist incidents in 54 countries that are "domestic" according to this coding rule.

[36] The MIPT data are very different from the Krueger and Laitin data for several countries, so finding different results will not be surprising. Differences are not limited to domestic terrorism.

[37] Mountainous terrain is another variable that is often included in civil war models, but it is not robust (Sambanis 2004a), so I exclude it to avoid losing several observations with missing data on this variable.

[38] The polity data come from Marshall and Jaggers (2000). This definition of democracy as polity > 5 is standard in the literature. Other measures also exist. I use the Polity measure because that is the one used by the civil war studies I engage with in this chapter.

Table 6.1a. *Logit model of the incidence of civil war, 1997–2003*

	Y * P = 1 if high GDP & high polity	Y * P = 1 if high GDP & low polity	Y * P = 1 if low GDP & low polity	Y * P = 1 if low GDP & high polity
Income * democracy (Y * P)	−1.23	−0.85	**1.11**	0.03
	(0.61)	(0.92)	(0.47)	(0.63)
Population (log)	**0.40**	**0.37**	**0.40**	**0.38**
	(0.16)	(0.16)	(0.16)	(0.15)
Ethnolinguistic frac.	**2.44**	**2.95**	**2.48**	**2.99**
	(0.91)	(0.90)	(0.92)	(0.90)
Oil dependence	0.34	0.87	0.55	0.58
	(0.63)	(0.69)	(0.63)	(0.63)
Constant	**−8.97**	**−9.10**	**−9.85**	**−9.27**
	(2.71)	(2.69)	(2.76)	(2.65)
Observations	147	147	147	147
Pseudo-**R**^{2}	0.17	0.14	0.18	0.14
Log likelihood	−60.71	−62.57	−60.20	−63.04

Note: Coefficients and standard errors (in parentheses). Significant at 0.05 = Bold; significant at 0.10.

Table 6.1b. *Logit model of the incidence of terrorism, 1997–2003 (excluding civil wars)*

	High GDP & high polity	High GDP & low polity	Low GDP & low polity	Low GDP & high polity
Income * democracy (Y * P)	−0.42	**1.49**	0.20	−1.15
	(0.46)	(0.64)	(0.48)	(0.80)
Population (log)	**0.45**	**0.52**	**0.43**	**0.43**
	(0.16)	(0.17)	(0.16)	(0.16)
Ethnolinguistic frac.	0.69	0.98	0.77	0.87
	(0.82)	(0.82)	(0.83)	(0.81)
Oil dependence	0.75	0.40	0.82	0.68
	(0.63)	(0.67)	(0.63)	(0.63)
Constant	**−8.37**	**−10.08**	**−8.38**	**−8.23**
	(2.65)	(2.83)	(2.64)	(2.63)
Observations	118	118	118	118
Pseudo-R^2	0.08	0.11	0.08	0.09
Log likelihood	−65.08	−62.80	−65.41	−64.24

Note: Coefficients and standard errors (in parentheses). Significant at 0.05 = Bold; significant at 0.10.

Nicholas Sambanis

Table 6.1c. *Logit model of terrorism or civil war with democracy-income interactions*

	Civil wars	All terrorism outside civil war	All terrorism outside civil war	Domestic terrorism (no civil war)
Democracy	−2.997	−0.54	−1.24	−1.01
	(2.78)	(2.40)	(0.87)	(0.93)
Log of income	−0.61	0.14	−	−
	(0.34)	(0.25)	−	−
High-income country	−	−	1.14	0.74
	−	−	(0.70)	(0.76)
Democracy * Income	0.38	−0.07	−0.34	0.43
	(0.41)	(0.32)	(1.09)	(1.15)
Population (log)	**0.39**	**0.48**	**0.51**	**0.73**
	(0.16)	(0.17)	(0.17)	(0.19)
Ethnolinguistic frac.	**2.05**	0.65	0.79	−0.56
	(0.97)	(0.87)	(0.86)	(0.87)
Oil dependence	0.74	0.38	0.24	−0.05
	(0.72)	(0.68)	(0.68)	(0.73)
Constant	−4.83	**−9.40**	**−9.44**	**−12.71**
	(3.45)	(3.61)	(2.88)	(3.25)
Observations	147	118	118	117
Pseudo-R^2	0.1918	0.1079	0.1305	−56.86
Log likelihood	−59.00	−63.21	−61.61	0.1595

Note: Coefficients and standard errors (in parentheses). Significant at 0.05 = Bold; significant at 0.10.

autocracies; and in column 4, for low-income democracies.[39] I do not control for the linear income and democracy terms in those regressions, but report results in footnotes. In Table 6.1c, I control for democracy and income separately, as well as for their interaction. In all regressions, I control for ethnic fractionalization, population size, and dependence on oil.

3.2. Discussion

An interesting result (Table 6.1a) is that ethnic fractionalization is very significant and positively correlated with civil war.[40] This is a sharp difference

[39] Out of 147 countries with nonmissing data on income or democracy, there are 55 high-income democracies, 18 high-income autocracies, 52 low-income autocracies, and 22 low-income democracies.

[40] Its coefficient is not affected significantly when we control for the linear democracy and income variables, and it is still significant.

from the rest of the literature and the result is robust to the addition of controls. The difference may be due to the cross-sectional format of the data (country-years are the most common way of organizing the data in other studies) or to particularities of the short time period I analyze here. Though intriguing, this result on the relationship between fractionalization and civil war is not of central concern to this chapter, so I do not discuss it further.

High-capacity democracies (Tilly's "zone of citizenship") are less likely to have civil war, whereas low-capacity nondemocracies (column 3) are more likely to have civil war.[41] The result is consistent with the rationalist model because in these regime type-capacity combinations there is both less demand for rebellion (high democracy should reduce grievances) and less opportunity (high capacity should improve policing). The result is also consistent with Tilly's arguments and suggests a refinement of existing results in the civil war literature, which look only at the effects of income and democracy in isolation.

There are only a few cases of high-capacity nondemocracies (Tilly's "zone of authoritarianism") and only two of them have had a civil war (Algeria and Russia). So, though the coefficient is negative (column 2, Table 6.1a), it will inevitably be affected by those two cases and it is not statistically significant.[42] Finally, low-capacity democracies (column 4) do not have a significant correlation with civil war – the ease of organization of an insurgency is apparently not enough to explain civil war and demand-side factors such as regime type may be much more relevant than previous studies have argued.

The model fits civil war much better than it does terrorism. Table 6.1b reports results on terrorism using all terrorist incidents in Krueger and Laitin's database. I have also restricted the analysis to domestic terrorism only but do not report those results because no variable except population size is significant in those regressions. But, I discuss those results in the text. Because I am interested in considering terrorism as a form of violence distinct from civil war, I conduct the analysis by dropping cases with civil war.

---

[41] Adding binary controls for high-income and democracy in the regression in column 1 introduces multicolinearity as the high-income-democracy variable is correlated with high-income at 78%. None of the variables is individually significant, but they are all jointly significant ($p = 0.08$), and democracy has a negative coefficient. In column 3, adding the corresponding linear terms (in this case for low-income and nondemocracies) has a similar effect, and all three variables are jointly significant ($p = 0.08$).

[42] Adding binary controls for high-income and nondemocracy in the regression in column 2 shows that high income has a significant negative coefficient when nondemocracies take the value 0.

High-capacity democracies are not significantly less likely to have terrorist incidents, particularly if we drop cases of civil war and look at the incidence of terrorism in isolation.[43] By contrast, high-capacity autocracies are much more likely to have terrorism.[44] In fact, only high-capacity nondemocracies are more likely than other regime type/capacity combinations to have terrorism *once civil war cases are dropped,* and this result disappears if we look only at cases of domestic terrorism (results not shown). Low-capacity autocracies are also more likely to have terrorism (p-value = 0.09), but only if we include cases where civil war is ongoing in the same period (result not shown). This is consistent with a view that grievances that motivate violence are more likely to escalate into civil war than be limited to terrorism if there are opportunities to organize an insurgency.

In Table 6.1c, I control for democracy and income separately as well as in interaction (multiplicative term). With respect to civil war (first column of Table 6.1c), the results show that the net effect of income on civil war becomes nonsignificant when we control for democracy.[45] Income's negative effect on civil war applies to nondemocracies only. The effect of income on all terrorism (column 2) is entirely nonsignificant when we drop cases of civil war.[46] This is consistent with the Krueger and Laitin chapter 5 (this volume) results, which show that richer countries are often the target of terrorism, particularly transnational terrorism. The effect of democracy outside the context of civil war, by contrast, is significant, reducing the risk of terrorism once we control for high-income countries (column 3).[47] With respect to domestic terrorism alone, however (column 4), neither democracy nor income has any significant effect.[48]

---

[43] The result is the same if I use data on domestic terrorism only from MIPT (only cases with at least one fatality are coded). Results available from the author. In column 1 of Table 6.1b, if we add the linear, high-income democracy variables, they are jointly significant with the interaction (p = 0.06) and income has a positive sign.

[44] The coefficient of the nondemocracy-high income interaction is jointly significant with the nondemocracy and high-income linear terms. If we run the regression without the interaction, we find a positive relationship between terrorism and nondemocracy (p = 0.01) and high income (p = 0.07).

[45] The net effect is computed by adding the coefficient of the income variable and its interaction with democracy (−0.23) and adjusting the standard error (taking the square root of the variance of each of the two estimate plus two times their covariance, which yields 0.25).

[46] Adjusted coefficient of 0.07 and standard error of 0.2.

[47] The adjusted coefficient of democracy is -1.6 with a standard error of 0.7.

[48] Democracy is also not significant using the MIPT data. Negative binomial regressions of the number of terrorist incidents on the same explanatory variables produce similar results, though the effects of democracy are stronger using the Krueger and Laitin data (domestic events with or without civil war).

Overall, the analysis so far and more results that I show later indicate that regime type is much more important than regime capacity/income in explaining terrorism whereas the opposite is true for civil war. Thus, a key difference between terrorism and civil war may be that terrorism is more demand driven – perhaps because it is "cheaper" to produce – and it is less responsive to supply-side factors that influence the incidence of civil war.

The fact that the model used here does not explain domestic terrorism may simply be because the model is too simplistic, possibly missing important variables. But the result is also consistent with an argument that the causes of "pure" terrorism are idiosyncratic – a point to which I return later. Interestingly, while some evidence suggests that democracies are less likely to have domestic terrorism by virtue of the lower "demand" for violence that freer political systems should generate, the four countries that have by far the highest number of domestic terrorist attacks are democracies – Israel, U.S.A., Colombia, and India.[49]

The different effect of income with respect to terrorism and civil war becomes clear in Table 6.2, where we see results from a multinomial logit model of political violence. The period covered is 1997–2002, and the dependent variable is coded 0 in countries with neither of the two forms of violence we examine here, 1 in countries that had terrorist attacks but no civil war, and 2 in countries that had civil war (which may or may not include terrorist acts). The same explanatory variables as models in Table 6.1 are used and this estimation method allows us to compare parameter estimates for civil war and terrorism. The estimates are clearly different: a test of similarity of coefficients rejects the null hypothesis of no difference (p-value below 0.05 for domestic terrorism and below 0.1 for all terrorism). Income clearly has a strong negative effect on civil war risk but not on terrorism.[50]

The picture that emerges from these simple tests is that civil war and terrorism are different. But we still do not have a good explanation of what causes terrorism outside the context of civil war.

Terrorism and civil war seem to differ with respect to the influence of ethnicity (fractionalization, as measured by the standard ELF index). The relationship is positive with respect to civil war, while no significant association exists with terrorism. The effects of income and democracy are also different. Income has a negative relationship with civil war, especially for nondemocracies. Its effect diminishes and becomes nonsignificant if we only

---

[49] Dropping these four countries does not affect the results reported here.

[50] These results are based on Krueger and Laitin's data. The difference between civil war and domestic terrorism is slightly stronger with MIPT data for the period from 1999 to 2003.

Nicholas Sambanis

Table 6.2. *Multinomial logit model of political terrorism and civil war*

	All terrorism (KL 2003)	Domestic terrorism (KL 2003)	Domestic terrorism (MIPT)
Terrorism			
Per capita income (log)	0.15	0.08	−0.18
	(0.18)	(0.19)	(0.19)
Democracy score	*−0.075*	−0.009	0.009
	(0.04)	(0.05)	(0.05)
Oil export dependence	−0.02	−0.04	−0.04
	(0.74)	(0.81)	(0.81)
Ethnolinguistic fractionalization	**2.14**	0.11	−0.01
	(1.06)	(1.03)	(1.02)
Population (log)	**0.43**	**0.64**	**0.56**
	(0.17)	(0.18)	(0.18)
Religious fractionalization	*−2.09*	−0.12	*−2.00*
	(1.18)	(1.17)	(1.15)
Constant	**−8.93**	**−12.00**	**−7.84**
	(3.20)	(3.35)	(3.11)
Civil war			
Per capita Income (log)	**−0.53**	**−0.56**	**−0.64**
	(0.25)	(0.25)	(0.25)
Democracy score	−0.03	−0.004	0.002
	(0.05)	(0.05)	(0.05)
Oil export dependence	0.58	0.55	0.53
	(0.84)	(0.81)	(0.83)
Ethnolinguistic fractionalization	**2.91**	*2.20*	*2.14*
	(1.23)	(1.21)	(1.23)
Population (log)	**0.50**	**0.55**	**0.55**
	(0.19)	(0.20)	(0.20)
Religious fractionalization	−1.57	−0.91	−1.52
	(1.37)	(1.33)	(1.34)
Constant	*−6.35*	−6.95	*−6.14*
	(3.71)	(3.73)	(3.68)
Observations	133	133	133
Pseudo-R^2	0.17	0.17	0.17
LR χ^2	44.06	42.77	44.67
Log likelihood	−109.995	−107.918	−109.689

Note: Coefficients and standard errors (in parentheses). Significant at 0.05 = Bold; significant at 0.10 = italics.

analyze the seventy-seven countries that are coded as democratic, but there are only nine cases of civil war in this group. By contrast, income does not have the same negative effect on terrorism (domestic or any type) in nondemocracies.[51]

The average level of democracy is higher in countries with no terrorist incidents of any kind.[52] If we compare instead the average number of terrorist incidents in democracies and nondemocracies, we find a significant difference (with fewer incidents in democracies) only if we drop India and Colombia – two democracies with very high numbers of terrorist incidents – or if we compare only countries that are not at civil war. But these differences become nonsignificant when we look only at domestic terrorism.[53]

The association between democracy and terrorism must be investigated further as it is sensitive to the database used. There are also theoretical reasons that we could expect the relationship to go either way. Terrorism may be more effective in democracies to the extent that democracies are more likely to shape their policies in response to public pressure.[54] Thus, Pape (2003), for example, explains suicide bombing as a rational strategy by terrorist elites who want to force concessions by democratic states. Another reason that democracies may have more terrorism is that terrorist groups capitalize on the greater freedom of the media in democracies to publicize their actions (Chai 1993; Li 2005).[55] Consistent with those arguments, Eubank and Weinberg (1994, 1998) show that democracies have more terrorist groups and that more transnational terrorist events are likely to occur

---

[51] Results available from the author.

[52] P-value = 0.00. This is also confirmed using MIPT data from 1998 to 2003 for transnational and domestic terrorism. Mean level of democracy for countries with no terrorism is higher (p-value = 0.04).

[53] These results are available from the author. With the MIPT data, we get similar results if we look only at domestic attacks with at least one fatality. The picture changes if we also consider nonlethal attacks, which seem to take place more frequently in more democratic countries. I exclude attacks in West Bank and Gaza from these comparisons because the MIPT database codes more than 1,000 domestic attacks whereas the Krueger and Laitin data code 28 total attacks. But there are extensive differences in the two datasets for many countries, and those differences are extreme if we also include nonlethal attacks from MIPT. The MIPT database seems to have a more inclusive definition of terrorism than other databases.

[54] Though the opposite might also occur if the public is convinced in the legitimacy of government policy and terrorism "backfires" in shoring up public support for the government.

[55] This logic should apply to domestic and transnational terrorism. Li (2005) argues that we should actually expect to see a positive relationship between civil liberties and transnational terrorism because of the higher level of institutional constraints placed on the government in countries with higher levels of civil liberties. These constraints imply that governments are less able to take action to limit terrorism because they cannot undercut civil liberties.

in democratic countries.[56] By contrast, autocracies should not only be more immune to public concerns over terrorism but also have greater freedom to violently repress dissent.[57]

But the democracy-terrorism link has a supply side and a demand side. The studies I referred to earlier in this chapter focus on the supply (likelihood of accommodation by the regime). Demand-side factors also matter: there should be fewer political grievances that support terrorism in democracies (Crenshaw 1981; Schmid 1992; Abadie 2004). The empirical results presented here suggest that the demand side may be more powerful than the supply side or, alternatively, that the relative ease of concessions to terrorists in democratic regimes may have been exaggerated in the literature.

On the whole, the analysis in this chapter suggests that in countries with low per capita income, violence is more likely to be organized as a civil war, particularly if the regime is undemocratic. By contrast, terrorism is more responsive to political freedoms. In nondemocracies with high capacities, freedom restrictions are likely to lead to terrorism (rather than civil war) because insurgency is harder to organize.

There is certainly much more to say – and more analysis to be done – to fully explain the conditions under which terrorism can transform into civil war. A number of intervening variables should matter, such as the technology of violence or the "geography" of the conflict. Terrorism is a form of violence that is most appropriate to urban warfare, perhaps as the first step of a revolution that must eventually spread to the countryside to win control of the country.[58] Thus, we might reasonably expect to see terrorism used more frequently in developed, urbanized environments, whereas guerilla warfare is the strategy most likely to be used in rural areas. This idea can be found in early writings on the organization of political violence, including Hibbs (1973) and Huntington (1968), who thought that high rates of urbanization provided terrorists easy access to large groups of potential victims, even if terrorists were relatively weak.[59]

---

[56] The relationship between democracy and terrorism is heavily debated in the literature. For analyses of the effect of democracy on transnational terrorism, see Eyerman (1998) and Eubank and Weinberg (2001).

[57] Though consistent with our definition of terrorism, autocracies' success at counterinsurgency might come at the cost of some state-incited terror.

[58] On terrorism and its links to insurgency, see in particular Marighela (1971) and Guillen (1973).

[59] Crenshaw (1981, 382). Hobsbawm (1973) writes that cities became the focal point of terrorism starting with barricades erected in protests after the urban renewal projects and boulevards built in Paris in the late nineteenth century. See, also, Jack Goldstone's research on early modern European states, which argues that high levels of urbanization increased the risk of conflict in countries with economies that were not doing well.

But, I would like to suggest another explanation for the fact that we can still see terrorism in several high-capacity democratic regimes: the causes of terrorism in developed states are likely to be idiosyncratic.

Terrorism is a way for aggrieved groups to make symbolic statements or take selective revenge against the state even when they know that their actions will not have a major effect on government policy. If we conceptualize terrorism as punishment or revenge, then it becomes clear that terrorist organizations can have a wide range of selective goals and the occurrence of domestic terrorism can be unpredictable. Though restrictions of political freedoms can motivate domestic terrorism, small-scale terrorist violence can be motivated by a wide range of private incentives that are not necessarily captured by the logic underlying rationalist models of civil war.[60] The key importance of democracy and political freedoms is that they undercut the opportunities for fringe groups to receive mass-level support and thus make it hard for most terrorist groups to transform themselves into rebel armies.

The rationalist model requires that potential members of a terrorist or rebel organization have a "reservation wage" that is determined by the expected benefits of violence relative to the opportunity costs of violence.[61] Because the average person in a high-capacity democracy has a high "reservation wage," terrorist organizations will be unable to generate the mass level participation they need for growth into rebellion. So, why do we still see terrorism in high-capacity democracies?

The rationalist model may have to be amended to answer this question. One amendment that might help explain terrorism-as-punishment is to consider how psychological or other emotional rewards motivate terrorists. Violence in this case need not depend on objective assessments of its likely success in shaping government policy.[62] Alternatively, we might consider how the rationalist model might work if people have radically different discount factors. The greater the material or psychological rewards from achieving terrorism's stated goals, the longer some ideologically committed people might be willing to wait to achieve those goals. If "reservation wages" are high for most people, then terrorist organizations that face long-time horizons before they can begin to reap rewards will only be able to attract people with an ability to defer gratification and invest in their future

---

[60] Several psychological perspectives have been proposed as explanations of terrorism (e.g., terrorism as martyrdom). See Juergensmeyer (2003), Kramer (1991), Zeidan (2001).

[61] For a rent-seeking model of terrorism, where violence is used as a way to extort rents from the government, see Kirk (1983). In such a model, as in rationalist models of civil war, violence will be used if it is cost effective.

[62] See Gurr (1983, 42–43). A related view is that terrorists and rebels may be seeking social approval. See Muller and Opp (1986).

and/or people who receive significant psychological benefits from violence regardless of the probability of success in their political agenda.

These ideas reflect some of the typological differences between terrorism and civil war that I outlined earlier: I described terrorism as a form of violence that is likely to be used when there is severe power asymmetry between the state and its challengers. The relative weakness of terrorist groups implies that, by its design, terrorism is based on the principle of deferred gratification and requires extreme discipline.[63]

In some cases, terrorism can be considered as an incomplete civil war, or a proto-civil war – an aspiring insurgency that cannot stir up enough mass-level support to reach the level of a civil war. Mass-level support cannot be won partly due to this power asymmetry that defines terrorism because terrorist organizations are unable to recruit members by promising material rewards that are conditional on victory (or on looting, or many of the other ways in which many rebel armies use to compensate their recruits). External assistance may help transform a terrorist group into a rebel army. But mass-level support might be hard to mobilize even when assistance is available because of the organization's extremist ideology. In democracies especially, terrorist groups will represent extreme ideological viewpoints, which limit the public appeal of the organization and make recruitment difficult.

These constraints imply that terrorists, just like early recruits in an insurgency, are a "front guard" – they are nationalist leaders or revolutionaries who are committed to a long-term, high-risk investment. Filled with such people, terrorist groups are top-heavy, elite-driven organizations. Because of their small size and top-heavy organization, terrorist groups will have on average a higher proportion of educated members than would be the case in the typical rebel movement that is based more heavily on grassroots support because it has to recruit large numbers of foot soldiers (nationalist leaders are usually well educated because it is through education that they have cultivated their nationalist beliefs).[64] This explanation is consistent with Crenshaw's (1981, 384) description of terrorism as "the result of elite

---

[63] By contrast, other violence (e.g., riots) offer more immediate emotional release (see Horowitz 2001).

[64] Crenshaw (1981, 384) writes that terrorists are generally well educated and middle class in background, or disillusioned young professionals. There is evidence from geographical regions other than the Middle East that perpetrators of terrorist events (e.g., suicide bombing) are relatively highly educated (e.g., Sri Lanka). There is also evidence that relatively highly educated people lead rebellions. For example, the leader of the SPLA in the Sudan has a PhD in Agricultural Economics from an American university. Educated Tamils who were disproportionately affected by the lack of economic opportunities in the south motivated the Sri Lankan rebellion. See Goodhand (2003).

disaffection" and can account for the microlevel empirical finding that education levels in some terrorist organizations are higher than the average education level in the general population (Krueger and Malecková 2003).

Ideological extremism cuts both ways: it inhibits the organization's capacity to grow into a mass movement, but it helps sustain the organization in the presence of extreme uncertainty about the outcome of terrorist action. If educated individuals populate terrorist groups, we have to explain why such individuals, who should be able to weigh the likely costs and benefits of their actions better than less educated foot soldiers, would participate in high-risk activities. An answer is that terrorists must believe that violence will work – eventually.[65] How can they believe that, given the immense power asymmetry that defines their struggle? This is not the result of private information or miscommunication. Rather, ideological commitment acts as a filter for the information that people will use to assess the likely effectiveness of their actions.

Russell Hardin (2002, 4) wrote "the fanatic never sleeps" to describe the need for constant reinforcement of a conscience and beliefs that can sustain extremism. Hardin focuses on how people come to hold their beliefs and argues that there are economic costs to acquiring the knowledge that is necessary to check the veracity of one's beliefs. But knowledge has value as a resource, so there are incentives to acquire knowledge even if this is costly. Because it is costly to acquire and process new information, our beliefs come to a large extent from experts or from other authorities who can manipulate our beliefs. Politically extreme views can be partly explained by such manipulation. But the more extreme the beliefs, the easier it will be to challenge them by exposing them to outside influences. Thus, extremist organizations have incentives to keep their numbers small to better manage their socialization process. Moreover, the norms of exclusion that prevail in extremist organizations tend to push moderates out of the group, and only the intensely committed remain. This makes it easy for the group to build mutually reinforcing exclusionary beliefs that are impervious to outside challenges. But it also makes it hard for the group to grow into a mass-level movement that can challenge the sovereignty of the state by providing credible alternatives to its members.[66]

---

[65] Consistent with this argument, Krueger and Malecková (2003) present evidence that the majority of the Palestinian population believe that terrorism has helped achieve Palestinian rights.

[66] An implication of Hardin's argument is that insurgent action in pursuit of nationalist goals is successful in recruiting mass-level support because of its ideological vagueness and "lack of programmatic content." Hardin (2002, 12–13) writes that "such vagueness often

This argument about the relationship between ideological commitment and the organizational structure of violent groups can help explain how terrorism can be sustained over long periods with little or no policy success. Terrorists have long horizons, and because beliefs about the likelihood of future victory are always subjective, the logic of terrorism is likely to persist as long as ideology filters events in ways that reinforce the terrorist's beliefs in eventual victory.

This argument also suggests that terrorism will typically not escalate to civil war. In some cases it will – and indeed it has. Reasons for such conflict transformation are partly captured by the civil war models that we studied earlier: if recruiting foot soldiers into a rebel army is feasible because of the combined effect of nondemocratic institutions and low levels of economic development, it is possible to see how the organizational constraints that terrorists face can be overcome or at least reduced.

But part of the reason that terrorism sometimes transforms itself into full-blown rebellion has to do with how states respond to terrorism – and these factors have until now been left out of rationalist models of civil war. Indiscriminate use of state repression in response to terrorism serves to mobilize the masses including moderates who would not otherwise support the terrorists. By contrast, there are theoretical arguments and some empirical evidence that targeted killings of terrorist elites are an effective counterterrorist strategy.[67]

Concessions to extremist groups may only embolden their demands. This follows from arguments that terrorist violence is a bargaining move and that concessions by the state may signal weakness. Terrorists may want escalation (if they are a proto-civil war type of movement). Part of the rationale of violence escalation may be to incite a disproportionate and indiscriminate response from the state, which could mobilize mass-level support for the terrorists (Lake 2002; Laqueur 1987). This "backfiring" of repression has been observed in detailed qualitative analyses of terrorist groups in Western Europe.[68] The mechanisms through which repression leads to conflict escalation are less clear. Partly, repression may cause emotional responses (fear, anger) or it may lead to "belief amplification" (Snow et al. 1986, 469–72), making people feel more strongly that they are being treated

---

underlies negative programs," such as nationalist wars aimed at overthrowing a colonial regime. By contrast, terrorism has clear programmatic content with a "positive" program, in the sense that it seeks to achieve specific goals, which restricts its support base and makes it more focused, but also more extremist.

[67] Tuvia Blumenthal (2004), "Targeted Killings Can Save Lives," *Haaretz*, March 16. For formal models consistent with this logic, see Ethan Bueno de Mesquita (2005a, 2005b).

[68] See, in particular, Della Porta (1995) and Tarrow (1998).

unjustly. Repression of nonviolent people generates new grievances and makes people believe that violence is relatively more effective than nonviolent protest (White 1989, 1293). State repression also creates opportunities for elites to galvanize people into supporting a cause (Jenkins and Perrow 1977; Tilly 1978). Thus, there can be several mechanisms through which states' overreaction to terrorist violence can explain the transformation of terrorism into something larger, including civil war. The obvious implication of this argument is that effective counterterrorist strategies must be targeted and must avoid radicalizing moderates. It takes an overreaction by the state to help terrorists overcome the organizational and ideological obstacles that stand in the way of conflict transformation.

4. Conclusion

Terrorism is a complex phenomenon. It can be a battlefield strategy during a civil war or a distinct form of violence with limited goals, designed to punish the state or seek revenge for prior abuses by the state. Terrorism can have merely symbolic value, or it can be part of a revolutionary strategy with clearly defined political goals. The complexity of terrorism speaks to its many motivations as well as to the impossibility of eradicating it. The fact that terrorism can occur in a variety of different contexts and used as a strategy by a number of actors, including state and nonstate political groups or criminal organizations, means that it is too broad and too heterogeneous a phenomenon to be captured by a single model. It is unlikely that the occurrence of terrorist incidents can be predicted with significant accuracy. The difficulty of predicting terrorist incidents is related to the limited scope of terrorist violence and the relative ease with which such violence can be used against soft targets. The implication for the study of terrorism is that we cannot rely on country-level characteristics such as income or democracy to predict the outbreak of terrorist violence. The potential for such violence is simply too abundant in any political system, so terrorism can occur for quite idiosyncratic reasons even in systems where we would not expect to find much violence.

This argument implies that economic development strategies that increase per capita income or education levels might help reduce terrorism if they help reduce the prevalence of civil war since terrorism can easily occur in civil war. But economic development alone is unlikely to succeed in reducing terrorism of the sort that takes place outside of the context of civil war.

A related point is made by Christina Paxson (2002, 3) who notes that, given that terrorist groups are small, even if higher education and income could reduce motives for terrorism in a population, fighting terrorism by increasing education or income levels would not be the most cost-effective strategy because it would require a massive shift in the distribution of income and education within countries. Thus, Paxson argues that terrorism might be fought more effectively by restricting violence-specific capital (e.g., access to weapons) or by restricting the demand for violence. This is plausible, but the success of such a policy would depend on how feasible it is to restrict access to military technology that is used most commonly in terrorist activity. But the broader point Paxson makes is consistent with the discussion in this chapter.

If terrorism is hard to predict, then perhaps policy makers can think instead about how to reduce the level of terrorist violence once it occurs and how to prevent the transformation of terrorism to civil war. I have touched on this question and have pointed to the fact that existing models of civil war offer little guidance on issues of conflict transformation.[69] Not all terrorist groups want to cause a civil war, and most are not able to do so. The ideological extremism that sustains them limits their ability to mobilize mass-level support. The small, versatile, decentralized, and fluid organizational structure that allows terrorist groups to operate in an asymmetric conflict also hinders their ability to grow into a rebel army by promoting factionalism and preventing coherent, large-scale attacks on the state and its military apparatus. But terrorists can overcome those problems at least partially if the state pushes people into their fold by overreacting to terrorist challenges. If terrorists gain ground in rural areas and begin to control territory and people, they can begin to undermine the state's sovereign authority more effectively as their barriers to recruitment will be lower. This, I have argued, is more likely to happen in low-capacity undemocratic regimes or when indiscriminate repression is used against the population, generating new grievances that play into the terrorists' rhetoric.

The typological differences between civil war and terrorism that I outlined are directly linked to the differences in the causes of the two phenomena. Where terrorism is a proto-civil war or when terrorist violence takes place within the context of civil war, we would not expect to see any significant differences between the two. But when we compare civil wars with cases of terrorism without civil war, then we find that the simple opportunity cost logic that may explain some of the individual decisions to join a rebellion does not fit terrorism. The economic logic of rebel recruitment certainly cannot capture all of the motives that explain recruitment into rebel armies.

---

[69] For such a study of conflict transformation in self-determination movements, see Sambanis and Zinn (2006).

But participation in terrorist action is likely to be systematically different, given the narrower scope, ideological extremism, lack of mass-level support, and significant power asymmetry that characterize terrorism. Yet terrorism and civil war are adjacent phenomena. Terrorists with legitimacy become revolutionaries and failed rebellions can give way to sporadic terrorist violence by the remnants of rebel armies. A key difference between the two phenomena is that terrorism typically cannot generate a tipping point that leads to mass-level support. Poor conflict management can facilitate the transformation of terrorism into civil war. Thus, better targeting of state responses to terrorism may help reduce the risk that terrorist violence will escalate by getting to that tipping point. Economic development as a strategy to reduce the prevalence of terrorism has limited effectiveness unless it is accompanied by – or stimulates – political openness.

References

Abadie, Alberto. 2004. "Poverty, Political Freedom, and the Roots of Terrorism," Unpublished paper, Harvard University, October.

Alesina, Alberto, and Roberto Perotti. 1996. "Income Distribution, Political Instability, and Investment." *European Economic Review* 40: 1203–1228.

Arjona, Ana M., and Stathis N. Kalyvas. 2006. "Testing Theories of Recruitment by Armed Groups: Survey Evidence from Colombia." Mimeo., George Washington University.

Becker, Gary. 1957. *Economics of Discrimination.* Chicago: University of Chicago Press.

Berrebi, Claude. 2003. "Evidence About the Link Between Education, Poverty, and Terrorism Among Palestinians." Princeton, NJ: Princeton University Industrial Relations Section Working Paper 477.

Blau, Judith R., and Peter M. Blau. 1982. "The Cost of Inequality: Metropolitan Structure and Violent Crime." *American Sociological Review* 47: 114–29.

Braithwaite, John. 1979. *Inequality, Crime, and Public Policy.* London, Boston: Routledge & Kegan Paul.

Bueno de Mesquita, Ethan. 2005a. "The Terrorist Endgame: A Model with Moral Hazard and Learning." *Journal of Conflict Resolution* 49: 237–258.

———. 2005b. "Conciliation, Counterterrorism, and Patterns of Terrorist Violence." *International Organization* 59: 145–176.

Chai, Sun-Ki. 1993. "An Organizational Economics Theory of Antigovernment Violence." *Comparative Politics* 26: 99–110.

Collier Paul, and Anke Hoeffler. 2004. "Greed and Grievance in Civil War." *Oxford Economic Papers* 56: 563–595.

Crenshaw, Martha. 1981. "The Causes of Terrorism." *Comparative Politics* 13: 379–399.

Darden, Keith. 2004. "The Scholastic Revolution: Explaining Nationalism in the USSR." Unpublished manuscript, Yale University.

Della Porta, Donatella. 1995. *Social Movements, Political Violence, and the State: A Comparative Analysis of Italy and Germany.* Cambridge: Cambridge University Press.

Deininger, Klaus, and Lynn Squire. 1996. "A New Dataset Measuring Income Inequality." *The World Bank Economic Review* 10: 565–591.

Drakos, Konstantinos, and Andreas Gofas. 2006. "The Devil You Know but Are Afraid to Face: Underreporting Bias and Its Distorting Effects on the Study of Terrorism." *Journal of Conflict Resolution* 50: 714–735.

Eubank, William, and Leonard Weinberg. 1994. "Does Democracy Encourage Terrorism?" *Terrorism and Political Violence* 6: 417–43.

————. 1998. "Terrorism and Democracy: What Recent Events Disclose." *Terrorism and Political Violence* 10: 108–18.

————. 2001. "Terrorism and Democracy: Perpetrators and Victims." *Terrorism and Political Violence* 13: 155–64.

Eyerman, Joe. 1998. "Terrorism and Democratic States: Soft Targets or Accessible Systems." *International Interactions* 24: 151–70.

Fearon, James D., and David D. Laitin. 2003. "Ethnicity, Insurgency, and Civil War." *American Political Science Review* 97: 75–90.

Finer, Samuel E. 1962. *The Man on Horseback.* London: Pall Mall.

Goodhand, Jonathan. 2003. "Enduring Disorder and Persistent Poverty: A Review of the Linkages Between War and Chronic Poverty." *World Development* 31: 629–646.

Grossman, Herschel I. 1991. "A General Equilibrium Model of Insurrections." *American Economic Review* 81: 912–21.

————. 1995. "Insurrections," In *Handbook of Defense Economics*, vol. 1, ed. Keith Hartley and Todd Sandler, 191–212. Amsterdam: Elsevier.

Guillen, Abraham. 1973. *Philosophy of the Urban Guerrilla: The Revolutionary Writings of Abraham Guillen*, translated and edited by Donald C. Hodges. New York: Morrow.

Gurr, Ted Robert. 1970. *Why Men Rebel.* Princeton, NJ: Princeton University Press.

————. 1983. "Some Characteristics of Political Terror in the 1960s." In *The Politics of Terrorism*, 2nd ed., Michael Stohl, 23–49. New York: Marcel Dekker.

Hardin, Russell. 2002. "The Crippled Epistemology of Extremism." In *Political Extremism and Rationality*, ed. Albert Breton, Gianluigi Galeotti, Pierre Salmon, and Ronald Wintrobe. Cambridge: Cambridge University Press.

Hassan, Nasra. 2001. "An Arsenal of Believers: Talking to the Human Bombs." *The New Yorker* 19 November.

Hegre, Håvard, and Nicholas Sambanis. 2006. "Sensitivity Analysis of Empirical Results on Civil War Onset." *Journal of Conflict Resolution* 50: 508–535.

Hibbs, Douglas. 1973. *Mass Political Violence: A Cross-National Causal Analysis.* New York: Wiley.

Hirschleifer, Jack. 1995. "Theorizing about Conflict." In *Handbook of Defense Economics*, vol. 1, ed. Keith Hartley and Todd Sandler, 165–92. Amsterdam: Elsevier.

Hobsbawm, Eric J. 1973. *Revolutionaries: Contemporary Essays.* New York: Pantheon Books.

Horowitz, Donald L. 2001. *The Deadly Ethnic Riot.* Berkeley: University of California Press.

Huntington, Samuel P. 1968. *Political Order in Changing Societies.* New Haven, CT: Yale University Press.

Jenkins, Craig J., and Charles Perrow. 1977. "Insurgency of the Powerless: Farm Worker Movements (1946–1972)." *American Sociological Review* 45: 191–213.

Juergensmeyer, Mark. 2003. *Terror in the Mind of God.* Berkeley: University of California Press.

Kalyvas, Stathis N. 2006. *The Logic of Violence in Civil War.* Cambridge: Cambridge University Press.

Kimhi, Shaul, and Shmuel Even. 2004. "Who Are the Palestinian Suicide Terrorists?" *Terrorism and Political Violence* 16(4): 815–840 (Winter).

Kirk, Richard M. 1983. "Political Terrorism and the Size of Government: A Positive Institutional Analysis of Violent Political Activity." *Public Choice* 40: 41–52.

Kramer, Martin. 1991. "Sacrifice and Fratricide in Shiite Lebanon." *Terrorism and Political Violence* 3: 30–47.

Krasner, Stephen D., and Carlos Pascual. 2005. "Addressing State Failure." *Foreign Affairs* 84: 153–163.

Krueger, Alan B., and Jitka Malecková. 2003. "Education, Poverty, and Terrorism: Is There a Causal Connection?" *Journal of Economic Perspectives* 17: 119–144.

Krueger, Alan, and David D. Laitin. (2007). "*Kto Kogo?*: A Cross-Country Study of the Origins and Targets of Terrorism." Chapter Five, this volume.

Laqueur, Walter. 1987. *The Age of Terrorism.* Boston: Little Brown.

————. 2003. No End to War: Terrorism in the Twenty-first Century. New York: Continuum.

Lake, David A. 2002. "Rational Extremism: Understanding Terrorism in the Twenty-first Century." *International Organization* 56: 15–29.

Li, Quan. 2005. "Does Democracy Promote or Reduce Transnational Terrorist Incidents?" *Journal of Conflict Resolution* 49: 278–297.

Londregan, John and Keith Poole. 1990. "Poverty the Coup Trap, and the Seizure of Executive Power." *World Politics* 42(2): 151–183 (January).

Luttwak, Edward. 1969. *Coup d'Etat: A Practical Handbook.* New York: Knopf.

Marighela, Carlos. 1971. *For the Liberation of Brazil.* Harmondsworth: Penguin Books.

Marshall, Monty, and Keith Jaggers. 2000. "Polity IV Project. Codebook and Data Files." www.bsos.umd.edu/cidcm/inscr/polity.

McAdam, Doug, Sidney Tarrow, and Charles Tilly. 2001. *Dynamics of Contention.* Cambridge: Cambridge University Press.

Merkl, Peter, ed. 1986. *Political Violence and Terror.* Berkeley: University of California Press.

Merton, Robert K. 1957. *Social Theory and Social Structure.* Glencoe, IL: Free Press.

Miguel Edward, Shanker Satyanath, and Ernest Sargenti. 2004. "Economic Shocks and Civil Conflict: An Instrumental Variables Approach. *Journal of Political Economy* 112: 725–753.

Muller, Edward N., and Karl-Dieter Opp. 1986. "Rational Choice and Rebellious Collective Action." *American Political Science Review* 80: 471–487.

Murdoch, James, and Todd Sandler. 2004. "Civil Wars and Economic Growth: Spatial Dispersion." *American Journal of Political Science* 48: 137–150.

Nafziger, Wayne E., and Juha Auvinen. 2002. "Economic Development, Inequality, War, and State Violence." *World Development* 30: 153–163.

Pape, Robert A. 2003. "The Strategic Logic of Suicide Terrorism." *American Political Science Review* 97: 343–361.

Paxson, Christina. 2002. "Comment on Alan Krueger and Jitka Maleckova, 'Education, Poverty, and Terrorism: Is There a Causal Connection?'" http://www.wws.princeton.edu/~rpds/downloads/paxson_krueger_comment.pdf.

Russell, D. E. H. 1974. *Rebellion, Revolution, and Armed Force: A Comparative Study of Fifteen Countries with Special Emphasis on Cuba and South Africa.* New York: Academic Press.

Rosendorff, Peter B., and Todd Sandler. 2005. "The Political Economy of Transnational Terrorism." *Journal of Conflict Resolution* 49: 171–182.

Sambanis, Nicholas. 2002. "A Review of Recent Advances and Future Directions in the Literature on Civil War." *Defense and Peace Economics* 13: 215–243.

———. 2004a. "What Is A Civil War? Conceptual and Empirical Complexities of an Operational Definition." *Journal of Conflict Resolution* 48: 814–858.

———. 2004b. "Expanding Economic Models of Civil War Using Case Studies." *Perspectives on Politics* 2: 259–280.

———. 2005. "Poverty and the Organization of Political Violence: A Review and Some Conjectures." In *Brookings Trade Forum 2004,* ed. Susan M. Collins and Carol Graham, 165–222. Washington, DC: Brookings Institution.

Sambanis, Nicholas, and Annalisa Zinn. 2006. "From Protest to Violence: An Analysis of Conflict Escalation with an Application to Self-Determination Movements." Unpublished manuscript, Political Science Department, Yale University.

Sandler, Todd. 2003. "Collective Action and Transnational Terrorism." *World Economy* 26: 779–802.

Schmid, Alex P. 1992. "Terrorism and Democracy." *Terrorism and Political Violence* 4: 14–25.

Skaperdas, Stergios. 2001. "An Economic Approach to Analyzing Civil Wars." Paper presented at the World Bank Conference on Civil Wars and Post-Conflict Transitions, University of California, Irvine, May 18–20.

Snow, David E., Burke Rochford, Jr., Steven K. Worden, and Robert D. Benford. 1986. "Frame Alignment Processes, Micromobilization, and Movement Participation." *American Sociological Review* 51: 464–81.

Tarrow, Sidney. 1998. *Power in Movement: Social Movements and Contentious Politics,* 2nd ed. Cambridge: Cambridge University Press.

Tilly, Charles. 1978. *From Mobilization to Revolution.* New York: Random House.

———. 2003. *The Politics of Collective Violence.* Cambridge: Cambridge University Press.

———. 2004. "Terror, Terrorism, Terrorists." *Sociological Theory* 22: 5–13.

White, Robert W. 1989. "From Peaceful Protest to Guerrilla War: Micromobilization of the Provisional Irish Republican Army." *American Journal of Sociology* 94: 1277–1302.

World Bank. 2003. "Two Years of Intifada, Closures, and Economic Costs: An Assessment." *World Bank Report No. 26314* (March).

Zeidan, David. 2001. "The Islamic Fundamentalist View of Life as a Perennial Battle." *Middle East Review of International Affairs* 5: 26–53.

PART THREE

THE ORIGINS OF TERRORISTS

SEVEN

The Political, Economic, and Organizational
Sources of Terrorism

David D. Laitin and Jacob N. Shapiro

This chapter organizes the conjectures from a rationalist literature on terrorist organizations, analyzing the strategic issues that they face and the
consequences of their actions. From this perspective, terrorism is seen as
one of a set of rebel tactics that is chosen in response to changes in five
factors: funding, popular support, competition against other rebel groups,
the type of regime against which they are fighting, and counterinsurgency
tactics. However, once groups adopt terrorist tactics over other, more traditional, tactics of insurgency, terrorism becomes self-perpetuating. This is
especially true when the use of terrorist tactics coincides with a shift into
underground modes of organization.

The value added by this literature, in conjunction with some standard
econometric analyses, is that it helps to identify the relevant actors, to
reckon their utilities and payoffs, and to highlight different factors that
affect when/where/and against whom terrorists strike. However, because
the studies under review are not, by and large, written as part of a coherent,
self-aware literature, a summary of the conjectures offered in the literature
will not lead to an internally consistent body of testable hypotheses. Instead,
we use the literature as a jumping off point to suggest a series of broad
hypotheses that should serve as a foundation for future theoretical analysis
and statistical testing. The emphasis here will be on developing hypotheses
to understand why, where, and when civilians are likely to become victims in
rebellions. Little will be said directly about economic development because
the literature on the relationship between terrorism and development has
focused on how to use development to mitigate terrorism, not on how terrorism affects development.[1] Abadie and Gardeazabal (2003) provide evidence

---

[1] This focus reflects myopia on the part of people analyzing the relationship of terrorism to
economic outcomes, one that deserves to be remedied.

that in a rich country (Spain), terrorist activities (by the Basque separatists) have significant negative macroeconomic consequences. Blomberg, Hess, and Orphanides (2004) show an inverse relationship between terrorism and investment in poor countries, especially in Africa. Despite these preliminary results, it has become a part of conventional wisdom that terrorist tactics are more often used against citizens in relatively rich states, in part because in these states soldiers are extremely "hard" targets. Under such conditions, intimidating the population by attacking not military but civilian targets – the essence of terror – is a second-best strategy, due to the fact that rebels are weak vis-à-vis the state they are confronting. If this is the case, terrorism is less a development issue than a police issue for advanced industrial states.

Even if the conventional wisdom is correct, the poor will suffer from increases in terrorism for several reasons. First, as Blomberg, Hess, and Orphanides (2004) show, terrorism is associated with a redirection of economic activity away from investment spending and toward government spending. Even though terrorist incidents appear considerably more frequently in developed nations, the negative influence of the distortion of economic activity due to terrorism likely falls most heavily on poor nations. Second, international terror distorts foreign investment and aid decisions. U.S. bilateral aid to Indonesia after the events of 9/11 shifted from health, education, and welfare issues to the building of institutions to limit money laundering.[2] To the extent that the former had positive welfare implications, the war on terror has been hazardous for the poor in less developed countries. Third, as terrorism increases, the borders of the rich states will be increasingly closed to immigrants from poor states. The more barriers that stand between the rich and the poor, the more the poor will suffer. Finally, if there is no upward bound on the cost OECD states are willing to pay to reduce the fear of terrorism, its citizens and policy makers become blind to the externalities (and who is paying for them) of their counterterrorism policies. These externalities are likely to fall on the poor. Therefore, even though econometrics have not identified a relationship of terror and low growth, increasing use of terror – and the resultant counterterror – should be considered a development issue.

This review has five sections. In the first, we defend the rationalist perspective in analyzing terror. In section two, we examine the conditions that favor terrorist tactics over other forms of rebellious and/or protest activities. In section three, we examine from an organizational perspective why

[2] Laura Bailey, World Bank seminar, May 27, 2005.

terrorism is so hard to end. Section four discusses the implications of the hypotheses articulated in sections two and three for theorizing and large-n data collection. The key issue here is that standard datasets do not allow for efficient testing of the principal hypotheses in the literature. Section five summarizes the previous sections.

1. A Defense of a Rationalist Perspective in Understanding Terrorism

Standard definitions of terrorism point to two criteria.[3] First, the action involves significant damage or death perpetrated by an organized group that seeks to undermine or challenge state authority.[4] Second, the attackers, through the killing of noncombatants or destruction of nonmilitary targets, intend to alter the expectations and daily routines of civilians through the mechanism of fear. This definition, by its focus on means and ends, favors a rationalist theory of terrorism.

Empirical evidence also supports a perspective that assumes rational actors seeking to maximize political goals. *First, terrorists are not psychologically deviant or ideologically blinded.* Hudson's review (1999) shows no consistent psychological profile to identify likely terrorists. For every study finding a purported psychological regularity, recruitment path, or social psychology, he reports a contradictory study. Zimbardo (2004) similarly discounts the notion that terrorist recruits fit a well-defined psychological profile, finding instead that situational factors dominate the decision to engage in terrorism. Tilly (2004) offers a general critique of a "dispositional" approach toward understanding terrorism as part of a critique of Stern's (2003) research that suggests radical Islamic schools increase the disposition toward terrorism. The most balanced account of psychological profiles (McCauley 2002, 5, 7) concludes that terrorists are not crazed or suicidal psychopaths but "emerge out of a normal psychology of emotional commitment to cause and comrades." In this light, he argues, we need to analyze terrorist motivations as a branch of normal psychology, in

---

[3] CENTRA Technology, Inc., under contract with the National Counter Terrorism Center has prepared a comprehensive review of the definitions of terrorism, under the direction of James Harris, Arlington, Virginia (Harris 2005). See also Bergesen and Lizardo (2004) for a discussion of definitions.

[4] This definition is a post-Cold War perspective. During the Cold War, many of the examples of terrorism, as Wickham-Crowley (1990) points out, were state induced. He gives the example of the Acción Democrática governments in Venezuela where "peasants were tied to jeeps and dragged on the ground; others were beaten to death or had their hands cut off; women were raped; huts and grain stores were burnt.... What the government wanted it got: the peasants are terrified" (207).

which terrorists kill for a combination of ideology and intense small-group dynamics.[5]

To be sure, terrorist organizations have a bias that leads them at key junctions to misperceive tactical victories as strategic successes (Petersen 2001; Laitin 1995). Heralding the ambush of a police convoy or the deep fear of urban populations that future terrorist attacks are imminent, rebel organizations lose sight of whether these results really bring them closer to their political goals. Such cognitive dynamics will be particularly strong in groups that must operate clandestinely, as the daily struggle to maintain operational security distort rebels' understanding of the world outside their organization (Bell 1990, 2002). Therefore, we should not expect the abandonment of terrorist tactics as rebel groups fall farther away from any hope for achieving their original political goals or assume that effective counterinsurgency will reduce monotonically terrorist incidents. These findings do not undermine a rationalist perspective because they do not point to any form of psychological deviance by rebel leaders. They merely point to cognitive limits that bias rebel choices. These limits should be built into the assumptions of any positive model of tactical choice.

The search for the causes of terrorism in psychological deviance is therefore misguided. But so is the search for the causes in ideologies such as radical Islam. Documents from Hamas show careful calibration of the use of violence rather than an ideologically driven view to drive enemies of Islam to the sea (Mishal and Sela 2002). Wilhelmsen's (2004) analysis of the second Chechen war shows that the use of Wahhibi Islam was instrumental based on funding availabilities rather than any deep feeling among the leadership for Islamic goals. Menkhaus's (2004) analysis of support for the al Qaeda-linked Al-Ittihad in Somalia shows it has far more to do with the provision of local services than any ideological connection to radical Islam. Finding the psychological and/or ideological foundation for a terrorist movement, according to these analyses, will provide few clues as to their tactical shifts.

Second, empirical work shows that terrorist organizations are tactically rational. Insurgent groups and opposition movements are more likely to adopt terrorist tactics when the benefits of other forms of violence decrease, when the costs of other forms of violence increase, or both.

This has been a fundamental theme in the work of Crenshaw (1985, 1987, and 1990) who traces the rise of terrorist tactics to the increase in American military power. To the extent that direct attacks on military targets by guerrilla forces are likely to fail and hence the benefits to traditional insurgent

---

[5] For a contrary view, postulating psychological traits of terrorists, see Post (1990).

tactics are reduced, rebel groups will go after softer civilian targets. Likewise, the costs to traditional insurgent tactics are lower where the physical terrain is rough and therefore amenable to guerrilla tactics such as ambushes and attacks on government armories (Fearon and Laitin 2003). Thus one possible explanation for low rates of terrorism in certain parts of the world, such as sub-Saharan Africa, is that insurgent organizations are simply less likely to choose terrorism where the terrain and weakness of state armies support the survival of small insurgent bands.

From this perspective of leadership decisions, the evidence is strong that (ignoring bias issues) terrorists attack targets strategically to maximize political goals. Scholars such as Pape (2005) point to data showing that when suicide missions are organized in coherent campaigns, they have generally been successful in bringing the terrorized state to a policy shift. This is the reason, according to Pape, that terrorist organizations rely on suicide tactics mostly against democracies, where popular fear drives policy shifts. Recent evidence from Islamist Web sites shows a clear recognition that Spain was a weak link in the U.S. coalition in Iraq and that the effect of a terrorist attack near an election would be consequential (Brynjar, Lia, and Hegghammer 2004). Mishal and Sela (2002) analyze documents showing that Hamas's leadership engaged in similar reasoning before the Palestinian elections that took place in the wake of the 1993 Oslo accords. Reuter (2004, 73) shows that the Hezbollah training program in Lebanon made clear that for them, suicide attacks are to be sparingly used and designed to generate the minimum number of martyrs and maximum effect. Calibration is a sign of rational maximization of political goals.

On the question of tactical choice, data also support a rationalist perspective. The stronger the state institutions, for example, the more rebels will choose terror over civil war. Blomberg, Hess, and Weerapana (2004) use ITERATE data to show that the U.S. and Western Europe suffer the most terrorism. The authors explain this by the large pie worth fighting over and the low probability of mounting a successful rebellion, relative to the probability of influencing the government through terrorism. Meanwhile, in the nondemocratic states of Africa, terrorizing civilians provides no direct or even indirect influence over the government. In these poorly institutionalized countries, unified resistance and resort to actual war with the opposing government is required for change. Similarly, while Burgoon (2004) finds social welfare to be negatively correlated with terrorist events, he finds that state strength is positively correlated with these events.[6]

---

[6] In a potentially contradictory finding, Brauer, Gómez-Sorzano, and Sethuraman (2004) show a link in Colombia between political unrest and politically motivated murder.

Finally, we should note that the expectation of short-term adjustments in terrorist tactics in reaction to strategic incentives is supported by econometric analysis. Enders and Sandler (2002) analyze several government interventions by antiterrorist state actions: metal detectors in U.S. airports (1973); fortification of U.S. embassies (1976); increases in spending because of the 1979 takeover of U.S. embassy in Tehran, and again in 1985; and the U.S. retaliation against Libya (1986). Using a variety of econometric techniques, they find inter alia that the effect of metal detectors in airports induced a change from skyjackings to more deadly tactics. They conclude that "efforts to secure U.S. airports and borders will cause terrorists to stage their attacks against Americans at other venues and in other countries...terrorists respond to 'higher prices' for one mode of attack stemming from a policy intervention (e.g., better metal detectors and security screening at airports) by substituting an alternative mode where measures have not been taken."

Terror cannot be explained in terms of psychological deviance. And terrorists are sensitive to the costs and benefits of different tactics for the fulfillment of revolutionary goals. It is therefore justified to develop hypotheses culled from the broad literature that can eventually be included in a rationalist theory of tactical choice.

2. Hypotheses on the Political and Economic Sources of Terrorist Campaigns

The most important conditions culled from the literature on the sources of terrorism include popular support (Hypothesis 1); the nature of the political regime (Hypothesis 2); the existence of political competitors for a rebel organization (Hypothesis 3); the sources of funding upon which a rebel organization relies (Hypothesis 4); and the nature of the counterinsurgency tactics of the target state (Hypothesis 5).

H1: *Terrorism is more likely to be chosen by groups that have lost popular support or that have strong popular support. It is less likely to be chosen by groups with moderate and stable levels of support due to the signals of weakness such a choice is likely to send to potential recruits.*

Terrorism by radical groups often begins when the group loses support from the social/cultural population it purports to represent. Wieviorka (1993) calls this phenomenon "inversion." It happens when the social group that radicals wish to mobilize rejects them. Inversion pushes them toward even more radical action, that is, terror. Crenshaw (1990, 12) was early to point out that several groups turned to terrorism when members were unwilling or unable to generate mass mobilization. In Germany and Italy, with left-wing terrorism, della Porta (1995) reports that the more radical wings came to dominate as membership in the overall social movement declined. Della Porta (120–133) uses descriptive statistics to show that over time an increasing portion of group actions – attacks – had to be oriented toward integrative aims, toward keeping the group together. These attacks were often counterproductive in terms of raising external support. More recently, de la Calle and Sánchez-Cuenca (2004) report that ETA militants moved from attacks on police to attacks on civilians when their principal enemy shifted from Basques who were collaborators with the government to competitors for power within Basque country. To the extent that the ETA mission was losing popular support, their violence became directed against civilian competitors and therefore qualified as terrorism.

If groups that have lost public support are likely to use terrorism, the question arises as to whether this is a continuous relationship. Is the probability of adopting terrorist tactics monotonically decreasing in popular support? It is not. Consider the argument that terrorism is actually used as a tactic to enhance popular support. Here the mechanism is one in which state overreaction helps terrorist recruitment; what the Basque terrorists in ETA called the "action/reaction cycle." The Provisional Irish Republic Army (PIRA), as reported by Jackson et al. (2005), sought to make the "Six Counties" ungovernable except by colonial military rule, seeking by their terrorist actions to convince moderate Catholics that the only way they could be ruled by the British would be as colonial subjects.[7] In light of this reasoning, Pape (2003) and Atran (2003) have argued that aggressive counterterrorism can be counterproductive by aiding recruitment and promoting radicalization of moderates among the population that rebel organizations purport to represent. Data collected and analyzed by Kaplan, Mintz, Mishal, and Samban (2005) support Pape and Atran. They find that preventive arrests by Israeli authorities are a better counterterror tool than military attacks against suicide cells because arrests do not enhance recruitment in the way that attacks do.

However, the fact that aggressive government counterterrorism can support recruitment does not show that the logic of the "action/reaction" cycle implies more terrorism by groups with lower popular support. That logic ignores the signal that such attacks sends to the population in whose name

---

[7] But note well that this tactic failed for the Egyptian Islamic Group (EIG) in 1997 according to Sageman (2004, 47, 148). Popular revolt did not follow from government crackdown on the EIG following its attack at Luxor.

the group is fighting. Suppose that terrorists expect states to overreact to their attacks, thereby "proving" to their unsupportive constituency that people of their type are not safe in the country that governs them. Then the very use of terrorist tactics designed to trigger government overreaction signals to the population that the movement lacks popular support. Therefore terrorist attacks, and especially suicide attacks, are risky for organizations that seek popular support. This signaling dynamic, plus the possibility of horrifying their own potential supporters by gruesome tactics, puts constraints on the use of terrorism by groups that do not have high levels of public support. For example, the PIRA and Basque ETA were deterred from using suicide attacks for these reasons (Kalyvas and Sánchez-Cuenca 2005). Likewise, Gurr (1990) reports that a terrorist campaign by the FLQ in Quebec in the 1970s generated a backlash among moderate Quebecois that led to the group's demise.[8]

Groups with strong popular support are not expected to have to worry about this signaling dynamic because they have a recruiting advantage. Bueno de Mesquita (2005b) presents a model to explain the finding that though terrorism is more common in impoverished societies (Blomberg, Hess, and Weerapana 2004; Burgoon 2004) terrorists tend not to come from the lower end of the socioeconomic distribution (Kreuger and Maleckova 2003; Berrebi 2003). His model suggests that terrorist groups select for quality in their recruits and will thus find more potential recruits in a poorer population, assuming that the distribution of competence doesn't decrease too quickly with average income. By a similar logic, groups with popular support will be able to recruit from a larger pool of potential operatives and may find it easier to identify the necessary expertise to adopt and sustain terrorist tactics.

Taken together, these findings suggest a complex relationship between popular support and the propensity of groups to adopt terrorist tactics. We expect the following: rebel groups that have lost popular support are more likely to engage in terrorism out of desperation; rebel groups that have achieved a high level of popular support are able to take advantage of the

---

[8] The signaling dynamic does not apply to international terrorism. Committing attacks on foreign soil can serve as a recruitment device for rebel organizations when it is difficult, due to lack of popular support, to recruit at home. Going after targets in prosperous states gives an organization élan, and makes it more attractive to potential recruits at home. Moreover, if underemployed migrant populations abroad continue to identify with the populations that terrorists claim to represent, they are an excellent pool of terrorists especially when government crackdowns in the home state have effectively deterred terrorist acts (Nesser 2004). Thus any groups' likelihood of adopting international terrorism as a tactic may be conditional on the supporting population identifying a foreign enemy and having recruits abroad who are eager to act in the name of the terrorist organization.

"action/reaction" cycle and therefore are also relatively likely to engage in terrorist tactics; but rebel groups with popular support between these two levels are relatively less likely to engage in terrorism because of the signaling dynamic.

H2: *Terrorism works by creating common knowledge among civilian populations that they are in danger. Thus, it is more effective in democracies where rule of law makes it easier for groups to survive and popular responsiveness makes it more likely that government will react to citizens' knowledge.*

The nature of the political regime affects both the costs and likely benefits of terrorism. The costs of terrorism appear to be decreasing in democracy because democracies tend to impose procedural limits on government counterterrorism tactics.[9] Li (2005) reports that countries with more institutional constraints on government (i.e., free press, many veto players, and the other "government restraint" indicators in the Polity IV index) experience more transnational terrorist incidents. In this case, a one-point increase in the government constraint variable leads to a 6.3 percent increase in number of incidents. He discounts the possibility that this pattern could come from any information-sharing role of the press in passing on terrorist expertise because independent tests of press freedom do not hold up statistically when combined with the government restraint index. This result buttresses nicely with the observation that illegal organizations known to the government survive best where government faces procedural restraints from wiping them out (Fearon n.d.).[10]

For reasons identified in Blomberg, Hess, and Weerapana (2004), democratic regimes are relatively more likely to make policy changes in response to terrorist campaigns.[11] We believe this dynamic is weakly supported

---

[9] In ongoing research Shapiro examines the fates of 243 individuals arrested for participation in the global salafi jihad between 1997 and 2003. Preliminary findings indicate that the average sentence in rich democratic countries is significantly lower than in autocratic states and that procedural safeguards such as restrictive extradition laws have prevented prosecutions in 6% of the cases.

[10] See also the decision by leaders of the main Egyptian Islamist organization, Jamaa Islamiya, to renounce the use of violence because of its failure against the authoritarian Egyptian state. Likewise al-Zawahiri (2001) argues that the *jihad* should focus on Western states supporting apostate Arab regimes because those regimes cannot be overthrown so long as they enjoy Western support.

[11] Gurr (1990) reports that most terrorist campaigns in democratic societies contain the seeds of their own demise, in part by leading to reforms that reduce support for terrorist activities.

by the finding that the richer the country, the more likely it will be the target for international terrorism. Krueger and Laitin (this volume) examine both terrorist incidents using data from *Patterns of Global Terrorism* and data on suicide missions to show that though the attackers tend to be from undemocratic countries, they tend to attack wealthy countries. This is consistent with Krueger and Maleckova's (2003) finding that terrorists do not come from the poorer segments of society. Given that organizations prefer to send competent terrorists, and thus select for high SES, these results are best interpreted as showing that not poverty but oppression is the underlying cause of terrorist incidents. While this work shows no direct relationship between democracy and being targeted, such a relationship may help indirectly, as country wealth is associated with democracy.

H3: *Rebel groups and opposition social movement organizations are more likely to adopt terrorist tactics when they face political competition within the opposition.*

Terrorism by separatist groups is often a function of competition among organizations seeking to become the monopoly representative of the cause. This phenomenon is referred to as outbidding, and it predicts that terrorism will rise with rebel fractionalization. Historical works on revolutionary organizations suggest that centrally controlled organizations tend to shun terrorism, in large part because it would divide the movement and weaken mass action. This is especially true of the Leninists in Russia (Newell 1981). Therefore terrorism is usually a function of a factionalized rebel movement. Aum Shinrikyo leader Asahara, as Jackson et al. (2005) reported, ordered his followers to pursue terrorist violence in competition with "rival" religious organizations that he feared would attract support away from Aum Shinrikyo if they were the first to use terror. Success in early uses of violence led his group to adopt terrorist violence as a more important tool and led it as well to seek chemical, biological, and nuclear capabilities. In Israel, the early Hamas decision to promote terrorist events was driven in part by competition with the Palestinian Islamic Jihad (PIJ), as Mishal and Sela (2000) report. Bloom (2004) reports that the suicide missions before the second Intifada were intended to undermine not only the peace process but also the legitimacy of the Palestinian Authority. After November 2000, in the second *Intifada*, Hamas and other radical organizations relied on the success of suicide missions as a key to gaining popular support. Fatah then invested in suicide attacks not so much as to win concessions from Israel but rather to stem the growing popularity on the street of Hamas. Therefore the dynamics of the factionalized internal politics within the Palestinian movement impelled suicide missions. Using a new and more complete database of suicide missions from 1981 to 2003 in the Israeli-Palestinian conflict, Ricolfi (2005) supports Bloom's focus on the factional splits among Palestinians as the impetus for the growing use of suicide attacks. He argues that the Palestinian Authority could only reestablish its authority given the challenge from Hamas by showing the population that it could play the suicide mission game.[12]

H4: *Terrorism is more likely to be used by rebel organizations and opposition social movements if most of their funding comes from a single source that is unable to monitor the group's activities.*

Hovil and Werker (2005) identify this dynamic, suggesting that when insurgents rely on foreign donors for financial support, terrorist tactics are more likely to be chosen. This is because foreign donors have a monitoring problem and cannot know for sure that insurgents are using their aid to further their revolutionary goals. To mollify donors, insurgents will rely on more visible violence – and this entails attacking civilians – than they would normally do for strategic purposes. They illustrate this dynamic in their study of the Allied Democratic Forces (ADF) in western Uganda that was receiving Libyan aid. The ADF engaged in terrorist violence against locals with a goal of maintaining their level of foreign aid. In consequence, the ADF lost local support and access to local resources as peasants fled the area, and fields (supplying rebels their food) were not replanted.

Though it seems intuitively appealing to think about the relationship of fundraising sources to terrorist activity, little empirical evidence exists to support hypotheses about this relationship. Existing empirical studies of financing terrorist activities either collect conjectures from government reports and press accounts (Piombo 2007) or consist of detailed enumerations of the wide range of methods used to raise, store, and transfer value without assessing the relative frequency of different techniques associated with those methods (Napoleoni 2003).

Given this weak evidence, the best that can be done is to generate hypotheses indirectly through first the relationship of funding sources to group organization and then from group organization to the propensity to adopt

---

[12] Kydd and Walter (2002) suggest that terrorist attacks are methods radicals use to spoil peace agreements. This would explain Hamas moving into terrorist activity but not Fatah entering into the game. Siqueira (2005) models the interaction of a military and political wing of a rebel organization, seeking to deduce the equilibrium level of militant action given different strategies by the counterterrorist state. Again, it is the interaction of rebel factions that provides one dynamic leading to terrorist activity.

terrorist tactics. Here Weinstein (2005) provides insight. His work suggests that the nature of control within rebel organizations depends to a large extent on the resources available to those organizations. Resource-poor groups need to sustain themselves by getting support from peasants in the countryside. If they engage in terrorism and scare the population, their revenue sources and cover from state surveillance will dry up. Resource-rich groups (e.g., those funded by outside powers or those that control valuable resources) will attract opportunistic cadres who will seek short-term maximization of their return to insurgency. In these cases, terrorizing local populations (and stealing from them) makes sense. By this logic, groups that begin with significant resources are more likely to engage in terrorist acts, even when such acts are politically counterproductive.

Shapiro (2005) offers a slightly different analysis but also suggests that the level of central control in cellular organizations depends on their funding sources. In groups that rely on funds raised from sources requiring coordinated effort, such as charitable contributions from diaspora populations, the leadership can maintain de facto control over the organization by conditioning the receipt of funds on certain behaviors.[13] The same is true when groups rely on a sole source of external funding and that source prefers to deal with a centralized organization rather than with a large number of independent factions.[14] However, where fundraising through decentralized means such as ad hoc criminality is feasible, leaders cannot use control over funds to achieve control over their members' activities. In such cases, groups are more likely to slip into terrorism because the leadership cannot prevent politically counterproductive violence by autonomous extremist elements.

H5: *Rebel organizations and opposition social movements become more likely to adopt terrorism as government efforts to end a movement or rebellion alter their internal organizational dynamics, or if patron states give visible support to the counterinsurgency policies of their clients.*

States and rebel organizations respond to each other's tactics, and the choice of terrorism is a function of the incentives created by the other side's choices.[15] In response to insurgent terror, governments often pressure

---

[13] Diaspora fundraising is most effective where subtle coercive efforts are made to pressure a community. For example, La (2004) describes coercive fundraising by the Liberation Tigers of Tamil Eelam (LTTE) in Tamil communities in Canada.

[14] Weinstein (2005) identifies this dynamic among rebel organizations relying on external sponsors.

[15] For a model of government use of terror in counterinsurgency, see Azam and Hoeffler (2002).

rebel organizations by working through social ties among a group's supporters. When this happens, terrorism becomes an organizational tool to prevent "information leakage" in the course of a rebellion. To the extent that informers penetrate rebel organizations, they will terrorize among the civilian population that they purport to represent to scare away future informants (Wickham-Crowley 1990; consistent with Kalyvas 1999). In a related phenomenon, as terrorist organizations decentralize in reaction to counterterrorist tactics, punishment of cell members who shirk becomes more costly, and therefore leaders will target through terror organizational members who defy leadership. Chai (1993) observes this phenomenon in the Japanese Red Army.

A different process comes into play when government offers concessions to ideologically heterogeneous organizations. In such cases, moderates are most likely to accept the buy-outs, leaving extremists in control, rendering the organization more likely to engage in terrorism. Bueno de Mesquita (2005a) develops a model of this process, showing that governments are willing to accept this adverse selection problem when the benefits of counterterror aid from moderate former terrorists outweigh the costs of heightened militancy in the rump organization. Moderates, according to the model, are willing to accept this deal as well because their knowledge of the groups' inner workings provides them with bargaining leverage. In other words, government can credibly commit to concessions because the moderates can withhold counterterror information if the government reneges. Several implications of the model are worth noting. First, if both the radical and moderate factions make concessions, government will renege, so there is no equilibrium level of terrorism where both factions accept concessions. Second, shifting of preferences by the moderate faction through recruiting more extreme members can lead to greater policy concessions by government. Bueno de Mesquita's article relies on selected examples, such as the British offering concessions to the Hagana, to illustrate the model's implications. In a similar vein, Wilhelmsen (2004) identifies a process of radicalization within the Chechen separatist movement as Russian handling of Chechnya contributed to the marginalization of more moderate elements. As we will see in section three, the dynamics illustrated in this model are one reason for the self-perpetuating nature of terrorist campaigns.

Groups that adopt limited nonterrorist uses of violence in response to government pressure can fall into the trap that concerned early Marxist leaders where insurgent organizations were forced to adopt more violent tactics than the strategic situation demanded to retain the allegiance of their most radical cells (Newell 1981). Della Porta (1995) observes a similar trap in her study of Italian and German left-wing terrorist groups. These groups' dependence on violent factions for survival given the tactics of state police pushed them into higher levels of violence against civilians, even when such violence was not politically ideal.

Government success in counterterrorism can have perverse effects. With the jailing of terrorist suspects, prisons in the target state become a prime recruiting ground for terrorist organizers (Cuthbertson 2004, 17; Kenney 2004, 21); this means that terrorist organizations will quickly adopt the skills built into prison survival culture as these men finish serving their sentences. Similarly, the deportation of Hamas operatives to Lebanon brought them conveniently to Hezbollah's school for suicide missions (Reuter 2004, 100).

External states' actions can also affect the level of terrorism. These states, for a variety of strategic reasons, support client states seeking to control terrorism. But to the extent that the patron states become identified with their clients, their populations become natural targets for terrorist actions. The interdicted attack by Algerian rebels in Strasbourg that targeted Notre Dame Cathedral as a symbol of French religion and nationalism is a well-documented example. Nesser (2004) concludes that on balance French support for the Algerian anti-Islamist campaign mainly motivated this attack, although the plotters' personal "diaspora" motivations contributed to their recruitment. French support for the Algerian government similarly motivated the 1995 wave of attacks Algerian Islamists in France carried out (Shapiro and Suzan 2003).

Government efforts to crack down can trigger terrorism, as can government deals with moderates to settle a movement or rebel organization's grievances. Any analysis of the choice of terrorist tactics needs to model state counterinsurgency tactics and as well the tactics of the patrons of states facing insurgencies.

3. Why Terrorism Persists

Analysis of the causes of terrorist tactics cannot explain why terrorism so often persists even when the returns to terrorist actions are declining. An organizational perspective on terrorist tactics is important to explain this persistence. Two hypotheses follow to develop this perspective.

H6: *Once a group engages in terrorism, there is a self-perpetuating logic; the tactic is self-reinforcing.*

There are five factors that support this hypothesis. First, once a terrorist is implicated in a dastardly act, he no longer has an option to freely join the legitimate economy. Second, as Fanon (1968) has noted, great psychological barriers must be overcome before someone can terrorize others. But the second time is much easier than the first. So as time goes on, the psychic costs of perpetrating terrorist acts goes down. Third, if a leadership group plots a terrorist course, its organizational culture becomes set for future terrorist plans, as Sprinzak (1990) identifies in left-wing militant organizations in the United States. All in all, any organization that chooses terrorist tactics will have a difficult time changing its repertoire (Wieviorka 1993, 53–54). Fourth, if funding depends on clear examples of success, a tactical shift toward peaceful negotiation dries up funds from regular contributors (Crenshaw 1991).[16] Fifth, membership in terrorist organizations offers a lifestyle that is often more exciting and meaningful than participants' other options. Recruitment thus suffers with a shift in tactics toward moderate bargaining (Stern 2003).

One implication of the self-perpetuating logic is that for members of terrorist organizations, terrorism becomes not a tactical device to achieve particular ends but a way of life. To the extent this occurs, deterrence strategies to control terrorism are less likely to succeed (Davis and Jenkins 2002).

H7: *Effective government actions have induced organizational shifts for terrorist groups from hierarchy to flattened networks. Counterterrorist success in flattening terrorist organizations, given agency problems, leads to a greater number of attacks in the short run, but attacks that are less carefully targeted, and therefore less successful in fulfilling political goals.*

The current trend in the industrial organization of terror has been away from centralized control and toward an organizational flattening.[17] This is largely driven by the difficulty of maintaining a terrorist organization in the face of American-led counterterrorism when few states are willing to provide safe havens.

The recent pattern is at odds with the modal pattern observed in the historical literature in which radical groups have enhanced central control and adopted more cellular organizational structures in response to government pressure (Shapiro 2005). A study of recent European terrorist organizations

---

[16] For a good rational choice account for the perpetuation of violent strategies, see Chai (1993).

[17] The pioneers in studying social movements from the point of view of their industrial organization are Zald and McCarthy (1980), and they recognized the implications for these movements of organizational fragmentation. Many of the recent studies on terrorist organizations are footnotes to Zald and McCarthy.

finds them to be involved in a "loosely organized collective conflict in which 'hundreds of groups and organizations – many of them short-lived, spatially scattered, and lacking direct communication, a single organization, and a common leadership – episodically take part in many different kinds of collective action" (della Porta 1995, quoting Oberschall 1980, 45–6).[18] Studies of al Qaeda reveal that after 1996, the group's central staff was no longer directly involved in most field operations (Sageman 2004, 138). Arquilla and Ronfeldt (2002) describe Salafi jihadism in similar terms. Evidence from the Madrid attack of March 2004 shows that locals unaffiliated with centralized networks can organize highly effective attacks on civilian targets. Though most had lived militant lives before their arrival in Spain, plans for the attack were ad hoc without central direction (Jordan and Horsburgh 2005).

Several reasons lie behind this reversal of organizational structure. First, the operational inefficiencies decentralization introduced have decreased as the market in weapons and information about the production of weapons has globalized, giving local networks without central direction an opportunity to take autonomous action in the name of the broader organization with which it empathizes.[19] Second, there are fewer safe havens provided by sanctuary states, and without such havens governments can more easily identify terrorist organizations' hierarchical links (Pillar 2004). Horgan and Taylor (1997) find that as British intelligence successfully penetrated the PIRA organizational hierarchy in the mid-1990s – a period when the leadership no longer had a safe haven in the Republic of Ireland – it was compelled to give greater autonomy to its local Active Service Units (ASU), something it had not done during earlier reorganizations. Kenney (2004) identifies a similar dynamic among Colombian narcoterrorists and al Qaeda, both of which have evolved "flat" organizational structures in response to government campaigns that targeted leadership and limited the availability of safe havens.

The flattening of terrorist structures leads to reduced communications between center and cells, exacerbating the agency problems inherent in underground organization. Less hierarchy means that middlemen (standing between the organizational leadership and local activists) will be more likely to appropriate organizational resources for private purposes (Shapiro

---

[18] To be sure, not all terrorist organizations factionalize. Wieviorka (1993) reports that the Red Brigades in Italy became *more* hierarchical and bureaucratized as the Italian police closed in on them. Mishal and Sela (2000) report similar changes by Hamas. Shapiro (2006) analyzes the core challenges driving the organizational choices of terrorist groups.

[19] Note well that there is no evidence that globalization itself has an impact on the number or target of incidents. See Li and Schaub (2004).

and Siegel 2007) and that more initiative will be given to local cells performing tasks with insufficient funds and direction. In light of these factors, organizations have a harder time preventing politically damaging civilian casualties. Given counterterrorist success in breaking up organizational hierarchy, as we hypothesized, we should expect an enhanced number of attacks, but attacks that are less well funded and less carefully targeted.

Consistent with this hypothesis, Bell's studies of European groups (1990) and Salafi jihadi groups (2002) show that flatter organizational structures and more secure operational patterns (in light of counterterrorist pressure) rendered these groups less able to coordinate actions, control operatives, and efficiently use group resources. Indeed, wildcatters may also have planned the al Qaeda attacks in London in July 2005.

Thus an increased number of (albeit indiscriminate) attacks may well be the result of greater "success" by counterterrorist states in identifying and disrupting rebel organizations. However, this success is merely tactical, because the uncoordinated attacks in which tactics are not adjusted to strategy and the political environment make it more likely that terrorists will fail to achieve their political goals.

A key policy implication of this analysis is that approaches that continue to think of a terrorist organization as a hierarchy – with success determined by rankings on a deck of cards – are no longer likely to be successful. Early evidence suggests that counterterrorist operations that resist head hunting have had success in undermining newly flattened terrorist networks.[20]

4. Issues of Formalization and Data

A general principle that follows from many of the hypotheses discussed herein is that terrorism is not an attribute of a group whose members have a specific psychological profile or who share a particular ideology. Rather terrorism is a tactic adopted by rebel groups given a set of internal and external constraints, and its further use is sensitive to resources and political constraints. Furthermore, terrorism in civil wars is sensitive to funding levels and sources, organizational dynamics, and government policies.

If this perspective is correct, it should influence how in the future we collect data for a war on terrorism. Counting "incidents" as separate

---

[20] See Shapiro and Suzan (2003) on France; and Finnegan (2005) on New York City and the successful terrorist adaptations. See also Arquilla and Ronfeldt (2002) and Cullison (2004) for excellent data on the organizational travails of terrorist groups in the face of state penetration.

observations may be the wrong way to code for the degree of terrorism in the world, because such data do not allow us to distinguish between factors leading to increases in terrorism due to substitution from traditional insurgency into terrorism and increases in terrorism due to an increase in the overall level of rebel activity. Instead, we need to collect data on terrorism as part of a family of related rebellious activities and acknowledge that groups under changing circumstances will switch strategically among these activities. We therefore need to know when groups move from one form of rebellion toward and away from terrorism.

The family of related activities upon which data should be collected to shed light on this strategic choice is broad. We list them here.

(a) **Organized Crime**. Silke (1998) reports that loyalist paramilitaries in Northern Ireland used extortion to raise funds. His paper is stunning in regard to how much terrorist groups resemble traditional organized crime. Examples of Mafia-style retaliation against those who rob businesses that pay protection money suggest that the provision of protection services is an oft-used tactic of rebel organizations.

(b) **Armed Robbery**. Silke (2000) reports that when extortion was insufficient, Irish paramilitaries relied on armed robbery to sustain their operations. Collusion with criminals is used to reduce the risks to the paramilitary organizations of fundraising, often by demanding a "tax" on criminal proceeds.

(c) **Drug Wars**. The Irish People's Liberation Organization, a splinter group within the nationalist movement, turned to drug dealing to finance a terrorist campaign. Wealth accrued this way quickly corrupted the organization, and plagued by internal feuds, it degenerated into gangsterism (Silke 2000). Hudson (2002) reports similarly for the FARC in Colombia and the Abu Sayyaf Group (ASG) in Philippines.

(d) **Homicides**. Brauer, Gómez-Sorzano, and Sethuraman (2004) show that the correlates of large-scale homicide are quite similar to violent rebellion. In McGarry and O'Leary (1995), the authors present data showing that though the sum of terrorist and homicidal killings in Northern Ireland has remained a constant, the latter go up during periods of truce. This suggests that criminal violence is a substitute for terrorist attacks under certain conditions.

(e) **Hate Crimes**. The difference between a terrorist act and a hate crime, as coders at the National Counterterrorism Center have found, is often a matter of whether there is a group behind the action with a wider political program. Therefore as hate crimes become more institutionalized in a society, they merge into the category of terror.

(f) **Standard Insurgency**. Rural-based guerrilla attacks generally involve ambushes of convoys, attacks on armories, mortaring or burning of villages, and selectively assassinating political and military authorities. Because these insurgencies seek to win the hearts and minds of local populations, leaders of rural insurgencies have discouraged the use of terrorism (Wickham-Crowley 1990). But of course the temptation to terrorize is always present, especially when support begins to wane.

(g) **Terrorism**. We should think about subcategories of terrorism. Hijacking airplanes, suicide attacks, the taking of hostages or kidnapping, and the bombing of official/commercial structures are a few of the many possible categories. Shifts between these tactics represent adaptations by organizations to changes in the effect of their actions and in the capabilities of security forces. Terrorist tactics, because their mechanism of affect is shock and awe, have limited life spans. Skyjacking, after initial successes, had declining marginal returns for rebel organizations because of the loss of the shock effect and the learning by counterterrorist forces on how best to mitigate its effects. Because of this adaptive dynamic, we should expect to see a cat-and-mouse adaptation of constantly new terrorist tactics over time.

A clear implication of this chapter is that counting terrorist incidents, the principal method of ITERATE, of MIPT, and of RAND, may not capture the dynamics of rebellion and the conditions under which terrorist tactics are chosen. An alternative data collection strategy would be to make the unit of observation "rebel goal, date, incident." Other columns would include organizational data, data on the annual homicide rate in the country in the year of the incident, and data on the number of hate crimes and army robberies not attributed to groups. We would also need columns for the government responses to these acts. Finally, we would need a column recording the number of incidents in that year attributed to rival groups representing the same cause. If the data were organized in this way, we would be able to track systematically the changing percentage of violent incidents that are terrorist for all rebel organizations and the conditions that lead organizations to choose terrorism over other means of influencing the state.

5. Summary and Conclusion

Though the literature identifies a number of factors affecting the costs and benefits to terrorist tactics, we believe the following are the most important:

(a) the strength of state institutions, (b) the democratic processes within the target state, (c) the degree of popular support for the terrorist organization within the population it purports to represent, (d) the degree to which rebel organizations within a state are factionalized, (e) the sources and magnitude of funding to the rebel organization, and (f) the tactics of the target state in response to a proto-insurgency.

But once an organization adopts terrorism within its tactical repertoire, adjustment to other tactics is difficult. While rebel organizations adapt to the changing opportunities in response to state tactics, the adaptations serve to reduce the costs of continued terrorist actions rather than to move toward other tactics. There is thus a self-reinforcing quality to the initial choice to adopt terrorist tactics.

Once terrorism is understood as a tactical choice for rebel groups, the most useful specification of the dependent variable would be the ratio of terrorist incidents compared with all incidents promoted by a rebel organization. Present data collection efforts are organized to count the raw number of terrorist incidents by groups and, therefore, cannot discern trends in the importance of terrorism in any group's repertoire of rebellion. This chapter recommends a change in the organization of terrorist data to allow for sharper analysis of terrorist trends, better theoretical development, and more effective hypothesis testing.

References

Abadie, Alberto, and Javier Gardeazabal. 2003. "The Economic Costs of Conflict: A Case Study of the Basque Country." *American Economic Review* 93:113–132.

al-Zawahiri, Ayman. 2001. "Knights Under the Prophet's Banner." *Al-Sahraq al-Awsat* (London), December 2. Foreign Broadcast Information Service (FBIS) translation available at http://www.fas.org/irp/world/para/ayman_bk.html.

Arquilla, John, and David Ronfeldt. 2002. "Netwar Revisited: The Fight for the Future Continues." *Low Intensity Conflict & Law Enforcement* 11:178–189.

Azam, Jean-Paul, and Anke Hoeffler. 2002. "Violence Against Civilians in Civil Wars: Looting or Terror." *Journal of Peace Research* 39:461–85.

Atran, Scott. 2003. "Genesis of Suicide Terrorism." *Science* 299: 1534–1539.

Bell, J. Bowyer. 1990. "Revolutionary Dynamics: The Inherent Inefficiencies of the Underground." *Terrorism and Political Violence* 2:193–211.

———. 2002. "The Organization of Islamic Terror: The Global Jihad." *Journal of Management Inquiry* 11:261–266.

Bergesen, Albert J., and Omar Lizardo 2004. "International Terrorism and the World-System." *Sociological Theory* 22:38–52.

Berrebi, Claude. 2003. "Evidence About the Link Between Education, Poverty and Terrorism Among Palestinians." Princeton University Industrial Relations Section Working Paper No. 477 (September).

Blomberg, S. Brock, Gregory D. Hess, and Athanasios Orphanides. 2004. "The Macroeconomic Consequences of Terrorism." *Journal of Monetary Economics* 51:1007–32.

Blomberg, S. Brock, Gregory D. Hess, and Akila Weerapana. 2004. "Economic Conditions and Terrorism." *European Journal of Political Economy* 20: 463–478.

Bloom, Mia M. 2005. *Dying to Kill.* New York: Columbia University Press.

———. 2004."Palestinian Suicide Bombing: Public Support, Market Share, and Outbidding." *Political Science Quarterly* 119:61–88.

Brauer, Jergen, Alejandro Gómez-Sorzano, and Sankar Sethuraman. 2004. "Decomposing Violence: Political Murder in Colombia, 1946–1999."*European Journal of Political Economy* 20:447–461.

Brynjar, Lia, and Kjok Ashild. 2001. "Islamist Insurgencies, Diasporic Support Networks, and Their Host States: The Case of the Algerian GIA in Europe 1993–2000." *FFI/Rapport* 2001/03789.

Brynjar, Lia, and Thomas Hegghamme. 2004. "Jihadi Strategic Studies: The Alleged Al Qaida Policy Study Preceding the Madrid Bombings." *Studies in Conflict and Terrorism* 27:355–375.

Bueno de Mesquita, Ethan. 2005a. "Concilliation, Counterterrorism, and Patterns of Terrorist Violence." *International Organization* 59:145–176.

———. 2005b. "The Quality of Terror." *American Journal of Political Science* 49:515–530.

Burgoon, Brian. 2004. "On Welfare and Terror: Social Welfare Policies and Political-economic Roots of Terrorism." Amsterdam School for Social Science Research, ASSR Working Paper 04/07.

Chai, Sun-Ki. 1993. "An Organizational Economics Theory of Antigovernment Violence." *Comparative Politics* 26:99–110.

Crenshaw, Martha. 1985. "An Organizational Approach to the Analysis of Political Terrorism." *Orbis* 29:465–89.

———. 1987. "Theories of Terrorism: Instrumental and Organizational Approaches." *Journal of Strategic Studies* 10:13–31.

———.1990. "The Logic of Terrorism: Terrorist Behavior as a Product of Strategic Choice." In *Origins of Terrorism*, ed. Walter Reich. Washington, DC: Woodrow Wilson Center Press, 7–24.

———. 1991. "How Terrorism Declines." *Terrorism and Political Violence* 3:379–399.

Cullison, Alan. 2004. "Inside Al-Qaeda's Hard Drive." *Atlantic Monthly* 294:55–70.

Cuthbertson, Ian M. 2004. "Prisons and the Education of Terrorists." *World Policy Journal* 21:15–22.

Davis, Paul K., and Brian Michael Jenkins. 2002. *Deterrence & Influence in Counterterrorism: A Component in the War on Al Qaeda.* Santa Monica, C.A.: RAND.

de la Calle, Luis, and Ignacio Sánchez-Cuenca. 2004. "La Selección de Víctimas en ETA." *Revista Española de Ciencia Política* 10:53–79.

della Porta, Donatella. 1995. *Social Movements, Political Violence, and the State: A Comparative Analysis of Italy and Germany.* New York: Cambridge University Press.

Enders, Walter, and Todd Sandler. 2002. "Patterns of Transnational Terrorism, 1970–1999: Alternative Time-Series Estimates." *International Studies Quarterly* 46:145–65.

Fanon, Frantz. 1968. *The Wretched of the Earth.* New York: Grove Press.

Fearon, James. n.d. "Civil War Since 1945: Some Facts and a Theory." Manuscript, Department of Political Science, Stanford University.

———— and David Laitin. 2003. "Ethnicity, Insurgency, and Civil War." *American Political Science Review* 97(1): 75–90.

Gurr, Ted Robert. 1990. "Terrorism in Democracies: Its Social and Political Basis." In *Origins of Terrorism*, ed. Walter Reich. Washington, DC: Woodrow Wilson Center Press, 86–102.

Harris, James. 2005. *Terrorism Metrics: A Compilation of Definitions.* Arlington, VA: Centra Technology.

Horgan, John, and Max Taylor. 1997. "The Provisional Irish Republican Army: Command and Functional Structure." *Terrorism and Political Violence* 9:1–32.

Hovil, Lucy, and Eric Werker. 2005. "Portrait of a Failed Rebellion: An Account of Rational, Sub-optimal Violence in Western Uganda." *Rationality and Society* 17:5–34.

Hudson, Rex A. 1999. *The Sociology and Psychology of Terrorism: Who Becomes a Terrorist and Why?* Washington, DC: Federal Research Division, Library of Congress.

————. 2002. *A Global Overview of Narcotics-Funded Terrorist and Other Extremist Groups.* Washington, DC: Federal Research Division, Library of Congress.

Jackson, Brian A., et al. 2005. *Aptitude for Destruction: Organizational Learning in Terrorist Groups and Its Implications for Combating Terrorism.* Santa Monica, CA: RAND.

Jordan, Javier, and Nicola Horsburgh. 2005. "Mapping Jihadist Terrorism in Spain." *Studies in Conflict and Terrorism* 28:169–191.

Kalyvas, Stathis. 1999. "Wanton and Senseless? The Logic of Massacres in Algeria." *Rationality and Society* 11:243–285.

———— and Ignacio Sánchez-Cuenca. 2005. "Killing Without Dying: The Absence of Suicide Missions." In Diego Gambetta (ed.) *Making Sense of Suicide Missions* (Oxford: Oxford University Press), 209–32.

Kaplan, Edward H., Alex Mintz, Shaul Mishal, and Claudio Samban. 2005. "What Happened to Suicide Bombings in Israel? Insights from a Terror Stock Model." *Studies in Conflict and Terrorism* 28:225–235.

Kenney, Michael. 2007. *From Pablo to Osama: Trafficking and Terrorist Networks, Government Bureaucracies, and Competitive Adaptation.* University Park, PA: Pennsylvania State University Press.

Kreuger, Alan B., and David D. Laitin. "*Kto Kogo?*: A Cross-Country Study of the Origins and Targets of Terrorism," chapter 5 this volume.

Krueger, Alan B., and Jitka Maleckova. 2003. "Education, Poverty and Terrorism: Is There a Causal Connection?" *Journal of Economic Perspectives* 17:119–144.

Kydd, Andrew, and Barbara F. Walter. 2002. "Sabotaging the Peace: The Politics of Extremist Violence." *International Organization* 56:263–96.

La, John. 2004. "Forced Remittances in Canada's Tamil Enclaves." *Peace Review* 16(3): 379–385.

Laitin, David D.. 1995. "National Revivals and Violence." *Archives Européennes de Sociologie* (Spring 1995), 3–43.

Li, Quan. 2005. "Does Democracy Promote or Reduce Transnational Terrorist Incidents?" *Journal of Conflict Resolution* 49:278–97.

Li, Quan, and Drew Schaub. 2004. "Economic Globalization and Transnational Terrorism: A Pooled Time-Series Analysis." *Journal of Conflict Resolution* 48:230–258.

McCauley, Clark 2002. "Psychological Issues in Understanding Terrorism and the Response to Terrorism," in Chris E. Stout (Ed.), *The Psychology of Terrorism, Volume III Theoretical Understandings and Perspectives.* Westport, CN: Praeger, 3–30.

McGarry, John, and Brendan O'Leary. 1995. *Explaining Northern Ireland: Broken Images.* Oxford: Basil Blackwell.

Menkhaus, Ken. 2004. *Somalia: State Collapse and the Threat of Terrorism.* Adelphi Paper 364. International Institute for Strategic Studies.

Mickolus, Edward F., Todd Sandler, Jean M. Murdock, and Peter Flemming. 2004. *International Terrorism: Attributes of Terrorist Events, 1968–2003* (ITERATE). Dunn Loring, VA: Vinyard Software.

Mishal, Shaul, and Avraham Sela. 2000. *The Palestinian Hamas.* New York: Columbia University Press.

———. 2002. "Participation without Presence: Hamas, the Palestinian Authority and the Politics of Negotiated Existence." *Middle Eastern Studies* 38:1–26.

Napoleoni, Loretta. 2003. *Modern Jihad: Tracing the Dollars Behind the Terror Networks.* New York: Pluto Press.

Nesser, Petter. 2004. *JIHAD IN EUROPE – A Survey of the Motivations for Sunni Islamist Terrorism in Post-millennium Europe.* FFI/Rapport-2004/01146.

Newell, David Allen. 1981. *The Russian Marxist Response to Terrorism: 1878–1917.* PhD Diss., Stanford University.

Oberschall, Anthony. 1980. "Loosely Structured Collective Conflict: A Theory and an Application." *Research in Social Movements, Conflicts and Change* 3:45–68.

Pape, Robert. 2005. *Dying to Win.* New York: Random House.

Petersen, Roger Dale. 2001. *Resistance and Rebellion: Lessons from Eastern Europe.* New York: Cambridge University Press.

Pillar, Paul R. 2004. "Counterterrorism after Al Qaeda." *The Washington Quarterly* 27:101–113.

Piombo, Jessica. 2007. "Terrorist Financing and Government Response in East Africa." In *Terrorist Financing in Comparative Perspective*, ed. Harold Trinkunas and Jeanne K. Giraldo. Stanford, CA: Stanford University Press.

Post, Jerrod M. 1990. "Terrorist Psycho-Logic: Terrorist Behavior as a Product of Psychological Forces." In *Origins of Terrorism*, ed. Walter Reich. Washington, DC: Woodrow Wilson Center Press, 25–42.

Reuter, Christopher. 2004. *My Life is a Weapon.* Princeton, NJ: Princeton University Press.

Ricolfi, Luca. 2005. "Palestinians, 1981–2003." In *Making Sense of Suicide Missions*, ed., Diego Gambetta, 77–129. London: Oxford University Press.

Sageman, Marc. 2004. *Understanding Terror Networks.* Philadelphia: University of Pennsylvania Press.

Shapiro, Jacob N. 2005. "Organizing Terror: Hierarchy and Networks in Covert Organizations." Manuscript, Department of Political Science, Stanford University.

———. 2006. "The Terrorist's Challenge: Security, Efficiency, Control." Manuscript, Department of Political Science, Stanford University.

Shapiro, Jacob N., and David A. Siegel. 2007. "Underfunding in Terrorist Organizations." *International Studies Quarterly.*

Shapiro, Jeremy, and Bénédicte Suzan. 2003. "The French Experience of Counterterrorism." *Survival* 45:67–98.

Silke, Andrew. 1998. "In Defense of the Realm: Financing Loyalist Terrorism in Northern Ireland – Part One: Extortion and Blackmail." *Studies in Conflict and Terrorism* 21:331–361.

———. 2000. "Drink, Drugs, and Rock'n'Roll: Financing Loyalist Terrorism in Northern Ireland – Part Two." *Studies in Conflict and Terrorism* 23:107–127.

Siqueira, Kevin. 2005. "Political and Militant Wings within Dissident Movements and Organizations." *Journal of Conflict Resolution* 49:218–236.

Sprinzak, Ehud. 1990. "The Psychopolitical Formation of Extreme Left Terrorism in a Democracy: The Case of the Weathermen." In *Origins of Terrorism*, ed. Walter Reich. Washington, DC: Woodrow Wilson Center Press, 65–85.

Stern, Jessica. 2003. *Terror in the Name of God: Why Religious Militants Kill.* New York: HarperCollins.

Tilly, Charles. 2004. "Terror as Strategy and Political Process." Manuscript, Department of Social Science, Columbia University.

Weinstein, Jeremy M. 2005. "Resources and the Information Problem in Rebel Recruitment." *Journal of Conflict Resolution* 49:598–624.

Wickham-Crowley, Timothy P. 1990. "Terror and Guerrilla Warfare in Latin America, 1956–1970." *Comparative Studies in Society and History* 32:201–37.

Wieviorka, Michel. 1993. *The Making of Terrorism.* Chicago: University of Chicago Press.

Wilhelmsen, Julie. 2004. *When Separatists Become Islamists: The Case of Chechnya.* FFI/RAPPORT 2004/00445.

Zald, Mayer N., and John D. McCarthy. 1980. "Social Movements and Industries: Competition and Cooperation Among Movement Organizations." *Research in Social Movements, Conflict and Change* 3:1–20.

Zimbardo, Philip G. 2004. "A Situationalist Perspective on the Psychology of Evil: Understanding How Good People are Transformed into Perpetrators." In *The Social Psychology of Good and Evil*, ed. Arthur G. Miller. New York: Guilford Press, 21–50.

EIGHT

Economics and Terrorism: What We Know, What We Should Know, and the Data We Need

Fernanda Llussá and José Tavares

1. Introduction

In the last seven years, terrorism, its consequences, and how to counteract it, have become a household discussion subject and the object of intense scrutiny by social scientists. This is the direct consequence of the attack of September 11, 2001, in the United States, the shape of the U.S. government's response in a variety of forms labeled the "war on terror," and the continuing occurrence of extremely violent attacks in various parts of the world. In economics, the literature on terrorism has made remarkable advances since 2001, building on important work that was available. The literature has been strengthened in the range of topics analyzed, as well as the data and methodologies employed. In spite of substantial progress, though, different strands of research remain insufficiently integrated. At this stage, charting the progress made so far and suggesting fruitful avenues for additional effort are key. This chapter puts forward a broad survey of the economic literature on terrorism, organized according to seven different topics. We identify what we think we know, highlight the key issues that remain to be answered and the data that might illuminate this research effort.

Any attempt at organizing existing knowledge on a topic should circumscribe the topic and adopt a definition. Terrorism, given its variety of objectives, methods, targets, and organizational forms, is elusive as far as definitions go. The word "terror," at least with its ominous sense of persistent and indiscriminate violence, has been traced to the Robespierre years of revolutionary France.[1] The word "terror" has remained associated with the actions of states against their own citizens, not least due to the historical record of Nazism and Stalinism. In discussing the issue of "terrorism,"

---

[1] See Harris (2005) and Bergesen and Lizardo (2004) for a discussion of the definitions of terrorism.

we ought to recognize that totalitarian experiments (in the worst sense of the word) have been responsible for millions of victims in the premeditated use of state-sponsored terror. Only recently does the word "terrorism" (no longer "terror") suggest an association with the actions of subnational groups.[2] Here, we adopt Enders and Sandler's (2002) view of terrorism as "the premeditated use or threat of use of extra-normal violence or brutality by sub-national groups to obtain a political, religious, or ideological objective through intimidation of a huge audience, usually not directly involved with the policymaking that the terrorists seek to influence," the most frequently used in studies of terrorism.[3] In this, as well as in most definitions of terrorism, four important elements come together to characterize it: the "underground" or even informal nature of the perpetrators of terrorist acts, be it individuals or organizations; the premeditated or "rational" element in the pursuit of objectives; the crucial role of violence, often of an extreme nature; finally and certainly not least, its intended influence on a broad audience beyond the direct targets.

Our examination of the economics literature on terrorism shows that most studies concentrate on the consequences of terrorist attacks at the aggregate level and in specific sectors of activity. An important share of the literature is empirical, using a limited number of available datasets. Notable examples are all those papers that examine the causes or consequences of terrorism in the context of theoretical models of individual, group, or aggregate economic behavior. The analysis of individual actors is severely constrained by data limitations. Another strand in the literature is clearly policy-oriented and, although presenting neither a theoretical model nor an empirical exercise, can provide very useful insights.[4]

---

[2] Irrespective of the breadth and legitimacy of the possible definitions of terrorism, we must acknowledge that data on terrorist attacks have one important limitation: they tend to refer to attacks by nonstate groups (even if sponsored by foreign states) on the citizens and the assets of a specific nation or economy.

[3] The official definition by the United States Department of State is compiled under title 22 of the United States Code as the "premeditated, politically motivated violence perpetrated against noncombatant targets by sub-national groups or clandestine agents, usually intended to influence an audience" (Office of the Coordinator for Counterterrorism [1997]). Interestingly, the Federal Bureau of Investigation (FBI) and the Department of Defense slightly change the definition to highlight the "*unlawful* use of force or violence" and explicitly include both people and property. Another possible definition, by Mickolus (1980, xiii), sees terrorism as "the use, or threat of use, of anxiety-inducing extra-normal violence for political purposes ... when such action is intended to influence the attitudes and behavior of a target group wider than the immediate victims and when ... its ramifications transcend national boundaries." See also Mickolus (1982) and Shugart (2007).

[4] See Llussá and Tavares (2007) for a "graphical" presentation of the breakdown of papers on the economics of terrorism regarding their micro versus macro and empirical versus theoretical approach.

In this chapter we organize the study of the economics of terrorism around seven different topics. Although some papers are relevant for more than one topic, our organization and comprehensive view of the literature is useful to identify the questions that remain unanswered. The topic areas are: The Measurement of Terrorist Activity, The Nature of Terrorists, The Utility Cost of Terrorism, The Effect of Terrorism on Aggregate Output, Terrorism and Specific Sectors of Activity, Terrorism and Economic Policy, and Counterterrorism. Thus, from measurement we proceed to studies on the characteristics of terrorists and terrorist organizations, the consequences of terrorism for individual utility and, at the aggregate level, the cost of terrorism in terms of output and output growth, the direct effect on specific sectors of activity, and the reflection of terrorism in fiscal and monetary policies. We conclude with an examination of the economics literature on counterterrorism measures.

In this chapter we discuss, for each of the topics listed, what the literature has achieved, important questions that remain open, and the type of data that would help researchers make progress. In our discussion, we identify the main papers in the literature and the issue(s) where each made a contribution. In the appendix we present a brief individual summary of the papers, in tables organized along the topic areas.

2. What We Know, What We Should Know, and the Data We Need

Next we present our assessment of the state of the literature on terrorism for which research in economics has (or should have) made a contribution. For each theme, we start with a brief summary of what we "know," and proceed to a discussion of the issues worth an extra research effort, pointing to data limitations when relevant.

2.1. The Measurement of Terrorist Activity

The measurement of terrorist activity has resulted in a limited number of datasets. Some provide a count of terrorist events and have been widely used, most notably those organized by Mickolus and associates – Mickolus (1980, 1982), Mickolus and Flemming (2003), Mickolus et al. (1989, 1993) – and the dataset from the International Policy Institute for Counter-Terrorism (2003). A wide group of datasets is based on sectoral or individual information and tends to be collected directly by researchers conducting a specific study and thus to be poorly disseminated. As mentioned in the introduction, the variety of objectives, means, targets, and organizations, in addition to the underground nature of terrorism, add to the difficulty of measuring terrorist activity. Terrorism ranges from ethnically motivated to state sponsored and religious or ideologically motivated and can directly target the government, the military or the civilian population, and extending from individual assassinations to the threat of use of weapons of mass destruction.[5] A simple count of events may seriously underestimate the phenomenon of terrorism. It is important to acknowledge the indirect and psychological costs of terrorism, whether or not translated into actual attacks. This is addressed in the subsection on the utility cost of terrorism.

The existing literature has established important facts about the occurrence of terrorism. First, terrorist attacks are relatively rare and extreme events. The number of actual attacks is highly volatile over time and across countries, as Enders and Sandler (2002) document.[6] There is some evidence of a cyclical pattern in terrorism, a higher prevalence during economic downturns – documented in Im et al. (1987) and Enders and Sandler (1995, 2000) and explained in Blomberg, Hess, and Weerapana (2004a) – or close to the occurrence of elections – electoral outcomes in Berrebi and Klor (2004) and electoral dates in Brauer et al. (2004). There is evidence that terrorist attacks have become more lethal over time – Enders and Sandler (2000) and Sandler and Enders (2004) present data that might be explained by a change in the motivation of terrorists, from ideological to religious, and a change in method, towards the use of suicide attackers, as documented in Berman and Laitin (2005). In addition, at least since the 1967 Arab-Israeli War, many acts of terrorism have acquired a transnational nature.[7]

Rich countries are frequent targets of terrorism. Israel and the United States are the most frequent targets, the latter also indirectly, through political and business interests – as documented in Blomberg, Hess, and Weerapana (2004a, 2004b), Blomberg and Hess (2007), Enders and Sandler (2002), and Krueger and Laitin (2007) – and this remains true when a count of events per capita is used – as in Tavares (2004).[8] It is unclear whether democracies are likelier targets – see Blomberg et al. (2004, 2007) for a "yes," Tavares (2004) for a "no," and Abadie (2004) for a nonmonotonic relationship where countries with intermediate levels of political rights are subject to more attacks. Blomberg and Hess (2007) use bilateral data to find that,

[5] See Enders and Sandler (1995; 2002) and Frey (2004) for a discussion. Shugart (2007) organizes an analytical history of terrorism around three "waves": the national liberation and ethnic separatism phase, the ideological, and the religious.
[6] Tavares (2004) shows that the time series on yearly terrorist attacks displays a substantially higher standard deviation than a similar series on natural disasters.
[7] See Enders and Sandler (2002).
[8] Laitin and Shapiro (2007) argue for the use of relative indicators of the intensity of terrorism.

while richer, more open, and more democratic countries seem more prone to be targeted, poorer, less democratic, and less open countries are more often the origin of terrorists – corroborated by Krueger and Laitin (2007).

The measurement of terrorist activity presents opportunities for research in at least three areas. To support research on the individual and aggregate costs of terrorism and the effectiveness of different counter-terrorism measures, there is a need to document the type and nature of attacks as far as number of events, type of targets, type of organization, number of dead and wounded, direct dollar cost of attacks, and, especially type of media coverage. A thorough documentation of how these different characteristics of attacks correlate and evolve over time is a precondition for identifying what it is that causes what and why. A reading of the literature strongly suggests that data constraints have limited the type of terrorism indicator used, and studies that compare the effects of different indicators are rare. A second issue deserving substantial attention is more technical in nature and appeals to a much broader use of statistical and econometric techniques that take account of outliers, censored and truncated data when assessing the incidence of terrorism. The incentives of governments and certainly of terrorist organizations go against transparency and toward manipulation of information, but this may be partly overcome by a more intense use of the techniques already discussed. A third important issue for research on the measurement of terrorism, for which econometric methods are useful, is a fuller account of the fact that terrorism does not always lead to terrorist acts. The task of measuring the underlying level of terrorist activity, as opposed to terror events, is an important step to assess the individual utility cost and the economic cost of terrorism.

2.2. The Nature of Terrorists

There are several explanations for the emergence of terrorist groups and the occurrence of terrorist attacks, ranging from those based on individual or group incentives to an examination of how aggregate variables correlate with the frequency of events. Both provide important insights. In general, what is known as to the individual motivations of terrorists goes against current prejudices that view terrorists as irrational misanthropes with low income and poor education.[9] Generalizations are extremely risky at the current stage of research, but, if anything, available evidence suggests that the support for and participation in terrorist acts is not associated with

---

[9] This does not mean they are not driven by political and religious ideologies.

lower educational or economic status – as in Krueger and Maleckova (2003), Berrebi (2003), and in Schelling (1991).[10]

As the presence of suicide actors dramatically illustrates, nontraditional explanations for terrorism may be required – as in Wintrobe (2006, 2007) on extreme tradeoffs, where one of the choice variables is whether to use your own life; Hardin (1995) on group identity theories; and Ferrero (2005) on the use of social sanctions. The use of club good theory – as in Berman (2003) and Berman and Laitin (2005) – is another important tool toward identifying group rationality, associating the process of recruiting terrorists to membership in a restricted group, with its associated costs and benefits.[11] More specifically, the existence of multiple terrorist groups, behaving "rationally" but pursuing different objectives, may confound conclusions. Kydd and Walter (2002) show how a minority of terrorist radicals may "rationally" delay a truce between the government and a majority of their own camp that desire peace as violent actions undermine the trust between the majorities of peace seekers on both sides of the conflict. Siqueira (2005) shows how the existence of different factions may instead decrease rather than increase terror activity.

As argued in Laitin and Shapiro (2007), the strength of state institutions, the democratic process in the target state, the degree of popular support for the terrorist organization, the degree to which terrorist organizations divide into factions, the sources and magnitude of funding, and the counterterrorist tactics, all affect the nature and intensity of terrorist activities. These authors put forward a series of hypotheses on the political, economic, and organizational determinants of terrorism, derived from the "rationalist" view that sees terrorists as calculating individuals reacting to incentives. Laitin and Shapiro (2007) propose that organizations with either dwindling support, or strong support but no political voice, are more prone to adopt terrorism as a tactic, especially in democratic states. Moreover, the

---

[10] As an example of an explanation for these counterintuitive results, education can signal an individual's ability to commit, a necessary input for extreme actions. Azam (2005) uses a dynastic model where the "benefits" of terrorism accrue to several generations to rationalize this result: higher income and higher educated individuals may be more sensitive to those future benefits. Bueno de Mesquita (2005b) models terrorist volunteers and terrorist organizations that screen for "quality," delivering results consistent with more terrorism in recessionary economies while actual terrorists are better educated than the average. For an interesting exercise based on a different view, see Berman and Stepanyan (2004), which assesses the number of potentially "radical" Muslim women, based on fertility, low returns to education, and religious education.

[11] The "demand" for suicide terrorists is easier to understand. See Wintrobe (2006) and Pape (2003).

adoption of terrorism tends to be reinforced by the emergence of perverse incentives once that path has been chosen. Several studies view terrorism as the result of tensions and new resources that arise with modernization – Crenshaw (1981) and Aziz (1995) – and the rise of religious-based fundamentalism – also Crenshaw (1981). Terrorism may be a substitute for other forms of political conflict in the internal fight over resources – as in Garfinkel (2004), Blomberg et al. (2004b), and Sambanis (2007)[12] – and terrorist acts as part of a signaling game where governments are uninformed of the terrorists' strength – Lapan and Sandler (1993)-or, in the case of international terrorism, a foreign policy tool used in foreign policy crises – O'Brien (1996). Individual hatred toward specific groups or nations can emerge from misinformation and manipulation by political leaders – as in Glaeser (2005) and Charney and Yakatan (2005) – who can enhance follower loyalty by promoting violence and terrorism – Epstein and Gang (2004).

What avenues for research are presented insofar as the characteristics and motivations of terrorists? First, and despite important progress, the analysis of individual motivations should proceed by encouraging interdisciplinary research, bringing economics into closer interaction with other disciplines, especially psychology, sociology, political science, and media studies. This can enrich the "rational" explanations for terrorist participation, helping build more plausible models of extreme behavior. In parallel, interdisciplinary research can result in further testing of the existing incentive theories of terrorist participation. Second, we need to know much more about the "industrial organization" of terrorist groups. Terrorists seldom act alone and are instead recruited, trained, supported, and protected by specific organizations and networks. These organizations have developed different organizational patterns over time, the study of which can help identify the source of terrorism and the best instruments to counter it. The fact that some terrorist organizations are twins to more easily scrutinized political parties or associations, with a line of discourse and reaction to events, opens possibilities for important documentation of the terrorists' motivations. Data collection on the internal organization of terrorism, on the role of different actors, technologies, and costs – financial, time, or otherwise – will help identify effective points for defusing it. A third promising line of research is the collection of survey data on the relationship among individual characteristics such as income, education, and support for terrorism. Detailed studies of this type could unveil the individual characteristics that groups

---

[12] Though Sambanis (2007) argues that development may decrease the risk of civil war without significantly altering the risk of terrorist activity.

delve into when recruiting terrorists, but also the public reaction to different terrorist goals, means, and activities, which terrorist groups probably take into account in their decisions.

2.3. The Utility Cost of Terrorism

No doubt, terrorist acts have a negative influence on individual utility and on the economy. However, their association with extreme random harm and a level of uncertainty that is difficult to ascertain suggests that terrorism's utility cost goes well beyond the direct and immediate damage. Terrorism entails costs linked to what some term a "nonrational" evaluation of risk on the part of individuals, namely, a decrease in utility that goes beyond the computable expectation of losses. The perception of this cost may be associated with an outcome-independent negative effect of "fear and loathing" that greatly exceeds the "objective" discounted harm – as in Becker and Rubinstein (2004) and Sunstein (2003).[13] Despite its "nonrational" nature, this perceived cost can be quite substantial. Viscusi and Zeckhauser (2003) suggest that there are several anomalies in people's evaluation of the cost of terrorism, and Frey et al. (2004) argue that people's utility losses from terrorism far exceed the expected consequences.

There are important lines of future research on the utility cost of terrorism. It is very important to assess directly, through individual surveys and contingent valuation techniques, the effect of terrorism on individual happiness. In the wake of successful applications of contingent valuation to public and environmental economics, researchers should evaluate the effect of terrorism on self-reported subjective well-being. Additionally, research should try to identify the characteristics of terrorist acts that entail the greatest subjective loss.

2.4. The Effect of Terrorism on Aggregate Output

A considerable number of articles on the economics of terrorism concentrate on the consequences of terrorist events on the macroeconomy, namely on

---

[13] Becker and Rubinstein (2004) argue that an exogenous shock to the probability of being harmed affects peoples' choice in two ways: a change in exposure to risk – the weights of "good" and "bad" states change – and in fear – in each state of nature, the utility level itself decreases in response to an increased probability of being harmed. Sunstein (2003) had shown that individuals focus on the "badness" of the result rather than on the probability of occurrence. This so-called "probability neglect" results in fear that greatly exceeds the discounted harm.

output.[14] The direct cost to output seems to be relatively low and short term – Hobijn (2002), International Monetary Fund (2001), Navarro and Spencer (2001), and Treverton et al. (2007) – and mostly associated with public expenditures for specific military operations abroad and protective measures at home – Treverton et al. (2007). Terrorist attacks do reduce economic growth, though its effect is estimated to be much smaller than that of violent internal conflict and external war – Blomberg et al. (2004) – or even natural disasters – Tavares (2004). However, high and persistent levels of terror – Eckstein and Tsiddon (2004) – or concentrated in specific regions – Abadie and Gardeazabal (2003) and World Bank (2002, 2003) – have a considerable effect. Moreover, although less often targeted, poorer countries suffer more from attacks – see Blomberg et al. (2004) and Sandler and Enders (2007) on poorer countries, World Bank (2002, 2003) on Israel versus the Palestinian territories.[15] Democratic countries show more resilience to attacks – Tavares (2004). Larger and more diversified economies are likely to suffer less – Sandler and Enders (2007).

An alternative way to look at the effect of terror on aggregate output is to examine its effect on the value of stocks of different companies. Here researchers have found evidence that the effect is relatively short term and may decrease over time – as in Choudhry (2003), Chen and Siems (2004), and Eldor and Melnick (2004). A possible explanation is that efficient markets diversify efficiently, diminishing the influence of risk on particular stocks.

The study of the effects of terrorist attacks on output and economic growth seems relatively consensual in that the cost is limited and short term, except in cases of extreme vulnerability. We believe a useful line of research stems from analyzing the cost of terrorism in light of what is known on the cost of other unlikely but extreme events such as natural disasters, which also are rather circumscribed in time. A second line of research should connect the cost of terrorism to the literature on volatility and growth,[16] which relates output changes to the fluctuations of consumption, investment, and trade. A third line of research that would draw on relatively inexpensive collection of new data would be to run event-studies on the performance of stock markets differentially affected by terrorism in periods of heightened terrorist activity.

---

[14] See Brück and Wickström (2004) for a survey on the consequences of terrorism.
[15] The World Bank (2002, 2003) estimates the cost of the Palestinian–Israeli conflict for both contenders: while the cost to Israel is estimated at 4 percent of GDP, the Palestinian territories suffered a 50 percent decline in income per capita between 1994 and 2002. In addition, specific sectors such as tourism and trade have been especially hurt.
[16] See Auffret (2003) and Hnatkovska and Loayza (2003).

2.5. Terrorism and Specific Sectors of Activity

In addition to the effects on aggregate output already mentioned, the economics literature provides ample evidence that terrorism is associated with significant differential effects on specific economic sectors. There are noticeable decreases in consumption following terror attacks – modeled and documented in Eckstein and Tsiddon (2004) and documented in Fielding (2003a) – and decreases in investment – modeled and documented in Eckstein and Tsiddon (2004), also documented in Blomberg et al. (2004) and in Fielding (2003b) –, the latter also consequence of a crowding out effect in response to increases in public spending, which we will cover in the next subsection. Capital flows and trade across borders also tend to decrease – as argued and documented in Abadie and Gardeazabal (2005) and documented in Enders and Sandler (1996) for capital flows; argued in Walkenhorst and Dihel (2002) and documented in Nitsch and Schumacher (2004) for trade.[17]

Tourism and airline demand, due to their specific vulnerability to terrorist attacks and to fluctuations in consumer sentiment, have received special attention by researchers. The consensus points to a clear negative effect on tourism and airline demand – Drakos and Kutan (2003), Enders et al. (1992), Enders and Sandler (1991, 1996), Sloboda (2003), and Fleischer and Buccola (2002) on tourism; Drakos (2004) and Ito and Lee (2004) on airline demand.

The concentration of economic and governmental activities and the large population density of urban areas hint at their greater vulnerability to terrorism. This can be compounded by the fact that media attention is naturally focused on events taking place in large, populated, identifiable geographical areas, that is, cities. If this view holds, terrorism can be viewed as a tax on cities. Several authors have discussed whether cities are particularly vulnerable, but the estimates put forward point to a very limited cost, especially in the long run – Bram et al. (2002), Glaeser and Shapiro (2002), Harrigan and Martin (2002), Mills (2002), and Rossi-Hansberg (2003).

Given the association of terrorism with risk in general, and the dramatic revisions in the risk profile that economic activities face, the insurance industry is likely to be affected, either positively or negatively, by terrorism.[18] In

[17] The contraction in trade may be in response to an increase in trade and transport costs, as argued in Organization for Economic Development and Cooperation (2002) and Lenain et al. (2002).

[18] Woo (2002) presents an analytical method to compute the risk of terrorism in actuarial terms. Lenain et al. (2002) argue for an effect on the insurance industry.

addition, changes in exposure may highlight market imperfections in the industry.[19] There is evidence that the stock of insurance companies reacts to increased terrorist risk – Cummins and Lewis (2003). There is a broad discussion on the appropriateness of government schemes that interfere with the insurance market, such as the Terrorism Risk Insurance Act (TRIA) in the United States. Chalk et al. (2005) examine the trends in terrorism and in the threat level to the United States and how the Terrorism Risk Insurance Act responded or not to those changes.[20] Kunreuther et al. (2003) show that the insurance system TRIA established is neither a complete nor a definitive response to increased risk. Brown et al. (2004) follow thirteen key legislative events leading to the Terrorism Risk Insurance Act (TRIA) in November 26, 2002, and document their effect on the stock price of firms in banking, construction, insurance, real estate investment trusts, transportation, and public utilities. Stock prices in the affected industries responded negatively to the legislative events. As to the differential effect of terror on other activities, Berrebi and Klor (2005) show strong evidence of a differential and positive effect on defense and security-related Israeli industries in response to terror attacks.[21]

The research agenda on the sectoral effects of terrorism is likely to yield interesting results in at least two directions. First, given the differential effect of terrorism on the components of output and different economic sectors, namely on consumption and investment, it is worthwhile to investigate which characteristics of terror events drive consumption and investment changes. This is compatible with the suggestion in subsection one on organizing existing data and collecting new data on terrorist actions. Given the different reasons for changes in consumption and in investment and the different motivations of the decision makers involved – consumers or firm managers – the use of a richer panel of characteristics of attacks may help

[19] Froot (1999) studies catastrophic events. According to risk management theory, reinsurance should cover the most severe events such as natural disasters. However, reinsurance is more prevalent for mid- and small-size risk events. Supply restrictions associated with capital market imperfections and market power exerted by reinsurers are the most reasonable explanations for the divergence of observed data from what is expected from theory.
[20] One of the reactions to the 2001 attacks on the World Trade Center was the enactment of the Terrorism Risk Insurance Act (TRIA), which requires insurance companies to provide terrorism insurance to customers in return for federal provision of reinsurance in case of losses due to terrorist attacks.
[21] This is true also of defense-related Israeli exports, which seem to have benefited from a boom following the attacks.

identify which characteristics affect different aggregates: victims, material losses, type of perpetrators, or a simple count of events. In addition, there are several sectors for which stock market data are available and which should react differently to terror, in line with Berrebi and Klor (2005). A second line of research is the collection of new aggregate data on tourist movements, including origin and destination and information on cost and length of stay, to evaluate more finely the effect and the substitution effect between destinations. Crossing this data with information on media coverage, which should vary substantially across countries, can also lead to important insights.

2.6. Terrorism and Economic Policy

Terrorism can affect fiscal and monetary policy, either as any other unexpected shock would, or as the result of the endogenous response of economic policy making to terrorist events. The increase in public spending in response to additional security needs is likely to be small – as argued in Lenain et al. (2002), Gupta et al. (2004), and Hobijn (2002) – and probably with little effect on budget deficits – Eichenbaum and Fisher (2004) and Wildasin (2002).

Another important issue is the reaction of the payments system in the face of an attack. Here there is at least one careful study of the consequences of the September 11 terrorist attacks on the monetary and payment systems, in the context of what is required knowledge on banking crises. Lacker (2004) shows how the Federal Reserve credit extension after September 11 increased the supply of banks' balances and attenuated the effects of the terrorist shock.

2.7. Counterterrorism

A final key question on terrorism and the economy, and probably the most important policy issue, is what can be done to reduce the incidence of terrorism. The two basic policy options are, in simplified terms, to counter terrorism by force – the "stick" – option or to increase the opportunity cost, to terrorists make the targets less attractive, or to adjust the media coverage to diminish the benefits – the "carrot" option.[22] In thinking about counter-terrorism, it is realistic to acknowledge beforehand that complete eradication of terrorist activity is unlikely, not only because of imperfect

---

[22] See Frey (2004) for a discussion of the relative attractiveness of these two counter-terrorism options.

information and cost asymmetry, which gives terrorist groups a strategic advantage, but also due to continuous innovation on both sides of the conflict.[23]

Evidence shows that terrorists substitute between means, targets, and across time – Im et al. (1987) for substitution away from military and governmental targets to tourists and over time.[24] This ability on the part of terrorists suggests the use of a portfolio rather than one specific antiterrorist measure – argued in Enders and Sandler (2004) and Frey (2004). Deterrence has been the main response of states to terrorist organizations but may not be the right strategy since it induces escalation and a negative sum game interaction – as argued in Frey (2004) and modeled in Arce and Sandler (2005) and Bueno de Mesquita (2005b).[25] Bueno de Mesquita (2007) argues that the observability of specific counter-terrorism measures and the voters' perceptions may explain a bias. For deterrence as highlighted in Rosendorff and Sandler (2004), proactive policies may be excessive and encourage more "dramatic" terrorist attacks, either at home or abroad. Economic sanctions may also be ineffective.[26] An important measure is active limitation of terrorist funding through better regulation – proposed in Fitzgerald (2004). Other counter-terrorist strategies that should be considered involve decreasing the benefits or raising the opportunity cost, rather than the material cost, of terrorist attacks – Frey and Luechinger (2003; 2004) and Frey (2004).[27] There is evidence that citizens realize the complexity of terrorism and are ready for more considered and more flexible policy responses – Downes and Hoffman (1993) – including during episodes involving hostage taking – Shambaugh and Josiger (2004).

---

[23] Mickolus et al. (1989) quote an IRA member who, after a near miss of the United Kingdom prime minister, bragged: "Today, we were unlucky. But remember we have only to be lucky once. You will have to be lucky always."

[24] In addition, there may be substitutability with other forms of violence, as argued in Garfinkel (2004) and Blomberg, Hess, and Weerapana (2004a, b). See 2.2.

[25] Frey (2004) lists a series of costs from overreliance on deterrence, including budgetary costs and political costs (in terms of possibly reduced support for counter-terrorism policy), exploitation by self-interested politicians to extend their stay in power, and reduced human rights and civil liberties. Deterrence also entails costs due to the response of terrorists, who gain in visibility and cohesion and substitute toward potentially deadlier modes of attack. Concessions may be important, even as they apparently result in more attacks in the immediate aftermath, as explained in Bueno de Mesquita (2005b).

[26] See Frey (2004).

[27] However, in a comparative analysis of the two forms of political violence, Sambanis (2007) argued that economic development may decrease the likelihood of civil war but not of terrorism.

Credible nonnegotiating policies are also key – Sandler and Enders (2004) – but time inconsistency is an issue, leading to a high risk of default – as explained in Lapan and Sandler (1993). At the other extreme, some states tolerate the activities of terrorist organizations in their territory in exchange for no direct harm, at the expense of other nations – a dominant strategy, according to Lee (1988) – which points to the desirability of multilateral coordination and institutions. Coordination is also described as desirable in Rosendorff and Sandler (2004), whenever there are incentives for too much or too little proactive counterterrorism, at the cost of more "dramatic" attacks, and in Sandler and Siqueira (2003), who argue that an efficient counterterrorist policy cannot be achieved through the leadership of one country.

One plausible response to terrorism is adjusting how political institutions – as discussed in Wilkinson (2001) – or legal institutions function – discussed in Garoupa et al. (2006) and, more skeptically, in Enders et al. (1990). Mueller (2004) argues that it is necessary instead to strengthen democratic institutions and increase citizens' understanding and support for those institutions.[28] Other options include decentralizing political institutions to decrease the attractiveness of targets – argued in Frey and Luechinger (2003) – and increase the cost to terrorists through screening – as in Viscusi and Zeckhauser (2003) and Garoupa et al. (2006).

We identified three important niches for research on counter-terrorism. First, we should learn more on the linkage between a country's legal and political institutions and both the incidence and the impact of terrorism. In the wake of September 11 and the qualified restrictions on civil liberties, a debate has ignited over the appropriate means that democracies should use in their fight against terrorists. Here we believe the history of terrorism in Israel provides a field for examining the comparative effectiveness of counter-terrorist measures through a case study analysis. A related issue is how to make democratic institutions less vulnerable to terrorism.[29] A second research path should model the asymmetries between the terrorists and the governments' actions, in terms of information and cost requirements, as an intermediate step toward increasing the effectiveness of counterterrorism. A particular issue worth investigating given the current level of the debate is how to coordinate among nations as far as information and means

---

[28] Tavares (2004) finds evidence that the more democratic a country, the lower the output decrease following a terror attack.

[29] Here, a useful linkage can be made with the literature arguing that more developed institutions lower the incidence or the cost of risk.

to combat terrorism, exploiting the existence of multiple equilibria in the coordination level among countries and in the incidence of terrorism. A third research area that we consider particularly promising is analysis of the media coverage of terrorist events. Foremost among the motives for terrorist activity is the publicity gained freely as a consequence of terror. Existing geographical variation in coverage – for example, in Europe versus the United States – and variation in its content and intensity – as to terrorist groups, motivation, victims mentioned, and so forth, can go a long way toward establishing what in terrorism drives (or not) media attention. By combining datasets on terrorist events and the associated news coverage, researchers can better understand how the media could be used to discourage terrorist activity.

3. Concluding Remarks

Probably, and unfortunately also for the worst reasons, terrorism will be high on the political agenda for years to come. Understanding the motivations of terrorists and terrorist groups and the policies to diminish the occurrence and the effects of violence must be a key element in the response to terrorism. This is only possible if we extend our knowledge on the intrinsic nature of the terrorist phenomena by collecting new data and methods to answer the remaining questions, thus decreasing the extent of our ignorance of its causes and consequences. In this general effort, the role of economics research as surveyed in this chapter, is likely to remain central.

References

Abadie, Alberto. 2004. "Poverty, Political Freedom and the Roots of Terrorism." Working Paper 10859, National Bureau of Economic Research, Cambridge, MA.

Abadie, Alberto, and Javier Gardeazabal. 2003. "The Economic Costs of Conflict: A Case Study of the Basque Country." *American Economic Review* 93:113–32.

_____. 2005. "Terrorism and the World Economy." Working Paper, Harvard University.

Air Transportation Association of America 2001. Annual Report. http://www.airlines. org/economics/review_and_outlook/annual+reports.htm.

Arce, Daniel G., and Todd Sandler. 2005. "Counterterrorism: A Game-Theoretic Analysis." *Journal of Conflict Resolution* 49:183–200.

Auffret, Phillipe. 2003. "High Consumption Volatility: The Impact of Natural Disasters?" Working Paper, 2962, World Bank Policy Research.

Azam, Jean Paul. 2005. "Suicide Bombing as Intergenerational Investment." *Public Choice* 122:177–98.

Aziz, Heba. 1995. "Understanding Attacks on Tourists in Egypt." *Tourism Management* 16:91–95.

Becker, Gary S., and Yona Rubinstein. 2004. "Fear and Response to Terrorism: An Economic Analysis." Working Paper, University of Chicago.

Bergesen, Albert J., and Omar Lizardo. 2004. "International Terrorism and the World-System." *Sociological Theory* 22:38–52.

Berman, E. 2003. "Hamas, Taliban and the Jewish Underground: An Economist's View of Radical Religious Militias." Working Paper 10004, National Bureau of Economic Research, Cambridge, MA.

Berman, E., and D. Laitin. 2005. "Hard Targets: Theory and Evidence on Suicide Attacks." Working Paper 11740, National Bureau of Economic Research, Cambridge, MA.

Berman, Eli, and Ara Stepanyan. 2004. "How Many Radical Islamists? Indirect Evidence from Five Countries." Working Paper, University of California, San Diego.

Berrebi, C., and E. Klor. 2005. "The Impact of Terrorism Across Industries: An Empirical Study." Discussion Paper 5360, Centre for Economic Policy Research, London.

Berrebi, Claude, and Esteban F. Klor. 2004. "On Terrorism and Electoral Outcomes: Theory and Evidence from the Israeli-Palestinian Conflict." Industrial Relations Section, Working Paper Series, Princeton University.

Berrebi, Claude. 2003. "Evidence About the Link Between Education, Poverty and Terrorism Among Palestinians." Industrial Relations Section, Working Paper Series, Princeton University.

Blomberg, S. Brock, Gregory Hess, and Athanasios Orphanides 2004. "The Macroeconomic Consequences of Terrorism." *Journal of Monetary Economics* 51:1007–32.

Blomberg, S. Brock, Gregory Hess, and Akila Weerapana. 2004a. "Economic Conditions and Terrorism." *European Journal of Political Economy* 20:463–78.

———. 2004b. "An Economic Model of Terrorism." *Conflict Management and Peace Science* 21:17–28.

Blomberg, S. Brock, and Gregory D. Hess. 2007. "The Lexus and the Olive Branch: Globalization, Democratization and Terrorism." In *Terrorism and Economic Development*, ed. P. Keefer and N. Loayza, chap. 4. Cambridge: Cambridge University Press.

Board of Governors of the Federal Reserve System. 2001. "Guide to the Federal Reserve's Payments System Risk Policy." Washington, DC: Federal Reserve Board.

Bram, Jason, Andrew Haughwout, and James Orr. 2002. "Has September 11 Affected New York City's Growth Potential?" *Economic Policy Review*, Federal Reserve Bank of New York 8:81–96.

Brauer, Jurgen, A. Gómez-Sorzano, S. Sethuraman. 2004. "Decomposing Violence: Political Murder in Colombia." *European Journal of Political Economy* 20:447–61.

Brown, Jeffrey R., J. David Cummins, Christopher M. Lewis, and Ran Wei. 2004. "An Empirical Analysis of the Economic Impact of Federal Terrorism Reinsurance." *Journal of Monetary Economics* 51:861–98.

Brück, T., and Bengt-Arne Wickström. 2004. "The Economic Consequences of Terror: A Brief Survey." Working Paper, University of Sussex.

Bueno de Mesquita, Ethan. 2005a. "Conciliation, Counterterrorism, and Patterns of Terrorist Violence." *International Organization* 59:145–76.

———. 2005b. "The Quality of Terror." *American Journal of Political Science* 49:515–30.

———. 2007. "Politics and the Suboptimal Provision of Counterterror." *International Organization* 61(1):9–36 (Winter).

Chalk, Peter, Bruce Hoffman, Robert Reville, and Anna-Britt Kasupski. 2005. *Trends in Terrorism: Threats to the United States and the Future of the Terrorism Risk Insurance Act.* Malibu, CA: Rand Center for Terrorism Risk Management Policy, Rand Corporation.

Charney, C., and Nicole Yakatan. 2005. "A New Beginning: Strategies for a More Fruitful Dialogue with the Muslim World." Council on Foreign Relations, CRS No. 7.

Chen, Andrew H., and Thomas F. Siems. 2004. "The Effects of Terrorism on Global Capital Markets." *European Journal of Political Economy* 20:349–66.

Choudhry, Taufiq. 2003. "September 11 and Time-Varying Beta of United States Companies." Mimeo., Bradford University School of Management.

Constitutional Rights Foundation. 2001. "Significant terrorist attacks." http://www.crf-usa.org/terror/.

Council of Insurance Agents & Brokers. 2003. "2003 Terrorism Insurance Survey." Washington, DC: Council of Insurance Agents & Brokers.

Crenshaw, Martha. 1981. "The Causes of Terrorism." *Comparative Politics* 13:379–99.

Cummins, J. David, and Christopher M. Lewis. 2003. "Catastrophic Events, Parameter Uncertainty and the Breakdown of Implicit Long-Term Contracting: The Case of Terrorism Insurance." *Journal of Risk and Uncertainty* 26:153–78.

Downes-Le Guin, Theodore, and Bruce Hoffman. 1993. "The Impact of Terrorism on Public Opinion, 1988 to 1989." Malibu, CA: RAND Corporation.

Drakos, Konstantinos. 2004. "Terrorism-Induced Structural Shifts in Financial Risk: Airline Stocks in the Aftermath of the September 11th Terror Attacks." *European Journal of Political Economy* 20:435–46.

Drakos, Konstantinos, and Ali M. Kutan, 2003. "Regional Effects of Terrorism on Tourism in Three Mediterranean Countries." *Journal of Conflict Resolution* 47:621–41.

Eckstein, Zvi, and Daniel Tsiddon, 2004. "Macroeconomic Consequences of Terror: Theory and the Case of Israel." *Journal of Monetary Economics* 51:971–1002.

Eichenbaum, Martin, and Jonas D. M. Fisher. 2004. "Fiscal Policy in the Aftermath of 9/11." Working Paper 10430, National Bureau of Economic Research, Cambridge, MA.

Eldor, Rafi, and Rafi Melnick. 2004. "Financial Markets and Terrorism." *European Journal of Political Economy* 20:367–386.

Enders, W., and T. Sandler. 2004. "What Do We Know about the Substitution Effect in Transnational Terrorism?" In *Research on Terrorism: Trends, Achievements, Failures*, ed. Andrew Silke, 119–37. London: Frank Cass.

Enders, Walter, and Todd Sandler. 2002. "Patterns of Transnational Terrorism, 1970–1999: Alternative Time-Series Estimates." *International Studies Quarterly* 46:145–65.

———. 2000. "Is Transnational Terrorism Becoming More Threatening?" *Journal of Conflict Resolution* 44:307–32.

———. 1996. "Terrorism and Foreign Direct Investment in Spain and Greece." *Kyklos* 49:331–52.

———. 1995. "Terrorism: Theory and Applications" In *Handbook of Defense Economics*, ed. Keith Hartley and Todd Sandler, vol. 1, 213–49, Amsterdam: Elsevier.

———. 1991. "Causality between Transnational Terrorism and Tourism: The Case of Spain." *Terrorism* 14:49–58.

Enders, Walter, Todd Sandler, and J. Cauley. 1990. "Assessing the Impact of Terrorist-Thwarting Policies: An Intervention Time Series Approach." *Defense Economics* 2:1–18.

Enders, Walter, Todd Sandler, and Gerald F. Parise. 1992. "An Econometric Analysis of the Impact of Terrorism on Tourism." *Kyklos* 45:531–54.

Epstein, Gil, and Ira N. Gang. 2004. "Understanding the Development of Fundamentalism." Discussion Paper 1227, IZA (Institute for the Study of Labor).

Ferrero, Mario. 2005. "Martyrdom Contracts." Working Paper, University of Eastern Piedmont.

Fielding, David. 2003a. "Counting the Cost of the Intifada: Consumption, Saving and Political Instability in Israel." *Public Choice* 116:297–312.

———. 2003b. "Modeling Political Instability and Economic Performance: Israeli Investment During the Intifada." *Economica* 70:159–86.

Figueiredo, Rui J. P. de Jr., and Barry R. Weingast. 2001. "Vicious Cycles: Endogenous Political Extremism and Political Violence." Working Paper 2001–9, Institute of Governmental Studies.

Fitzgerald, Valpy. 2004. "Global Financial Information, Compliance Incentives and Terrorist Funding." *European Journal of Political Economy*, 20:387–401.

Fleischer, Aliza, and Steven Buccola. 2002. "War, Terror and the Tourism Market in Israel." *Applied Economics* 34:1335–43.

Frey, Bruno. 2004. *Dealing With Terrorism: Stick or Carrot?* Cheltenham, UK: Edward Elgar Publishers.

Frey, Bruno S., and Simon Luechinger. 2004. "Decentralization as a Disincentive for Terror." *European Journal of Political Economy* 20:509–51.

———. 2003. "How to Fight Terrorism: Alternatives to Deterrence." *Defense and Peace Economics* 14:237–49.

Frey, Bruno S., Simon Luechinger, and Alois Stutzer. 2004. "Calculating Tragedy: Assessing the Costs of Terrorism." Working Paper 205, Institute for Empirical Research in Economics, University of Zurich.

Froot, Kenneth. A., and Paul G. J. O'Connell. 1999. "The Pricing of U.S. Catastrophe Reinsurance." In *The Financing of Catastrophe Risk*, ed. Kenneth Froot, 195–227. Chicago: University of Chicago Press.

Garfinkel, Michelle R. 2004. "Global Threats and the Domestic Struggle for Power." *European Journal of Political Economy* 20:495–508.

Garoupa, Nuno, Jonathan Klick, and Francesco Parisi. 2006. "A Law and Economics Perspective on Terrorism." *Public Choice* 128(1–2): 147–168.

Glaeser, Edward L. 2005. "The Political Economy of Hatred." *Quarterly Journal of Economics* 120:45–86.

Glaeser, Edward L., and Jesse M. Shapiro. 2002. "Cities and Warfare: The Impact of Terrorism on Urban Form." *Journal of Urban Economics* 51:205–224.

Gupta, Sanjeev, Benedict Clements, Rina Bhattacharya, and Shamit Chakravarti. 2004. "Fiscal Consequences of Armed Conflict and Terrorism in Low and Middle Income Countries." *European Journal of Political Economy* 20:403–421.

Hardin, R. 1995. "One for All: The Logic of Group Conflict." Princeton, NJ: Princeton University Press.

Harrigan, James, and Philippe Martin. 2002. "Terrorism and the Resilience of Cities." *Economic Policy Review*, Federal Reserve Bank of New York, 8:97–116.

Harris, James. 2005. *Terrorism Metrics: A Compilation of Definitions.* Arlington, VA: Centra Technology.

Hnatkovska, V., and N. Loayza. 2003. "Volatility and Growth." Mimeo., World Bank, Washington DC.

Hobijn, Bart. 2002. "What Will Homeland Security Cost?" *Federal Reserve Bank of New York Economic Policy Review* 8:21–33.

Im, Eric Iksoon, Jon Cauley, and Todd Sandler. 1987. "Cycles and Substitutions in Terrorist Activities: A Spectral Approach." *Kyklos* 40:238–55.

International Policy Institute for Counter-Terrorism. 2003. Terrorism Database, http://www.ict.org.il.

International Monetary Fund. 2001. "How Has September 11 Influenced the Global Economy." World Economic Outlook 2001, chap. 2. Washington DC: International Monetary Fund.

Ito, Harumi, and Darin Lee. 2004. "Assessing the Impact of the September 11 Terrorist Attacks on U.S. Airline Demand." *Journal of Economics and Business* 57:75–95.

Krueger, Alan B., and David D. Laitin. 2007. "*Kto Kogo?*: A Cross-Country Study of the Origins and Targets of Terrorism." In *Terrorism and Economic Development*, ed. P. Keefer and N. Loayza, chap. 5. Cambridge: Cambridge University Press.

Krueger, Alan B., and Jitka Maleckova. 2003. "Education, Poverty and Terrorism: Is There a Causal Connection?" *Journal of Economic Perspectives* 17:119–44.

Kunreuther, Howard, Erwann Michel-Kerjan, and Beverly Porter. 2003. "Assessing, Managing, and Financing Extreme Events: Dealing with Terrorism." Working Paper 10179, National Bureau of Economic Research, Cambridge, MA.

Kydd, Andrew, and Barbara F. Walter. 2002. "Sabotaging the Peace: The Politics of Extremist Violence." *International Organization* 56:263–96.

Lacker, Jeffrey M. 2004. "Payment System Disruptions and the Federal Reserve Following September 11, 2001." *Journal of Monetary Economics* 51:935–65.

Laitin, David D., and Jacob N. Shapiro. 2007. "The Political, Economic and Organizational Sources of Terrorism." In *Terrorism and Economic Development*, ed. P. Keefer and N. Loayza, chap. 7. Cambridge: Cambridge University Press.

Lapan, Harvey E., and Todd Sandler. 1993. "Terrorism and Signaling." *European Journal of Political Economy* 9:383–97.

Lee, Dwight R. 1988. "Free Riding and Paid Riding in the Fight against Terrorism." *American Economic Review* 78:22–26.

Lenain, Patrick, M. Bonturi, and V. Koen. 2002. "The Economic Consequences of Terrorism." OECD Working Paper 334. Paris: Organization for Economic Cooperation and Development.

Llussá, Fernanda, and José Tavares. 2007. "Economics and Terrorism: A Synopsis." *The Economics of Peace and Security Journal*, 2(1).

Mickolus, Edward F. 1980. *Transnational Terrorism*. Westport, CT: Greenwood Press.

———. 1982. *International Terrorism: Attributes of Terrorist Events, 1968–1977* (ITERATE 2). Dunn Loring, VA: Vinyard Software.

Mickolus, Edward F., and Peter Flemming. 2003. *International Terrorism: Attributes of Terrorist Events*, 1992–2002 (ITERATE). Dunn Loring, VA: Vinyard Software.

Mickolus, Edward F., Todd Sandler, Jean M. Murdock, and Peter Flemming. 1993. *International Terrorism: Attributes of Terrorist Events*, 1988–1991 (ITERATE 4). Dunn Loring, VA: Vinyard Software.

————. 1989. *International Terrorism: Attributes of Terrorist Events, 1978–1987* (ITERATE 3). Dunn Loring, VA: Vinyard Software.

Mills, Edwin S. 2002. "Terrorism and U.S. Real Estate." *Journal of Urban Economics* 51:198–204.

Mueller, D. C. 2004. "Rights and Citizenship in a World of Global Terrorism." *European Journal of Political Economy* 20:335–48.

Navarro, Peter, and Aron Spencer. 2001. "September 2001: Assessing the Cost of Terrorism." *Milken Institute Review* 2:16–31.

Nitsch, Volker, and Dieter Schumacher. 2004. "Terrorism and International Trade: An Empirical Investigation." *European Journal of Political Economy* 20:423–33.

Office of the Coordinator of Counterterrorism. 1997. *Patterns of Global Terrorism, 1986.* Publication 10433, U.S. Department of State, Washington, DC.

Organization for Economic Development and Cooperation (OECD). 2002. *The Impact of the Terrorist Attacks of 11 September 2001 on International Trading and Transport Activities.* Paris: OECD Publications.

O'Brien, Sean P. 1996. "Foreign Policy Crisis and the Resort to Terrorism: A Time Series Analysis of Conflict Linkages." *Journal of Conflict Resolution* 40:320–35.

Pape, Robert A. 2003. "The Strategic Logic of Suicide Terrorism." *American Political Science Review* 97:343–61.

Rosendorff, Peter, and Todd Sandler. 2004. "Too Much of a Good Thing? The Proactive Response Dilemma." *Journal of Conflict Resolution* 48:657–71.

Rossi-Hansberg, Esteban. 2003. "Cities Under Stress." *Journal of Monetary Economics* 51:903–27.

Sambanis, Nicholas. 2007. "Terrorism and Civil War." In *Terrorism and Economic Development*, ed. P. Keefer and N. Loayza, chap. 6. Cambridge: Cambridge University Press.

Sandler, Todd, and Walter Enders. 2004. "An Economic Perspective on Transnational Terrorism." *European Journal of Political Economy* 20:301–16.

————. 2007. "Economic Consequences of Terrorism in Developed and Developing Countries: An Overview," In *Terrorism and Economic Development*, ed. P. Keefer and N. Loayza, chap. 1. Cambridge: Cambridge University Press.

Sandler, Todd, and Kevin Siqueira. 2003. "Global Terrorism: Deterrence versus Preemption." Working Paper, University of Texas.

Schelling, Thomas C. 1991. "What Purposes Can "International Terrorism" Serve?" In *Violence, Terrorism and Justice*, ed. R. C. Frey and C. W. Morris, 18–32. Cambridge: Cambridge University Press.

Shambaugh, George, and William Josiger. 2004. "Public Prudence, the Policy Salience of Terrorism and Presidential Approval following Terrorist Incidents." Mimeo, Annual Joint Conference of the International Security and Arms Control Section of the American Political Science Association.

Shugart, William F. 2007. "An Analytical History of Terrorism, 1945–2000." Working Paper, University of Mississippi.

Siqueira, Kevin. 2005. "Political and Militant Wings within Dissident Movements and Organizations." *Journal of Conflict Resolution* 49:218–36.

Sloboda, Brian W. 2003. "Assessing the Effects of Terrorism on Tourism by Use of Time Series Methods." *Tourism Economics* 9:179–90.

Summers, Robert, and Alan Heston. 1991. "The Penn World Table (Mark 5): An Expanded Set of International Comparisons." *Quarterly Journal of Economics* 106:327–68.

Sunstein, Cass R. 2003. "Terrorism and Probability Neglect." *Journal of Risk and Uncertainty* 26:121–36.

Tavares, José. 2004. "The Open Society Assesses Its Enemies: Shocks, Disasters and Terrorist Attacks." *Journal of Monetary Economics* 51:1039–70.

Treverton, Gregory F., Justin Adams, James Dertouzos, Arindam Dutta, Susan S. Everingham, and Eric V. Larson. 2007. "Costing Rich Country Responses to the Terrorist Threat."In *Terrorism and Economic Development*, ed. P. Keefer and N. Loayza, chap. 2. Cambridge: Cambridge University Press.

Viscusi, W. Kip, and Richard J. Zeckhauser. 2003. "Sacrificing Civil Liberties to Reduce Terrorism Risks." *Journal of Risk and Uncertainty* 26:99–120.

Walkenhorst, Peter, and Nora Dihel. 2002. "Trade Impacts of the Terrorist Attacks of 11 September 2001: A Quantitative Assessment." Mimeo., Workshop on the Economic Consequences of Global Terrorism, German Institute for Economic Research (DIW Berlin), June 14–15.

Wildasin, David E. 2002. "Local Public Finance in the Aftermath of September 11." *Journal of Urban Economics* 51:225–37.

Wilkinson, Paul. 2001. *Terrorism versus Democracy: The Liberal State Response*. London: Frank Cass.

Wintrobe, R. 2006. "Can Suicide Bombers Be Rational?" In *Rational Extremism: The Political Economy of Radicalism*, ed. R. Wintrobe. Cambridge: Cambridge University Press.

———. 2007. *Rational Extremism: The Political Economy of Radicalism*. Cambridge: Cambridge University Press.

Woo, Gordon. 2002. "Quantifying Insurance Terrorism Risk." Working Paper, National Bureau of Economic Research.

World Bank. 2002. *Fifteen Months Intifada, Closures and Palestinian Economic Crisis: An Assessment*. Washington, DC: World Bank.

———. 2003. *Two Years of Intifada, Closures and Palestinian Economic Crisis: An Assessment*. Washington, D.C: World Bank.

Appendix

Table 8.1. *Measurement of terrorist activity: Paper overview*

Author(s) and title	Brief summary	Model	Data
Abadie, Alberto. (2004). "Poverty, Political Freedom, and the Roots of Terrorism." Working Paper.	An empirical investigation of the determinants of terrorism at the country level using a new measure of terrorism that encompasses both domestic and transnational terrorism. Terrorist risk is not significantly higher for poorer countries, once the effects of other country-specific characteristics such as the level of political freedom are taken into account. Political freedom is shown to explain terrorism, but it does so in a nonmonotonic way: countries in some intermediate range of political freedom are shown to be more prone to terrorism than countries with high levels of political freedom or countries with highly authoritarian regimes. Finally, the results suggest that geographic factors are important in sustaining terrorist activities.	No	Yes
Berman, E. and D. Laitin. (2005). "Hard Targets: Theory and Evidence on Suicide Attacks." *National Bureau of Economic Research*.	Insurgency typically occurs in poor countries but suicide attacks are as likely in rich democracies and favored by the radical religious. The authors model the choice of tactics by rebel groups, considering that a successful suicide attack imposes a large and definitive cost on the attacker and the organization. The attacker and other operatives are embedded in a club-good model emphasizing the provision of benign local public goods. The ultimate sacrifice demanded serves as a regulator of entry and solves a free-rider problem. The model predicts that suicides will be used when targets are well protected and when damage is great.	Yes	International Policy Institute for Counter-Terrorism (2003) and from Pape (2003).

(*continued*)

Table 8.1 *(continued)*

Author(s) and title	Brief summary	Model	Data
Berrebi, Claude and Esteban F. Klor. (2004). "On Terrorism and Electoral Outcomes: Theory and Evidence from the Israeli-Palestinian Conflict." Working Paper.	The interaction between terrorist attacks and electoral outcomes in Israel is studied based on a dynamic model of reputation with two equilibrias: in the first one, support for the rightist party increases after periods with high levels of terrorism and decreases after relatively calm periods; and in the second one, the expected level of terrorism is higher during the leftist party's tenure in office compared to the one expected during the rightist party's term in office. The empirical results support the theoretical model for three of the four Israeli governments in the period between 1990 and 2003: terrorist attacks increase during leftist governments and decrease during rightist governments.	Yes	Public opinion polls and a new dataset on terrorist attacks in Israel and the occupied territories between 1990 and 2003.
Blomberg, S. Brock, Gregory Hess, and Athanasios Orphanides. (2004). "The Macroeconomic Consequences of Terrorism." *Journal of Monetary Economics.*	The authors examine a panel dataset of 177 countries from 1968 to 2000 to evaluate the macroeconomic consequences of terrorism, using three different econometric procedures: cross-section, panel growth regression analysis, and a structural VAR model. Terrorism reduces growth and the country fixed effects are an important explanatory variable. The negative effect of terrorism on growth is stronger and statistically significant in developing countries, not statistically significant in OECD economies. The incidence of terrorism correlates with increases in government spending and a crowding out of investment. Violent internal conflict and external wars have a stronger and more persistent negative effect on economic growth than terrorism.	No	Data on terrorism from "International Terrorism: Attributes of Terrorist Events" – ITERATE from Mickolus et al. (2003).

Citation	Description		Data and sources
Blomberg, S. Brock, Gregory Hess, and Akila Weerapana. (2004a). "Economic Conditions and Terrorism." *European Journal of Political Economy.*	The theoretical model used in this paper sees terrorism as initiated by groups that are discontent with their current economic situation but are unable to drastically change it or affect the present political and institutional order that are responsible for their situation. The model predictions are: (a) conflict is more likely in bad times when the economic resources shrink and the dissident groups are less likely to be satisfied and (b) the choice between a rebellion and a terrorist attack depends on the responses of the government to these actions. Richer countries that have better institutions, stronger economies, and well-equipped armies increase the cost of rebellion to the point that dissident groups prefer to resort to terrorism. These predictions are tested in a panel of 127 countries from 1968 to 1991. It is observed that in richer democratic countries terrorism is more likely during economic downturns. This is consistent with the model predictions.	No	Data and sources: the terrorist activities data are the ITERATE dataset from Mickolus et al. (1993) with 159 countries over 24 years providing 3,816 observations, and the economic data are obtained from the update to the Summers and Heston (1991) dataset, which is given for 152 countries over 25 years providing 3,800 observations. Combining both datasets results in a panel of 3,014 observations (127 countries from 1968 to 1991).
Brauer, J., A. Gómez-Sorzano, and S. Sethuraman. (2004). "Decomposing Violence: Political Murder in Colombia." *European Journal of Political Economy.*	Demonstrates the role of cyclical political variables and permanent nonpolitical variables applying the Hodrick-Prescott and Beveridge-Nelson business-cycle decomposition methods to a time-series of homicides in Colombia (1946–1999).	No	Crime statistics from Colombian National Police, between 1946 and 1999.

(*continued*)

Table 8.1 (continued)

Author(s) and title	Brief summary	Model	Data
Enders, Walter, and Todd Sandler. (2002). "Patterns of Transnational Terrorism, 1970–1999: Alternative Time-Series Estimates." *International Studies Quarterly*.	This paper uses time-series methods to evaluate some of the consequences of transnational terrorism and finds that: (a) transnational terrorism tends to result in relatively few deaths, especially as compared with more frequent events such as accidents on roads and highways; (b) terrorist attacks have become more threatening and lethal in recent years; (c) there seems to be a cyclical pattern in the incidence of terrorism, with a large fraction of casualties associated with a small number of events; and (d) attacks aimed at the United States or U.S. interests constitute a substantial portion of total attacks.	Yes	Data on transnational terrorism incidents. They are drawn from International Terrorism Attributes of Terrorist Events (ITERATE): ITERATE 2 covers 1968–77 (Mickolus, 1982); ITERATE 3 covers 1978–87 (Mickolus et al. 1989); and ITERATE 4 covers 1988–91 (Mickolus et al. 1993).
Enders, Walter. and Todd Sandler. (2000). "Is Transnational Terrorism Becoming More Threatening? A Time Series Investigation." *Journal of Conflict Resolution*.	This study applies time-series techniques to investigate the current threat posed by transnational terrorist incidents. Although the number of incidents has dropped dramatically during the post-cold war period, transnational terrorism still presents a significant threat. In recent years, each incident is almost 17 percentage points more likely to result in death or injuries. Three alternative casualties' series (incidents with injuries and/or deaths, the proportion of incidents with casualties, and incidents with deaths) are investigated. These series increased in November 1979 with the takeover of the U.S. embassy in Tehran and again after the fourth quarter of 1991. The growth of religious terrorism appears to account for the increased severity of terrorist attacks since the last quarter of 1991. All three casualties' series displayed more deterministic factors than the noncasualties series, which is largely random after detrending. Cycles in the aggregate incident series are attributable solely to the underlying casualties' series.	No	Data on transnational terrorist incidents and casualties.

Enders, Walter, and Todd Sandler. (1995). "Terrorism: Theory and Applications." In *Handbook of Defense Economics*, ed. Keith Hartley and Todd Sandler.	Reviews game-theoretic and choice-theoretic depictions of terrorist behavior. A simple game-theoretic framework is presented to ascertain under what circumstances a government would want to precommit itself to a no-negotiation strategy. In another game model, the authors analyze whether two governments (nations) that are targeted by the same terrorist group would over-deter or under-deter terrorist attacks. Moreover, they demonstrate that piecemeal policy, which allows the governments to share intelligence but not deterrence decisions, can be worse than no coordination. Choice-theoretic models identify possibilities for substitution and complementarity among diverse modes of terrorist attacks as terrorists respond optimally to government actions. A host of time-series techniques are used to study the effectiveness of alternative antiterrorism policies. Vector-autoregression intervention procedures are particularly suited. Time-series analyses are also used to identify cycles, trends, and irregular components for forecasting purposes.	No	Data on transnational terrorist incidents.
Figueiredo, Rui J. P. de Jr., and Barry R. Weingast. (2001). "Vicious Cycles: Endogenous Political Extremism and Political Violence." Working Paper.	The authors develop a model of radical political violence with three players: a dominant in-group, moderate and radical subgroups of the out-group, showing that persistent violence is most likely when moderates are truly moderate (not too close to either the dominant group or to the radicals) and a provocation motive interacts with other explanations as an incentive for terrorist violence as the radicals must have an incentive to terrorize *beyond* the provocation motive so that the threat of future violence is credible.	Yes	No

259

(*continued*)

Table 8.1 (continued)

Author(s) and title	Brief summary	Model	Data
Im, Eric Iksoon, Jon Cauley, and Todd Sandler. (1987). "Cycles and Substitutions in Terrorist Activities: A Spectral Approach." *Kyklos.*	By using spectral analysis this paper shows that all terrorist events series had a cycle of 28 months. Skyjackings had two periodicities: 41 and 28 months. The periodicity of a barricade and hostage events were 72 and 48 months, respectively. It is also shown that tighter security measures for military and government facilities made tourists relatively more attractive for terrorist attacks. There is also some evidence that terrorists substitute in the short run between similar events (e.g., kidnapping and skyjacking).	No	Yes.
Sandler, Todd, and Walter Enders. (2004). "An Economic Perspective on Transnational Terrorism." *European Journal of Political Economy.*	In the period from 1960 to 1980, nationalism, separatism, Marxist ideology, and nihilism basically motivated terrorism. In the 1990s, motivation changed and an increased proportion of terrorist attacks were from religious-based fundamentalist groups. In terms of cycles and trends, the series of incidents tended to rise in the late 1960s and decline in the late 1990s (inverted U-shaped pattern). Also, in recent years the probability of death or injury in a terrorist incident increased by about 17%. In addition, this study shows that transnational externalities and market failures are present in the case of transnational terrorism. Given the data, this paper summarizes some studies on terrorism in order to understand what antiterrorist policies can do. Studies support that if terrorists know ahead of time that they have nothing to gain – there will be no concessions and deals with terrorists – they will never abduct hostages. Game theory accounts for uncertainty and strategic interactions of opposing interests, which could help the understanding of terrorism. Every policy to thwart terrorism would entail its own stream of benefits and costs that must be taken into account.	No	Transnational terrorism annual data from U.S. Department of State (1988–2002) and the ITERATE dataset (International Terrorism: Attributes of Terrorist Events – 1968–2002) from Mickolus (1982), Mickolus et al. (1989, 1993), and Mickolus and Flemming (2003).

Tavares, José. (2004). "The Open Society Assesses Its Enemies: Shocks, Disasters, and Terrorist Attacks." *Journal of Monetary Economics*.	This paper uses datasets on terrorist attacks, natural disasters, and currency crises to answer three different questions: what the determinants of terrorism are, if there is an output cost following a terrorist attack, and if that cost is larger or smaller in the case of democracies. We find that rich countries are the most prone to suffer attacks while democracies are, if anything, less vulnerable than other countries. The cost to output of a terrorist attack is quantitatively small and closely associated with the occurrence of an event rather than the number of casualties. The paper finds robust evidence that a terrorist attack imposes a lower output cost the more democratic a country is.	No	Data on terrorism incidence International Policy Institute for Counter-Terrorism.

Table 8.2. *Nature of terrorists: Paper overview*

Author(s) and title	Brief summary	Model	Data
Azam, Jean Paul. (2005). "Suicide Bombing as Intergenerational Investment." *Public Choice*.	Models terrorism as a phenomenon where the current generation is linked to the next one as in standard dynastic family models: bombing today increases the probability of some public good accruing to the next generation. The model is used to explain the fact that suicide bombers have been found by Krueger and Maleckova (2003) to come disproportionately from wealthy families and have an above-average education level. Income and education increase the opportunity cost of "investing" in a suicide bombing but may also increase the sensitivity to the future generation's welfare.	Yes	No
Aziz, Heba. (1995). "Understanding Attacks on Tourists in Egypt." *Tourism Management*.	The author argues that the terrorist attacks carried out by Muslim groups in Egypt (1991–1993) could be a reaction to irresponsible tourism development in the region.	No	No
Berman, E. (2003). "Hamas, Taliban, and the Jewish Underground: An Economist's View of Radical Religious Militias." *NBER*.	The paper proposes a club-good framework that emphasizes the function of voluntary religious organizations as efficient providers of local public goods. The sacrifices these groups demand are economically efficient and suitable for solving the extreme principal-agent problems present in militia production. Seemingly gratuitous acts of violence by group members destroy their outside options, increasing the incentive compatibility of loyalty.	Yes	No
Berman, Eli, and Stepanyan, Ara. (2004). "How Many Radical	High-fertility and low-market returns to schooling have been pointed to as characteristics of religious sects. The authors investigate fertility and returns to education in families of graduates of Muslim religious schools	No	Datasets on religious education, fertility, and earnings in Indonesia,

Islamists? Indirect Evidence from Five Countries." Working Paper.	in five countries with a Muslim population. It is found that fertility is indeed higher among these families, and there is evidence of lower market returns to education. The results provide a rough estimate of the individual prevalence of a well-defined strand of "radical Islamism," which ranges from 2 to 18% of the female population.		Bangladesh, India, Cote D'Ivoire, and Pakistan.
Berrebi, Claude. (2003). "Evidence About the Link Between Education, Poverty, and Terrorism Among Palestinians." Working Paper.	The paper investigates whether participation in terrorist activity can be linked to low schooling, to poverty at the individual level, or various economic difficulties at the societal level. It analyzes the determinants of participation in terrorist activities in Israel from the late 1980s to the present day, as well as a time-series relationship between terrorist attacks in Israel and economic conditions. Both higher standards of living and higher levels of education are *positively* associated with participation in terrorist activities. The analysis of the determinants of self-selection as a suicide bomber provides evidence that suicide bombers tend to be of higher economic status and higher educational attainment than the typical individual in the population but come from lower socioeconomic groups than other, nonsuicidal terrorists.	No	Data on Hamas and Palestinian Islamic Jihad terrorist cells.
Blomberg, S. Brock, Gregory Hess, and Akila Weerapana. (2004b). "An Economic Model of Terrorism." *Conflict Management and Peace Science.*	In this model, terrorism is initiated by groups unhappy with their current economic status and unable to change it drastically through political and institutional means. The prediction is that conflicts are more frequent in bad times, when economic resources shrink and dissident groups are dissatisfied. The choice between a rebellion and a terrorist attack depends on the governments' ability to respond and richer countries, with better institutions, stronger economies, and better-equipped armies, increase the relative cost of rebellion to the point that dissident groups resort to terrorism.	Yes	Yes

(*continued*)

Table 8.2 *(continued)*

Author(s) and title	Brief summary	Model	Data
Blomberg, S. Brock, and Gregory D. Hess. (2007). "The Lexus and the Olive Branch: Globalization, Democratization, and Terrorism." This volume.	This paper employs a gravity model to investigate the relative importance of globalization and democratization on transnational terrorism, using a database of more than 200,000 bilateral observations on economic, political, and historical factors that may influence the likelihood of citizens from one country to engage in terrorist activities against citizens of another. The advent of democratic institutions, high income, and more openness in a "source" country significantly reduces terrorism, but the exact same factors in "target" countries actually increase terrorism. For a "source" country, being a democracy or a participating member of the World Trade Organization decreases the number of transnational terrorist attacks by about 2 to 3 per year, more than two standard deviations above the average number of attacks between any two countries in a given year.	No	Yes. Cross-section of bilateral data for 179 "source" and "target" countries, from 1968 to 2003.
Bueno de Mesquita, Ethan. (2005b). "The Quality of Terror." *American Journal of Political Science.*	As the result of the interaction of a government, a terrorist organization, and terrorist volunteers, while individuals with low ability or little education are most likely to volunteer to join the terrorist organization, especially in recessionary economies with lack of economic opportunities, screening for quality by terrorist organizations may lead to better educated terrorist operatives. Government crackdowns have opposing effects on mobilization as they fuel the ideological war (which attracts volunteers) but also makes attacks less effective (which discourages volunteers).	Yes	No

Charney, C., and Nicole Yakatan. (2005). "A New Beginning: Strategies for a More Fruitful Dialogue with the Muslim World." Working Paper.	Draws on focus groups of adult, university-educated Muslims responding to open-ended questions and statements put forward by a trained moderator. The discussions are transcribed and analyzed and results are seen as qualitative, not quantitative. The major factors behind the hostility that dominates Muslim thinking on America are identified, including: American military action in recent years – including the invasion of Iraq and the war on terror – which has cast the United States as domineering and unpredictable; the rise of local satellite networks that openly criticize U.S. policy; the lack of visibility of U.S. development aid. An overturn of the situation will probably involve an emphasis on bilateral communication, including an ability to listen, focus on bilateral aid and partnership and tolerating disagreement on controversial issues.	No	Focus groups of adult, university-educated Muslim citizens from Morocco, Egypt, and Indonesia. Focus groups are small, homogeneous in social terms – age, gender, education – led by a moderator and responding to open-ended questions. Results are qualitative.
Crenshaw, Martha. (1981). "The Causes of Terrorism." Comparative Politics.	Identifies aggregate causes of terrorism as modernization, which can increase inequality and group segregation while providing cost-effective ways of equipping them for violence – social sanctioning of violence and the spread of disruptive forms of nationalism and religiosity.	No	No
Epstein, Gil, and Ira N. Gang. (2004). "Understanding the Development of Fundamentalism." Working Paper.	Develops a model to explain the creation and development of fundamentalist groups under which leaders compete to enhance the observance of their followers. The model explains the result of competition among fundamentalist groups leading, over time, to extremism and terrorist activity.	Yes	No

(continued)

Table 8.2 (continued)

Author(s) and title	Brief summary	Model	Data
Ferrero, Mario. (2005). "Martyrdom Contracts." Working Paper.	Highlights the similarities between different instances of the use of suicide to advance group interests and ideology, from the Christian martyrs under the Roman Empire to the Islamic martyrs of yesterday and today, and including the Japanese *kamikaze* of World War II, and the Tamil Tigers of Sri Lanka. Presents a two-period, expected-utility model of a martyrdom contract, under which volunteers sign up in the expectation of probabilistic earthly rewards. Contract enforcement is ensured through a social sanction (or stigma) placed on possible renegades. Counterterrorism policy would be effective if it could reduce this sanction and turn prospective martyrs into apostates.	Yes	No
Garfinkel, M. (2004). "Global Threats and the Domestic Struggle for Power." *European Journal of Political Economy*.	Presents a theoretical model on the interaction of terrorism and internal conflict where groups compete over the redistribution of future income. An increase in terrorist threats reduces the expected value of future income and, accordingly, the intensity of internal conflict. Terrorism may also imply a greater sense of group security against external threats and a greater struggle for power at home.	Yes	No
Glaeser, Edward L. (2005). "The Political Economy of Hatred." *Quarterly Journal of Economics*.	An attempt to explain the origins of hatred, a necessary input for terrorist activities. Three "case studies" are examined: anti-Americanism in the Arab world; antiblack sentiment in the south of the United States, and episodes of anti-Semitism in Europe. Hatred is fostered by stories that derive their effect from repetition rather than objectivity and politicians are the suppliers of such hate-creating stories as tools to discredit their opponents. Individual citizens are willing to accept such stories as valid generalizations if the cost of acquiring information is	Yes	Data on the lynching of African Americans between 1868 and 1930.

	higher than its return. Hatred reduces the presence of strong private incentives to learn the truth, such as when the interactions with minorities in peaceful settings are frequent. Thus, hatred emerges if minorities are politically relevant but socially segregated.		
Krueger, Alan B. and David D. Laitin. (2007). "Kto Kogo?: A Cross-Country Study of the Origins and Targets of Terrorism." This volume.	This paper links the country of origin and the target country of the terrorist event and finds that, after controlling for political regime, there is little economic foundation for terrorist origins. Rather, the economic story for terrorism is in the characteristics of the target. The data suggest that the origins of terrorism are in countries that suffer from political oppression while the targets are countries that bask in economic success.	No	Yes. Suicide attacks.
Krueger, Alan B., and Jitka Maleckova. (2003). "Education, Poverty, and Terrorism: Is There a Causal Connection?" Journal of Economic Perspectives.	Analyzes opinion polls conducted in the Palestinian Territories on support for attacks against Israeli targets and finds that support does not decrease with higher education and living standards. The paper also provides a statistical analysis of the determinants of participation in Hezbollah militant activities in Lebanon: a living standard above the poverty line or a secondary or higher education is positively associated with participation. Israeli Jewish settlers who attacked Palestinians in the West Bank in the early 1980s originated overwhelmingly in high-paying occupations.	No	Individual microdata from public opinion polls and characteristics of terrorists in the Israel and the Palestinian Territories.
Kydd, Andrew, and Barbara F. Walter. (2002). "Sabotaging the Peace: The Politics of Extremist Violence." International Organization.	The authors present a game theoretic model analyzing terrorism as a problem of trust between the moderate opposition group and the targeted government as to the ability of the former to carry out a peace treaty. A small minority of radicals may be able to provoke the continuation of conflict even if majorities on both sides would rather conclude an agreement. This is because the actions of the radical minority affect the trust the government places in the moderates' ability to enforce a successful agreement.	Yes	No

(continued)

Table 8.2 *(continued)*

Author(s) and title	Brief summary	Model	Data
Laitin, David D., and Jacob N. Shapiro. (2007). "The Political, Economic, and Organizational Sources of Terrorism." This volume.	This paper reviews the "rationalist" view of terrorist organizations, their strategic options, actions and consequences. This view sees terrorists as conditioning their decisions to five factors: funding, popular support, competition against other terrorist groups, the regime type against which they fight, and the counter-insurgency tactics by states. The literature shows how terrorist tactics self-perpetuate after they are chosen over other, more traditional, tactics of insurgency. Because the literature was not written as a coherent piece, we use it as a starting point to suggest a series of hypotheses that should serve as a foundation for future analyses and statistical tests.		
Lapan, Harvey, and Todd Sandler. (1993). "Terrorism and Signaling." *European Journal of Political Economy*.	Presents an analysis of terrorism based on a signaling game in which an uninformed government uses the first-period attacks of the (informed) terrorist to assess terrorists' capabilities. Based on posterior beliefs, the government decides in period 2 whether to resist or to capitulate. A perfect Bayesian equilibrium for the two-period signaling game is derived in which the government prefers the associated partial-pooling equilibrium associated with probabilistic regret owing to ex-post wrong inferences.	Yes	No
O'Brien, Sean P. (1996). "Foreign Policy Crisis and the Resort to Terrorism: A Time Series Analysis of Conflict Linkages." *Journal of Conflict Resolution*.	This study tests the validity of opposing arguments regarding superpower state sponsorship of international crises by exploring the linkages between the monthly foreign policy crisis behavior of nation-states and the occurrence of international terrorism over a 228-month period from 1968 to 1986 using data drawn from ITERATE 2 and 3 and the International Crisis Behavior (ICB) datasets. Using time-series ARIMA modeling techniques, superpower involvement in	No	Yes

(continued)

Pape, Robert A. (2003). "The Strategic Logic of Suicide Terrorism." *American Political Science Review*.

international crises, attitudes toward superpower crisis intervention, and the victory and defeat patterns of democracies and nondemocracies are considered for their short-term and long-term influences on the amount and occurrence of international terrorism in the global system. The analysis lends support to the view that the Soviet Union and other authoritarian regimes are more likely than the U.S. and other democracies to resort to international terrorism as a foreign policy tool.

The widening range of socioeconomic backgrounds of suicide terrorists has contradicted existing psychological explanations. To advance our understanding of this growing phenomenon, this study collects the universe of suicide terrorist attacks worldwide from 1980 to 2001, 187 in all. In contrast to the existing explanations, this study shows that suicide terrorism follows a strategic logic, one specifically designed to coerce modern liberal democracies to make significant territorial concessions. Moreover, over the past two decades, suicide terrorism has been rising largely because terrorists have learned that it pays. Suicide terrorists sought to compel American and French military forces to abandon Lebanon in 1983, Israeli forces to leave Lebanon in 1985, Israeli forces to quit the Gaza Strip and the West Bank in 1994 and 1995, the Sri Lankan government to create an independent Tamil state from 1990 on, and the Turkish government to grant autonomy to the Kurds in the late 1990s. In all but the case of Turkey, the terrorist political cause made more gains after the resort to suicide operations than it had before. Thus, Western democracies should pursue policies that teach terrorists that the lesson of the 1980s and 1990s no longer holds, policies which in practice may have more to do with improving homeland security than with offensive military action.

Yes

Data on suicide terrorist attacks worldwide from 1980 to 2001.

269

Table 8.2 (*continued*)

Author(s) and title	Brief summary	Model	Data
Sambanis, Nicholas. (2007). "Terrorism and Civil War." This volume.	The author argues that there is a link between terrorism and widespread political violence, but the former is unlikely to evolve into civil war, as there are key differences between the conditions that favor the organization of violence as terrorism as opposed to civil war. The paper provides a conceptual discussion for the differences between terrorism and civil war and empirically tests if a rationalist model of civil war can explain terrorism in the same countries and years. A key policy implication of this analysis is that strategies of economic development, which are likely to reduce the prevalence of civil war in the world, are unlikely to eliminate the incidence of terrorism.	No	Yes. Data on the incidence of terrorism and civil war from 1997 to 2002.
Siqueira, Kevin. (2005). "Political and Militant Wings within Dissident Movements and Organizations." *Journal of Conflict Resolution.*	A model provides a basis for investigating the interrelationships between factions and their supporters under conditions of competition and cooperation. When factions act competitively and independently of one another, the existence of several factions does not necessarily lead to increased terrorist activity and violence if compared with the case where factions act jointly and in a coordinated way.	Yes	No
Wintrobe, R. (2006). "Can Suicide Bombers Be Rational?" In *Rational Extremism: The Political Economy of Radicalism,* ed. R. Wintrobe.	Suicide attacks are particularly difficult to understand. The readiness to sacrifice oneself increases its effectiveness and influence dramatically. One reason such acts are committed is to obtain solidarity, typically acquired through group-directed activity in gangs, cults, unions, political parties or movements, and religious sects. The author analyses the production of solidarity through a simple formal model. The central	Yes	No

idea is that of a "solidarity multiplier" through which an individual chooses *more* solidarity by identifying with a leader's utility. In these circumstances, rational suicide for the group is possible.

See Also Papers Below, From Other Tables

Author(s) and Title	Table
Abadie, Alberto. (2004). "Poverty, Political Freedom, and the Roots of Terrorism." Working Paper.	1
Berman, E., and Laitin, D. (2005). "Hard Targets: Theory and Evidence on Suicide Attacks." National Bureau of Economic Research.	1

271

Table 8.3. *Utility cost of terrorism: Paper overview*

Author(s) and title	Brief summary	Model	Data
Becker, Gary S., and Yona Rubinstein. (2004). "Fear and the Response to Terrorism: An Economic Analysis." Working Paper.	A rational choice model of fear where an exogenous shock on the probability of being harmed affects people's choice due to the changes in the risk – the weights of the "good" and "bad" states change – and fear – persons' utility decreases in all states of nature, regardless of outcomes. People can invest and accumulate skills to overcome their fears if they derive other benefits from undertaking the risky activity. Otherwise, individuals substitute away from the risky activity. Assuming a constant relative risk aversion utility function (CRRA), the authors calibrate the fear and risk aversion parameters and find that the higher the fear factor is the lower people's risk aversion should be in order to explain their response to terror. Terror is found to have a large effect on the "quality" of life – by increasing fear – rather than the "quantity" of life.	Yes	Micro- and macrolevel data series from public sources in the United States and Israel and terror events and casualties collected by authors.
Frey, Bruno S., Simon Luechinger, and Alois Stutzer. (2004). "Calculating Tragedy: Assessing the Costs of Terrorism." Working Paper.	Aims to show that the damage done by terrorism can be empirically measured. In the authors' opinion, terrorism can be measured through the life satisfaction approach in which individual utility is approximated by self-reported subjective well-being (surveys with large representative questionnaire studies, where individuals are asked about their level of life satisfaction or happiness), suggest that people's utility losses may far exceed the purely economic consequences.	No	No
Sunstein, Cass R. (2003). "Terrorism and Probability Neglect." *Journal of Risk and Uncertainty.*	Shows that individuals focus on the badness of the outcome of terrorism rather than on the probability that it will occur. The "probability neglect" results in fear that greatly exceeds discounted harm.	Yes	No
Viscusi, W. Kip. and Richard J. Zeckhauser. (2003). "Sacrificing Civil Liberties to Reduce Terrorism Risks." *Journal of Risk and Uncertainty.*	The paper surveys people's willingness to sacrifice civil liberties to reduce terrorism risks. The results show that support for targeted screening of airline passengers increases if the cost delays to other passengers is controlled. Perceptions of terrorism risk are highly diffuse: people are subject to a propensity to predict worst-case scenarios in the case of terrorism and anomalies known from other risk perception contexts.	No	Yes, survey data on willingness to sacrifice civil liberties as part of an effort to reduce the risk of terrorism.

Table 8.4. *Effect of terrorism on aggregate output: Paper overview*

Author(s) and title	Brief summary	Model	Data
Abadie, Alberto, and Javier Gardeazabal. (2003). "The Economic Costs of Conflict: A Case Study of the Basque Country." *American Economic Review.*	To evaluate the effect of terrorism in the Basque Country in Spain, the authors create a synthetic Spanish region based on the region's characteristics that closely resembles the actual region in the absence of terrorism. Based on this comparison, terrorism is estimated to decrease regional output by 10%. The authors use information on ETA's 1998–1999 truce as a natural experiment to estimate the effect of terrorism. Stocks of firms with a significant share of their business activity in the Basque region showed a positive relative performance when the truce began and as the truce gained credibility and a relative negative performance when the truce ended.	No	Data on ETA terrorist activities between 1968 and 1997, a list of Basque and non-Basque firm stocks collected from the Spanish Ministry of Interior (2002), Fundación BBV (1999), and Madrid Stock Exchange online data.
Brück, T., and Bengt-Arne Wickström. (2004). "The Economic Consequences of Terror: A Brief Survey." Working Paper.	This paper is a very short summary of what has been studied by other authors on the consequences of terrorism in terms of data availability, costs of terror on financial markets and on international trade, fiscal and growth effects of terrorism, and policy implications for developed and developing countries. The indirect effects of terrorism (i.e., the changes in risk, transaction costs, demand, public finances, and growth) may outweigh the direct effects.	No	No
Chen, Andrew H., and Thomas F. Siems. (2004). "The Effects of Terrorism on Global Capital Markets." *European Journal of Political Economy.*	Using an event study methodology, the authors study the global market's response to terrorist attacks and observe that the U.S. capital markets in the recent two episodes (Iraq's invasion of Kuwait in 1990 and the September 11, 2001, terrorist attack) are more resilient and recover sooner compared with what happened in the past 14 terrorist/military attacks dating back to 1915. This can be partially explained by a more developed and stable banking and financial sector providing liquidity in order to have market stability.	No	Data from Constitutional Rights Foundation and the U.S. Department of State.

(continued)

273

Table 8.4 (*continued*)

Author(s) and title	Brief summary	Model	Data
Choudhry, Taufiq. (2003). "September 11 and Time-Varying Beta of United States Companies." Working Paper.	This paper evaluates the effect of September 11, 2001, on the time-varying beta for 20 United States firms. The results show that the September 11 terrorist attack affected most of the United States firms. The size and direction of the effect varies according to the companies, but none of them had a significant increase in beta in the period following the terrorist attack.	No	Daily stock price data from 20 United States companies (1/1/1991–7/31/2002) from DataStream dataset.
Eckstein, Zvi, and Daniel Tsiddon. (2004). "Macroeconomic Consequences of Terror: Theory and the Case of Israel." *Journal of Monetary Economics*.	A theoretical model is presented to predict the effect of terrorism on output. An increase in terror results in a decrease in investment, consumption, and income in the long run. A government that acts optimally increases the proportion of output spent on defense. These predictions are assessed for the case of the Israeli economy using a VAR methodology for the period 1980–2003. The negative effect of continued terror in the economy results in a decrease of annual consumption per capita in the Israeli economy by about 5% in 2004. According to the authors' calculations, the Israeli output per capita in March 2003 is 10–15% lower due to the terrorist attacks that occurred from 2000 to that date.	Yes	Public data sources including the International Policy Institute for Counter-Terrorism.
Eldor, Rafi, and Rafi Melnick. (2004). "Financial Markets and Terrorism." *European Journal of Political Economy*.	This paper evaluates the reaction of the stock and foreign exchange market to terrorist attacks in Israel between 1990 and 2003. Results show that the intensification of Palestinian attacks after 9/27/2000 had a negative effect on the stock market but not in the foreign currency market. Also, it is observed that markets continue to perform efficiently. Market liberalization helped the economy to cope with terrorism.	No	Data from 1990 to 2003 on terror attacks in Israel.

Hobijn, Bart. (2002). "What Will Homeland Security Cost?" *Federal Reserve Bank of New York Economic Policy Review.*	This paper estimates the costs of extra security measures imposed after 9/11. Evidence suggests that the economic costs of homeland security will be relatively small with no major effects on the fiscal discipline of the government. It is expected that government spending on homeland security will be about 0.35% GDP in 2003. If we add to this amount the private sector spending on security-related inputs, the total direct cost of homeland security would be 0.66% of GDP. Also, the private sector productivity levels will decrease by only 1.12.	No	Data from 2003 Homeland Security Budget on share of inputs devoted directly to protective services, hours lost due to airport delays, road congestion, and security-check waiting times at ten major U.S. airports from the Air Transportation Association of America (2001).
International Monetary Fund. (2001). "How Has September 11 Influenced the Global Economy." *World Economic Outlook.*	The total direct loss of the terrorist attacks on September 11, 2001, is estimated at $21.4 billion.	No	Yes
Navarro, Peter, and Aron Spencer. (2001). "September 2001: Assessing the Cost of Terrorism." *Milken Institute Review.*	This paper estimates the human capital loss to be $40 billion and the property loss to be between $10 and $13 billion due to the September 11, 2001, terrorist attacks.	No	Yes

(continued)

Table 8.4 (continued)

Author(s) and title	Brief summary	Model	Data
Sandler, Todd, and Walter Enders. (2007). "Economic Consequences of Terrorism in Developed and Developing Countries: an Overview." This volume.	This paper reviews the literature on the economic consequences of terrorism and evaluates the methodology used to date, distinguishing macroeconomic from microeconomic or sector-specific influences of terrorism. The authors evaluate the effect of terrorism in developed and developing countries, suggesting its costs are greater in the latter, especially when economies are smaller and less diversified.	No	No
Treverton, Gregory F., Justin Adams, James Dertouzos, Arindam Dutta, Susan S. Everingham, and Eric V. Larson (2007). "Costing Rich Country Responses to the Terrorist Threat." This volume.	The new terrorist threat implies renewed costs for both rich and poor states. This report takes a first step by examining the costs to the rich states of addressing the terrorism threat, not the wider costs of terrorism itself or the narrower costs of the immediate response to an attack. In that sense, the costs might be thought of as the "secondary" cost of countering terrorism, rather than the "proximate" costs of terrorism. Costs, estimated as those costs that would not have been incurred had it not been for the threat of terrorism, are found to be incremental in the case of the United States. Direct costs are those associated with security activities and mostly borne by the government. Indirect costs, mainly private, are those incurred through changes made to lower the threat level, for instance, the diminished level of travel and increased inspection of goods. There are also opportunity costs associated with the shifting of resources away from activities to those in which there are larger threats. The analysis distinguishes between rich country actions at home, most of them nonmilitary, and rich country actions abroad, most	No	Yes

276

Author(s) and Title				Table
	of them military. The increment in homeland security spending for the United States is not very large in total and is mostly associated with public expenditures for specific military operations abroad and protective measures at home.			
World Bank. (2002). "Fifteen Months – Intifada, Closures, and Palestinian Economic Crisis: An Assessment." World Bank.	Studies the large cost to the Palestinian–Israeli conflict: estimates the cost to the Israeli economy as 4% of GDP.	No	Yes	
World Bank. (2003). "Two Years of Intifada, Closures and Palestinian Economic Crisis: An Assessment." World Bank.	Estimates that the Palestinian territories suffered a 50% fall in income per capita between 1994 and 2002. In addition to the aggregate costs, some specific sectors, such as tourist and trade activities, may be especially hurt.	No	Yes	
Blomberg, S. Brock, Gregory Hess, and Athanasios Orphanides. (2004). "The Macroeconomic Consequences of Terrorism." *Journal of Monetary Economics*.				1
Tavares, José. (2004). "The Open Society Assesses Its Enemies: Shocks, Disasters, and Terrorist Attacks." *Journal of Monetary Economics*.				1

277

Table 8.5. *Terrorism and specific sectors of activity: Paper overview*

Author(s) and title	Brief summary	Model	Data
Abadie, Alberto, and Javier Gardeazabal. (2005). "Terrorism and the World Economy." Working Paper.	A two-country stochastic version of the AK endogenous growth model is used to show that terrorism may have a long-run affect on international capital flows. According to the model, even if terrorist attacks destroy only a small fraction of the productive capital of a country, increases in terrorist risk may greatly affect the level of international investment. In the empirical work, it is shown that higher levels of terrorist risk are associated with lower net foreign direct investment after controlling for country risk. Estimates suggest that a one standard deviation increase in the intensity of terrorism leads to a 5% fall in the net FDI position of the country.	Yes	Data on country terrorism risk from the World Markets Research Centre's Global Terrorism Index for the period 2003/4.
Berrebi, C. and Klor, E. (2005). "The Impact of Terrorism Across Industries: An Empirical Study." Working Paper.	Uses data on the Israeli-Palestinian conflict to assess the effect of terrorist activities on Israeli companies related to the defense, security, or antiterrorism industries and on other companies. The findings show that terrorism has a significant negative effect on non-defense-related companies and a significant positive effect on defense and security-related companies. The authors also find that terror fatalities in Israel have a positive effect on Israeli exports of defense products.	No	Yes
Bram, Jason, Andrew Haughwout, and James Orr. (2002). "Has September 11 Affected New York City's Growth Potential?" *Federal Reserve Bank of New York Economic Policy Review.*	This article studies the effects of September 11, 2001, terrorist attack on the New York City economy in the long run. According to the author, the worst-case scenario is the possibility that financial firms will leave the city having an effect on the number of jobs and on the city's economic growth. After evaluating some key growth fundamentals prior to September 11 (the city's industrial structure and its quality-of-life amenities), the conclusion is that the ability to manage relatively large budget deficits and rebuild New York City's destroyed infrastructure – while maintaining the productivity of the capital stock – will be crucial to allow future economic growth.	No	Yes

278

| Brown, Jeffrey R., J. David Cummins, Christopher M. Lewis, and Ran Wei. (2004). "An Empirical Analysis of the Economic Impact of Federal Terrorism Reinsurance." *Journal of Monetary Economics*. | This paper examines the effects of 13 key legislative events related to federal reinsurance that resulted in the signing of the Terrorism Risk Insurance Act (TRIA) on November 26, 2002, on the stock price of firms in the industries most affected by the Act (banking, construction, insurance, real estate investment trusts (REITs), transportation, and public utilities). The period covered is from October 2001 to November 2002. The TRIA aimed at providing a federal reinsurance backstop for U.S. commercial property – casualty insurers for "free," preventing the reemergence of private sector reinsurance for terrorism losses. In the months following September 11, 2001, insurers eliminated terrorism coverage. After the TRIA, U.S. insurers are now required to cover terrorism but are unable to buy private reinsurance to cover the loss exposure created by TRIA. In addition, TRIA eliminated the possibility of more efficient private market solutions and reduced market expectations of federal assistance following future terrorist attacks. As a result, stock prices in the affected industries responded negatively to the legislative events. | No | Thirteen legislative events related to the enactment of TRIA, prices and returns of insurance, banks, construction, utilities, and transportation stocks from the Center for Research in Security Prices (CRSP), Council of Insurance Agents and Brokers (CIAB) (2003), U.S. Census Bureau. |
| Chalk, Peter, Bruce Hoffman, Robert Reville, and Anna-Britt Kasupski. (2005). "Trends in Terrorism: Threats to the United States and the Future of the Terrorism Risk Insurance Act." *Rand Center for Terrorism Risk Management Policy*. | The book analyzes the present and future trends in terrorism and whether developments that could affect the probabilities of a future terrorist attack within the borders of the continental United States are addressed or not by the TRIA (Terrorism Risk Insurance Act). The TRIA legislation requires insurance companies to make terrorism insurance available to customers and, in return, provides federal reinsurance for losses from terrorist attacks. | No | No |

(*continued*)

279

Table 8.5 (*continued*)

Author(s) and title	Brief summary	Model	Data
Cummins, J. David, and Christopher M. Lewis. (2003). "Catastrophic Events, Parameter Uncertainty, and the Breakdown of Implicit Long-Term Contracting: The Case of Terrorism Insurance." *Journal of Risk and Uncertainty.*	Investigates similarities between terrorist attacks and other types of catastrophic events by comparing the response of the U.S. equity markets to the WTC attack and earlier large loss shocks (the WTC attack, Hurricane Andrew, and the Northridge earthquake). The authors conduct an event study analysis of the response of equity markets to the three large loss events. They differentiate the effect of event-induced uncertainty – e.g., parameter uncertainty – and flight to quality in determining the market's valuation of different insurance companies in an attempt to better understand the process by which the industry moves toward a new market equilibrium following a crisis.	No	Yes
Drakos, Konstantinos. (2004). "Terrorism-Induced Structural Shifts in Financial Risk: Airline Stocks in the Aftermath of the September 11th Terror Attacks." *European Journal of Political Economy.*	This paper investigates the effects of the terror attacks of September 11 on a set of airline stocks listed at various international stock markets. Based on the market model, the author observes an increase in stock returns' volatility following the terrorist attack. Also, the ratio of systematic risk to total risk shows an increase of 72% in its share in the total decomposition of risk. The systematic risk accounted for about 10% and 19% of total risk before and after 9/11, respectively. These results have implications in terms of increasing the difficulty and the costs of airlines in raising capital. In terms of portfolio diversification, managers who hold airline stocks now have a sizeable increase in the undiversifiable risk and will seriously consider a portfolio reshuffling.	No	Yes

Drakos, Konstantinos, and Ali M. Kutan. (2003). "Regional Effects of Terrorism on Tourism in Three Mediterranean Countries." *Journal of Conflict Resolution.*	Based on the theoretical model of Enders, Sandler, and Parise (1992), the authors use the seemingly unrelated regression model to study the effect of terrorism in Greece, Israel, and Turkey on each other's market share, with Italy serving as a control country, being a proxy for tourist activities in the rest of the Mediterranean region and being a tourist destination itself from January 1996 to December 1999. The results show that there are significant substitution effects. But there is also empirical evidence for the contagion effect: only around 11% of aggregate loss in market shares is directed toward other destinations within the group of countries under consideration, whereas around 89% flows out of the region.	No	Data on terrorist attacks were obtained from the International Terrorism Database (ITD) of the International Policy Institute (http://www.ict.org.il/).
Enders, Walter, and Todd Sandler. (1991). "Causality between Transnational Terrorism and Tourism: The Case of Spain." *Terrorism.*	Using a VAR, the authors estimate that a typical terrorist act in Spain scares away more than 140,000 tourists, when all the monthly effects are combined. In 1988, 5.392 million foreigners visited Spain, and 18 international terrorist incidents took place. Hence without these incidents, 1.5 times as many tourists would have visited Spain in 1988.	No	Monthly data on terrorist incidents.
Enders, Walter, and Todd Sandler. (1996). "Terrorism and Foreign Direct Investment in Spain and Greece." *Kyklos.*	The authors study the effect of terrorism in reducing foreign direct investment in Spain and Greece. Using a VAR methodology, it is estimated that terrorism reduced annual FDI flow by 13.5% in Spain in the period 1975–1991 (about $500 million) and by 11.9% in Greece in the period 1976–1991 (about $400 million). As a consequence of the reduced FDI, investment and economic growth were negatively affected. Also, the reduced transfer of technological know-how contributed to a decrease in the countries' growth.	No	Quarterly data on terrorism.

(*continued*)

281

Table 8.5 (continued)

Author(s) and title	Brief summary	Model	Data
Enders, Walter, Todd Sandler, and Gerald F. Parise. (1992). "An Econometric Analysis of the Impact of Terrorism on Tourism." *Kyklos.*	The authors quantify the present value of loss in tourism revenues for a sample of European countries. According to their calculations, Austria, Italy, and Greece lost $4.538 billion, $1.159 billion, and $0.77 billion, respectively, between 1974 and 1988 (in 1988 terms, using a real interest rate of 5%). Continental Europe as a whole lost $16.145 billion due to terrorism.	No	Yes. Tourism revenues.
Fielding, David. (2003a). "Counting the Cost of the Intifada: Consumption, Saving, and Political Instability in Israel." *Public Choice.*	The author studies the effects of political instability and violence in Israel in aggregate consumption and savings since 1987. An estimated consumption function for Israel in the period 1989–1999 including data that reflect insecurity (basically the number of Israelis killed, the number of Palestinians killed, and the rate of growth of the Jewish settlements in the West Bank and Gaza areas) allows the author to conclude that savings would double with an end to the terrorist attacks in the area.	No	Yes
Fielding, David. (2003b). "Modeling Political Instability and Economic Performance: Israeli Investment During the Intifada." *Economica.*	The author investigates the effects of political instability and violence in Israel on the level and composition of investments by estimating two investment equations (one for non-traded capital goods and one for machinery and equipment) including data that reflect insecurity – which are the number of Israelis killed, the number of Palestinians killed, and the rate of growth of the Jewish settlements in the West Bank and Gaza areas. The results show that the terrorist attacks have a huge effect on the construction and machinery and equipment investments, which would be 27.9% and 14.7% higher, respectively, with an end to the terror attacks.	No	Yes

Fleischer, Aliza and Steven Buccola. (2002). "War, Terror, and the Tourism Market in Israel." *Applied Economics*.	The author uses a supply and demand model of the Israeli hotel industry to study the influence of terrorism on tourist activity and hotel revenues. The model has four equations: supply and demand in the local market and supply and demand in the foreign market. A lagged monthly terror index influences foreign demand and, thus, the equilibrium prices. From 1992 to 1998 annual averages of monthly revenue losses from terror events in the foreign and local markets were approximately $48.6 million or 1.27% and $0.3 million or less than 1% of total revenues, respectively. The losses increase in both markets with the deterioration of the situation. In addition, because local market demand is inelastic, hotels have little incentive to reduce prices in the case of a terrorist outbreak to compensate reduction in the number of foreign tourists and revenue losses.	No	Data on the index were taken from the International Terrorism Web site (http://www.ict.org.il).
Glaeser, Edward L., and Jesse M. Shapiro. (2002). "Cities and Warfare: The Impact of Terrorism on Urban Form." *Journal of Urban Economics*.	Focusing on the effect of war and terrorism on cities, the authors conclude that the costs on urban structure are limited. Though there is a positive relationship between terrorism and the extent of urbanization in the period 1968 to 1977, Glaeser and Shapiro (2002) assert that "this link is small, statistically weak, and causally dubious" (p. 223). No evidence is found for an effect of terrorism on the number of tall buildings built in a country.	No	Data from 1968 to 1977 on the number of terrorist incidents, the extent of urbanization in 1978, and the number of skyscrapers built.
Harrigan, James, and Philippe Martin. (2002). "Terrorism and the Resilience of Cities." *Federal Reserve Bank of New York Economic Policy Review*.	The authors study the resilience of cities to terrorist shocks. They conclude that "the same forces that are thought to lead to the formation of cities – namely, the gains derived from the proximity of firms to markets, suppliers, and a large labor pool – will help preserve cities in the face of an attack." In the case of a continued threat, the costs are certainly higher, but even in this case, the gains from producing and consuming in large agglomerations such as New York City largely overwhelm the "tax-like" cost of higher vulnerability to terrorist attacks.	No	No

283

(*continued*)

Table 8.5 (continued)

Author(s) and title	Brief summary	Model	Data
Ito, Harumi, and Darin Lee. (2004). "Assessing the Impact of the September 11 Terrorist Attacks on U.S. Airline Demand." *Journal of Economics and Business*.	The authors estimate a reduced form model of demand for air services with monthly time-series data since 1986 and model the post-September 11 period as an attenuating shock process, which has both a transitory and an ongoing component. After controlling for cyclical, seasonal, and other unique events influencing the industry, the initial demand shock is estimated to be more than 30%, measured in revenue passenger miles (RPMs), and 7.3%, measured in yields. The decline in yield is smaller because a large number of airline tickets are purchased well in advance (transitory component). There is also an ongoing downward shift in the demand of 7.4% measured in RPMs and of 10% measured in yields. On the basis of a counterfactual demand prediction, the authors conclude that the terror attacks and security measures account for roughly 94% of the decline in RPMs from the historical peak.	No	Data on U.S. airline industry demand from the Air Transport Association.
Kunreuther, H., Erwann Michel-Kerjan, and Beverly Porter. (2003). "Assessing, Managing, and Financing Extreme Events: Dealing with Terrorism." Working Paper.	This paper shows that the temporary insurance system established by TRIA is neither a complete answer nor a definitive one. It raises fundamental questions for U.S. insurers as to how they will estimate the risk to set premiums for terrorist coverage that they must now offer to their clients. Since the passage of TRIA, the current level of demand for insurance coverage has remained low, and some factors that may contribute to it are discussed. After presenting alternative foreign public-private partnerships and discussing the potential role for terrorist catastrophe bonds, some features of a more sustainable program for terrorism insurance in the U.S. after December 31, 2005, are provided.	No	No
Lenain, Patrick, M. Bonturi, and V. Koen. (2002).	This paper identifies three possible channels through which terrorism may influence macroeconomic activity: through decreased insurance	No	No

Reference			
"The Economic Consequences of Terrorism." Working Paper.	coverage as a result of the perception of increased risk, through higher trade costs possibly leading to lower levels of international transactions, through greater security and defense spending.	No	No
Mills, Edwin S. (2002). "Terrorism and U.S. Real Estate." *Journal of Urban Economics.*	The author considers the effect of a terrorist threat on the returns to investments in structures. The main results are similar to Esteban Rossi-Hansberg (2003).	No	No
Nitsch, Volker, and Dieter Schumacher. (2004). "Terrorism and International Trade: An Empirical Investigation." *European Journal of Political Economy.*	This paper studies the effect of terrorism on international trade among 217 countries in the period 1968–1979 using an extended gravity model. The results are that countries affected by a large number of terrorist attacks trade significantly less with each other than countries that are not affected by terrorism. Also, doubling the number of terrorist attacks reduces bilateral trade flows by 4%.	No	Yes
Organization for Economic Development and Cooperation. (2002). "The Impact of the Terrorist Attacks of 11 September 2001 on International Trading and Transport Activities." Working Paper.	There were major disruptions of trade flows in the immediate aftermath of the terrorist attacks, but over time, trade operations returned to normal. Some modest increase in frictional costs due to increased security concerns is likely to persist, even though the exact amount is hard to predict. Some have likened these higher frictional trading costs to taxes on business activity or increases in border tariffs, but a comparison with business spending on mandatory pollution abatement equipment would be more appropriate. Not all commodities and countries will be affected to the same extent by the increases in frictional costs. Differences across products are due to varying ratios of transport and insurance costs to goods-value, divergences in prevailing transport modes, and differing roles in the production process.	No	No

(*continued*)

Table 8.5 (continued)

Author(s) and title	Brief summary	Model	Data
Rossi-Hansberg, Esteban. (2003). "Cities under Stress." *Journal of Monetary Economics*.	Studies the effect of terrorist attacks on the internal structure of cities. Develops an urban framework with suitable capital structures. In the long run, a terrorist attack will affect urban structure only modestly, relative to the potentially large decrease in the level of economic activity in the city. In the short run, agglomeration forces will amplify the effect of the original destruction and will reduce urban economic activity temporarily.	Yes	No
Sloboda, Brian W. (2003). "Assessing the Effects of Terrorism on Tourism by Use of Time Series Methods." *Tourism Economics*.	This paper studies the effects of terrorism on tourism using the ARMAX (autoregressive moving average with explanatory variables) model for the period 1988–2001. It also studies the effect of the Gulf War in 1991 and the increase in anti-American attacks on tourism revenues. The number of terrorism attacks on U.S. interests almost doubled in 1991, and this shock had a long effect on the tourism revenues until 2000. The total losses in revenue due to it were about $57 billion (1996 present value discounted at 5%).	No	Yes. Tourism.
Walkenhorst, Peter, and Nora Dihel. (2002). "Trade Impacts of the Terrorist Attacks of 11 September 2001: A Quantitative Assessment." Working Paper.	The author studies the effects of September 11, 2001, terrorist attacks on welfare and international trade using a general equilibrium model (the GTAP: Global Trade Analysis Project). The tightened security measures implemented following the terrorist attacks resulted in additional frictional trading costs, which made international trade more expensive. The largest trade and welfare losses due to increased frictional costs are in regions with high trade to GDP ratios (South Asia, North Africa, and the Middle East). Agriculture and food products, textiles and leather, nonmetallic minerals and machinery are the products that have the greatest reduction in the volume of trade.	No	GTAP-5 database; Organization for Economic Development and Cooperation. (2002).

Woo, G. (2002). "Quantifying Insurance Terrorism Risk." Working Paper.

No

No

Terrorism risk quantification must take into account the following aspects: "(a) the frequency and severity of planned attacks will depend critically on the network architecture of the terrorist organization; (b) pressurized increasingly by counter-terrorist forces, terrorist organizations may adapt to form emergent swarm clusters. These rapidly forming virtual cells, communicating via Internet, will be very hard to detect and stop; (c) emergent networks will facilitate the execution of more frequent but less ambitious and generally less damaging, planned attacks; (d) an event-tree may be constructed to estimate the probability that a planned attack will succeed, depending on the availability and usage of intelligence, the effectiveness of security barriers and technical and logistical mishaps; (e) the loss severity distribution may be derived by mapping losses from realistic showpiece terrorism scenarios and assigning a cost function to each. The cost function reflects practical logistical factors such as planning time, technical difficulty, and consumption of scarce resources; (f) the overall computation of a terrorism loss excess curve can be achieved, provided that the assignment of subjective input probabilities is made using the formal elicitation of expert judgment, such as has been invoked already by government security agencies." Even if there is uncertainty about the loss curves they will help insurers to price terrorism coverage.

(continued)

287

Table 8.5 *(continued)*

Author(s) and title	Brief summary	Model	Data

See Also Papers Below, From Other Tables

Author(s) and Title			Table
Blomberg, S. Brock, Gregory Hess, and Athanasios Orphanides, (2004), "The Macroeconomic Consequences of Terrorism." *Journal of Monetary Economics.*			1
Brück, T., and Bengt-Arne Wickström, (2004), "The Economic Consequences of Terror: A Brief Survey," Working Paper.			4
Eckstein, Zvi, and Daniel Tsiddon, (2004), "Macroeconomic Consequences of Terror: Theory and the Case of Israel," *Journal of Monetary Economics.*			4
Frey, Bruno S., Simon Luechinger, and Alois Stutzer, (2004), "Calculating Tragedy: Assessing the Costs of Terrorism," Working Paper.			3

Table 8.6. *Terrorism and economic policy: Paper overview*

Author(s) and title	Brief summary	Model	Data
Eichenbaum, Martin, and Jonas D. M. Fisher, (2004), "Fiscal Policy in the Aftermath of 9/11." NBER Working Paper.	The dramatic fall in the government surplus in the aftermath of 9/11 is not due to the large exogenous increase in military spending, but the driving force was the large fall in tax rates.	No	Data on real defense spending – consumption and investment components.
Gupta, Sanjeev, Benedict Clements, Rina Bhattacharya, and Shamit Chakravarti. (2004). "Fiscal Consequences of Armed Conflict and Terrorism in Low- and Middle-Income Countries." *European Journal of Political Economy.*	The paper examines the fiscal effects of armed conflict and terrorism on low- and middle-income countries and concludes that conflict and terrorism have a negative affect on growth. Higher government spending on defense tends to be financed through macroeconomic instability (higher inflation and lower investment) rather than in a decrease in spending on education and health.	No	Data from Yearbooks of the Stockholm International Peace Research Institute (SIPRI rating for major armed conflicts).
Lacker, Jeffrey M. (2004). "Payment System Disruptions and the Federal Reserve Following September 11, 2001." *Journal of Monetary Economics.*	This paper evaluates the consequences of the 9/11 terrorist attacks on the monetary and payment systems, comparing it with U.S. banking crises. A common characteristic of all these crises is the disruptions in the interbank payment. In the case of September 11, 2001, terrorist attacks the Federal Reserve credit extension increased the supply of banks' balances, mitigating the effects of the shock.	No	Data on the behavior of the federal reserve system, depository institutions, and retail stores during September 2001, including data from the Board of Governors of the Federal Reserve System (2001).

(continued)

289

Table 8.6 *(continued)*

Author(s) and title	Brief summary	Model	Data
Wildasin, David E. (2002). "Local Public Finance in the Aftermath of September 11." *Journal of Urban Economics.*	The author describes the effect on local public finances of terrorist shocks. Because terrorism seems to present acute risks for core urban areas, it may affect the spatial distribution of population and economic activity. These effects, however, will depend importantly on the assignment of responsibilities among Federal, state, and local governments for dealing with terrorism, and on the distribution of the costs of these responsibilities. Issues for further research should include fiscal competition in the metropolitan area and funded versus unfunded mandates. In its efforts to improve security throughout the nation, the Federal government might insist on costly security upgrades for subway systems, nuclear power plants, harbor and port facilities, and the like. Will and should these mandates be subsidized by the Federal government?	No	No

See Also Papers Below, From Other Tables

Author(s) and Title			Table
Hobijn, Bart. (2002). "What Will Homeland Security Cost?" *Federal Reserve Bank of New York Economic Policy Review.*			4
Lenain, Patrick, M. Bonturi, and V. Koen. (2002). "The Economic Consequences of Terrorism." Working Paper.			5

Table 8.7. *Counterterrorism: Paper overview*

Author(s) and title	Brief summary	Model	Data
Arce, Daniel G., and Todd Sandler. (2005). "Counterterrorism: A Game-Theoretic Analysis." *Journal of Conflict Resolution.*	This model establishes the general tendency for governments to provide too much deterrence over preemption, resulting in equilibrium with socially inferior payoffs. Proactive policies provide mostly purely public benefits to all those potentially targeted, while defensive policies provide mostly provider-specific benefits. When a disproportionate number of attacks are directed at one government, the overreliance on defensive measures can disappear. In other words, in this latter case, terrorists assist governments in overcoming coordination problems.	Yes	No
Bueno de Mesquita, Ethan. (2005a). "Conciliation, Counterterrorism, and Patterns of Terrorist Violence." *International Organization.*	The model explains the benefits of concessions to terrorists even if a surge in attacks follows. Terrorist organizations increase militancy after concessions because it is the moderate terrorists who accept them, while extremists gain control. Governments, on the other hand, are willing to make concessions when they increase their counterterror capabilities with the collusion of former terrorists.	Yes	No
Bueno de Mesquita, Ethan. (2007). "Politics and the Suboptimal Provision of Counterterror." *International Organization.*	In this model, interactions between voters, government, and a terrorist organization lead to an overreliance on some observable counterterrorism measures despite their relative ineffectiveness. Terrorists have a diversity of tactics available, governments also have a menu of counterterrorism measures, but voters decide on the basis of observable spending on counterterrorism and their inferred success, inducing the government to overspend on observable counterterror. When voters are less demanding as to nonsecurity-related public goods, government spending on covert operations, and counterterrorism effectiveness may increase.	Yes	No
Downes Le Guin, Theodore, and Bruce Hoffman. (1993). "The Impact of Terrorism on Public Opinion, 1988 to 1989." RAND Corporation.	Examines the relationship between terrorism and public opinion on two levels: how the public reacts to terrorism and the preferences for terrorism countermeasures. The study concludes that the majority of people realize the complexity of terrorism and are ready for more considered and more flexible policy responses. There is support for more flexible policy in dealing with hostage episodes.	No	Poll data.

(continued)

Table 8.7 (continued)

Author(s) and title	Brief summary	Model	Data
Enders, W., and T. Sandler. (2004). "What Do We Know about the Substitution Effect in Transnational Terrorism?" In *Researching Terrorism: Trends, Achievements, Failures*, ed. A. Silke and G. Ilardi.	The authors investigate the substitution effect in terrorist activities and find strong evidence in favor of its existence. Piecemeal approaches to counterterrorism or technological advances can be overcome by terrorists, though still useful if they induce substitution toward less deadly attacks. The authors suggest that the right approach is a continued effort to reduce total resources available to terrorists – financial, leadership, and otherwise.	No	Yes
Enders, Walter, Todd Sandler, and Jon Cauley. (1990). "Assessing the Impact of Terrorist-Thwarting Policies: An Intervention Time Series Approach." *Defence Economics.*	Discusses the effectiveness of terrorist-thwarting policies on reducing the incidence of terrorism. Legal actions seem particularly ineffective and disappointing in results.	No	Yes
Fitzgerald, Valpy. (2004). "Global Financial Information, Compliance Incentives, and Terrorist Funding." *European Journal of Political Economy.*	The author considers as a priority the interdiction of international transactions supporting global terrorism. However, the current obstacles to transactions made by targeted individuals or groups have had limited success, mainly due to economic disincentives for the disclosure of the identity and purpose of transacting agents, or the transactions are reported too late for the effective intervention. A solution to this problem could be policies of disincentives for undertaking terrorist financial transactions and improving systems for channeling migrant remittances.	No	No
Frey, Bruno S., and Simon Luechinger. (2004). "Decentralization as a Disincentive for Terror." *European Journal of Political Economy.*	Consideration of antiterrorism policy has focused almost exclusively on deterrence that seeks to fend off terrorism by raising the costs of undertaking terrorist acts. This paper suggests an alternative approach to antiterrorism policy that is based on reducing the expected benefits of undertaking terrorist acts to prospective terrorists, rather than raising the costs of doing so. Specifically, it is argued that strengthening decentralized decision making in the polity and economy provides disincentives for terrorist attacks.	No	No

Frey, Bruno S., and Simon Luechinger. (2003). "How to Fight Terrorism: Alternatives to Deterrence." *Defense and Peace Economics*.	Deterrence has been a crucial element in fighting terrorism, both in actual politics and rational choice analyses of terrorism. But there are better strategies for deterrence. One is to make terrorist attacks less attractive. Another is to raise the opportunity cost – rather than the material cost – to terrorists. These alternative strategies effectively dissuade potential terrorists. The strategies suggested here build on the "benevolence" system and tend to produce a positive sum game among the interacting parties. In contrast, the deterrence system is based on "threats" and tends to produce a negative sum game interaction.	No	No
Garoupa, Nuno, Jonathan Klick, and Francesco Parisi. (2006). "A Law and Economics Perspective on Terrorism." *Public Choice*.	This paper reviews the existing law and economics literature on crime, noting where various models might apply to the terror context. Specifically, it focuses on two strands of the literature, deterrence and incapacitation. Challenging the conventional application of the basic rational agent model of crime in the context of terrorism, it considers antiterror measures enacted by different countries, highlighting how the details of the laws correspond to the insights from economic models of crime. In conclusion, the paper proposes an efficient sorting mechanism in which individuals will be provided with adequate incentives to reveal their type to law enforcement authorities.	No	No
Lee, Dwight R. (1988). "Free Riding and Paid Riding in the Fight against Terrorism." *American Economic Review*.	Analyzes the accommodation between terrorists and a government, where the terrorist organization may operate with impunity in the host country, provided it does not create collateral damage there. Nations have three options before terrorists: do nothing, retaliate, or accommodate, this last option being to help the terrorists at the expense of the cooperating nations. This third option dominates the other two, thereby resulting in a prisoner's dilemma where some nations seek accommodation and, in so doing, undermine the efforts of others to curtail terrorist activity.	Yes	No

(continued)

293

Table 8.7 (continued)

Author(s) and title	Brief summary	Model	Data
Mueller, D. C. (2004). "Rights and Citizenship in a World of Global Terrorism." *European Journal of Political Economy.*	Studies policy implications of 9/11, asking whether global terrorism should lead to a reevaluation of how to design constitutions, how to award citizenship, and how to protect property rights. Mueller's premise is that global terrorism seriously challenges the democratic constitutional state. Thus, it is necessary to strengthen both the democratic institutions and the citizens' understanding and support for these institutions.	No	No
Rosendorff, Peter, and Todd Sandler. (2004). "Too Much of a Good Thing? The Proactive Response Dilemma." *Journal of Conflict Resolution.*	The authors model the amount of proactive counterterrorist activity where the choice of the terrorist target is endogenized, as well as the type of terrorist attack – "normal" or "dramatic." Proactive policy has a downside by increasing grievances and terrorist recruitment if the government responds too harshly. Aggressive antiterrorist actions may result in "dramatic" terrorist attacks. The paper explains why target nations may engage in a modest level of offense but a prime target can choose too large a level of proactive counterterrorism when "dramatic" attacks can be transferred abroad to softer targets.	Yes	No
Sandler, Todd, and Kevin Siqueira. (2003). "Global Terrorism: Deterrence versus Preemption." Working Paper.	This paper analyzes two antiterrorism policies when a government's nationals are attacked at home and abroad. Deterrence involves external benefits and costs. When damages are limited to home interests, countries will overdeter, while, for globalized terror, they will underdeter while preemption is usually undersupplied. Leader-follower behavior may lessen inefficiency for deterrence, but worsens inefficiency for preemption as compared with coordinated equilibria, so that targeted nations cannot achieve the proper counterterrorism policy through leadership.	Yes	No

Author(s) and Title	No	Poll data.
Shambaugh, George, and William Josiger. (2004). "Public Prudence, the Policy Salience of Terrorism, and Presidential Approval Following Terrorist Incidents." Working Paper.	The public is assumed to rally around the flag in the event of national emergencies, granting greater executive powers to promote national security. This paper indicates that the importance the public assigns to terrorism as a policy issue and the rallying effect terrorist activity has on public support for the president and his policies vary as a function of the costs of the attacks in human and material terms, the types of people targeted and the weapons used by terrorists. Even in the context of a terrorist attack, the public exercises prudence when lending support to the president.	

See Also Papers Below, From Other Tables

Author(s) and Title	Table
Blomberg, S. Brock, Gregory Hess, and Akila Weerapana. (2004a). "Economic Conditions and Terrorism." *European Journal of Political Economy.*	1
Blomberg, S. Brock, Gregory Hess, and Akila Weerapana. (2004b). "An Economic Model of Terrorism." *Conflict Management and Peace Science.*	2
Bueno de Mesquita, Ethan. (2005b). "The Quality of Terror." *American Journal of Political Science.*	2
Garfinkel, M. (2004). "Global Threats and the Domestic Struggle for Power." *European Journal of Political Economy.*	2
Im, Eric Iksoon, Jon Cauley, and Todd Sandler. (1987). "Cycles and Substitutions in Terrorist Activities: A Spectral Approach." *Kyklos.*	1

(continued)

Table 8.7 (continued)

Author(s) and title	Brief summary	Model	Data
Kydd, Andrew, and Barbara F. Walter. (2002). "Sabotaging the Peace: The Politics of Extremist Violence." *International Organization*.			2
Laitin, David D., and Jacob N. Shapiro. (2007). "The Political, Economic, and Organizational Sources of Terrorism." This volume.			2
Lapan, Harvey, and Todd Sandler. (1993). "Terrorism and Signaling." *European Journal of Political Economy*.			2
Sambanis, Nicholas. (2007). "Terrorism and Civil War." This volume.			2
Sandler, Todd, and Walter Enders. (2004). "An Economic Perspective on Transnational Terrorism." *European Journal of Political Economy*.			1
Siqueira, Kevin. (2005). "Political and Militant Wings within Dissident Movements and Organizations." *Journal of Conflict Resolution*.			2
Tavares, José. (2004). "The Open Society Assesses Its Enemies: Shocks, Disasters and Terrorist Attacks." *Journal of Monetary Economics*.			1
Viscusi, W. Kip, and Richard J. Zeckhauser. (2003). "Sacrificing Civil Liberties to Reduce Terrorism Risks." *Journal of Risk and Uncertainty*.			3

Index

Even, S., 187
Everingham, S. S., 48, 240–241, 273
Eyerman, J., 196

Fair, C. C., 5
Fajnzylber, P., 11
FALN (Armed Front for National Liberation), 96
Fanon, F., 223
Fatah, 219
FDI. *See* Foreign direct investment (FDI)
Fearon, J., 161, 166, 181–182, 184, 186, 188, 213, 217
Federal Bureau of Investigation (FBI), cost increases in response to terrorism, 58
Ferrero, M., 238, 262
Fielding, D., 242, 278
Figueiredo, Rui J. P. de, 255
Financial markets, terrorism's impact on, 39–40
Finer, S. E., 186
Fisher, J. D. M., 244, 289
Fitzgerald, V., 245, 291
Fleischer, A., 242, 278
Flemming, P., 22, 88, 90, 119, 235, 245
Foreign direct investment (FDI)
    global trends in, 93, 116–117
    study methodologies, 36–38
    terrorism's impact on, 18, 26, 210, 242
    violence/globalization's impact on, 118
Foreign intelligence service, cost increases in response to terrorism, 58
France
    domestic terrorism trends in, 110
    NFDI, impacts on, 38–39
    as terrorism target, 128
    terrorist incident trends in, 95–98
    terrorist incidents per capita, 154
Frey, B. S., 236, 240, 244–246, 272, 291
Froot, K. A., 243

Gang, I. N., 239, 262
Gardeazabal, J., 25, 32–33, 35, 209–210, 240–242, 273, 278
Garfinkel, M. R., 239, 254, 262
Garoupa, N., 246, 291
Germany
    domestic terrorism trends in, 110, 215
    NFDI, impacts on, 38–39
    terrorist incident trends in, 96–97
    terrorist incidents per capita, 154

Glaeser, E. L., 239, 242, 262, 278
Glick, R., 86, 117
Globalization
    and terrorism
        cross country regression analysis, 99–103
        as deterrent, 92–93
        gravity model analysis, 119–120, 135–138
        as motivation, 93–94, 122–125, 134, 145–146
        panel estimation analysis, 118
        terrorism trends by, 95, 124, 135–138, 145
        terrorist activity support by, 134
    and transnational terrorism, 5–6, 117
Gofas, A., 178
Gómez-Sorzano, A., 213, 226, 236, 255
Goodhand, J., 198
Government openness and terrorism
    cross-country regression analysis, 99–103
    as deterrent, 5, 87, 133, 145–146
    elections, 8–9
    as motivation, 87–88, 120–121, 158–161, 165–166, 217–218
    panel regression analysis, 103–108
    trends
        by development and governance, 94
        domestic terrorism, 107–108
Great Britain
    9/11 economic impact on, 21
    response to terrorism, economic impact of, 3
    security expenditures, 72–74
    as terrorism target, 128
Greece
    ARIMA analysis, 37–38, 40
    domestic terrorism trends in, 110
    NFDI, impacts on, 38–39
    terrorist incidents per capita, 154
Grossman, H. I., 86
Guillen, A., 196
Gupta, D., 156
Gupta, S., 244, 289
Gurr, T. R., 98, 184, 197, 216–217

Hamas, 212–213, 218–219, 224
Haqqani, H., 5
Hardin, R., 199–200, 238
Harrigan, J., 242, 278
Hassan, N., 186
Haughwout, A., 242, 278
Hegghamme, T., 213
Hegre, H., 18–19, 185